THE MARYLAND

CALENDAR OF WILLS

COMPILED AND EDITED

BY

JANE BALDWIN

(JANE BALDWIN COTTON)

AND

ROBERTA BOLLING HENRY

Wills from 1713 to 1720

VOLUME IV.

FAMILY LINE PUBLICATIONS
WESTMINSTER, MARYLAND

1988

Originally published: Baltimore, Maryland, 1914
Reprinted: Family Line Publications,
    Westminster, Maryland, 1988
International Standard Book Number: 0-940907-07-0
Made in the United States of America

INTRODUCTION

With much pleasure, the fourth volume of THE MARY-LAND CALENDAR OF WILLS is at last placed before its public; a volume of great interest, containing, as it does, the wills of some of the most important men and women of the early days of the Province. It may be fitting to offer an apology for the long hiatus between the publication of this and the preceding volume and also to give some explanation of the reason.

Many obstacles have arisen, which have had to be overcome in the preparation of this number of the series, but the most important one has been geographical.

With the Will Books in the Land Office at Annapolis, and the compiler living in Boston, obtaining the data has been no easy task. Indeed, at one time it seemed almost inevitable that the work would have to be abandoned. At last, however, a Maryland woman responded to my need of a collaborator, who should possess enthusiasm as well as the trained ability necessary, and thus Mrs. Roberta Bolling Henry became associated with the work.

These qualities are indeed requisite, for the presentation of these volumes requires conscientious, painstaking effort as well as selective sense, and our reward is the realization that by means of the series all data in the colonial wills, which is of historical or genealogical value, or of importance in tracing properties, is given in condensed form to our contemporaries, and their substance is preserved to posterity even should the old books crumble away.

Some wills which have been found in other records than the Will Books have been added as an appendix, as they would be out of place in the body of the book.

Our thanks are ever due to the Commissioner of the Land Office and the gentlemen associated with him for the courtesy and assistance they constantly extend to us.

JANE BALDWIN COTTON.

KEY

The name of the testator is in **Bold Type**; those persons bearing relationship to the testator, if stated in the will, are in bold type also. All others are in Roman Type. The county of testator follows the name in the same line if it is given in the will itself, and if none appears in the abstract the inference must be drawn that it is lacking in the will.

The dates of drawing and of the probate of each are placed one above the other, opposite the name of testator; that of probate under that of drawing. If either date does not appear in the Calendar a line of dashes is placed in the respective place to indicate the fact that it is lacking in the will as recorded, and if, as is the case in a few instances, neither date or drawing nor that of probate appears in the will, a double line of dashes is substituted.

The numbers at the foot of each abstract give the number of the book and the page from which it has been taken. The book numbers and not the old liber numbers are used, this being in accordance with the system usual with genealogists in making notes from these books.

It will be seen that in many instances overseers or trustees are named by testators. The custom now being obsolete it is best explained by a quotation from one of the wills where a testator, after designating several friends for the office, adds: "who shall assist the executrix in the care of the estate that neither she nor the children be wronged!"

Nunc. placed after a name indicates that the will was a nuncupative one.

Young. is used in the calendar as the abbreviation of youngest.

Test., the abbreviation of testis and testes, has been adopted in accordance with the custom of the times rather than the more modern term of witnesses. The other abbreviations and terms are so simple that explanation of them seems needless, since they do not differ from those in ordinary use.

MARYLAND CALENDAR OF WILLS

Leach, Jno., Calvert Co.,   16th Nov., 1713;
                                            12th Mch., 1713-14.

> To 2 sons, **Jno.** and **Samuell,** and their hrs., jointly, 100 A., "Rattlesnake."
> "   dau. **Mary,** 150 A., "Mary's Green."
> "   dau. **Eliza:,** personalty.
> "   child., viz., **Margarett,** extx., **Alice, Mary, Eliza:, John** and **Samuell,** residue of estate, real and personal.
> Test: Mary Dodd, William Burford, Thos. Jones.   13. 625.

Bromley, Mile (Mich), (nunc.), Chas. Co.,   —— —— ——;
                                                  6th Nov., 1713.

> To boy Jno. Hall, personalty at 21 yrs.
> "   John Penn, residue of estate (personal).
> Test: Grace Gemmett, Edward Roberts.   13. 626.

Warren, Jno., Chas. Co.,   12th Aug., 1713;
                                              13th Feb., 1713.

> To dau. **Mary** and hrs., "Rich Thicketts," with tract 50 A., ——, adjacent, also "The Hills," "Warren's Discovery" and personalty.
> "   dau. **Anne,** tract, ——, formerly belonging to John Gooch, "The Tanyard," "Smoot's Purchase," now in tenure of Edward Lloyd, and personalty. Should either dau. afsd. die during minority, sd. lands to pass to survivor.
> "   wife **Judith,** extx., and hrs., dwelling plantation and land "Hatton's Point," she being reversionary legatee in event of daus. afsd. dying during minority.
> Test: Jno. Maddox, Alex. Contee, Thos. Lewis.   13. 627.

Lynn (Line), Francis, Chas. Co.,   10th Dec., 1713;
                                                 26th Jan., 1713.
>
> (Illeg.)
> To son **Richard** and hrs., 159 A., "—— Choice."
> "   dau. **Eliza:** and sister **Anne Martin,** personalty.
> "   wife **Margery** and child. afsd., residue of estate (personal).
> Test: Gustavus Brown, Maria Brown, Ann Fraser.   13. 628.

Causine, Ignatius, Port Tobacco, Chas. Co.,
25th Dec., 1713;
25th Jan., 1713.

To 2 brothers **John** and **William,** joint exs., entire estate, real and personal, including 300 A., testator's part of ''Causin's Manor.''

Test: Mary Dawson, Thos. Reeves, Jr., Eliza: Hope, Ubgate Reeves.   13. 629.

Groves, George, Chas. Co.,   11th Nov., 1713;
3rd Jan., 1713.

To sister **Mary,** brother **Matthew,** minors, personalty, and to brother **John,** certain personalty belonging to deceased brother, **Wm. Groves.**

''   John Guyun, ex., residue of estate in trust for son **William** at majority.

Test: Mary Posey, Nicholas Wyetts, Thos. Howard, Edward Miles.   13. 630.

Howard, Edmund, gent., Chas. Co.,   3rd Dec., 1709;
5th Jan., 1713.

To eld. son **Wm. Stevens (Howard)** and hrs., 100 A., ——, where he now lives.

''   2nd son **Thomas** and hrs., dwelling plantation ——, and addition thereto, tract to contain 150 A.

''   3rd son **John** and hrs., 100 A. layed out by Joseph Manning, surveyor.

''   only dau. **Eliza:** and hrs., that part of ''Saturday Work'' belonging to testator, at 16 yrs. or marriage, and negro as per recorded deed of gift in Chas. Co.

''   young. son **George** at 21 yrs. and hrs., residue of lands not already devised and land devised dau. **Eliza:,** should she die without issue.

''   little granddau. **Margaret Howard,** personalty, including mourning ring in memory of late deceased brother, **Geo. Dent,** and ring in memory of her grandmother, deceased, marked M. H.

''   brother **Rich'd Eyton,** merchant in London, and only sister, **Mrs. Hester Tyndale,** wife of **Athelstand Tyndale,** upholsterer in Bristol, personalty.

''   4 sons and dau. afsd., residue of estate. No lands to pass out of name while there is a male survivor.

Exs.: 2 eld. sons.

Test: Geo. Dentt, Rachell Smoot, Mary Posey, Jane Thompson, Anne Dodd.   13. 632.

By codicil ——, 1712—In event of birth of certain negress, she is devised to **Edmund Howard** at 21 yrs., son of eld. son

Wm. Stevens Howard, and **Eliza:,** his wife; and provisionally, certain personalty to his sister **Margarett** afsd., dau. of same.

Test: Jno. Fendall, Jane Coe, Rich'd Coe.

Norris, Henry, Chas. Co., 5th Jan., 1713;
26th Jan., 1713.

To son-in-law **John Fairfax,** ex., to pass to grandchild, son of same, entire estate, real and personal, including "Kitts Choice" in Chas. Co., nr. Gilbert's Bridges.

Test: Robert Saintclar, Jon Slye, Peter Cartwright. 13. 637.

Yates, Robert, Sr., Chas. Co., 19th Nov., 1713;
26th Dec., 1713.

To eld. son **Robert,** ex., and hrs., 250 A., ——, on Wickocomyco R., bought of Benony Foning and Hannah, his wife.

" son **Charles** and hrs., 180 A., "Charles Yates," 180 A.. "Manchester," and 150 A., "Herds Mountains," also 50 A., "Arabia."

" wife **Lydia,** absolutely, 160 A., "Wollring Field" and personalty belonging to Mr. Hatton's estate.

Test: Jno. Maddox, Wm. Goody, Chas. Jones. 13. 638.

Whitticar, Jno., Balto. Co., 27th Nov., 1713;
23rd Dec., 1713.

To sons **Jno.,** ex., and **Charles,** equally, and their hrs., 250 A., "Whittacar's Ridge."

" sons **Peter** and **Abraham** and hrs., rights in "Inlargement."

" son **Isaac,** unborn child, and wife, 150 A., "Whittacar's Ridge"; son **Isaac** to live with mother during his minority.

" daus. **Elizabeth, Sarah** and **Hannah,** personalty.

Exs.: Wife and son **John.**

Test: Jno. Macomus, Thos. Ramsey, Edward Harry. 13. 639.

Jones, Barbara, Chas. Co., 1st Jan., 1713;
27th Feb., 1713.

To son **Richard Chapman** and to his dau., **Eliza: Chapman,** to son-in-law **John Suttle,** to dau. **Ann Suttle** and to **Eliza: Suttle,** personalty.

" son **Thos. Goletie,** personalty formerly belonging to son **William Chapman.**

Exs.: 2 sons, **Jno. Chapman** and **Thos. Goletie.**

Test: Wm. Chandler, Mary Frawner. 13. 640.

Robinson, Peter, Chas. Co.,   8th Sept., 1712;
                                                   16th Jan., 1713.
John Browne, ex. and sole legatee of estate.
Test: Jno. Craxson, Thos. Craxson.   13. 641.

Talbott, William, Balto. Co.,   8th Nov., 1713;
                                                   16th Nov., 1713.
To dau. **Margarett** and hrs., plantation "Oldton's Garrison"
    and "Credentia" adjoining it and "Hurd's Camp," all
    lying on Garryson Ridge.
"   possible unborn child, 400 A., "Melinda," and 200 A.,
    "Middle Ridge," on n. branch Jones Falls; sd. lands to
    revert to dau. afsd. if no other child be born. Should
    dau. afsd. die without issue, to wife **Katharine** and hrs.,
    plantation and "Credentia" afsd.; to brother-in-law **Geo.
    Ogg, Jr.,** "Hurd's Camp," and to child. of brother **Thos.
    Talbot,** in Lancastershire, and hrs., other lands named
    above. In event of Jno. Pattison paying for same, he is
    to have 75 A., ——.
"   wife and dau. afsd., all personalty.
Exs.: Rich'd Colegate, Edward Stevenson and father-in-law
    Geo. Ogg, Sr.
Test: Thos. Hammond, Job Evan, James Crooke.   13. 642.

Lambert, Joseph, Queen Anne's Co.,   25th Oct., 1713;
                                                   19th Dec., 1713.
To Mrs. Jane Wells and hrs., "The Plaines," contiguous to
    land belonging to her.
"   Carpenter Lillingston, Frances Lillingston, exs., and to
    sd. Jane Wells, all personalty.
Exs.: Carpenter Lillingston and Jno. Wells.
Test: Nathan'll Comegys, Jno. Houlton, Robt. Phillips.
                                                            13. 643.

Cassey, James, Queen Anne's Co.,   24th Sept., 1713;
                                                   23rd Mch., 1713.
To wife ——, extx., dower rights in estate, real and personal.
"   brother **Joseph Carsey,** 100 A., ——.
"   child., **John, James** and **Eliza:,** residue of personalty.
Test: Joshua Nichols, Nich. Marsey, Thos. French.   13. 644.

Hindman, James, Rector, St. Paul's Parish, Queen Anne's
            Co.,   10th Aug., 1713;
                                                   25th Nov., 1713.
To wife **Mary,** extx., plantation recently bought from John
    Loveday and land belonging to same and personalty.

To son **Jacob,** residue of personalty. In event of birth of
another child sd. bequest to be divided among both child.
Rev. Jacob Henderson to have charge of son afsd.
Test: Chris. Denny, Anna Denny, Sam'll Wade, John Lawson.
13. 645.

Note—By codicil, 30th Aug., 1713, to brother **William (Hindman),** Revs. Henry Nichols and Wm. Glen, and to neighbor Madan Tilghman, personalty.

Imbert, Andrew, apothecary, Queen Anne's Co.,
5th Mch., 1711;
28th Nov., 1713.

To wife **Elizabeth,** extx., entire estate, real and personal,
unless child shall be born, in which event estate to be
divided between wife and child. Wife is empowered to
sell estate should she desire to return to Grt. Brittain.
Overseers: Col. Edward Lloyd, Col. William Coursey.
Test: Thom. Price, Jr., Eliza: Price, Jr., Otho Coursey. 13. 647.

Cox, Christopher, Balto. Co.,   10th Nov., 1710;
3rd Mch., 1713-14.

To son **Joseph** and hrs., dwelling plantation at decease of his
mother. He dying without issue, said plantation to pass
to Nich. Day, Jr., and hrs.
"   wife **Mary,** dau. **Eliza: Day** and son **Joseph (Cox),** residue
of estate.
Ex.: Nicholas Day.
Test: Chas. Rose, Sarah Day, Eliza: Day.   13. 649.

Smithson, Thos., Talbot Co.,   1st Nov., 1713;
9th Apr., 1714.

To wife **Mary,** extx., during life, dwelling plantation and lands
adjacent, viz., "Holden," "Holden's Addition," "Holden's Range," part of "Mill Road" and part of "Mill
Road Addition," including "Vaux's Land;" sd. lands to
pass at her decease to vestry of St. Michael's parish, to
be used as dwelling place for pastor and as glebe lands
forever; also, to wife, personalty, including certain pieces
of silver which are, at her decease, to be converted into
plate for Communion table of parish afsd.
"   kinswoman **Mary,** wife of **John Wrightson,** and hrs., "Reviving Spring" at Chester, Dorchester Co.
"   sister **Dorothy,** wife of **Michael Fletcher,** of Richmond,
Yorkshire, Gt. Brittain, and to **Michael,** her husband, and
hrs., "Surveyors Forrest" in Dorchester Co.; they dying
without issue, to pass to visitors of free schools in Maryland.

Test: William Wood, Robt. Goldsborough, Ambrous Wood.

13. 649.

Donnoghoe, Jno., Jr., planter, Langford's Bay, Kent Co.,
27th Nov., 1713;
23rd Dec., 1713.

To cous. **Dan'll (Donnoghoe)** and **Jno. Donnoghoe, Sr.,** and Thos. Jones (servant), personalty.

" wife **Elinor**, extx., son **John** at 18 yrs. and son **Matthew** at 18 yrs., residue of estate, personal. Son **John's** portion to be managed by Thos. Mansfield.

Test: Wm. Scott, **Jno. Donnoghoe, Dan'll Donnoghoe.** 13. 653.

Frisby, William, Sr., Kent Co.,   29th Nov., 1713;
4th Jan., 1713.

To son **William** and hrs., "Frisby's Purchase," 400 A., bought of Stephen Coleman and formerly belonging to Jno. Vanheck, nr. Farley Creek, Kent Co., on the Bayside, adjoining land of Wm. Ellmes; also, "Bay-neck," nr. Swan Point. (For description see will.)

" son **James** and hrs., 100 A., "The Island" between Swan and Tavern Creeks, bought from old Robt. Parke; 18 A., "Swan Island," nr. Swan Pt., and 300 A., "Frisby's Conveniency," bought from Wm. Hambleton, of Talbot Co., being part of "Hinchingham," between Thos. Lewis and Wm. Glanvill.

" son **Stephen** and hrs., 400 A., "Swan Point," and dwelling plantation (land, "Bay Neck" afsd., devised son **William,** having been taken out of sd. "Swan Point"); also, 150 A., "Cornliv's Hills" and "Frisby's Purchase," on n. side Sassafras R., nr. the Court House, the upper part adjoining land of Thos. Kellton. He (son **Stephen)** to be kept at school for two yrs.

In event of death of sons afsd., next of kin to inherit lands.

To wife **Ann,** use of ½ dwelling plantation and other lands during life.

" grandson **Rich'd Frisby,** personalty.

" wife and sons afsd., residue of estate.

Exs.: Sons **Wm.** and **James** afsd., the last one named to be of age at decease of testator.

Test: Alex. Williamson, Chas. Fitzpabuck, Hugh Perry.

13. 654.

Note—By codicil, terms of will are confirmed excepting **gift** to grandson **Richard** is revoked and to unborn child, if male, is devised tract on n. side Sassafras R., bequeathed son **Stephen** in will, in lieu of which to son **Stephen and** hrs. is devised a parcel of land adjoining dwelling plantation, and given in will to son **William.**

Bond, Benjamin, Kent Co.,   16th Oct., 1712;

To grandson **Charles Smyth,** personalty.
"   wife **Eliza:,** during widowhood, use of ½ land and dwelling plantation and ⅓ personalty.
"   son **Benja.,** residue of estate, and all lands at decease of wife afsd.; he to be joint ex. with her.
Test: Rich'd Louther, M. Miller, Martha Miller.   13. 659.

Trew, William, Sr., Kent Co.,   2nd Sept., 1712;
                                       14th Nov., 1713.
To son **William,** 10 shillings.
"   granddau. **Rebecka Clarke,** personalty.
"   wife **Eliza:** and son **John,** joint exs., and to daus. **Mary, Ealce** and **Eliza:,** residue of estate.
Test: George Holladay, Giles Porter, Thos. Savidge, D. Pearce.
                                                 13. 660.

James, John, gent., Kent Co.,   1st. Nov., 1713;
                                       16th Nov., 1713.
To son **John** and hrs., at majority, dwelling plantation "Lyn" and tract "Petton."
"   dau. **Ann Ewbanks,** part of "Petton," and jointly with her husband, **Rich'd Eubanks,** use of dwelling-house for 4 yrs.
"   dau. **Ellinor James** and hrs., "James Inspection."
Richard Campbell, ex., and to have charge of son **John** during his minority.
Test: Jno. Williams, Geo. Read, Nicho. Typpett.   13. 662.

Attwood, John, planter, St. James Parish, A. A. Co.,
                                         15th Nov., 1713;
                                         20th May, 1714.
To wife **Eliza:** and son **Henry,** ex., entire estate, personal.
Test: Eliza: Farmer, James Marr, Chr. Vernon.   13. 664.

Preston, Jno., Talbot Co.   9th Dec., 1712;
                                       13th Jan., 1713.
To dau. **Anne Preston,** ½ of 300 A., "Hatton," according to division line between self and Wm. Dickenson, adjoining great neck "Crooked Lane," binding Robert Stapleford's land.
"   grandson **John Hutchinson** at 21 yrs., dwelling plantation ——. (For description see will.)
"   2 grandsons, viz., **Willoby Goforth** and eld. son of dau. **Eliza:,** and **Robert Miller,** her husband, equally, residue of lands, and to **Mary,** dau. of sd. **Robert,** personalty.

To wife **Jone**, extx., use of dwelling-house and plantation during widowhood.
" daus. **Sarah Goforth, Mary Hutchinson, Eliza: Miller** and **Ann Preston,** residue of personalty.
Test: Rob't Stapleford.   13. 665.

Betty, Arthur, planter, Dorchester Co.,
26th Feb., 1713-14;
9th Mch., 1713-14.

To wife's child., **Joseph Wooderd, Benja. Woodard** and **James Wooderd, Martha Person, Mary Parck** and **Rachell Vickars,** entire estate.
Ex.: **Joseph Woodward.**
Test: Godfrey Moettig, Thos. Brannock, Joshua Kennerly.
13. 667.

Fisher, Dorrington, Dorchester Co.,
—— —— ——;
3rd Dec., 1713.

To Pategrew Salsbury and hrs., part of ''Fisher's Choyce'' (for description see will), and to have charge of child. should wife die during their minority.
" dau. **Mary (Fisher),** dwelling plantation and residue of land, she paying to her two sisters at 16 yrs. certain amount of tobacco. In event of her death during minority, eld. dau. **Sarah** to have sd. real estate, to make payment as afsd. to her young. sister ——.
" wife **Rachell,** extx., personal estate.
Test: John Flowry, Jos. Woodward, Rich'd Boxwell.   13. 668.

Clarke, Roger, Dorchester Co.,
13th Dec., 1713;
24th Jan., 1713.

To Eliza:, wife of Geo. Furgusson; Mary, wife of Charles Robson, and to her sister Ann Philips, personalty.
" godson Peter Makings at 21 yrs. of age and hrs., 30 A., ——, upon Blackwater R., adjoining tract which Jno. Brambley bought of Jno. Smith. He dying without issue, sd. land to pass to young. son of Geo. Farguson and hrs.
" Benony Philips, ex., residue of estate, real and personal; Wm. Philips to have use of orchard for 7 yrs.
Test: Sarah Joanes, Edw'd Elliot, Rich'd Roberts.   13. 669.

*Woolcoat (Woolcott), John, Kent Co.,
13th Mch., 1669;
28th Jan., 1713.

To wife **Sarah,** extx., entire estate.
Overseers: Thos. Taylor of Kent, Peter Sharpe of the Cliffts and Wm. Berry of Patuxent.
Test: Francis Neale, John Denan, John Barrett.   13. 671.

---

* Francis Neale, aged 28 yrs., proved this will, 18th Dec., 1677.

Fairbanck, David, Sr., Second Creek, Talbot Co.,
25th Sept., 1713;
28th Jan., 1713.

To son **David,** 100 A., "Belfast," to descend to his hrs., excepting to the child born to him by the wife of **Thos. Camper.**
" Mary White, dau. of Dennis White, Sr., and to granddau. **Hannah Fairbanck,** dau. of son **David,** personalty.
" dau. **Bridgett Shahan** and hrs., 60 A., "Wisbick," and 50 A., "Upholden."
" son **John** and hrs., residue of lands, and plantation at decease of wife.
" wife **Ann** and son **John,** joint exs., residue of personalty.
Test: James Auld, Wm. Hambleton, Sr., Robt. Harrison.
13. 672.

Digges, Edward, Prince George's Co., 10th Apr., 1714;
19th Apr., 1714.

To brother **John (Digges)** and hrs., plantation and land "Barbadoes," also "Bangiah," devised testator by mother, **Eliza: (Digges).**
" sister **Mary Digges,** sister **Darnall,** certain negroes.
" brother **Notley Rozer** and hrs., 1000 A., "Elizabeth's Delight," at the eastern branch.
" nephews **Henry** and **Edward Neale,** and their hrs., watermill at head of Port Tobacco Creek.
" each Jesuit priest in the province, and to Rev. James Haddock, priest, personalty.
" nephew **Francis,** son of brother **Benjamin Hall,** 50 A., part of land bought of Rich'd Harrison, adjoining land of sd. **Benjamin.**
" Col. Wm. Whittington and hrs., 2 tracts on eastern shore, viz., "Cedar Neck" and "Digges Point," for which he has already paid; also, to John Sinnet and hrs., "Denby" in St. Mary's Co., for which he has paid, and to Alexander Hamilton part of "Bangiah Manor," at head of Portobacco branch, provided he pay remainder of purchase money, otherwise to be sold for benefit of estate.
Exs. are desired to finish paying for land bought of Rich'd Harrison on tract of Collington Branch, Prince George's Co., also to sell 1000 A., more or less, in Cecil Co., devised testator by Col. Henry Darnall, half of proceeds to be given to Rev. Thomas Mansell, priest, and residue for benefit of estate, and to sell 1050 A., "Brandferd," on Tuckahoe branch, eastern shore, proceeds to be used to benefit of estate.

In event of there remaining any claim for lands, negroes, stock, etc., bought from cous. **Charles Pye**, sd. claim to be placed against brother **William Digges** and hrs., for whose use sd. purchases were made.

Exs. are empowered to pay all money due at college of St. Omers, to Feb., 1711, for education of brother **Dudley Digges**, provided he make no claim against test. as ex. of estate of father or of mother; and to him is devised, if he return to the province within 3 yrs. and shall not take holy orders, certain negroes.

To brothers **Charles, William, John** and **Dudley Diggs**, and sister **Mary** and child. of sister **Mary Neale**, i. e., niece **Mary** and her brothers ——, residue of personal estate.

Residue of realty to be sold and distributed to 3 brothers, **Chas., William** and **John,** to niece **Mary Wharton**, child. afsd. of sister **Neale**, and to niece and goddau. **Eliza: Rozer** and to William Hunter and brother **Robert Brooke**, priests, for holy purposes, proceeds which shall accrue from sale of residue of lands.

Exs.: Brothers **Charles** and **William Digges**, **Henry Darnall, Anthony Neale** and **Benja. Hall.**

Test: Thos. Brooke, Clement Brooke, Randall Garland, Anthony Hudson, John De Witt.   13. 673.

Phoenix, Edward, planter, Prince George's Co.,
8th Apr., 1713;
25th May, 1714.

To dau. **Jane Hynde**, wife of **Thos. Hynde**, personalty.
"   Major Josiah Wilson, all land ——, at decease of wife.
"   wife **Dinah**, extx., residue of estate and life interest in land afsd.

Test: Walter Thomson, William Shillingsworth, John Auston.
13. 677.

Thomas, Benony, Chas. Co.,
10th Oct., 1711;
25th Feb., 1713.

To wife **Katharine**, extx., and hrs., entire estate, real and personal, including tract of land in Stafford Co., Virginia, at hd. of Poluck Creek, "Acquinkekas Hill" at Pomokey, Prince George's Co., and dwelling land ——, at head of Bordick's Creek.

Test: Samuel Boughton, Francis Goodman, Thomas Perry.
13. 678.

Musslebrook, James, Prince George's Co., 13th Apr., 1714;
29th May, 1714.

To Geo. Nailer, Jr., ex., and his dau. Martha, entire estate, equally.

Test: Peter Brightwell, Thos. Ellet. 13. 680.

Pearson, Francis, Prince George's Co., 16th July, 1713;
26th Sept., 1713.

To wife Eliza:, extx., part of 166 A., "Collington," bought of Eliza: Beall, late wife of Ninian Beall.

Test: John Barrett, Sr., Edward Wellett, John Henry. 13. 681.

Lamar, Thomas, Sr., Prince George's Co., 4th Oct., 1712;
29th May, 1714.

To son Thomas and hrs., plantation where he now lives.
" son John and hrs., dwelling plantation.
" wife Ann, extx., interest in all land and personalty during widowhood; if she shall marr., ⅓ of personalty and residue to sons afsd.
" priest, Mr. Thurrel, personalty.

Test: John Pottenger, Jr., Samuel Pottenger, Jno. Turner, Jr.
13. 682.

Jones, Richard, Jr., A. A. Co., 30th Sept., 1704;
4th May, 1714.

To sons-in-law John, Nicholas and Gassaway Watkins, and to dau.-in-law Elizabeth Watkins, personalty.
" dau. Ann (Jones) and hrs., 224 A., ——, in Balto. Co., also personalty.
" wife Ann, extx., and dau. Ann at 16 yrs. of age, equally, residue of estate.

Test: Eliza: Grose, Grace Lewis, Matthew Clarke, James Sanders, Jr. 13. 684.

Currier, John, Talbot Co., 29th Mch., 1713;
25th Nov., 1713.

To son-in-law John Beach, personalty.
" dau. Eliza: (Currier), residue of estate.

Ex.: John Robinson, of Talbot Co.

Test: Eliza: Buckley, James Buckley, Michael Mackginney.
13. 685.

Stephens (Stevens), Richard, Somerset Co.,

—— —— ——;
3rd Nov., 1713.

To son Richard, part of "Gotherd's Folley," beginning at mouth of Back Creek and running down to Wickocomaco Crk. (For further description see will.)

To wife **Abigail,** residue of ''Gotherd's Folley'' during life, to pass at her decease to son **Isaack** and hrs.

"   dau. **Sarah Bounds,** 300 A., ''Cowes Six.'' At her decease to pass to her son **Jonathan Bounds** and his hrs.; he dying without issue, to next male hr. of his mother, and lacking such to his sister **Sarah Bounds,** and if she die without issue, to 3 daus., **Ann Stephens, Abygale Stephens** and **Hanna Stephens** and their hrs.

"   son **Isaack** afsd., and hrs., at 18 yrs., 80 to 100 A., ''Stephen's Conquest,'' and jointly with grandson **Jonathan Bounds** afsd., the great marsh belonging to 300 A. afsd.

"   son **John** and hrs., part of ''Fairfields,'' also land, the old plantation adjoining same.

"   son **Richard** and hrs., residue of 900 A., ''Fairfields.'' Should any dispute arise among sons named regarding their land, such disputes to be settled at meeting of Quakers.

"   sons and dau. **Hannah** afsd., and to dau. **Eliza: Emnit,** personalty.

"   wife **Abagail,** extx., dower rights and personal estate during widowhood.

Overseers: Rich'd Waters, Benja. Cotman, William Cobble.

Test: Jno. Benson, Rich'd Waters, Thos. Barnit, Benja. Tull, Geo. Downs.   13. 686.

Brooks, John, Chas. Co.,   30th June, 1712; 30th Mch., 1714.

To eld. son **John,** young. son **Matthew,** dau. **Eliza:,** wife of **Abel Wakefield,** dau. **Sarah Brook** and dau. **Mary Tennisson,** 1 shilling each.

"   dau. **Jane (Brooks),** personalty.

"   son **William Gody,** ex., and dau. **Margaret,** his wife, residue of estate, upon condition that they provide testator with necessaries of life.

Test: Rachel Eaty, Rachel Skeen, Katharine Gate, Josias Cuttance.   13. 690.

Brandt, Charles, Chas. Co.,   12th Feb., 1713-14; 10th Mch., 1713-14.

To son **Jacob,** daus, **Eliza:** and **Sarah,** personalty.

"   wife **Eliza:,** extx., residue of personal estate.

Test: William Harbert, John Thomkings.   13. 692.

Hopkins, William, planter, Talbot Co.,   28th Mch., 1710; 8th Mch., 1713.

To son **William** and hrs., land " Marshars Point," being part of larger tract ''Marshey Point,'' as per deed of gift from testator's mother, **Eliza: Hopkins**; he dying without issue, to pass to his sister, **Amie Hopkins**, and hrs.

To son **Edward** and hrs., plantation ——, on Tred Haven Creek, given testator by father's, ——, will; he dying without issue, to pass to dau. **Amie** afsd.

" wife **Susannah**, extx., and child. afsd., and any that shall be born, personal estate. Estate to revert to wife should child. die without issue. Sons to be of age at 21 yrs., dau. at 18 or marriage.

Test: Thomas Higgins, Eliza: Kinnimont, Eliza: Spry, John Cape. 13. 693.

Osborne, William, Somerset Co., 23rd Feb., 1711; 25th Nov., 1713.

Henry Smith, ex. and sole legatee of estate (personal), including interest in sloop "Michael and William," except £5 bequeathed to god-son Jno. Hall.

Test: Marcy Fountaine, Nicholas Fountaine, John Fountaine. 13. 695.

Anderton, Francis, Dorchester Co., 7th Dec., 1713; 10th Mch., 1713-14.

To eld. son **John**, 295 A., part of "Bath," and 50 A., part of "Westward," including dwelling plantation at decease of wife.

" son **Francis** and hrs., 200 A., "York," and 50 A., part of "Westward" afsd.

Land in Talbot Co., "Walkers Chance," which is bargained for with William Carr, to be made over in fee simple to son **James** and hrs.

To wife **Mary**, extx., life interest in lands devised son **John**, and personal estate for maintenance of 2 daus., **Mary** and **Sarah**.

Test: Abigail Ricks, John Ricks, John Kicke, Edmund Mackeel. 13. 697.

Fenwick, Richard, St. Mary's Co., 1st Apr., 1714; 26th Apr., 1714.

To sons **Rich'd, Cuthbert, John, Enoch** and **Ignatius**, joint exs., and their hrs., entire estate, real and personal. Sons by 2nd wife, ——, and by 1st wife, ——, to share equally in division. Should sons **Enoch** and **Ignatius** die during minority, their estate to pass to survivors.

Should disagreement arise, brother **John Fenwick** to make division.

Test: Joseph Alvey, George Plowden, Cuthbert Sawell. 13. 699.

Collins, Mary, Somerset Co., 24th Sept., 1713;
　　　　　　　　　　　　　　　　27th Nov., 1713.

To kinsman **Collins Adames** and hrs., 200 A., "Snowes Hill."
"　mother-in-law **Eliza: Cox,** personalty.
"　brother **Samuel Collins,** sister **Sarah Clifton,** extx., Ann
　　Adames, Dan'll Donoghue, and to their child., residue of
　　estate.
Test: Wm. Powell, Matthew Tat——, Ralph Mill——. 13. 700.

Rogers, Joseph, Talbot Co., 26th Nov., 1713;
　　　　　　　　　　　　　　　　6th Apr., 1714.

To wife **Eliza:,** extx., dwelling plantation ——, during life,
　to pass at her decease to son **Samuel** and dau. **Mary.**
Trustee: Peter Harwood.
Test: Rich'd Ratcliff, Thos. Spry, Marmaduke Harrison.
　　　　　　　　　　　　　　　　　　　　　　13. 701.

Note—Administration upon this estate was granted to Peter
　Harwod, the widow, **Eliza:,** having died before probate of
　will.

Skinner, Ann, widow, Calvert Co., 4th May, 1713;
　　　　　　　　　　　　　　　　　19th June, 1714.

To dau. **Greenfield,** dau. **Elizabeth Green** and each grandchild,
　　——, personalty.
"　eld. son **Clarke (Skinner),** ½ residue of estate, balance
　　to be divided between 2 young. sons **William** and **Adderton.**
Exs.: 3 sons afsd.
Test: Jno. Mackall, Mary Monk, Gabriel Parker. 13. 703.

By codicil, 30th July, 1713—To young. son **Adderton Skinner,**
　testator's portion of "The Reserve" as devised her by
　last husband, **Robert Skinner.**

Knowles, Henry, planter, Balto. Co., 4th Jan., 1713;
　　　　　　　　　　　　　　　　　　15th May, 1714.

To dau.-in-law **Sarah Owings** and hrs., 310 A., "Knowle's Pur-
　chase," being part of larger tract "Andower," on s. side
　Patapsco R.
"　dau.-in-law **Mary Scutt** and hrs., 2 tracts, 100 A., "Combes
　　Adventure," and 244 A., "Margarett's Delight."
"　wife **Catherine,** extx., and hrs., all personal estate.
Test: Jno. Israell, Robert Parker, Dan'll Bosworth, Jno. Nor-
　wood.　　　　　　　　　　　　　　　　　13. 705.

King, Peter, Cecil Co., 26th Dec., 1713;
8th Jan., 1713.

Wife **Susannah Slover,** extx., sole legatee of estate during
widowhood; if she marry, plantation is devised to 4 child.,
viz., **Jacob, Sarah, Isaac** and **Susannah,** and in event of
death of wife without naming an ex., brother-in-law **Hendrick Van Levenigh** is named as administrator.

Test: Derick Colakman, Petrus Bouchelle, Henry Sluter.
13. 707.

Note—To this will the widow, **Susannah Slover,** adds that,
being ill, she confirms the will of her late husband and
appoints, in conjunction with brother-in-law **Hendrick Van
Leuvening,** as guardian of child., **Thos. Heyerd** and **Jacob
King.**

N. B. The exs. named in will of **Peter King** refused to administer, being residents of Penna., and administration
was granted to **Jacob King,** his eld. son. Matthias Van
Bibber appointed his guardian. Page 710.

Penrice (Pinrice), Jno., Gunpowder R., Balto. Co.,
15th May, 1714;
2nd June, 1714.

To godson James Deminit (son of Wm. Deminit and Eliza:,
his wife), personalty.

" Charles Symonds, ex., and hrs., residue of estate.

Test: William Gallaway, Fran. Whitehead, Rich'd Robinson.
13. 709.

Bray, Pierce, Pocomoke, Somerset Co., 14th Oct., 1713;
4th June, 1714.

To Jno. White and Archibald White, orphans of Archibald
White of this Co., 62 A., part of "Corke."

" son **Edward** and hrs., residue of lands. 2 daus., **Mary** and
Martha, to live with him.

" wife and 3 child. afsd., personal estate.

Exs.: Wife and son afsd.

Test: Jno. Henry, Wm. Jones, Sarah Marshall, Robert Nairne.
13. 711.

Toole, Patrick, Cecil Co., 5th Oct., 1713;
26th Nov., 1713.

To child., **Patrick** and **Jane,** entire estate. The former, aged
2 yrs., to be cared for by Wm. Douglas, the latter, aged
6 yrs., by Patrick Burke, during minority.

Testator desires to be buried by deceased wife ——.

Ex.: Wm. Douglas afsd.

Test: Sam'll Bayard, John O'Cahan.   13. 712.
By codicil, 5th Oct., 1713—Will ratified, except dau. is com-
    mitted to Mrs. Anne Douglass, Jr., and son to Geo. Doug-
    lass.

Gilbert, Thos., Balto. Co.,

24th Oct., 1713;
2nd June, 1714.

To son **Thomas**, dwelling plantation.
"   son **Michaell**, "Gilbert's Adventure," commonly called
    "Stony Hill."
"   wife **Hannah**, ⅓ of estate.
"   child. (unnamed), all personalty.
Test: Lawrence Draper, Edward Hurtt, Thos. Simpson. 13. 714.

Battershell, Henry, planter, Kent Co.,

4th Jan., 1713-14;
28th Apr., 1714.

To sons **William** and **Jno.** and their hrs., "Arcadia"; in event
    of their death without issue, to pass to **Thos.** and **Susannah**
    Russh. Sons to be sent to school when they are 10 or 11
    yrs. of age. In event of marriage of wife to unkind per-
    son, sons afsd. to live with their godfather, ——, or with
    their brother **Rush.**
"   wife **Rachell**, extx., and 2 sons afsd., personalty.
Test: Jno. Rolph, Jacob Glen, Jno. Lee.   13. 715.

Parsons, John, Kent Co.,

25th Nov., 1713;
2nd June, 1714.

To sons **Charles** and **Sam'll** and their hrs., "Parson's Chance."
"   **Benja. Parsons** and **Francis Baker** and their hrs., "Frank-
    ford."
"   **Jno.** and **Solomon Parsons** and their hrs., "Frankford's
    Addition."
"   son **Joseph**, dwelling plantation at decease of wife.
"   son **Nicholas** and dau. **Abigail** and their hrs., residue of
    tract; in event of death of either, survivor to inherit por-
    tion of deceased.
"   wife **Agnes**, extx., all personal estate.
Test: Thos. Nutt, Mary Clarke, Anne Hamilton.   13. 716.

Coursey, James, Talbot Co.,

1st Jan., 1703;
5th May, 1714.

To brother **John**, ex., and hrs., entire estate, real and personal,
    he to pay testator's debts and those of deceased mother,
    ——.
Test: W. Clayland, Wm. Fisher, Joana Wood.   13. 717.

Hanson, John, planter, Chas. Co.,   12th Dec., 1713;
5th July, 1714.

To son **Robert,** ex., and hrs., dwelling plantation.
" son **Benjamin,** dau. **Mary,** wife of **Rev. Wm. Maconchie.**
" daus. **Ann** and **Sarah (Hanson),** and grandson **Sam'll Hanson,** personalty.
" 7 child., viz., **Robert, John, Sam'll Eenja., Mary, Ann** and **Sarah,** residue of personalty.
Test: Jane Rose, Alex. Contee, John Cockain.   13. 719.

Chapell, John, A. A. Co.,   31st Dec., 1706;
26th June, 1714.

To Col. Wm. Holland, personalty. To Anne Roberts, wife of Henry Roberts and dau. of Gerrard Hopkins, the elder, personalty; to pass at her decease to her son Jno. Roberts and hrs.
" John Welch, who married Thomasin Hopkins, personalty.
" Mary Wells, extx., wife of Thos. Wells and dau. of Gerrard Hopkins afsd., and Thomasin, his wife, residue of estate, real and personal.
Test: Thos. Hughes, Jno. Sutten, Robt. Conant.   13. 720.

Brocke, Edward, Prince George's Co.,   5th Mch., 1712;
19th June, 1714.

To granddau. **Mary Nicholls** and hrs., that part of "Brock," or "Rock Hall" on e. side Collington branch.
" grandson **Mathew Mogbee** and hrs., 100 A., being other part of "Rock Hall" on w. side Collington.
" grandson **Brock Mogbee** and hrs., dwelling plantation and land adjoining that devised his brother **Mathew** afsd. Should granddau. **Mary Nicholls** die, land devised to her to go to her brother **Mathew,** and he dying without issue, to grandson **Brock Mogbee** afsd.
" grandchild. by dau. **Offet,** viz., **Edward, William, James** and **Thos. Offett,** sons of **William Offett** and dau. **Mary,** his wife, residue of "Brock Hall" on n. side Brock branch. Should any of grandsons afsd. die, his portion of sd. land to pass to other grandson, **John Offett,** and hrs.
Ex.: Son-in-law **Wm. Offett** afsd. Personal estate to be used for education of grandsons **Mogbee** afsd.
Overseers: Alexander Beale and Jno. Gerrard.
Test: Mareen Duvall, Sr., Ninian Beall, Jno. Wall.   13. 723.

Greenwell, James, St. Mary's Co.,   28th Nov., 1709;
14th Aug., 1714.

To wife **Grace,** extx., during widowhood, ½ of 200 A., "Pileswood Lane," it being the dwelling place; she to have charge of younger child. until they are 18 yrs. of age.

To son **John** and hrs., residue of land afsd.; he to have charge
of child. should wife marry or die. In event of his death
without issue, his estate to pass in succession to sons
Justinian and **Ignatius** and hrs., to son **Stephen** and hrs.,
son **Charles** and hrs., and then to 3 sons **Henry, Thos.** and
William and hrs. To sons afsd., personalty.
"   son **James**, 1 shilling in full of his share of estate.
"   3 daus., **Mary Heard, Grace Clarke** and **Jane (Greenwell),**
at 18 yrs., personalty.
Test: Jo. Mason, Henry Taylor, James Gough, Peter Gahart.
13. 725.

Nuthall, John, Sr., gentleman, St. Mary's Co.,
22nd Nov., 1713;
28th Sept., 1714.
To grandson **Breaht Nuthall,** at 21 yrs., and granddau. **Elinor**
Nuthall, at 16 yrs., personalty.
"   son **John,** ex., residue of estate, real and personal, and re-
versionary legatee in event of death of either grandchild
afsd. during minority.
Test: Edmund Plowden, Thos. Sprigg, Dorothy Ashe.   13. 728.

Monro, Robert, Dr., Annapolis, A. A. Co.,   31st Oct., 1714;
8th Nov., 1714.
To Ann Noads, widow, extx., estate in trust for wife **Rebecca**
and only son **Robert.**
Test: Ann Tasker, Thos. Macnemara, Amos Garrett.   13. 729.

Mortemore, John, gent., Calvert Co.,   14th Apr., 1714;
——— ——— ———.
To wife **Eliza:,** extx., and hrs., entire estate, real and personal.
Test: James Mackall, B. Mackall, Thos. Holdsworth.   13. 731.

Cloud, Nicholas, St. Mary's Co.,   12th June, 1714;
11th Aug., 1714.
To brother **Benja. Cloud** and hrs., 350 A., ———, on Chester R.
"   Notley Maddox, Jr., Mary Goldsmith and Gerard Jordan,
personalty.
Cousin **Justinian Jordan,** ex. and residuary legatee of personal
estate.
Test: Robt. Scott, Thos. Notley Goldsmith, Rich'd Burroughs.
13. 731.

Gale, Elizabeth (nunc.), Balto. Co.,   5th Sept., 1714;
6th Sept., 1714.
To brother **William Crumwell,** personalty; that part of estate
which is in hands of brother **Joshua Cromwell** to be used
in paying debts of husband ———, and self.

Brother, **John Ashman**, ex., and residuary legatee.

Test: Joshua Crumwell, Jane Williams. 13. 732.

Hardy, Henry, Chas. Co., 21st Dec., 1705;
20th Sept., 1714.

To wife **Ann,** extx., and hrs., ⅓ of personal estate.

" dau. **Ann,** all land, tenements, etc., of "Hardy's Purchase," and ⅓ of personalty at 16 yrs. of age; she to be brought up in Protestant Church as established by law.

" kinsman **Henry,** son of **George Hardy,** and hrs., of Loughborow, Lessester Co., residue of personalty and land afsd. Should dau. **Ann** die without issue and he dying without issue, to pass to his brother **George** and hrs., and successively to the family of **Hardy** and to next of kin.

Exs.: Philip Briscoe and his son John.

Overseer: Walter Story.

Test: Richard Coe, Richard Beaumont, Magins Sinclair, Mary Sinckelair. 13. 733.

Numan, William, Chas. Co., 21st Feb., 1710-11;
3rd Aug., 1714.

To wife **Mary,** extx., entire estate, real and personal.

Test: *Mary Contee, Judith Warren, D. Dulany. 13. 736.

* Proceedings show that at date of proving will **Mary Contee** had become **Mary Hemsley.**

Davis, Henry, Balto Co., 24th Dec., 1713;
31st July, 1714.

To wife ——, extx., and hrs., entire estate, real and personal.

Son **Henry** to be of age at 18 yrs. if his mother die during his minority, and dau. ——, at 16 yrs., in which event she to live with Hector Macklaine.

Test: Jno. Marcarty, Jos. Harp, Wm. Hamilton (Hambleton). 13. 737.

Panter, John, Somerset Co., 6th Feb., 1713-14;
2nd Aug., 1714.

To Benja. Sauser, Jr., during life, 200 A., "Rowder," 50 A., "Newport Paywell," and 50 A., "Hausloop," also lower part of 100 A., "Wolfs Harbour." At his decease sd. lands to pass to his sons Thomas and Panter Sauser and their hrs.

" Jno. Hall, Jr., residue of "Wolf's Harbour" and 150 A. adjoining part of "Somethingworth," also 50 A. of marsh adjoining Pigeon House Creek.

" William Sauser and hrs., 150 A., part of "Somethingworth."

To **William Laws**, son of **Robt. Laws**, and hrs., 50 A., "Littleworth," and residue of "Somethingworth."

" **Ann**, wife of **Sam'll Rensha**, personalty.

Wife **Dorothy** to live at dwelling plantation and land "Panter's Den," provided she allows cous. **Robt. Laws** afsd. to live there, otherwise to have dower rights only; they to be joint exs. Sd. plantation to descend to cous. **Catherine Laws** and her children.

Overseers: Wm. Jones and John Jones.

Test: Robt. Skein, Jno. Jones, John Waller, Major Waller.

13. 738.

Watts, John, planter, A. A. Co., 29th Oct., 1714; 5th Jan., 1714.

To wife **Ann**, extx., entire estate, real and personal, in Md. and England.

Test: Thos. Moore, Constance Young. 13. 740.

Baltimore, Charles, Lord, 29th July, 1714;

To wife, **Lady Margaret**, daughter of **Thos. Carleton**, of Hixham, Northumberland, extx., entire personal estate, including certain plate and jewels now held in trust for testator by Thomas Vernon, Wm. Carleton and Nathan'll Pigatt, and all rents due testator in the Province.

Test: Nathan'll Pigott, Chas. Busby, Chas. Umgreville, Wm. Davis. 13. 741.

Wells, John, Kt. Island, Queen Anne's Co., 10th Mch., 1713-14; 15th Nov., 1714.

To wife **Jane** and unborn child, 300 A., "Broadfield," at point Cacoway at Langford's Bay, Kent Co., and 250 A., "Winchester" at the wading place, also lands which were her own.

" son **John** and hrs., dwelling plantation "Broad Creek" and 700 A., "Broad Knox Creek" at Pt. Cacoway; also, 100 A., "New France," on Kent Island, devised testator by father-in-law, **Lewis Blangy**.

" John Stevens and hrs., "Tarkill," on Kent Island, provided he make over to his brother Charles Stevens (carpenter) certain tract, ——, in southern neck of island. Should sd. John die, "Tarkill" to revert to son **John** afsd. and hrs. Should sd. son die without issue, "Broad Creek" to descend to sd. John Stevens, provided he give his brother Charles and hrs. "Tarkill."

To dau.-in-law **Jane Coursey** and hrs., all rights in "Smith's Meadows," at the narrows, taken up jointly with Capt. Thos. Smith.

" nephews **Andrew** and **Rich'd Tollson,** 700 A. at Cacoway Pt. afsd. should son **John** die without issue, and to brother **Jacob Blangey** and his son **Jacob, Jr.,** "New France" in event of death of son **John;** to pass at their decease, if without issue, to his brother, **Lewis Blangy.**

" William Rakes, Philip Conner, of the island, Rebecca Goodman, Geo. Goldhawk, William Willson and Edward Fanning, personalty.

Son **John** to be under tuition of brother **James Harris,** and remain with wife as long as there are good schools on the island.

Exs.: Wife, brother **Harriss** and Jno. Stevens.

Test: Thos. Goodman, Robt. Blunt, Geo. Mather, Wm. Rakes, Mathew Griffith. 14. 1.

Smith, Elizabeth, widow, Langford's Bay,

21st Dec., 1713;
28th July, 1714.

To son **Thos. Parker,** personalty.

" dau. **Mary Sheele,** to **William Sheele** and Richard West, joint exs., residue of estate.

Test: Wm. Scott, Wm. Bryum, Edward Huskins. 14. 3.

Taylor, William, St. Mary's Co.,

1st Mch., 1714;
5th June, 1714.

To daus. **Mary, Grace, Elizabeth** and **Ann** and son **Upgate** at 16 yrs., personalty.

Wife **Ann** extx. and residuary legatee; should she die, Thos. Revves, Jr., to administer upon estate.

Test: Wm. Willis, Torle Gillimore, Wm. Hoskins. 14. 4.

Cartwright, Mathew,

6th May, 1714;
15th May, 1714;

To son **John** and hrs., plantation, to pass to dau. **Mary** should son die without issue.

" wife **Susannah,** extx., life interest in plantation, and personal estate jointly with son and dau. afsd. Brother **Peter Cartwright** to have charge of dau.'s share until she attains 16 yrs. of age or marry.

Test: Jno. Sanders, Thos. Orphin, Michael Wikley. 14. 5.

Hanson, Thos., Balto. Co., 29th Oct., 1713;
3rd Oct., 1714.

To eld. son **Benja.,** 40 A., part of 100 A., "Common Garden,"
to be laid out of land adjoining the old plantation of
Roger Matthews.

" dau. **Sibell Wheatherly** and hrs., personalty.

" sons **Thos.** and **Jacob,** equally, residue of 2 tracts bought
of James Philips, except 40 A. afsd., and personalty.

" wife **Sarah,** extx., and hrs., all right in lands left by her
father, **Jno. Ray,** and residue of personal estate.

Test: Roger Matthews, Henry Matthews, Rich'd Rust, Sarah
Matthews.   14. 6.

Sheppard, Catherine, St. Mary's Co., 10th May, 1714;
26th May, 1714.

To son **William Wilkinsson,** ex., son **John Wilkisson,** dau.
Catherine Taney, grandson **Robert Hutchins,** granddau.
Catherine Hutchins, and to Frances Hutchins, Wm. Hutch-
ins, Mary Paine, Catherine Wıllkisson, John Hutchins,
Catherine Willson, Mary Taney and Quill Hutchins, per-
sonal estate.

Test: Andrew Bumvally, Mary Sample, Wm. Read.   14. 7.

Clarke, Edward, St. Mary's Co., 30th Apr., 1713;
24th June, 1714.

To sons **Jno., Edward, Clement** and dau. **Mary Clarke,** acknow-
ledgments made of certain live stock.

Wife **Mary,** extx. and residuary legatee; she being empowered
to sell all land, viz., 202 A., "Turvey," 25 A., "Houndslow's Addition," but if sd. lands are not sold they are
to pass at decease of wife to 3 sons afsd., son **John** to be
of age at 16 yrs. and other sons at 18 yrs. If son **John**
go to live at plantation he is to take his sister **Henrietta**
with him.

Test: Robert Ford, John Jones, James Thompson.   14. 8.

Lann *(Lane)**, John,** Tuckhow, Queen Anne's Co.,
16th Mch., 1713;
23rd Nov., 1714.

To wife **Judith,** extx., dwelling plantation "Lann's Delight"
during life, to pass at her decease to son **Walter** and hrs.

" dau. **Easter** and hrs., 100 A., ——, part of tract ——, sold
to Thos. Anderson.

* Lane in Testa. Proc. See Book 22, ps. 473 and 500.

To dau. **Mary** and hrs., 100 A., part of "Killcray."

" grandson **Jno. Lann** and hrs., personalty.

" wife **Judith**, residuary legatee of estate, real and personal, 250 A., ——, where Wm. Draper lived, and 200 A., part of "Lambert," to be sold for benefit of estate.

Test: Jeremiah Jadwyn, Jno. Gregory, Rich'd Smith, Mary Burk, Jno. Willson.   14. 10.

Tippin, William, planter, Queen Anne's Co.,
24th Apr., 1714;
29th Oct., 1714.

To sons-in-law **Wm. Austin** and **James Williams,** grandchild **William Austin** and dau. **Mary Tippin,** personalty.

Wife **Ann** and afsd. legatees, excepting grandchild, to be joint exs. Residue of estate to be divided among same and rest of child. (undesignated).

Test: Thos. Hynson Wright, Mich'll Hussey, John Alley.
14. 11.

Willis, John,
18th Sept., 1712;
24th Nov., 1714.

To son **William** and hrs., all lands and personalty.

" dau. **Grace,** personal estate and lands afsd. should son die without issue.

" dau. **Eliza:**, personalty.

" son **John,** 12 pence.

Exs.: Wm. Jones, Rice Levena.

Test: Wm. Kirke, Wm. Jones.   14. 12.

N. B.—**John Willis,** eld. son of deceased, prayed that administration should not be granted to exs., there being but two witnesses to will, and that there were two more child. not mentioned in same.

Bigger, John, Calvert Co.,
26th Dec., 1713;
18th Nov., 1714.

To **Kendall Head,** son of **Wm. Head,** by **Ann,** his present wife, dwelling plantation and lands adjoining, formerly called "Hambleton," "Hardfortune," part of "Cuckold's Miss," "Goosey's Addition," "Goosey's Comeagain," "Goosey's Lott," "Goosey's Choice," part of "Catterton's Lott," part of "Barber's Delight," "Bigger's Chance" and land adjoining containing 1060 A., "Bigger," also 150 A., "South Louthian," adjoining land of Charles Bowen. Sd. **Kendall** to be educated at expense of estate and to be of age at 21 yrs.

To **Bigger Head,** as 21 yrs., and hrs., son of afsd. **Wm.** and **Ann,** 441 A., "Landover," in Prince George's Co., residue of which having been made over to his brother **Kendall.**

" **Mary, Ann** and **Katharine Head,** daus. of **Wm.** and **Ann** afsd., personalty at 16 yrs. or marriage.

" kinsman **James Gibson** (who lives with testator), and hrs., personal estate and 690 A., "Beale's Chance," and 320 A., "Brooke Grove," in Prince George's Co.; he dying under 21 yrs., sd. lands to pass to **Kendall Head** afsd., and hrs.

100 A., part of "Beale's Chance," to be used by **William Head** and **Ann,** his wife, during life, as also is bequeathed them 4 square acres where their dwelling-house stands.

To wife **Ann,** extx., life interest in lands afsd., and personalty. Should she claim interest in estate other than as devised, all legacies to her son **Wm. Head** and **Ann,** his wife, and to all child. of sd. **William,** excepting those to **Kendall,** shall be null and void. She, together with **James Gibson,** residuary legatees of estate.

Trustees: Adderton Skinner, Wm. Head.

Extx. and trustees empowered to sell 300 A., "Back Camp," in Prince George's Co., to pay English debts, and residue of proceeds devised to **Kendall Head.**

Test: Geo. Gray, Joshua Sutcliff, John Godsgrace.   14. 14.

Stunnard, Abell, St. Mary's Co.,   23rd Sept., 1714; 30th Nov., 1714.

To David Evans, Jr., Suener (?) Evans, Sr., and David Evans Sr., personalty.

Test: Hannah Foy, Vincent Trewman, Abell Stannard. 14. 22.

Parker, Mary, Sr., Calvert Co.,   18th Oct., 1714; 15th Jan., 1714.

To sons **Henry Elt, William Elt, Jno. Elt, Wm. Henry Parker** and **Fielder Parker,** and to daus. **Mary Parker, Margarett Morgan,** and **Eliza: Parker,** personalty.

Ex.: Son **Wm. Elt** afsd.

Test: Cathe. Montgomery, Wm. Angell, Hannah Billingsley, Wm. Skinner.   14. 23.

Day, Geo., planter, Somerset Co.,   2nd Dec., 1714; 20th Dec., 1714.

To cous. **Geo. Day,** brother **Wm. Day** and 5 child. of sd. brother. viz., **Geo., John, William, Mary** and **Margarett Day,** and to **Ann,** dau. of brother ——, to Joseph Wooldhave, brother **Robert** and sister **Mary,** personalty.

Brothers **William** and **Robert** residuary legatees, nast named being appointed ex.

Test: Jno. Patrick, Ellis Fleming, Wm. Richards.   14. 23.

Morris, Thomas, planter, Somerset Co.,   22nd Feb., 1713;
                                                     3rd. Dec., 1714.

To eld. sons **William** and **Thomas** and their hrs., dwelling land
    and plantation "Linnath," provided they pay to sons
    Joseph and **Edward** certain amount of tobacco at majority.

"   John Burbage, of Somerset Co., 2 tracts, viz., "Hoggs
    Norton," having a plantation thereon, and 200 A., "Baw-
    marrigs," provided he pay to Jno. Hampton, or his hrs.,
    certain amount of tobacco.

"   wife **Parthenia**, extx., ⅓ of personalty, residue to be
    divided among sons afsd. and dau. **Parthenia.**

Overseers: Geo. Truitt, John Truitt.

Test: Henry Smock, Job Jerman, Gavin Hutchison.   14. 25.

Dorsey, John, Honorable, Balto. Co.,   26th Nov., 1714;
                                          22nd Mch., 1714-15.

To wife **Pleasance**, ⅓ of estate, real and personal, she to make
    choice of plantation ——, on South R., or dwelling plan-
    tation ——, on Elk Ridge.

"   grandson **John**, son of son **Edward**, deceased, and his hrs.,
    the Patuxent plantation "Dorsey's Search," in Balto.
    Co.; he dying without issue, to pass to grandson **Edward,**
    son of son **Edward,** and he dying without issue, to 3
    young. child., ——, of dau. **Deborah Clegat.**

"   grandson **Edward** afsd., and hrs., plantation "Dorsey's
    Adventure" on Elk Ridge, Balto. Co., also "Whiteaker's
    Purchase," bought of James Barley; He dying without
    issue, sd. land to pass to grandson **John** afsd. and hrs.,
    and then to child. of dau. **Deborah** as afsd.

"   grandsons **Charles** and **Wm. Ridgley,** sons of dau. **Deborah,**
    equally, and their hrs., "White Wine and Claret," on s.
    side Patuxent R., in Balto Co.; they dying without issue,
    sd. tract to pass to **Martha, Elinor** and **Edward Clegatr,**
    child. of dau. **Deborah,** and hrs.

"   grandsons **Sam'll** and **Rich'd Dorsey,** sons of son **Caleb,**
    and hrs., plantation "South River Quarter," being residue
    of a tract given by deed of gift to son **Caleb.**   Sd. land
    to be in possession of wife during life as afsd. should
    she so select; and should grandsons afsd. die without issue,
    to pass to granddaus. **Acksah** and **Sophia** and their hrs.

"   grandson **Bazill** and hrs., son of son **Caleb,** plantation
    "Troy," in Balto. Co.; he dying without issue, to pass
    to grandsons Jno. and **Caleb Dorsey,** sons of son **Caleb** afsd.

"   grandson **John**, son of **Edward**, deceased, personalty, to
    be held by his mother, ——, until he is 21 yrs. of age; and

to grandchild. **Charles, Ridgely,** 2nd son of dau. **Deborah,**
and other grandchild. afsd., personalty. Boys to receive
their estate at 21 yrs.

To dau. **Deborah Clegatt,** personalty.

Son **Caleb,** ex. and residuary legatee of estate.

Test: Joseph Howard, Thos. Higgens, Sam'll Dorsey, Thos.
Rogers, Jno. Beale, Vachell Denton.   14. 26.

Baldwin, John, gent., A. A. Co.,   27th Feb., 1714;
26th Mch., 1715.

To son **John** and hrs., 105 A., part of ''Baldwin's Chance,''
adjoining land of **Robert Lusby** and dau. **Mary Lusby,**
and 200 A. in Prince George's Co., adjoining land ''Bear
Neck,'' belonging to Benja. Williams in Prince George's
Co.; also, to sd. son, house and lot in London town.

''   son afsd. and dau. **Katharine Baldwin,** lott and houses in
Annapolis, and to sd. dau., 50 A., part of ''Baldwin's
Chance,'' also 80 A., part of ''Littleton.''

''   dau. **Mary Lusby** afsd. and her husband **Robert,** 50 A.,
part of ''Baldwin's Chance,'' where they now live, and
100 A., ''Littleton,'' on Patuxent R.

''   son **James** and hrs., 105 A., part of ''Baldwin's Chance''
afsd., and 200 A., ——, in Prince George's Co., adjoining
''Bear Neck'' as afsd.

''   **Thomas** and hrs., 105 A., sd. ''Baldwin's Chance,'' and
100 A., part of ''Littleton'' afsd.

''   wife **Hester,** life interest in real estate afsd. and personal
property jointly with child. afsd.

Exs.: Wife **Hester** and son **John.**

Test: Barnett Nuby, Edmond Benson, Rich'd Freeborne. 14. 30.

Smallwood, Col. James, Sr., Chas. Co.,   16th Sept., 1712;
12th Jan., 1714.

To wife **Mary,** extx., ⅔ of personal estate on plantation ''Bew
Plains,'' in Prince George's Co.*

''   child., viz., **James, Thomas, Prier** and **Leadstone Smallwood, Mary Tayler** and **Sarah More,** residue of estate on
sd. plantation.

Test: Jno. Done, Jno. Doddson.   14. 31.

Gott, Richard, A. A. Co.,   28th Dec., 1713;
16th Apr., 1715.

To eld. son **Rich'd,** aged about 23 yrs., and to 2nd son **Robert,**
aged 20 yrs., personalty.

---

* **Mary,** widow of **James Smallwood,** relinquished her right to bequests as provided by his will, 12th Jan., 1714.

To 3rd son **Anthony**, aged 18 yrs., land sold to father-in-law, **Anthony Holland**, but which came to testator again by right of wife.

" 4th son **Matthew**, aged 16 or 17 yrs., personalty.

" 5th son **John**, aged 13 yrs., ½ of plantation, wife's interest being reserved therefrom.

" 6th son **Samuell**, aged 7 yrs., residue of dwelling plantation. Should son **John** die without issue, son **Matthew** to inherit his share. Should son **Sam'll** die without issue, son **Robert** to inherit his portion.

" 7th son **Capell**, aged about 4 yrs., and dau. **Sarah**, aged about 9 yrs., interest in certain negroes devised by will of brother-in-law **Jno. Willoughby**.

" dau. **Susannah Hill**, personalty.

Ex.: Son-in-law **John Chesheir**.

Test: Chr. Vernon, Henry Attwood, Thos. Woodfield.   14. 33.

Merriken, Joshua, boatwright, A. A. Co.,   27th Dec., 1712;
27th May, 1713.

To sons **John** and **Joshua** and their hrs., plantation and land belonging thereto, part of 600 A., "Scotland."

" son **Hugh** and hrs., 262 A., plantation ——, on Patapsco R. Should sons die without issue, sd. land afsd. to pass to surviving child. and their hrs.

" dau. **Mary** at 18 yrs., to **Comfort Merriken** at 18 yrs., dau. **Sarah** at 18 yrs., and cous. **John Jones, Sr.,** personalty.

Wife **Grace** and son **John** joint executors.

Test: Jno. Jnoson, David Rablin, Thos. Grayham.   14. 35.

Dorrington, Joseph, Kent Co.,   11th Mch., 1713;
9th Mch., 1714.

To wife **Mary**, extx., and son **Thomas**, entire personal estate. Wife is empowered to make over to Wilks Churn and hrs., 50 A., ——, on Swan Creek as per agreement.

Test: Thos. Sunkey, Wilks Churn, Joseph Dorrington, Wm. Yearley.   14. 36.

Butt, Richard,   —— —— ——;
28th Apr., 1715.

To eld. son **Richard** and son **Thomas** and their hrs., all land, about 103 A., ——, at decease of their mother.

" other 4 child., viz., **Dinah, Mary, Sam'll** and **Nicholas (Butt)**, personal estate.

Wife ——, extx.

Test: Jno. Banks, Jno. Child, Sam'll Swearingen.   14. 37.

Orrick, James, A. A. Co.,   25th Mch., 1715;
               2nd May, 1715.

To wife **Priscilla,** extx., dau. **Mary** at 16 yrs. and son **Ezekiel**
 at 18 yrs., estate equally.
Test: Rebecca Ruley, Sarah Stevens, Henry Hill. 14. 38.

Usher, Thos. Kent Co.,   5th Nov., 1714;
               17th Jan., 1714.

To son **Jno.** and daus. **Eliza:, Jean** and **Sarah,** equally, and
 their hrs., land ———, where John Pickett lives.
" dau. **Mary** and son **George** and their hrs., 100 A., ——,
 with plantation, etc., where Oliver Mitchell lived.
" son (not christened) and hrs., 100 A., ——.
" son **Thomas** at 21 yrs., personalty and grist mill at head
 of Prickell Pear Creek.
" wife **Eliza:,** extx., ½ personalty, life interest in ½ grist
 mill afsd. and in plantation, which is also to pass to son
 Thos. afsd. at her decease.
Child. to be cared for by wife during their minority.
Test: Thos. Swynley, Joseph Langley, Den. Sullivane. 14. 39.

Sanders, Joseph, freeholder, A. A. Co., 18th Mch., 1714-15;
               22nd Apr., 1715.

Wife **Elizabeth,** extx. and sole legatee of estate.
Test: Joseph Wright, Henry Eden.   14. 40.

Orme, Robert, Sr., planter, Prince George's Co.,
               17th Jan., 1713;
               22nd Apr., 1722.

To son **Robert, Jr.,** and hrs., 2 tracts, 125 A., "Dunbar," and
 31 A., "Anglese," he to pay his brother, **John,** certain
 money; should he not do so, sd. **John** to inherit lands
 afsd.; son **Moses** to inherit sd. land should son **John** die
 without issue.
" sons **Moses** and **Aaron,** 200 A., part of "Brookfield" dwelling plantation; either dying without issue, survivor and
 hrs. to have portion of deceased.
" grandson **John Tanyhill,** son of dau. **Sarah Tanyhill,** and
 grandson **Robert Orme,** personal estate; dau. **Sarah** to live
 on dwelling plantation and take charge of sons **Moses**
 and **Aaron** during their minority.
" 5 child. afsd., residue of estate, personal, and to son **Aaron,**
 also, certain personalty devised him by Deborah Kiniston.
Exs.: Brother **Geo. Ransome,** and son **Robert.**
Test: Wm. Ransom, Josh. Cecell, Robt. Hurdle. 14. 41.

Samson, Rich'd, Balto. Co.,   6th Feb., 1714;
                                         8th Mch., 1714-15.

To son **Richard** and hrs., 100 A., "Ardin's Adventure," on s. side Back R.

"   dau. **Constant** and hrs., sd. land should he die without issue.

"   son **Jno.** and hrs., 50 A., "Samson's Addition."

"   wife ——, and child. afsd., all personal estate.

Test: Mary Baxter, Edmund Baxter, S. Hinton.   14. 43.

Lynch, Robt., Kent Co.,   15th Oct., 1714;
                                         2nd Nov., 1714.

To Thos. Mansell, land, "Dublin," at Sassafras Mill Branch.

"   Ann Headen, James Bronard, personalty.

Ex.: John Headon.

Test: Wm. Comegys, Rich'd Fulston, Dennis Briant.   14. 44.

Knolman, Anthony, Kent Co.,   21st Dec., 1714;
                                         9th Mch., 1714.

To son **Anthony Knowlman** and hrs., dwelling plantation ——; he dying without issue, to pass to son **Richard** and hrs. and in succession to son **Jno. Knowlman** and hrs. and to dau. **Rachell** and hrs.

"   **Richard** and hrs., plantation "Knaves Choyce," on Farloe Creek.

"   Eleanor Cole and Richard Cole, at day of freedom, personalty.

"   child. afsd., residue of estate.

Ex.: Son **Anthony** afsd., who is to be of age at 18 yrs.

No testes.   14. 45.

Stourton, Robert, St. Mary's Co.,   4th Dec., 1714;
                                         15th Mch., 1714-15.

To godson Stourton Edwards and hrs., 190 A., "St. Thomas," bought of James Hay, they to keep the name of Stourton.

"   Parish Church of "All Faith," silver tankard, to be used as sacramental ornament.

"   wife **Margery,** extx., and hrs., 300 A., dwelling plantation land, "The Parting Path," 100 A., "Hopewell," and residue of estate, real and personal.

Overseers: Joseph Edwards, Capt. Thos, Truman Greenfield.

Test: Chas. Smith, Cosmas Parsons, Robert Scott.   14. 46.

Lilley, Thos., chirurgeon barber, Chas. Co.,
                                         25th Dec., 1714;
                                         14th Mch., 1714-15.

Jacob Miller, ex. and sole legatee of estate.

Test: Sam'll Luckett, Jno. Neall, Jno. Beale.   14. 47.

Dawkins, Joseph, Calvert Co.,   30th Dec., 1714;
2nd Apr., 1715.

To brother **Wm. Dawkins** and hrs., 200 A., ''Joseph's Place.''
    ''   son **William** and hrs., ''Joseph's Reserve.''
    ''   son **Joseph** and hrs., dwelling plantation ''Bathler Hall.''
    ''   son **James** and hrs., residue of lands, including ''Haphazard.'' Son **William** to make over to him ''Mary's Duckdome,'' also, which is now in possession of James Duke.
    ''   daus. **Mary, Sarah** and **Maragarett,** at 16 yrs., and young. dau. **Dorcas,** personalty.
Ex.: Son **Wm.,** and residuary legatee.
Overseers: Col. Jno. Mack, and brothers, **Wm. Dawkins** and **Jno. Howe.**
Test: James Duke, Jr., Joseph Pinder, Andrew Duke.   14. 48.

Collson, Robert, gent., Chas. Co.,   28th Mch., 1715;
20th Apr., 1715.

To daus. **Eliza: Connill, Frances Daniell,** wife of **Wm. Daniell,** and **Eleanor Collson,** personalty.
    ''   wife **Ann** and her hrs., residue of estate, real and personal.
Test: Jno. Marloe, Lochle Mackleane, Wm. Godfrey.   14. 50.

Shiles, John, Somerset Co.,   17th Aug., 1714;
3rd Nov., 1714.

To Thos. Carey and hrs., land ——, mentioned in certain bond to Jno. Collins and purchased by Thos. Carey.
    ''   Sarah Green, personalty.
    ''   **Thos. Rensher** and **Bridgett,** his wife, personalty, including John Reynolds.
    ''   godson **John Shiles,** personalty.
    ''   son **John Shiles** at majority, all lands, including dwelling plantation ——, and residue of personal estate jointly with **Thos.** and **Bridgett Rensher** afsd.
Exs.: Brother-in-law **Jno. Irvin** and son-in-law **Thos. Rensher.**
Test: Thos. Shiles, Jno. Collins, Sam'll Worthington.   14. 51.

Sharp, Rob't, Dorchester Co.,   28th Jan., 1714;
14th Mch., 1714-15.

To daus. **Elizabeth, Mary** and son **John** at 18 yrs., personalty.
    ''   wife **Mary,** extx., residue of estate, personal.
Test: Henry Conyers, James Kidder, Basell Rose, Francis Fleharty.   14. 52.

Sharp, Mary, Dorchester Co.,   5th Feb., 1714;
14th Mch., 1714-15.

To daus. **Eliza:** and **Mary** and son **Jno.,** certain stock to be recorded for them at 18 yrs. of age.

Brother **John Sharp**, ex. and residuary legatee.

Test: James Kidder, Sarah Conyers, Henry Conyers.   14. 53.

Browne, Thos., Sr., A. A. Co.,   22nd Mch., 1714-15;
                                     4th June, 1715.

To son **Jno.**, ex., and hrs., land belonging to dwelling-house on Annarundell R.

"   son **Valentine** and hrs., Patuxent plantation.

"   son **Joshua** and hrs., 400 A., "Ranter's Ridge."

"   dau. **Hannah (Brown)**, all land adjoining son **Jno. Stevens** and Samuel Dryers.

"   brother-in-law **Jno. Somerland**, personalty.

Test: Abraham Childs, Jno. Somerland, Susannah Johnson, William Vinecome.   14. 54.

Lamb, John, A. A. Co.,   27th Dec., 1714;
                                    14th June, 1715.

To dau. **Margaret Lamb**, personalty.

"   son-in-law **Jeremiah Belt** and **Sarah Belt** and their hrs., personalty, and to sd. **Jeremiah** 150 A., part of "The Widow's Purchase," on n. side Beaver Dam Branch in fork of Patuxent R., in Prince George's Co.

"   wife **Eliza:**, extx., residue of estate.

Test: Eliner Mariate, Jno. Belt, W. Wootton.   14. 55.

Dossey, William, planter, Dorchester Co., 25th Aug., 1714;
                                            18th Dec., 1714.

To son **William** and hrs., residue of "The End of Controversy."

"   son **John** and hrs., 50 A., "Olive Branch."

"   son **Edward** and hrs., personalty and tract afsd. devised to son **William**, should he die without issue.

"   wife ——, extx., residue of estate.

Test: Joshua Kennerly, Thos. (Viegers) Vickors, Walter Campbell, John Vinson.   14. 57.

Croft, Edward, Somerset Co.,   19th Oct., 1714;
                                     2nd Mch., 1714.

To Thos. Studd and Sarah Murumrenough, personalty.

"   Sampson Wheatley, son of Wm. Wheatley, residue of estate, real and personal.

Ex.: Wm. Wheatley afsd.

Test: Stephen Horsey, Jno. Horsey, J. West.   14. 58.

Kenny (Kenney), William,   23rd Apr., 1708;
     11th Nov., 1708.

To sons **Joseph** and **Sam'll** and their hrs., all land; former to
     have dwelling plantation. Should either son die without
     issue, survivor to inherit portion of deceased.
"   dau.-in-law **Elizabeth** ——, personalty; should she marry,
     her husband to live on dwelling plantation during minority
     of son **Joseph** afsd.
"   son **Sam'll** and former sons unnamed, personalty.
Ex.: John Freeman.
Jno. Richetts to take charge of certain personalty for son
     Joseph, and Wm. Ricketts of that for son **Sam'll.**
Test: Eliza: Foskell, Wm. Robinson, Jno. Freeman.   14. 59.

Beck, Lanslett, Dorchester Co.,   23rd June, 1706;
     —— —— 1707.

To John Brannock, ex., estate, real and personal, in Md. and in
     colony of Penna.; also, 2 lots in Whore Kill Town, now
     the town of Lewis, bought from Charles Hyne.
Test: Jno. Trippe, Charles Harrison, Humphrey Hubart. 14. 60.

Harman, Henry, tailor, Dorchester Co.,   29th Oct., 1702;
     18th May, 1714.

To Barbary Johnson, extx., and hrs., entire estate, real and
     personal, including dwelling plantation and tract "Tiden-
     ton."
Test: Abell Pride, Robert Hobbs, Jr., Ann Hobbs.   14. 61.

Coale, William, A. A. Co.,   5th July, 1713;
     24th June, 1715.

To wife **Eliza:,** dwelling plantation and certain part of "Hill's
     Chance" and "Talbott's Angles."   (For metes and
     bounds see will.)
"   son **Samuell** and hrs., 200 A., "Martinton" and "Martin's
     Addition," in Balto. Co. Should he die without issue, to
     pass to son **Thomas** and hrs.
"   son **Thomas** afsd. and hrs., "The Young Man's Adven-
     ture," in Balto. Co.; he dying without issue, to revert to
     son **Sam'll** and hrs.
"   son **William** and sons afsd., and daus. **Eliza: Snowden** and
     Mary, Hannah, Priscilla, Sarah, Ann and **Margaret Coale,**
     personalty.
Exs.: Wife afsd. and eld. son **William.**
Overseers: Bros. **Rich'd Gallaway** and **Gerrard Hopkins** and
     friend Wm. Richardson.
Test: Rich'd Jones, Jr., Abell Hill, Jno. Gouldsberry.   14. 62.

Brent, Martha, Chas. Co., 7th Apr., 1715;
12th May, 1715.

To brother **William Chandler,** ex., sister **Mary Neale,** nephew **Wm. Brent,** personalty.

" brother **Robert Brent,** personal estate, including that due from brother **Nicholas Brent;** also that due from estate of deceased father, **Capt. Geo. Brent.**

Bros. **Oswell Neale** and **Wm. Chandler** to pay to Rev. Wm. Hunter certain sum for benefit of poor Catholics.

Test: Jane Brent, Sarah Mudd. 14. 63.

Price, Robt., planter, Chas. Co., 8th Dec., 1714;
22nd June, 1715.

To dau. **Eliza:** and dau. **Mary,** by 2nd and last marriage, all land ——; dau. **Mary** to have dwelling plantation. Either of afsd. dying without issue, survivor to inherit portion of deceased.

" wife **Julianah,** extx., and daus. afsd., personal estate. Daus. to remain with their mother during minority or until marriage.

" dau. **Mary Shaw,** personalty.

Test: Thos. Rogers, Thos. Cantwell, Wm. Colley. 14. 64.

Lane, Sam'll, A. A. Co., 13th May, 1715;
19th Aug., 1715.

To wife **Sarah,** extx., ⅓ of estate, real and personal.

" child. born, or to be born, residue of estate. Sons to have portion at 18 yrs., and dau. or daus., if there be more than one, at 16 yrs. of age or marriage.

" dau. **Eliza:** and hrs., ⅓ of real estate afsd. devised to wife. In event of decease of wife during minority of child., father-in-law **Rich'd Harrison** and Rich'd Galloway, Sr., and Wm. Richardson, Sr., to take charge of them and estate. Child. to be brought up in Quaker belief.

Test: Wm. Berry, Jno. Parrish, Alexander Watts. 14. 66.

Andrews, Nicholas, St. Peters Parish, Talbot Co.,
5th Aug., 1715;
11th Aug., 1715.

To wife **Mary,** entire estate, ½ absolutely, residue in trust for 2 child., **Rich'd** and **John;** she to be assisted in executorship by sd. sons and by Oliver Kranivit.

Test: Wm. Matthews, Thos. Beswick, Nicholas Lurty. 14. 67.

Arey, David, planter, Talbot Co.,   19th Jan., 1714;
                                           1st Mch., 1714.

To son **John,** personalty.

"   child., **John** afsd., **Esther** and **Deborah,** residue of personal
     estate; son **John** to inherit at decease of testator, daus. at
     18 yrs.

"   brother **Joseph,** plantation "Sinefield," where he now
     lives; he and his wife to have charge of daus. during
     minority. If they are not properly cared for, Geo. Bowers
     to take them in charge, and if he be deceased, they to be
     under care of Quaker Quarterly Meeting.

Test: Dan'll Thompson, Alse Thompson, Margaret Scully.

                                                      14. 68.

Ellis, Patrick, mariner, belonging to His Maj's Sloop
          "Nightingale," A. A. Co.,   24th Aug., 1715;
                                          16th Sept., 1715.

To Joseph Cannell, personalty.

"   Wm. Brymer and wife ——, joint exs., residue of estate.

Test: Jos. Boson, Jos. Cannell, James Green.   14. 69.

Young, David, Kent Co.,   20th Aug., 1715;
                                 7th Sept., 1715.

To Edward Crew, personalty.

"   wife **Sarah,** extx., residue of estate, real and personal.

Test: Jno. Casley, Rachell Fitzgarritt, Abraham Redgrave.

                                                      14. 70.

Briscoe, John, Kent Co.,   20th June, 1709;
                                  27th June, 1715.

To eld. son. **Alexander** and to son **John** and their hrs., each,
     100 A., part of "Providence."

"   dau. **Rachell Ford** and hrs., 65 A., "Chance;" she dying
     before her husband, **Robert Ford,** he to have use of sd.
     land during life.

"   wife **Mary,** personalty, and joint ex. with son **Alex.** afsd.

Test: Francis Kenccey, Jno. Porter, Abraham Redgrave.

                                                      14. 71.

Cary, Sary, Queen Anne's Co.,   9th Mch., 1714-15;
                                       —— —— ——.

To John Solsbury, plantation in trust for son **Joseph Thrill;**
     sd. son being now 8 yrs. of age.

Estate of dau. **Eliza: Thrill** to be in charge of Mrs. Sarah
     Wright.

Test. Geo. Mattershaw, Eliza: Mattershaw, Margaret Brown.

                                                      14. 72.

Thompson, George, Calvert Co.,   7th Mch., 1714-15;
—— ——.

To son **George** and hrs., dwelling plantation and land "Brook's Discovery," bought of John Brooks; should he die without issue, sd. land to be divided between eld. dau. **Eliza:** and hrs. and dau. **Margaret** and hrs.; either dying without issue, survivor to inherit portion of deceased.

" wife **Johanna,** extx., personal estate jointly with child. afsd.

Test. Thos. Harrison, James Brown, Jno. Pierreville.   14. 73.

Sturmey (Sturney), William, carpenter, Calvert Co.,
12th July, 1714;
31st Oct., 1715.

To daus. **Priscilla,** wife of **Dan'll Sillavan,** and **Mary,** wife of **Thos. Godsgrace Robinson,** each 1 shilling.

" granddau. **Priscilla Sillavan,** dau. of afsd. **Dan'll** and **Priscilla,** and to grandson **Dan'll,** son of same, and to grandson **William Robinson,** son of **Thos. Godsgrace** and **Mary** afsd., personalty.

" wife **Catherine** and son **William,** joint exs., residue of estate. Should wife marry, she to have dower rights only, residue to be possessed by son **Wm.,** of whom Wm. Skinner and Adderton Skinner are appointed guardians.   Tract "Rattle Snake Hill" to be sold with consent of wife for benefit of estate.

Test: George Young, Wm. Angell.   14. 74.

Langley, Joseph (nunc.), Kent Co.,   10th Jan., 1714;
3rd Mch., 1714.

To sons **Jno.** and **Joseph** and dau. **Sarah,** to sister **Shaw's** 2 child., ——, and to Thos. Curey's dau. ——, if she return, personalty.

" wife **Rachell,** residue of estate.

Attested by affidavits of Dan'll Mullican and wife ——, Ambrose Gload and wife and Eliza: Usher.   14. 76.

Copedge, John, Kent Island, Queen Anne's Co.,
30th Oct., 1709;
12th Dec., 1715.

To Wm. and Jno. Roales and their hrs., tract ——, on which they live.

" brother **Philip** and hrs., plantation "Enden Spring." Should brother die without hrs., sd. plantation to revert to testator's child. (undesignated).

" dau. **Eliza:** and unborn child and their hrs., residue of lands.

To Church on Kent Island, personalty.
"   wife ——, extx., and child., residue of estate.
Test: Jno. Wells, Darby Dullany, Louis Deroch Brune.   14. 76.

Sanders, James, Road River, A. A. Co.,   13th Dec., 1710; 25th Feb., 1715-16.

To wife **Jane,** extx., and hrs., entire estate, real and personal.
Test: Robt. Browne, Sam'll Batter, Thos. Gassaway.   14. 77.

Salter, John, Queen Anne's Co.,   29th June, 1715; —— —— ——.

To dau. **Sarah Thompson,** all real estate, including 600 A.,
"Coursey's Town," and 80 A., addition to same, bought by
Col. Wm. Coursey, of the Hamiltons; also, "Hemsley's
Brickland," adjoining "Coursey's Town," bought of
Capt. Jno. Gaudy, but conveyed to testator by Jno. Whit-
tington and wife, of whom sd. Gaudy bought it.
Should dau. afsd. die without issue, sd. lands to pass to sister's
son, **Jonathan Gunthrope,** Racliff Cross, nr. London, and
hrs., and in succession to **Sam'll Gunthrope** and hrs.
To church at head of s. e. branch of Chester R., godson Thos.
Hacket, goddau. Rachell Jenkins, at 18 yrs., personalty.
Dau. **Sarah** afsd., residuary legatee and joint ex. with her hus-
band, **Augustine Thompson.**
Test: Chris. Willkinson, Francis Halfpenny, Jno. Salsbury.

                               14. 77.

Brotton, Jno., Calvert Co.,   10th Nov., 1715; 19th Dec., 1715.

To son **Jno.** and hrs., all land ——, mentioned in patent; he
dying without issue, to pass to dau. **Eliza: Brotton** and hrs.
Wm. Morgan, ex., to have lands during minority of son.
Test: Robt. Lang, Jno. Holshott, Rachell Gloid.   14. 79.

French, Sam'll, Queen Anne's Co.,   1st Dec., 1714; 23rd Aug., 1715.

To son **Thomas,** ex., and hrs., dwelling land and plantation.
"   dau. **Mary** and hrs. and son **Zerubabell,** personalty; last
named to be bound out to a trade in Philadelphia, if
possible.
Test: Nich. Clouds, Wm. Pindar, A. Hamilton.   14. 80.

Houlson, John, Queen Anne's Co.,   7th Sept., 1715; 3rd Oct., 1715.

To son **Henry** and hrs., dwelling plantation, 100 A., part òf
"Hawkin's Pharsalia."
"   sons **Andrew** and **Thos.,** 100 A., on s. side plantation of
son **Abraham.**

Mention is made of eld. son **Thos.**, deceased.

To wife **Eals**, extx., and hrs., personal estate.

Test: Mary Scott, Ann Young, Mich'll Hussey. 14. 81.

Alward, John, Chas. Co., 5th Jan., 1715;
19th Jan., 1715.

To dau. **Margaret Malow,** to Dorothy Brown and granddau. **Sarah Yopp,** personalty.

" granddau. **Jane Yopp** at marriage, ''More's Hope,'' ''Good Luck,'' and ''Partnership.''

" grandson **Charles Yopp,** residue of estate, and lands afsd. should **Jane** afsd. die without issue.

Test: Thos. Thompson, Roger Yopp, Wm. Pecock. 14. 81.

Reed, Hugh, planter, Queen Anne's Co.,
—— ——, 1715;
7th Jan., 1715.

To son **Benja.**, entire estate. He to be under care of Geo. Mathershaw, ex., during minority.

Test: Jno. Wood, James Berry, Jno. Gibb. 14. 82.

Smith, Richard, St. Leonard's, St. Mary's Co.,
31st July, 1710;
19th Mch., 1714.

Mention is made of lands conveyed to son **Richard** by deed of gift, viz., 500 A., ''Smith's Fort,'' 2000 A., ''Smith's Forrest,'' as also personalty already given him.

To dau. **Elizabeth,** wife of **William Tom,** and hrs., plantation, ''Locust Thicket,'' being testator's part of ''Brook Ridge''; and to dau. **Ann,** wife of **Wm. Dawkins,** and hrs., 2500 A., jointly, ''Valley of Jehosophat,'' also to sd. dau. **Ann,** 500 A., ''The Addition to the Valley of Jehosophat.''

" son **Walter** at 21 yrs., dwelling-house and plantation, bought by father, ——, from Mr. Stone, and land adjoining which was Robt. Taylor's; also, tract ''Hogg Pen,'' between dwelling-house and the mill at head of St. Leonard's Creek, 300 A., ''Blinkhorne'' on sd. creek, and 300 A., ''Wolfe's Quarter,'' adjoining thereto, 800 A., ''Stedmore'' in Talbot Co., also, Stone Island in Patuxent R., at mouth of Island Creek.

" Thos. Johnson and Mary, his wife, certain plantation ——, on which they live; to pass to their son Thomas and hrs., and he dying without issue, to revert to son **Walter** and hrs.

To dau. **Barbary Smith** and hrs., residue of "Brook Partition," after portion sold to John Sollers and to John
Sunderlin, deceased, shall have been made over to them
or their hrs.; also, to sd. **Barbary,** "Upper Cock Town,"
commonly called "Vines Neck," 150 A., "Cock's Comb,"
50 A., "Cock's Head," and 185 A., "Smith's Conveniency," also, 2000 A., "The First Part of Free Gift," in
the forest behind Sassafrax and Chester Rs.

"   son **Charles Somerset Smith** and hrs., 2 tracts, 1000 A. and
4000 A., to be entered as 1 tract, "Beaver Dam," at head
of Chester R., and 725 A., part of "Calverton Manor";
he dying without issue, to revert to son **Walter** and hrs.,
and both sd. sons dying without issue, all lands devised
them to be equally divided amongst three daus., **Elizabeth,
Ann** and **Barbary,** and hrs.; also, to son **Charles Somerset,**
punchbowl bearing coat-of-arms of Somerset.

"   5 child. last named, residue of personalty.

Testator mentions son **Rousby** in certain business transactions.

Ex.: Brother **Walter Smith.**

Test: Wm. Creed, John Stennet, Jno. Easterling, Thos. Tucker,
James Mackall, Wm. Gray, Jno. Brome.   14. 83.

Durden, John, A. A. Co.,   9th Oct., 1715;
                                                9th Mch., 1715.

To wife **Elizabeth,** extx., and hrs., entire estate, real and personal, including 100 A., "Cheney's Hazard," and 50 A.,
"Clarcking's Wells," which are to be entailed upon sd.
devisees; should wife have no child., land afsd. to descend
to son —— of Dorothy Callinsworth, and hrs.

Test: Dorrity Holbrook, Jos. Holbrook, Margaret Catterwood.
                                                    14. 87.

Gardner, Frances, wife of **Alex. Gardner,** A. A. Co.,
                                            13th Mch., 1713-14;
                                            6th Mch., 1715.

To dau. **Tebbra Gardner** and hrs., ½ of 3 tracts, "Brush
Neck," "Bottom of Forked Pt." and "Chance"; sd.
lands having been obtained from father, **Robt. Tyler.**

"   dau. **Frances Gardner** and hrs., residue of sd. lands.
Should both daus. die without issue, lands to pass to grandson **William Hawkins** and hrs.

Husband not to be molested in use of above estate during life.

Test: Mary Ingram, Jno. Ingram, Sarah Dawson.   14. 87.

Greenfield, Thomas, planter, Prince George's Co.,
17th Aug., 1715;
7th Nov., 1715.

To dau. **Jone Greenfield** and hrs., residue of "Archer's Pasture," a portion of same having already been given to son-in-law **Gabriel Parker** and his wife and their hrs.; also, tract "Pheasant Tree" adjoining same, 73 A. adjoining thereto (as per deed of conveyance from son **Thomas Truman (Greenfield)** to self, her mother to have benefit of last named tract during life), and 100 A., part of "Retalliation," running from the cabin branch to boundary of tract given son-in-law **Basil Waring** (for further metes and bounds see will); also, bequest of personalty at 21 yrs.

" son **James** and hrs., 52 A., "Pheasant Hills" adjoining tract where he lives, and Salt Store house in Nottingham Town.

" townsman John Brent and hrs., 50 A., part of "Juxta Stadium Aureolum."

" **Benja. Gale,** son of kinsman **Jno. Gale,** decsd., and his hrs., part of last named tract; lacking hrs., to pass to the poor of Gedling, nr. Nottingham; he to be under guardianship of Richard Groon.

" William Olliver, of whom testator was formerly guardian, 50 A. adjoining land of **Benja. Gale.**

" dau. **Jone** afsd., and hrs., residue of "Juxta Stadium Aureolum."

" wife **Martha,** dwelling plantation during life, and absolutely plantation and land, 200 A., "Golden Race"; also, house and lot in "Mills Town," where tenant Evan Jones lives, and, as well, certain lease recorded from Wm. Mills.

" son **Thos. Truman Greenfield** and hrs., "Stokebardolph," in St. Mary's Co., and jointly with his young. brother **Micajah Greenfield,** ⅓ of 500 A., "Truman's Acquaintance" in Gunpowder Neck, to be held under guardianship of John Hall, of Balto. Co., during minority of sd. 2 sons.

" son-in-law **John Wight** and **Ann,** his wife, part of "Anchovis Hills," it being a lease bought of Nath'll Magruder.

" daus. **Martha Waring** and **Eliza: Parker,** personalty, including certain stock on plantation "Gledling Pt.," where she lives.

" niece **Mrs. Margery Covington** and daus.-in-law ——, personalty. Also, to kinsman **James Hollyday,** when of age, personal estate in lieu of some belonging to estate of his deceased father, ——. Mention made also of cous. **Leonard (Holladay)**.

To son **Truman**, at decease of wife, and male hrs., dwelling plantation "Billingsley's Point," and "Trent Neck"; lacking such hrs., to pass to son **James** and male hrs., and in succession to son **Thos. Truman** and male hrs., they dying without such hrs., to the poor of native town Gedling, in Grt. Brittain.

Exs.: Sons **Thos., Truman** and **James** afsd. In event of death of **James**, son **Truman** to take his place. Exs. empowered to sell 200 A., part of "Billingsley's Point," in fork of Patuxent, bought of Barnaby Kearne, of James R., Va.; "Pascuum," lying next "Anchovies Hills," and "Nutwell's Adventure," west of his lordship's manor in Chas. Co., where Edward Thomas lives; ⅓ of land, ——, in Cecil Co., bought from Nicholas Sproul by self, Chas. Carroll and Joshua Cecil; also, to sell part of "Taylor's Coast" (for metes and bounds of land see will), and to sell 80 A., ——, adjoining Ann Guin's land, bounding on "Bullington," for benefit of estate.

Test: Joseph Perry, Nicholas Davis, Jr., Wm. Badger.   14. 89.

Bowen, John, planter, A. A. Co.,   4th Jan., 1715; 11th Apr., 1716.

To eld. son **John**, and **Milcah**, his wife, ½ dwelling plantation "Gover's Hills."

"   2nd son **Geo.**, and **Eliza:**, his wife, residue of sd. plantation.

"   dau. **Margaret Deucey**, personalty.

"   grandson **Claxton Bowen**, plantation at decease of legatees afsd. and residue of estate.

Exs.: Sons **Jno.** and **George** and grandson **Claxton** afsd.

Test: Jno. Ward, John Walter, John Peteete.   14. 94.

Chew, Eliza:, A. A. Co.,   23rd Apr., 1716; 29th May, 1716.

To sister **Susanna Gassaway**, grandsons **Joseph** and **Henry Chew**, and granddau. **Eliza: Chew** at 16 yrs. or marriage, personalty.

"   sons **Sam'll Battee, Joseph** and **Henry Chew**, residue of estate.

Ex.: Brother **Thos. Gassaway**. Desires to be buried in meetinghouse grave-yard at Herring Creek.

Test: Sam'll Battee, Henry Chew, Susannah Gassaway, Jno. Brown.   14. 96.

Long, Benja., Prince George's Co.,   15th Dec., 1715; 19th Jan., 1715.

To son **Thos.** and hrs., 50 A., dwelling plantation; he dying without issue, to pass to son **Benja.** and hrs., and he lacking such, to daus. and their hrs. in natural succession. Dau. **Jane** to be of age at decease of testator. Son **Thos.,** now 12 yrs. old, to be under care of ex., **Benja.** Berry, during minority, as also dau. **Anne,** she being 10 yrs. of age. Rich'd Keen to care for dau. **Mary,** she being aged 8, and Robt. Orum of dau. **Susanna,** she being about 7 yrs. Son **Benja.** to remain with wife, his mother.

" wife **Eliza:** and child. afsd., residue of estate.

Test: Rich'd Keen, Chas. Beavan, Loyd Harris.   14. 98.

Lane, John, Prince George's Co.,   13th Sept., 1712; 17th Dec., 1715.

To Elinor, wife of Sam'll Magruder, and Sarah, their dau., and Samuell and Robert, their sons, personalty at majority.

Sam'll Magruder, ex., and residuary legatee of estate.

Test: Joseph Story, John James, Weedon Jefferson.   14. 99.

Grear, Joseph, Prince George's Co.,   8th Aug., 1715; 14th Dec., 1715.

To wife ——, extx., ⅓ of estate, real and personal. At her decease plantation and land to be divided amongst 6 sons equally.

" 5 sons, **Joseph, Benja., James, Henry, Annanias** and 2 daus., ——, residue of personalty, son **John** having already received his share.

In event of death of any child or child. without issue, survivors to inherit portion of deceased.

Test. desires to be buried according to rites of Church of England.

Test: Owen Ellis, Thos. Padgett, James Nuttwell.   14. 100.

Scamper (Scamport), (Scampord), Peter, Prince George's Co.,   27th Feb., 1715; 15th Mch., 1715-16.

To Edward Liston and Jno. Wheeler, personalty.

" wife **Jane,** extx., residue of estate, real and personal; dwelling plantation to pass to Eliza: Henly and hrs., at decease of wife.

Test: Sam'll Bresshier, Edward Holmes, Jno. Mills, Jno. Mawdesley.   14. 102.

Scamper (Scamport), Jane, Prince George's Co.,
1st Mch., 1715;
15th Mch., 1715-16.

To servant Jno. Wheeler and to Edward Reston, ex., personal
estate.

Test: Clement Hill, Sam'll Breshire, Rich'd Pile.   14. 102.

Lewis, William, Kent Co.,
20th Jan., 1715;
6th Feb., 1715.

To Wm. Trew, William Poape, Timothy Mulken and John
Yardly, personalty.

"   Dennis Clark, Sr., ex., all land ——, in Kent Co., nr. head
of Chester R.

Test: Edward Comegys, Sam'll Clark, Jno. Willson.   14. 103.

Catherwood, Robert, Somerset Parish, Somerset Co.,
27th Apr., 1715;
23rd Aug., 1715.

To wife **Anne,** extx., and dau. **Anne,** entire estate, personal,
equally. Dau. afsd. to live with her sd. mother-in-law
during minority.

Brother-in-law **Sam'll Worthington,** and **Alice,** his wife, to
have charge of dau. should wife die during her minority.

Test: William Caldwell, Margaret Fitzgerald, Jno. Elzey,
Sam'll Worthington.   14. 104.

Wood, Jno., Sr., Chas. Co.,
5th Jan., 1709;
6th Apr., 1716.

To wife **Margaret,** extx., and hrs., 50 A., ——, between Goose
and Nanjemy Creeks, on n. side Rotterdam.

"   son **John,** daus. **Mary Williams** and **Eliza: Killingsworth,**
1 shilling each, they having received their portions.

"   child. **Elijah, Jane, Ann, Sarah** and **Hannah Wood** and
their hrs., residue of land in Stafford Co., Va., also personal estate.*

Test: Mark Attkins, Jno. Ragon, Edward Chapman.   14. 106.

Maddox, Notley, St. Mary's Co.,
24th Feb., 1715;
3rd Apr., 1716.

To son **Samuell** and hrs., dwelling plantation and land; lacking
sd. hrs., land to pass to next hr.-at-law in succession.

---

*10th Dec., 1715—Dau. **Margaret,** born after making of will, to share with
child. named in sd. land in Virginia, and son **Elijah** live with his mother
until he is 21 yrs. of age.

To son **Notley** and hrs., 100 A., ——, in Chas. Co., bought by
brother, **William Notley,** from Benja. Fanning.
" son **John** and daus. **Ann, Sarah** and **Jane,** personalty.
" wife **Margaret,** extx., personalty.
Trustees of child. during minority, Thos. Nottley Goldsmith,
Sam'll Maddox, Jno. Maddox and Sam'll Williamson.
Test: Wm. Willis, Thos. Tippitt, Joseph Artley. 14. 108.

Willson, Alexander, Chas. Co., 8th Feb., 1715-16;
3rd Apr., 1716.
To William, Ignatius, James and Mary Sympson (Simpson),
entire estate, real and personal.
Ex.: Rich'd Edling.
Test: Thos. Sympson, Sam'll Noe, Elias Harrington. 14. 109.

Salsbury, William, Talbot Co., 18th Dec., 1715;
19th Mch., 1715.
To 2 sons, **Thos.** and **Joseph,** at 21 yrs. and their hrs., 250 A.,
"Swineyard," and "Scagspring."
" dau. **Eliza:,** house and lot in Philadelphia.
" dau. **Mary** and sons **James** and **Samuel,** personalty.
" wife **Elizabeth,** life interest in dwelling plantation, which,
at her decease, is to pass to son **John,** they being joint exs.
Test: Christopher Wilkinson, Matthew Collins, Edward Tubrid.
14. 110.

*Jennings, Joseph, Queen Anne's Co., 22nd Dec., 1715;
7th Jan., 1715.
Son **Bartholomew Jennings** to be under care of Jonn Sewence
until 18 yrs. of age, daus. **Ann** and **Mary** under that of
Susannah Sulevane.
Ex.: Charles Seth.
Test: Wm. Denton, John Lanahan, Wm. Camell. 14. 111.

Bayley, Thomas, Queen Anne's Co., 23rd Nov., 1715;
19th Mch., 1715·
To son **Thomas** and hrs., dwelling plantation and 100 A. adjoining, at decease of his mother.
" son **Jacob,** 50 A., adjoining to **John Meriday, Jr.**
" son-in-law **Jno. Merriday (Meryday)** and hrs., 50 A., where
he now lives.
" sons-in-law **Henry Wright** and **Henry Green,** personalty.
" wife **Mary,** extx., residuary legatee of estate.
Test: Robt. Walker, Thomas Ruth, Henry Green. 14. 113.

---

* In this will testator or scribe in preamble writes "I, Joseph Pennington."

Ball, Edward, Calvert Co.,   5th Jan., 1715;
                                               3rd Apr., 1716.

To 3 sons, **Edward, William** and **Michael,** and their hrs., dwelling plantation and land. Sons to be of age at 18 yrs.
" dau. **Catherine (Ball),** personalty.
" wife **Ann,** extx., life interest in plantation.
Test: Henry Austen, Wm. Lyle, Jno. Fowler.   14. 113.

Ellt, William, Calvert Co.,   10th Jan., 1715;
                                               21st Apr., 1716.

To wife **Elinor,** extx., entire estate, real and personal; at her decease estate to be divided amongst son **Wm.,** dau. **Mary** and possible unborn child.
Test: Benja. Harris, Wm. Harriss, Joseph Harris.   14. 114.

Burle, Stephen, A. A. Co.,   8th Aug., 1716;
                                               27th Aug., 1716.

To son **John,** "Pettibones Rest," bought of Thos. Pottobone.
" son **Stephen,** dwelling plantation "Burle's Hills."
" daus. **Mary** and **Rachell** at 18 yrs. of age, personalty.
" brother **John,** personalty.
Wife **Sarah,** extx.
Test: Robt. Jubb, Nathan'll Stinchecomb, Jno. Bucknoll.
                                                     14. 115.

Twiford (Twyford), Richard, shipwright, A. A. Co.,
                                               30th Sept., 1716;
                                               6th Oct., 1716.

To brother **John Soward,** of Dorchester Co., sister **Mary Pattison,** cous. **Mary (Soward),** eld. dau. of **Wm. Soward,** deceased, and to Henry Hill, Jr., personalty.
" Henry Hill, ex., residue of estate.
Test: Rich'd Whitehead, Moses Adney, Wm. Whitehead.
                                                     14. 116.

Boothby, Charles, merchant, Annapolis, A. A. Co.,
                                               2nd Oct., 1716;
                                               9th Oct., 1716.

To Alex Steward, of Annapolis, personalty.
" Margarett Stewart, wife of afsd., extx., residue of estate, real and personal.
Test: Jno. Connoway, Geo. Valentine, Wm. Brymer.   14. 117.

Raymond, Jno.,   5th Mch., 1713-14;
                                               19th Mch., 1713.

Wife **Susannah,** extx., sole legatee of estate, real and personal.
Test: Abraham Child, Rich'd Broadway, Mary Hollingshead.
                                                     14. 118.

Horne, William, A. A. Co.,   8th Feb., 1704-5;
                                                  19th Oct., 1719.

To granddau. **Constelvus Horne** at 16 yrs. or marriage, and
    daus. **Sarah** and **Margaret (Horne)**, personalty.
" wife **Margaratt**, extx., residue of estate.
Test: Sam'll Galloway, Jr., Robt. Franklin, Joseph Ror.
                                                14. 119.

West, John, Sr., Somerset Co.,   25th Nov., 1715;
                                                  9th June, 1716.

To wife **Catoron** and hrs., ⅓ of personal estate and ⅕ of 3
    tracts, viz., "Cattiron's Content," "Great Hopes," and
    "Brothers United."
" 4 sons and hrs., viz., **John, Thomas, Randall** and **Anthony**,
    residue of sd. lands; eld. son **John** to have dwelling plan-
    tation.
" son **William**, 1 shilling.
" daus. **Mary, Cattiron** and **Elizabeth**, and their hrs., per-
    sonalty.
Lands "Beverly" and "Winser Cassell" to be sold for bene-
    fit of estate.
Wife and sons **John, Thomas, Randall** and **Anthony** afsd., joint
    exs. and residuary legatees.
Test: Nath'll Horsey, Geo. Bosman, Stephen Horsey.   14. 120.

Stockdall, Edward, yeoman, Somerset Co.,
                                                  30th July, 1710;
                                                  20th June, 1716.

To wife **Jean (Boyce)**, extx., entire estate, real and personal,
    during life, or as long as she remains unmarried.
" son **Edward**, plantation at wife's decease, dwelling plan-
    tation and land belonging to same, also tract land ——.
" dau. **Jane**, land ——, on east side Busses Bridge, and per-
    sonalty; should either child afsd. die without issue, sur-
    vivor to inherit portion of deceased, and both dying with-
    out issue, lands to pass to Mary Long and hrs.
" dau. **Eliza: Wine**, 1 shilling.
Test: Thos. Stockwell, Wm. Cuttling, Edmund Cullen, Eph.
    Willson.
Note—Widow **Jeanne** takes her thirds of estate and revokes
    will.   14. 121.

Winder, John, Somerset Co.,   30th Apr., 1716;
                                                  13th July, 1716.

To wife **Jean** and hrs., ⅓ of personal estate, residue to be
    divided between .. child. (undesignated).
" **John Watts** and hrs., 75 A., part of "Little Belew."

To John and William Wenables and their hrs., residue of sd.
tract.

" John Stewart, 200 A., part of "Pimberton's Good Will,"
at head of river running up s. side of n. branch at Forrest
Landing.

" London Walton, residue of "Pimberton's Goodwill" upon
payment of certain sum of money; if he does not pay for
same it is to be sold for benefit of son **William.**

" son **Thomas** and hrs., 300 A., ——, adjoining James Mackmore.

" son **John** and hrs., residue of real estate.

Sons **John** and **Thos.** afsd. to live with brother-in-law **Joseph
Wenables,** and if he die with son-in-law **James Dashiel.**
Dau. **Eliza**: to be under care of wife; dau. **Rachell,** under
that of wife, her mother-in-law or her sister, **Bridget
Dashiel.**

Exs.: Wife **Jean** afsd. and son-in-law **Robert Dashiel.**

Test: Wm. Skirvan, Jno. Twigger, Wm. Richardson.   14. 123.

Hill, Rich'd, Somerset Co.,   18th Mch., 1715-16; 11th June, 1716.

To Joseph Schoofield and hrs., land ——, in "Wallops Neck";
also, 100 A., part of tract at head of "Husborne Forest."

" son **Richard** and hrs., residue of lands at 18 yrs. of age,
including dwelling plantation "Husborne Forest."

" wife **Elce,** extx., life interest in 1/3 dwelling plantation,
and all personal estate jointly with sons afsd.

Test: Benja. Scholfield, Robt. Perrie, Thos. Nath'll Williams.

14. 124.

Ryan, William, planter, Somerset Co.,   31st Mch., 1715; 22nd June, 1715.

To Benja., son of Jno. Mitchell, ex., and Mary, his wife, and
hrs., dwelling plantation.

" Wm. Ross, personalty.

Test: Jno. Noble, Benja. Cottman, Wm. Ross.   14. 126.

Derrickson, Andreas, Somerset Co.,   7th Sept., 1715; 13th June, 1716.

To dau. **Mary,** wife of **Wm. Tayler,** sons **Samuel, Joseph Andreas, Benja.,** dau. **Temperance,** and young. son **Andreas,**
personalty; also, land adjoining that of son **Samuel,** which
is to be included in warrant applied for.

" wife **Mary,** extx., personalty; she being desired to leave
land ——, patented in her name to one of young. child.
(undesignated).

Test: Sam'll Johnson, Jno. Morriss, Wm. Samonds.   14. 127.

Carter, Philip, Stepney Parish, Somerset Co.,
9th Nov., 1715;
10th Jan., 1715-16.

To wife **Mary,** ⅓ personalty and life interest in dwelling plantation ''Whetstone.''
" Sarah Acwith, Jr., and hrs., 200 A., part of ''Whettstone.''
" John Rickards, Jr., and hrs., 100 A., west of ''Whetstone'' afsd., and certain tract formerly belonging to Manasses Morriss.
" Tabitha More, Eliza: Rickards, Phil. Rickards, Sarah Acwith and her unborn child, personalty.
" Jno. Rickards, Sr., ex., and hrs., residue of ''Whettstone'' afsd.
Test: David Shehe, Jno. Kinler, Robt. Downs, Alex. Carlile.
14. 129.

Stockley, John, gentleman, All Hallows Parish, Somerset
Co., 23rd Nov., 1715;
12th June, 1716.

To Robert Johnson and hrs., 250 A., part of ''North Paterton.''
" son **Thos.,** 100 A., ——, and plantation at head of Cedar Neck Creek.
" son **William** and hrs., 100 A., dwelling plantation.
" son-in-law **Jonathan Sturges,** personalty.
" wife **Mary,** extx., and hrs., 150 A., ''The Beach'' on n. side Rehoboth Inlet, and personalty with sons afsd.
Test: Jones Rickards, Jos. Godwin, Jno. Rickards. 14. 130.

Sauser (Saser), Benja., Sr., Somerset Co.,
19th Apr., 1712;
20th June, 1716.

To son **Wm.** and hrs., 100 A., ''Sauser's Folly,'' and 50 A., ''Sauser's Addition.''
" son **John** and daus. **Mary Hall** and **Ann Rensher,** 1 shilling.
" grandson **Panter Sauser** and hrs., personalty.
" sons **Benjamin** and **William,** exs., residue of estate.
Test: Jno. Law's, Geo. Martin, Robt. Law's, Geo. Law's.
14. 131.

Sommers, Benja., Somerset Co., —— Feb., 1709;
22nd Dec., 1715.

To sons **William, Thomas** and **John** and their hrs., 250 A., ''Emissex'' (for description see will), and 200 A., ''Musketo Hammock.''
" granddau. **Mary Giddins,** cattle bearing mark of **Thos. Giddins.**

To **Eliza:**, wife of **Thos. Giddins**, and to dau. **Ann Scott**, personalty.

" wife **Mary**, dwelling-house during life and residue of personalty; she appointed ex. jointly with sons **William** and **John.**

Test: John Lane, Cornelius Ward, Thos. Ward, Samuell Ward. Ann Ward.   · 14. 132.

Harris, John, Perrahawkin, Somerset Co.,

7th Mch., 1710;
24th Mch., 1715-16.

To son **John** and hrs., 200 A., part of 600 A., ''Friend's Choice,'' with 150 A., ——.

" son-in-law **Richard Knight** and hrs., 350 A., part of ''Friend's Choice.''

" son **James** and hrs., 50 A., part of ''Harrises Venture.''

" son **Caleb** and hrs., 175 A., ''Middle Town,'' and 50 A., residue of ''Harrises Adventure.'' Should **son Caleb** die without issue, sd. land to be sold and proceeds divided between his 4 sisters, viz., **Priscilla, Esther, Sarah** and **Patience.**

" Jeremiah Harris, Ambrose Riggen, Randall Smuelling, Robert Harriss, Hugh Coligan and Thos. Prittchett each 1 shilling, in full of their portion of estate.

Wife **Judith**, extx. and residuary legatee of estate.

Test: Jno. West, Randall West, Eliner Lee.   14. 134.

Round, Sam'll, merchant, Maryland and Barbadoes,

15th Sept., 1715;
7th Oct., 1715.

To uncle **William Round**, all estate, real and personal, in Maryland and the Barbadoes, and estate in England to be divided among brothers and sisters, ——.

Ex.: Wm. Bradie, who is instructed to sell effects and forward proceeds to uncle **William** afsd.

Test: Geo. Gillespie, James Crosbie, Wm. Maxwell.   14. 135.

Smith, John, Somerset Co.,   13th Mch., 1716;
3rd Apr., 1716.

To wife **Mareen**, extx., dwelling-house and plantation; to pass at her decease to **Thomas**, son of brother **Robert (Smith)**, and hrs.

" mother, ——, brothers **Edward** and **William**, and to Robert, son of Isaac Stitts, personalty.

Test: Jno. Brown, Robert Stitt, Jno. Gray.   14. 136.

Davis, Thomas, Annimessex, Somerset Co.,
23rd Oct., 1715;
23rd Mch., 1715-16.

To son **Thomas** and hrs., upper part of "Unduce," on Davis
Inlet, and 150 A., "Long Town."

" son **John,** lower part of "Unduce," and 100 A., ——,
bought of Jno. Carter.

" wife **Sarah,** extx., "Waterford," in Marrumscoe, and personalty.

Test: Thos. Stockwell, Jno. Cullin, Abraham Trice, Rich'd
Barnes, Sarah Martin. 14. 137.

Roberson, John, Somerset Co., 2nd Nov., 1715;
3rd Nov., 1715.

To 2 sons, **Wm.** and **Jno.,** and their hrs., all land ——; former
to be under care of brother-in-law **James Whetherly** and
sister **Elizabeth,** his wife, during minority; latter under
that of father-in-law **Benja. Cottman** and mother, ——.

" dau. **Elizabeth,** personalty, including that which belonged
to her mother, ——; she to be under care of brother-in-
law **Richd. Samuells** and sister-in-law **Ann,** his wife.

" 3 child. afsd., residue of estate.

Exs.: **Benja. Cottman** and **James Wheatherly** afsd.

Test: Thos. Serman, Wm. Willson, Jr., Wm. Vaughan. 14. 138.

Acworth, Henry, Stepney Parish, Somerset Co.,
12th Oct., 1715;
16th Nov., 1715.

To sons **John, Samuell** and **Henry** and their hrs., 600 A., "Ac-
worths Purchase" and "Friend's Discovery"; young. son
Henry to have dwelling plantation, son **John** the middle
portion and son **Samuell** residue. Should any son die
during minority, deceased's portion to pass to survivor or
survivors.

" dau. **Mary,** personalty.

Wife **Sarah,** extx.

Overseers: Brothers **James Mathole** and **James Train.**

Test: Robt. Givan, Wm. Whetherly, John Robertson. 14. 139.

Davis, John, Back Creek, Somerset Co., 8th Aug., 1713;
16th Nov., 1715.

To cous. **David Willson,** 400 A., plantation and land on s. side
Back Creek, devised testator by will of brother **Rich'd
Davis,** and being greatest part of "Berray's Lott."

Kinsman **Ephraim Wilson,** ex. and residuary legatee.

Test: Andrew Thompson, Mary Sanders, Rich'd Sanders, Mary
Gordon. 14. 140.

Hill, Wm., Somerset Co.,   16th Jan., 1715-16;
                                                29th Feb., 1715-16.

To Elizabeth, dau. of Wm. Bouland, and Margarett, dau. of
    Thos. Pollet, personalty.

Wm. Bouland and Pat. Daley, joint exs. and residuary legatees.

Test: Thos. Pollet, Wm. Heath, Wm. Owens.   14. 142.

Harrison, Rich'd, Calvert Co.,   10th Sept., 1713;
                                                15th Feb., 1716-17.

To wife **Elizabeth,** during life, dwelling plantation and lands,
    350 A., "Hornisham," 30 A., part of "Popingay," bought
    of Benja. Chew, and 48 A., "Harrison's Pasture."

"   son **Samuell** and hrs., 1342 A. nr. Herring's Creek, on bay
    viz., "Holland's Hills," "Benjamin's Choyce," "Ben-
    jamin's Addition," "Bednall Green," "Marley Lott,"
    and "Harrison's Lott"; also, water-mill and 100 A. mill
    land, 136 A., "Birckhead's Right," lately bought of
    Abraham Birckhead, and part of "Birckhead's Lott,"
    bought of Solomon Birckhead.

"   son **Richard** and hrs., "Abington Manor," and "Dowls-
    dall," nr. Patuxent River, in Calvert Co.

"   grandson **Rich'd Lane** and hrs., at decease of wife afsd.,
    lands devised her, and 96½ A., part of "Birckhead's
    Lott," 100 A., "Gramer's Chance."

"   grandson **Harrison Lane** and hrs., residue of "Birckhead's
    Lott" and personalty.

"   grandsons **Sam'll** and **Joseph Lane** and their hrs., residue
    of 600 A., "Gramer's Chance" and land adjoining; also,
    200 A., part of "Birckhead's Chance," in A. A. Co.,
    bought of Abraham Birckhead.

"   grandson **Benja. Lane** and hrs., 300 A., "Pork Hall,"
    300 A. on n. branch Patuxent, in Prince George's Co.

"   dau. **Mary Chew,** wife of **Sam'll Chew, Jr.,** and dau.
    Eliza:, wife of **Jno. Chew,** and their male hrs., 800 A.,
    "Hall's Lott" and "Hall's Choice," in Cecil Co.

"   Sarah Lane, dau.-in-law **Eliza: Bond** and to Elizabeth
    Chew, widow of Joseph Chew, to the poor **Quakers** on
    western shore and to the poor of Herring Creek, person-
    alty.

"   wife afsd., ⅓ of residue; balance to be divided between
    son **Samuell,** ex., and son **Rich'd** and their hrs.

Overseers: Rich'd Johns, Sr., Wm. Richardson, Sr.

Test: Nehemiah Birckhead, Henry Child, Richd. Bond, Dan'll
    Robertson.   14. 142.

Curtis, Michael, St. Mary's Co.,   13th July, 1716;
                                           19th July, 1716.

To Sarah, wife of Jno. Turner, ½ tract "Salleys" on Clements Bay during life, and personalty.

" goddau. Mary Anderson, residue of sd. tract and entire tract at decease of Sarah Turner afsd., and personalty.

" goddau. Thomasin Stonestreet, King and Queen Parish; Thomas Bencraft, Sr., the widow of Thomas Greenfield, Sr.; ——, widow of Wm. Joseph; Henry Peregrine Jowles, Edward Field, Sr.; Edward Farr, Priscilla, wife of Robt. Saintclaire; Sarah, wife of Roderick Loyd; Mary, wife of Thos. Reaves, Sr.; Eliza: Bolt, widow Searson, Jno. Baker of St. Mary's; Frances, wife of Thos. Jordan; Thos. Notley Goldsmith and Justinian and Gerrard Jordain, personalty.

Philip Briscoe, Sam'l Williamson, and Elizabeth, wife of Thos. Jordain, Sr., exs. and residuary legatees of estate.

Test: George Winnett, Thos. Kindelan, John Donaldson.

                                         14. 146.

Dansey, John, collector of Patuxent District.
                                   18th Sept., 1716;
                                   27th Sept., 1716.

To brother **Robert Dansey** and hrs., plantation "Radner"; he dying without issue, land to be sold and proceeds to be given to male hrs. of Jane Lancelot and Eliza: Bridgeman.

" Mary Greenfield and Rev. Robt. Scott, personalty.

" the poor of All Faith Parish, 12 A., ——, in bottom of Town Neck, and to Poplar Hill Church, personalty.

Ante-nuptial agreement with **Martha Dansey,** made by Major Dent, confirmed.

Brother **Robert,** ex. and residuary legatee.

Test: Adam Bell, Wm. Swale, Rich'd Wise, Diannah Wise.

                                         14. 150.

Todd, Thomas, "the younger," Balto. Co.,
                                   11th Jan., 1714-15;
                                  *3rd June, 1715.

To son **Thomas** and male hrs., all lands——, in neck below head of Bare Creek and head of Back R.; he lacking male hrs., lands to pass to male hrs. of son **Robert,** and brothers **William Todd, Philip Todd** and **Christopher Todd** in succession.

" son **Robert** and hrs., 1500 A. in "Showan Hunting Ground," on draughts of Gunpowder R.

---

* Probated also in Essex Co., 20th Sept., 1715.

To brother **William** and **Martha**, his wife, personalty. The
tract of land on which testator lived in Virginia is devised to whomsoever testator's father, ——, shall devise
his plantation, provisionally; rest of lands there to be
sold and proceeds divided between wife **Elizabeth** and
child., together with residue of estate. Children to have
estate at majority.

Exs.: In Maryland, Rich'd Colegate, James Philips and wife.
Exs. in Va., brothers **Wm. Todd** and **Jonathan Hide.**

Test: Jacob Bull, Parle Phillpotts, Rich'd Ruff.   14. 152.

Jones, Thomas, A. A. Co., 20th Oct., 1716; 6th Nov., 1716.

To Samuel Dorsey and Francis Mercier, personalty.
Jane Burnell, extx. and residuary legatee of estate, real and
personal.

Test: Chas. Kilburne, F. Mercier.   14. 154.

Marsh (Mash), Thomas, Kent Island, Queen Anne's Co., 10th Jan., 1715; 27th June, 1716.

To possible unborn child, if male, upper plantation, "Cabin
Neck."
"   son **Thomas** and hrs., residue of lands and that afsd.
should no other son be born.
"   daus. **Mary** and **Sarah**, personalty.
"   wife **Eliza:**, extx., personal estate jointly with child afsd.,
and use of plantation during minority of same.

Overseers: Father and uncle, **Jno. Hawkins** and **Wm. Coursey.**
Test: **Wm. Coursey**, Jno. Johnson, Vincent Hemsley. 14. 154.

Jackson, Thomas, Queen Anne's Co., 2nd June, 1715; 29th Aug., 1716.

To wife **Barbara**, extx., dwelling plantation and land "Barbara's Choyce" and "Winchester Moyety"; to pass to
son **George** and hrs. at her decease.
"   son **Francis** and hrs., 200 A., "Jasper's Lott," at head of
Red Lyon's Branch on Chester R.
"   son **Joseph** and hrs., 200 A., "Barbara's Inlet," or Jones'
Neck.
"   dau. **Barbara Hyat**, at decease of her mother, provided
she be a widow, real estate.

Test: Mary Sanders, Sarah Sweet, Thos. Jones.   14. 156.

Pott, William, planter, Kent Co., 8th Sept., 1716; 27th Sept., 1716.

To Geo. Hanson and Ann Glen, "Langford's Neck" during
term of lease and personalty.

To Martha Decowdra, personalty bequeathed her by her godfather, Col. Hans. Hanson. Deed of gift of personalty
to Philip Church and dau.-in-law **Tabitha Church,** confirmed, they to receive it at ages of 21 and 16 respectively,
same to be paid in cattle, etc., according to appraisement
of their father's estate.
" cous. **John Pott** and sister-in-law **Sarah Hopkins,** personalty.
" son **Joseph** and hrs., residue of estate. Should he die
without issue, cous. **Jno. Pott** afsd. to have ½ of same,
and George Hanson, Frederick Hanson and Ann Glen to
have residue.
Ex.: Brother-in-law **Gideon Pierce.**
Test: Alex. Williamson, Jno. Rogers, Jno. Marsh. 14. 158.

Beans, Christopher, Prince George's Co., 11th Dec., 1716; 24th Dec., 1716.

To son **Charles** and hrs., all that land at head of branch of
Charles Branch at Mt. Calvert road, etc. (For description see will.)
" Josiah Willson and hrs., houses and lots in Charlestown,
for which he has paid.
" Edward Henebry and hrs., 21 A., part of "Beard's Landing," on n. side Charles Branch. Should suit pending in
prov. court go against testator, and brother **William,** as
security, "have to pay certain sum of money," sd. **William** then to have plantation "New Designe" for seven
years.
Brother-in-law **Jno. Boon** to have charge of 4 child., and use
seats of land belonging to sons until they attain 19 yrs.,
viz., that one given son **Charles** and one belonging by
heirship to son **Christopher.** Daus., ——, to be of age
at 16 yrs.
Ex.: Jno. Deakins.
Test: Rich'd Scurlock, Benja. Allen, Mary Miles. 14. 159.

Jones, Jane, Charles Co., 6th Aug., 1716; 12th Sept., 1716.

To son **James Tyre,** personalty; to be taken out of testatrix's
thirds.
" other 3 child., **Mary Jones, Eliza: Jones** and **Charles Jones;**
share of Mr. Jones' estate.
Also, to last named, land, ——, taken up by testatrix, land
to be granted in name of afsd. son.
Exs.: Brothers **Robert** and **Charles Yates.**
Test: Jno. Beale, Jno. Phelpes, Ann Gwinn. 14. 161.

Tovey, Sam'll, Kent Co.,   4th Dec., 1712;
                                            11th Jan., 1716.

To son **Sam'll** and hrs., dwelling plantation ''Tovey's Lott.''
  ''   dau. **Mary** and hrs., 50 A., ——, bought by father, **Samuell.**
  ''   dau. **Eliza:** and to Rev. Thos. Lodge, in or near Bristol,
       personalty.
Wife **Eliza:**, extx., she to have charge of son **Sam'l** until he
       is 18 yrs. of age and of dau. **Mary** until she attains 16
       yrs.
Test: Jno. Talbott, Geo. Hanson, Thos. Smyth.   14. 162.

Mahaney, Timothy, Talbot Co.,   27th Feb., 1716;
                                            5th Mch., 1716.

To son **Timothy,** personalty.
  ''   son **Thos. Edge** and dau. **Margaret Edge** is committed care
       of daus. **Hannah** and **Martha Neale,** during minority of
       last named daus.
Exs.: Son **Thomas** afsd., Jno. Morgan and Morty Roe.
Test: Robt. Sutton, Wm. Turner, Edward Turner.   14. 163.

Wicks, Benjamin, Kent Island, Queen Anne's Co.,
                                            17th Nov., 1715;
                                            20th Mch., 1715.

To son **Joseph** and (younger) **Sam'll,** ''Lovepoint'' on Kent
       Island jointly. (For description see will.)
  ''   cous. **John Ingram** and to Francis Stevens, personalty.
  ''   wife **Mary,** extx., dower rights and dwelling plantation
       during widowhood.
  ''   child., viz., **Joseph, Samuell, Anna** and **Mary,** residue of es-
       tate, they to be in charge of wife afsd. during minority.
Test: Edward Browne, Wm. Loramur, Wm. Rakes.   14. 164.

Man, William (nunc.), Dorchester Co.,   14th Oct., 1716;
                                            17th Oct., 1716.

To Wm. Ennall, ex., entire estate.
Test: Wm. Rawley, Semour Moore.   14. 165.

Evans (Evens), John, planter, Talbot Co.,
                                            16th Feb., 1716;
                                            5th Mch., 1716.

To John, Jr., Thos. and James Kemp, child. of Jno. and Mary
       Kemp; Thos. Mooth and Eliza: Weeb, child. of Catherine
       Dulany, entire estate, equally.
Ex.: John Kemp, Sr.,
Test: John Munfield, Hannah Hueit, Dan'll Richardson.
                                                     14. 166.

Lone, John, Dorchester Co., 9th Feb., 1716;
13th Mch., 1716.

To Henry (Harre) Edgar, son of James Edgar, 50 A., ——.
" Jacob Gray, Sr., ex., residue of estate, real and personal.
Test: Lewes Griffin, Elianor Adams, James Edgar. 14. 167.

Neale, Francis, Sr., planter, Talbot Co., 19th Oct., 1716;
27th Nov., 1716.

To eld. son **Francis** and hrs., 100 A., part of "Hickory Ridge,"
where he now lives.
" 3 sons, **Jerimy, Jonathan** and **Sam'll,** 300 A., equally, of
"Cabe" and "The Adventure."
" dau. **Mary Neal,** 70 A., part of "Cabe."
" dau. **Sarah,** wife of **Robert Register,** 100 A., part of
"Shadewell's Addition."
" dau. **Johannah,** wife of **Charles Climar,** 100 A., part of
"Shadewell's Addition."
" grandson **Francis Neal** and hrs., 100 A., "Shadewell," in
Tuckahoe, Queen Anne's Co.
" wife **Ann,** dwelling plantation during life; to pass at her
decease to son **Edward** and hrs., sd. **Edward** to live with
his mother during minority.
" child. afsd., residue of estate, all sons being appointed
joint exs.
Test: Thos. Wiles, James Merrick, Theodorus Bonner. 14. 168.

Edwin, William, Kent Co., 34th Oct., 1716;
—— —— ——.

To brother **Michaell Edwin** and hrs., 100 A., being ½ "Crab
Tree Neck," near Swan Creek.
" wife **Mary,** extx., dwelling plantation during life; to pass
at her decease to son **William** and hrs.; he to inherit
residue of lands at 18 yrs. of age.
Test: Wm. Deane, Tamer Hodges. 14. 170.

Brown, William, merchant, Susquehannah Hundred, Cecil
Co., 23rd July, 1716;
13th Aug., 1716.

To wife **Hester,** extx., and hrs., ½ estate, real and personal.
Lands in Balto. Co. to be sold, also those in Cecil, at discretion of extx.
" sons ——, and daus. ——, at 21 yrs. of age, residue of
estate.

Should wife die during minority of children, brothers **Jonathan
Brown** and **Nathan Baker** to care for estate and place
children with Quakers.

Test: James Collins, Jno. Piggott, John Mattason, Sarah
Baker.   14. 171.

Whipps, John, Calvert Co.,   10th Dec., 1716;
                                                 26th Dec., 1716.

To wife **Eliza:**, ⅓ part of dwelling plantation ——, and
⅓ of personal estate.

"   child. **Abigall Evans, Jane Jones, Sarah Busey, Susannah
Stanford** and **Jno. Whipps, Jr.,** 20s. each.

"   dau. **Eliza:**, when of age, 20s.

Son **John** afsd., ex. and residuary legatee.

Test: Mary Chew, Henry Johnson, Wm. Preston.   14. 172.

Note—In absence of son **John**, friends Thomas Smith and
Samuel Griffith are appointed to execute will.

Thornwell, Robert, Dorchester Co.,   15th Jan., 1716;
                                                31st Jan., 1716.

To son **Robert**, dwelling plantation "Oyle of Beasom," and
personalty.

"   son **William**, "Mazereen Hall," on Ireland Creek, and
personalty.

"   dau. **Leath**, personalty.

Wife **Mary**. extx.

Sons **Robert** and **William** to remain with their mother-in-law.
Should she marry and they prefer not to remain with her,
friend Richard Willis to have charge of them till they
reach age of 20 yrs.

Overseers: Rich. Willis and Thos. Smith.

Test: Peter Cornelius, Robt. Bazell.   14. 173.

Nowell, Septimus, Great Choptank Parish, Dorchester Co.,
                                                23rd Oct., 1716;
                                                28th Jan., 1716.

To brother **Bazwell**, ex. and hrs., dwelling plantation "Five
Pines"; he dying without issue, his portion to pass to
sister **Ann Kempston**.

"   brother **James** and sister **Hannah**, sister **Ann Kempston**
and Sarah, dau. of Jno. Stevens, personalty.

"   son-in-law **Thomas Taylor**, residue of personal estate at
age of 21. Should he die without issue, his portion to
pass to brother **Bazwell** afsd., to whose care he is left;

sd. **Bazwell** to be allowed 2,000 lbs. of tobacco yearly for 4 yrs. for maintenance and education of sd. **Thomas Taylor.**

Testator desires to be buried beside his wife, ——.

Test: Chas. Eareckson (Erreckson), Jno. Harwood, Joseph Richson.   **14. 175.**

Pope, Eliza:, widow, Dorchester Co.,   6th Aug., 1716; 2nd. Dec., 1716.

To daus. **Rosanna Cannon, Katherine Willy, Ann Rumley, Judy Wingate, Dianna Willy, Sarah Willis, Mary Wingate,** 1s. each.

" son-in-law **John Willy,** ex. and hrs., all real estate, being 130 A. "Widow's Purchase."

" grand-dau. **Dorcas Allen,** residue of personal estate at age of 16 yrs.

Test: Wm. Evans, Jr., Frances Willey.   **14. 176.**

Millington, Samuel, planter, Dorchester Co.,
31st Dec., 1715; 2nd Dec., 1716.

To Bridget, wife of James Edger (Edgar), and her hrs., 50 A., "Cabbin Quarter," after decease of wife.

" John Lun, after decease of wife, 100 A. dwelling plantation, "Moorfields," during life; after his decease to pass to Samuel Harper.

" wife **Ruth,** extx., real estate during life and residue of personal estate absolutely.

Overseer: Lewis Griffin.

Test: Jno. Robson, Jacob Gray, Rich. Lane.   **14. 177.**

Rogers, David, chirurgeon, Dorchester Co.,
22nd Feb., 1714-15; 14th July, 1716.

To son **David,** entire estate, real and personal, including dwelling plantation, "East Town"; son to be in charge of Neomy Atkinson and of age at 18 yrs.

Exs.: Jno. Flower and Christopher Short.

Test: Thos. Shilton, Niamy Attkinson, Anthony Rawlings.   **14. 179.**

Thomas, William, planter, Dorchester Co.,
12th Nov., 1714; 6th Dec., 1715.

To son **John,** upper part of "Springg Garden," given testator by his father, ——, and personalty.

To son **William,** dwelling plantation part of "Springg Garden," and personalty.

    (Note—A branch or run constitutes the dividing line between the two portions of "Springg Garden".)

"   daus. **Mary** and **Catherine,** personalty.

"   wife **Mary,** extx., residue of personal estate.

Test: Rich. Webster, Joshua Kennerly, Charles Wheeler.

14. 180.

Willson, Andrew, planter, Somerset Co.,   7th Nov., 1713; 10th June, 1715.

To cousin, **Thomas Wilson,** and hrs. (son of bro. **Thomas,** deceased), "Middlesex," on e. side of Nanticoke R.; he dying without issue, sd. land to pass to the nearest in blood to sd. **Thomas Willson.**

"   James Langrill and hrs., 50 A. Black Wallnut Island, at mouth of Island Creek, Dorchester Co.

"   Peter Samnell and hrs., 50 A. Mulberry Island, near mouth of Nanticoke R. in Dorchester Co.

"   brother-in-law, **Robert Bowditch,** and **Ann,** his wife, "Poplar Island" on s. side of Fishing Bay, and personalty.

"   wife **Abigall,** residue of estate, provided she lives with **Robt.** and **Ann Bowditch;** and should she choose to leave them, her thirds only.

Exs.: **Robt.** and **Ann Bowditch,** jointly.

Test: Wm. Acworth, James Story, Joana Storey.   14. 181.

Wattson (Whatson), William, planter, Dorchester Co., 6th July, 1714; 10th Jan., 1715.

To son **Robert,** 1s.

"   son **William,** 100 A., part dwelling plantation.

"   son **Benony,** 50 A. of same tract.

"   son **Francis,** 50 A., "Contention," at head of Marshy Ck.

"   dau. **Eliza: Green,** 1s. 6d.

"   John Kirk, personalty; he to be guardian of child. during their minority.

"   wife ——, extx., real and personal estate during life, with power to sell any land for her maintenance when necessary, also interest in bond of Govin Lockerman.

Test: Wm. Therenton (Thorneton), Wm. Munn (Mann).

14. 182.

Harper, Edward, Dorchester Co.,   16th Dec., 1714;
9th June, ——.

To sons **Francis, Edward** and **John,** 12d.
" sons **Henry** and **Richard,** personalty.
" wife **Sarah,** extx., residue of personal estate absolutely
and dwelling plantation ——, with land joining, on Nanticoke R. during life; at her death to pass to son **William**
if he be living. Should ʰhe be dead, to be equally divided
among daus. (unnamed).

Test. Henry Benson, Jno. Wine. Abra Covington.   14. 183.

Costin, Mathias, Dorchester Co.,   9th June, 1715-6;
13th June, 1716.

To daus. **Rebecca, Roody** and **Sarah,** 400 A. on n. side St.
Martin's R., in equal portions. (For description see will.)
" daus. **Mary** and **Elizabeth,** 300 A. in equal portions, being
Manor plantation on n. side Nanticoke R. (For description see will.)
" dau. **Rebecca,** 50 A., part of "Costin's Trouble" on w.
side Dividing creek.
" wife **Sarah,** extx., personalᵗy.

Test: Rich. Chambers, Jr., **Stephen Costin, Isaac Costin** and
Thos. Pool.   14. 184.

Linch, Robuck, Baltimore Co.,   16th June, 1714;
12th Nov., 1716.

To four child., **Patrick, Anne, William** and **Mary** and their
hrs., all real estate; to pass in succession to name and
line of **Linch.** Should son **Patrick** refuse to live with
mother-in-law (testator's wife), during minority, he to
lose his share of estate.
" wife **Mary,** extx., entire personal estate.

Test: Mary Hampton, John Norton, S. Hinton.   14. 186.

Howard, Elizabeth, Charles Co.,   7th July, 1716;
8th Oct., 1716.

To niece and god-dau. **Elizabeth** (dau. of eldest bro. **William
Stevens Howard**), personalty.
" god-daus. **Rebecka,** dau. of cousin **Geo. Dent,** and Ann
dau. of Thos. Skinner, personalty.
" nephew **Thomas,** ex. (son of bro. **Thomas Howard),** residue of estate.

Test: Benj. Douglass, Jno. Groves, Ann Dent, Jno. Scrogin,
Edw. Gardiner.   14. 187.

Shaw, Mathew, Kent Co.,   26th April 1714;
                                                    21st Aug., 1716.

To Elizabeth Merefield, personalty at age.
"   wife **Elinor,** entire real, and residue of personal estate,
     during life, at her decease to pass to her sons, **William**
     and **Humphrey Best.**
Test: Ann Jones, Wm. Robinson.   14. 188.

Keld (Kelld), John, cooper, Talbot Co.,   ·21st July, 1716;
                                                    28th Aug., 1716.

To wife **Elinor,** extx., ⅓ estate, real and personal, her portion
     to pass to son **John** and hrs. at her decease.
"   sons **Thomas** and **Simon,** residue of realty and to sd. sons
     and dau. **Mary Hebb Keld,** residue of personalty. Should
     any of three sons die during minority, his portion of estate
     to be divided between survivors equally. Should widow
     marry again, sons to be of age at 18 yrs.
Test: Rich. Dudley, Wm. Dudley, Wm. Tharpe, Jno. Pem-
     berton.   14. 189.

Buckley, William, ·planter, Talbot Co.,   28th Nov., 1708;
                                                    8th Aug., 1716.

To sons **William, James** and grandchild **Nick. Buckley,** dwell-
     ing plantation equally divided, son **William** to have first
     choice. Should grandson **Nich. Buckley** die without issue,
     his share to revert to son **William.**
"   sons **Richard** and **Robert,** personalty at marriage or 20
     yrs. of age.
Testator directs that **Margaret Buckley,** widow of son **Nich.,**
     have a reasonable maintenance during widowhood.
To wife **Elizabeth,** extx., residue of estate, real and personal,
     during widowhood. Should she marry, dower rights only.
Test: Walter Quinton, Jno. Robinson, Edw. Hambleton.
                                                    14. 190.

Giddins, Benjamin, Talbot Co.,   27th Aug., 1716;
                                                    20th Oct., 1716.

To son **Maurice** and hrs., ½ dwelling plantation, "New Scot·
     land," and personalty.
"   son **Benjamin** and hrs., remaining ½ "New Scotland"
     and personalty. Sons to be of age at 21 yrs. Should either
     of sd. sons die without issue, his share of "New Scot-
     land" to revert to survivor and ·his hrs.
Wife **Catherine,** residuary legatee and joint ex. with brother,
     Edw. Hardin.

Test: Jno. Blamour (Blamer), Mary Blamer, Wm. Stevens,
M. Giddins. 14. 191.

Willicoxon (Willicoxen), John, Prince George's Co., 6th Mar., 1712; 27th Sept., 1716.

To wife **Magdalen,** and three sons, **John, Lewis** and **Thomas,** estate, real and personal, equally. Son **John,** ex.

Friends Wm. Glover, Wm. Dent and Mr. Nick. Dawson to divide estate.

Test: Wm. Lee, Stephen Garman, Tho. Addison. 14. 192.

Cooper, Nicholas, Charles Co., 7th Nov., 1716; 4th Dec., 1716.

To sons **Jno.** and **Philip** and hrs., ''Wattson's Purchase,'' ''Cowsking'' and personalty.

'' son **William** and hrs., ''Middle Green'' and personalty; to be in charge of Jos. Harrison and of age at 21 yrs.

'' daus. **Prudence Sanders** 10s., **Ann King,** 2s. Former gifts to both confirmed.

Wife **Penelope** to be maintained by estate.

Exs.: Wife and son **Philip,** jointly.

To trustees, Mr. Gerard Fooke, 20s., and Jos. Harrison (son of Rich.) and hrs., all real estate in Durham Town.

Test: Jos. Harrison, Eliz. Chapman, Jno. Cutts. 14. 193.

Smith, Jno., Charles Co., 13th April, 1716; 16th Nov., 1716.

To son **Jno.** and hrs., dwelling plantation, ——, 300 A., and personalty after decease of testator's wife.

'' son **Martha** (son of son **Jno.**), personalty.

'' dau. **Priscilla** (wife of **Jno. More**) and hrs., 200 A. adj. the 200 A. deeded to **Jno. More** (for description see will), and personalty.

'' dau. **Elizabeth** and hrs., 300 A. adj. **Jno. More's** and running from Suckia Swamp westward to outside line of the Manor, and personalty.

'' dau. **Sarah** and hrs., 300 A. on s. side Jordan's Branch, and personalty.

'' wife **Ann,** dwelling plantation, ——, during life; at her decease to son **Jno.** and hrs., and residue of personalty during life. After her decease to child. afsd. (for description of portions allotted to child. see will).

Exs.: Sons **Jno. Smith** and **Jno. More,** jointly.

Test: Owen Reed, Thos. Allin, Jno. Brymer, Sam'l Smith.

14. 195.

Robson, Richard, planter, Prince George's Co.,

23rd Oct., 1716;
15th Dec., 1716.

To sons **Mathew** and **Richard** and their hrs., personalty and dwelling plantation. Son **Mathew** to have dwelling and half the land. Should either of sd. sons die without issue, his portion to pass to survivor. Sons of age at 18 yrs.

"   son **John** and dau. **Mary,** personalty.

"   wife **Eliza:,** ⅓ dwelling plantation and ⅓ personal es-tate during life.

Residue of estate to child. **Mathew, Richard, John** and **Mary,** equally.

Ex.: John Turner, Sr.,

Test: Rich. Duckett, Ambrose Bourne, Grace Wheeler.

14. 198.

Dickson (Dixon), John, Queen Anne's Co.,

—— —— 1712;
20th Oct., 1716.

To wife **Elizabeth,** extx., and hrs., entire estate, excepting 100 A., ''Wenfield,'' bought from Esq. Smith. To pass at decease of wife to William Sutterfield (a young man raised from infancy by testator and wife).

Test: Mich. Hussey, Dan. Walker, Edw. Sutterfield.   14. 199.

Smith, Mathew, planter, Queen Anne's Co.,

16th Jan., 1715;
10th Mar., 1715.

To sons **James,** 1s., and **Thomas,** 40s.

"   grandson **James Griffin,** personalty.

"   grandson **Thos. Smith** and hrs. (son of **Mathew Smith),** 200 A. ''Content'' on Tuckahoe Branch, and personalty.

"   grandson **Jno. Smith** and hrs., dwelling plantation, 200 A., being part of ''Coursey's Range.''

"   dau. **Mary Ingram,** 40s.

"   son **Mathew,** ex., residue of personal estate.

Test: Thos. Hynson Wright, Wm. Delany (Dullany), **James Griffin.**   14. 200.

Brown, Edward, Kent Island, Queen Anne's Co.,

6th Nov., 1713;
9th June, 1716.

To son **John** and hrs., ''Belshew,'' purchased of Frances Barnes, and part of tract, ''Scilla,'' with dwelling house and personalty.

To son **Mathew** and hrs., 100 A., part of "Scilla," now in tenure of Wm. Rakes, and personalty.

" daus. **Mary** and **Rachel,** personalty.

" wife **Mary,** extx., use of dwelling plantation during widowhood, and personalty.

" Joseph (son of Benjamin Wicks), Benjamin Wickes and William Rakes, personalty.

Testator directs that £13 due him from Randall Janney of Philadelphia (merchant), together with cash at hand, be used in purchasing a young negro for dau. **Sarah.** Sons to be of age at 18, daus. at 16 or marriage.

Residue of personalty estate to child. afsd., equally.

Overseer: Mr. Jno. Wells.

Test: B. Ball, B. Wickes, Wm. Rakes. 14. 201.

Sturney, Catherine, (nunc.), Calvert Co., 6th Dec., 1716;
—— —— ——.

To son **William,** entire estate.

Mention is made in proceedings of dau. **Priscilla,** wife of **Daniel Swillavant.**

Test: Wm. Miller, Grace Miller, Adderton Skinner. 14. 203.

Howes, Charles, Calvert Co., —— —— ——;
4th Aug., 1716.

To Elizabeth Weems, Jean Adams, **Henry** and **Edw. Howes,** James, Thos., Eliza:, Ann, Wm. and John Willymott and **Charles Dorin,** John and Elizabeth Richardson, child. of Wm. Richardson, Jane Charleton and **Susannah** and **Jane Howes,** personalty.

" sister **Neomy Dorin** and Wm. Stuart, Jr., Charles and David Steward, personalty.

Wm. Willymott ex. and residuary legatee.

(Not signed.)

Test: Not mentioned.

Note—James Willimott swears to will being in testator's own handwriting. 14. 204.

Turner, John, Calvert Co., 12th Mar., 1715; 28th July, 1716.

Testator directs that "Bodell's Chance" (near land of David Hellen and joining land formerly owned by Edward Blackborn) be sold for benefit of estate.

To son **John** and hrs., remainder of real estate; should he die without issue, sd. land to go to son **Thomas;** he failing issue, to son **Gidion** and hrs. Sons to be of age at 19 yrs.

To wife **Johana,** extx., use of real estate during life and ⅓
personal estate absolutely; the other ⅔ to be equally
divided among child.

Test: James Mackall, Wm. Dawkins, Wm. Blackborn.

14. 205.

Roberts, James, planter, Calvert Co.,   16th Mar., 1716;
25th June, 1716.

To son **James** and hrs., 100 A., part of estate bought of John
Manning.

"   son **Jacob** and hrs., 132 A. bought of Mary Mitchell, and
formerly owned by James Craford.

"   wife **Elizabeth,** entire estate, real and personal, during
life.

Personal estate at decease of wife divided among three child.
viz.: **James, Jacob** and dau. **Ruth.** Should any child die
their portion to go to survivor or survivors.

Test: James Bourne, Thos. Little, Nath. Dare.   14. 205.

Brooke, Robert, Calvert Co.,   17th Jan., 1715;
10th April, 1716.

To wife **Grace,** extx., ⅓ part of "Brooke Place Manor," containing 300 A., during life; at her death to son **Robert**
and hrs.; 200 A. joining land of **Roger Brooke** to be sold
for benefit of estate.

"   son **Robert** and hrs., the other ⅔ of "Brooke Place
Manor."

"   dau. **Eliza: Fenwick** and hrs., 100 A. on n. side of Island
Ck.

"   son **Charles** and hrs., 100 A. adjoining land given dau.
Eliza: Fenwick. Should he die without issue, sd. land to
revert to son **Robert** and hrs.

Test: Wm. Thacker, Grace Mackgill, Stephen Dunn, Jno.
Dorrumple.   14. 207.

Whittington, Wm., Sr., planter, Calvert Co.,
31st Mar., 1716;
19th May, 1716.

To son **Francis** and hrs., part of two tracts, 70 A., "Coxes
Freehold," 80 A., "Capthall," at decease of his mother
or at age of 21 yrs., and personalty.

"   son **William** and hrs., part of two tracts, "Lowerey's
Rut," containing 100 A., and "Bullens Right," containing 175 A.

To dau. **Mary,** personalty.
"   wife **Charity,** extx., residue of estate during life; to pass
to child. at her decease.
Test: Rich. Pool, Jno. Camwell.   14. 208.

Tucker, Thos., Calvert Co.,   12th April, 1716;
                                                       5th July, 1716.

To sons **Thos.** and **John** and hrs., tract of land "Adventer."
Residue of real estate and personalty to be divided between
wife **Ann,** extx., and child.
Test: James Duke, Joshua Sedwicks, Gilbard Deaver.
                                                              14. 209.

Jones, David, Calvert Co.,   3Cth Dec., 1715;
                                                       8th Mar., 1715-6.

To wife **Mary,** extx., entire estate absolutely, excepting 50
A. "Good Luck," which at her decease is to pass to
brother **William (Jones)** and hrs.; he failing issue, to pass
in turn to brothers, **Jacob** and **Benj.**
Test: Charles King, Temperance Jones, Elizabeth Jones.
                                                              14. 209.

Davis, Jno., Calvert Co.,   12th Aug., 1712;
                                                       8th Mar. 1715.

To son-in-law **James Cranford,** personalty at age of 21 yrs.
"   wife **Martha,** extx., ⅓ of estate.
"   son **Thomas** and dau. **Martha** residue of estate equally;
son to be of age at 18 yrs., dau. at 16 or marriage.
Test: Henry Ellt, Michel Dainell (Daniell).   14. 210.

Burton, Wm., Calvert Co.,   14th Feb., 1715;
                                                       26th July, 1716.

To nephew **Wm. Mackdowell** and to Thomas Collins, personalty.
"   wife **Ann,** extx., residue of estate, real and personal, during life. At her decease to child. of sister **Jane** ——,
equally.
Test: James Mackall, Mary Mackdowell, Cath. Henry.
                                                              14. 211.

Johnson, Daniel, planter, Baltimore Co.,   12th Sept., 1715;
                                                       30th Jan., 1715.

To wife **Frances,** extx., personalty, some of which was purchased of Wm. Cook, and dwelling plantation during life.
Should unborn child be a boy, he to enjoy same at her
decease in fee simple.

To **Jno. Low** and hrs., water mill on n. side Susquehanna R., and personalty.

Residue of estate, real and personal, equally divided among all child. and wife of testator, excepting wife of **Jno Low,** who is to have no part.

Extx. is empowered to dispose of tract "Rycraffs Choyce" for benefit of estate. Should wife not be contented with her legacy and child's portion and claim her thirds, sd. legacy to be divided with other estate, as law directs; wife of **John Low** to have no share in same.

Test: Mary Bellshair, Thos. Russell.   14. 212.

Hagoe, Thos., planter, Charles Co.,   29th Mar., 1714; 21st Feb., 1716.

To wife **Mary**, extx., dwelling plantation, 300 A., "St. James," also 15 A. bought of Major Wm. Boarman and 60 A. bought of Wm. Boarman, during life, to pass at her decease to son **William.**

"   son **James** and hrs., 350 A., part of "Good Intent." (For description see will.)

"   son **Ignatius** and hrs., 200 A., part of "Good Intent," also 65 A. bought of Major Wm. Boarman and made over to testator by codicil to will.

"   son **Thomas** and hrs., 250 A. "Clare," adjoining "Good Intent."

"   dau. **Mary Baggott**, 100 A., part of "Good Intent," adjoining the place she has already seated.

"   sons **Thos.** and **Ignatius** afsd., 150 A. "Correck Measure," in St. Mary's Co.

"   four. daus., **Sarah Edelen, Charity Green, Ann Smith** and **Eliza: Clarkson,** each 10s.

"   wife afsd., entire personal estate to pass to son **William** at her decease.

Test: Wm. Boarman, Jr., Thos. Dison, Jno. Gates, Joseph Gates.   14. 213.

Taylor, Sam'l, Queen Anne's Co.,   17th Feb., 1715; 19th Mar., 1715.

To son **Ruben** and hrs., 100 A., being easternmost hind part of "Arcadia," and lying next land sold to Solomon Wright.

"   son **Nebuchadnezer** and hrs., 100 A. "Arcadia." (For description see will.)

"   three sons and three daus., 5s.

To wife **Jane**, extx., remaining part of "Arcadia" and residue of estate. Should wife marry before sons arrive at age of 21 yrs., they are to be of age at 18.

Test: Thos. Shoebrooke, Ann Wright, Solomon Wright.

14. 214.

Kenton, Wm., planter, Tuckahoe, Queen Anne's Co.,
2nd April, 1716;
28th April, 1716.

To sons **Solomon** and **James** and their hrs., 200 A., e. end "Upland," equally; in event of death of either son before majority, his share to pass to survivor.

" sons **Wm., Jno.** and **Thos.** and their hrs., remainder of "Upland" and tract adjoining, "Upland Addition," equally.

" son **Wm.** afsd., personalty.

" dau. **Lidia** and hrs., ½ "Blomesberry," 200 A., Talbot Co. Other half to sons **Solomon** and **James** afsd., and their hrs.

" wife **Rebecka**, extx., ⅓ personal estate absolutely, and dwelling plantation for life, which at her decease passes to son **John** and hrs., he not to sell it. Residue of personal estate to six child. afsd. Sons of age at 20, dau. at 18 or marriage.

Test: Jno. Hill, Frances Hill, Wm. Rowe (Roe), Abigale Rowe (Roe), Jno. Willson. 14. 216.

Brown, Jno., Prince George's Co., 9th Feb., 1714;
28th Apr., 1716.

To son **Francis** and dau. **Mary Phippard**, 1s. each.

" son **Jacob**, ex., and hrs., dwelling plantation bought of Jacob Stanley, "Stanleys Choice," and residue of entire estate. Should son **Jacob** die without issue, land to pass to grandson **Jno. Phippard** and hrs.; he failing issue, to granddau. **Ursilla Phippard** and hrs.; she failing issue, to grandson **Wm. Phippard** and hrs.; he failing issue, to pass to Ann (dau. of Owen Ellis) and hrs.; should she have no issue, to the hrs. of Owen; he failing issue, to parish of St. Paul's as Glebe Land.

Test: Owen Ellis, Wm. Jones, Jane Addams, Thos. Cockshutt (Rect. All Sts. Parish, Calv. Co.), Charles Somersett Smith, Jos. Hall. 14. 217.

Winlock, Wm., planter, Kent Island, Queen Anne's Co.,
$$\text{1st Jan., 1715;}$$
$$\text{10th Mar., 1715.}$$
To cous. **Rich. More, Jr.**, niece **Sarah More**, Mrs. Hanah, and
    father, ——, personalty.
Residue of estate to 3 child. of **Richard Moore (More)**, equally.
Test: Jno. Godman, Wm. Elliott, Jno. Holland.   14. 219.

Mason, Mathew, Queen Anne's Co.,   7th May, 1715;
To sons **Mathew (Matha)** and **Richard** and their hrs., per-
    sonalty. "Now depending in House of Assembly."
  "   4 sons, **Matha, Rich., Joseph** and **Solomon** and their hrs.,
    interest now pending in House of Assembly. Sons to be
    of age at 18.
  "   dau. **Mary Jones Mason** and hrs., dwelling plantation.
  "   **Elizabeth** (dau. of Thos. Parsons), Thos. Parsons and
    Joseph Renshaw, personalty.
Exs.: Wife **Elinor** and son **Matha**, jointly.
Test: Thos. Parsons, Oliver Kranivet, Chas. Vanderford.
                                            14. 219.
Note—This name is written **Matha** throughout and marked
    by copyist as "being so in original," but will is signed
    Mathew Mason.

Dant, Wm., planter, St. Mary's Co.,   31st Jan., 1714;
                                            16th May, 1715.
To cousins **Jno. Dant** and **Wm. Mills** and their hrs., "Poplar
    Neck" with land adjoining, 76 A., "Annstroder," equally.
    Should **Jno. Dant** afsd. die without issue, then to **Jno.
    Mills** and his hrs.
  "   bro. **Peter Mills**, ex., **Peter Mills, Jr.**, cousin **Elinor Nevet**,
    personalty.
Test: Wm. Coode, Eliza: Hooke, Stephen Vinall, Hanah Vinall.
                                            14. 221.

Mattingly, Thos., Sr., planter, St. Mary's Co.,
                                            9th Oct., 1714;
                                            12th Jan., 1714.
To son **Thos.** and hrs., "Mount Misery," where he now lives,
    and personalty.
  "   son **James** and hrs., 130 A., e. side dwelling plantation,
    being part of a 200 A. tract; also 52 A. adjoining, called
    "Mattingly's Purchase," and personalty.

To grandson **James Clark** and hrs., 70 A., the plantation
where his father now lives, after decease of his father and
mother. This tract being the west side of testator's
dwelling plantation.

" daus. **Eliza: Clark** and **Judith Parker**, personalty.

In event of death of son **James** without issue, his share to
pass to son **Charles**, he to pay to his 3 bros. and sister,
Wm., Luke, Ignatius and **Ann**, 4,000 lbs. tobacco. Should
son **Chas.** die without issue, son **William** to succeed to
estate and pay as afsd. to surviving bros. and sister.
Sons to be of age at 18, and dau. at 16 or at marriage.
Residue of estate divided into six equal parts to five
child., viz.: **Charles, William, Luke, Ignatius** and **Ann**,
the sixth part to wife **Elizabeth**, extx. Should she reject
a child's portion and claim her thirds, sons **Thos.** and
James to be exs. and deliver to her a third part of estate,
to pay to sd. five children personalty, and divide residue
between themselves.

Overseers: Robt. Cole and son **Thomas**.

Test: Adam Boyde (Boyd), Thos. Dillon, Rich. Miller.

14. 222.

Guibert, Elizabeth, St. Mary's Co.,   19th Dec., 1715;
17th Sept., 1716.

To son **John Blackiston** and male hrs. (being Protestants),
dwelling plantation, "Langworth Point," on Potomac
River in St. Clement's Hundred, and all real estate except 150 A.

" dau. **Mary Mason** and hrs., being Protestant, and for want
of such issue to next surviving Protestant heir, 150 A.
afsd., it being a part of tract of waste land bought of
Mich. Curtis of St. Clements Hund. Should son **John**
die without Protestant issue, land given to sd. son to
be equally divided among grandchild. and their hrs.

" daus. **Susanah Attoway, Rebecka Walters, Mary Mason**
and **Ann Blackiston**, granddau. **Elizabeth Blackiston** and
grandson **Nehemiah Blackiston**, personalty.

" son **John** afsd., ex., ½ personal estate, other half to be
equally divided among daus. above mentioned and their hrs.

" church for ornaments, as vestry shall see fit, 2,000 lbs.
tobacco.

Test: John Coode, Wm. Gibson, James Brian, Katherine Gibson.   14. 224.

Cole, Valentine, planter, St. Mary's Co.,   26th May, 1716;
17th Sept., 1716.

To son **John,** ex., entire estate.

Guardian: Francis Hopewell.

Test: Wm. Hebb, Wm. Thomas, Edw. Askins, Her. Sweeny.

14. 225.

Attoway, Thos., carpenter, St. Mary's Co.,

17th Feb., 1715;
6th June, 1716.

To Wm. Hardy, personalty.

" wife **Ann,** extx., residue of estate.

Bro. **John Attoway** to be acquitted of indebtedness to testator
of 1,300 lbs. tobacco.

Test: Jno. Bullock, Joseph Hopkins and Benj. Reeder 14. 226.

Powell, Jno., Jr., son of **Jno. Powell,** deceased, A. A. Co.,

7th Nov., 1715;
6th Apr., 1716.

To mother, **Eliza: Jacks,** "Powell's Inheritance" on South
R., during life; after her decease to pass to brother
Joseph and hrs. Should **Joseph** lack issue, sd. land to
pass to **Richard Jacks** and hrs.

" brothers **Christopher Walters** and **Thos. Jacks, Jr.** (son
and sole heir of **Thos. Jacks, Sr.**), 200 A., equally.

" **Christo. Walters, Eliza:** (dau. of **Thos. Jacks**) and **Barbary Jacks,** personalty.

Ex. unnamed.

Test: Wm. Wayger, Robt. Nickols, Jno. Nickolson, Jr.

14. 227.

Parsons, Edward,   12th Dec., 1715;
21st April, 1716.

To wife **Mary** and 4 child. viz.: **Robert, Jno., Charles** and
Eliza:, dwelling plantation "Worrell," 240 A. in St.
Mary's Co. equally among them; also to wife **Mary** and
her afsd. child., all that tract on Kenebeck R., New England, containing 500 A., and personalty.

" son and dau., **Edw.** and **Mary,** child. by former wife
Phillis, 1s. each.

Exs.: wife **Mary** and brother **Robert Hopkins.**

Testator directs that the widow Pope should have her maintenance during life, according to covenant.

Test: Henry Reynolds, Randall Broom, Jno. Harwood. 14. 228.

Green, Mary (widow), St. Mary's Co., 12th May, 1716;

—— —— ——.

To sons **Thos.** and **James** and hrs., "Guyther's Purchase" as now divided, between them. Should sd. sons die without issue, their share to pass to their widows during widowhood, then to grandson **Thos. Squires** and hrs. Should he die without issue, to next hr. of dau. **Squires.**

" dau. **Sarah Squires,** personalty; she to enjoy part of the tract belonging to son **James. Jno. Squires** to have liberty to clear and plant same at his wife's pleasure.

" **Jane Campbell,** personalty.

" grandson **Thos. Squires,** personalty at age of 18.

Ex.: Son **James.**

Test: Danll. Clocker, Alice Clocker, Jno. Baker. 14. 229.

Knowles, Catherine (widow), Balto. Co.,
8th June, 1716;
15th June, 1716-7.

To daus. **Mary Douglass** and **Sarah Owens** and hrs., personalty.

" three grandchildren, **Rich, Ruth** and **Steven Owens** (children of dau. **Sarah),** £60 each.

" granddau. **Ruth Owens,** personalty.

" sons-in-law **Wm. Douglass** and **Rich. Owings,** joint exs., residue of estate, equally.

Test: Wm. Hamillton, Robert Parker, Thos. Beavans. 14. 230.

Cooke, Thomas, planter, St. Mary's Co., 3rd June, 1715;
3rd May, 1716.

To eld. son **Thomas** and hrs., personalty and tract —— on which he is now seated, and, if necessary, part of dwelling plantation ——; division to be made by Major William Watts, Peter Watts and John Mason.

" sons **John** and **Henry,** personalty and residue of dwelling plantation. Should either of last named sons die during minority or without issue, survivor to inherit portion of deceased.

" son **William** and daus. **Margaret, Bethe, Elinor** and **Mary,** personalty.

" wife **Elizabeth,** extx., residue of personal estate and use of part of dwelling plantation ——, during life.

Test: Jno. Mason, Robt. Moseley, Jno. Stacey, Sam'l Johnson. 14. 232.

Barrons, Thos., Sr.,   28th Nov., 1716;
4th Feb., 1716.

To son **Rich.** and hrs., 100 A. "Cochells Hall."
"   son **Thos.**, 100 A., part of "Doggwood Springs."
"   dau. **Alloner** and hrs., 50 A. "Doggwood Springs."
"   youngest daus., **Margaret** and **Ann**, residue of sd. land.
Ex. unnamed.

Test: Wm. Prickard, Rich. Breen, Thos. Huntt.   14. 233.

Thompson, Wm., Britain's Bay, St. Mary's Co.,
10th Feb., 1716;
7th Mar., 1716.

To son **Michael** and hrs., 40 A., dwelling plantation (leased
by father, ——, from Jno. Sheircliffe for 90 yrs.), during
remaining time of lease. Also 100 A., being ½ of "Hat-
field Hills." Should sd. son die without issue, this tract
to be equally divided—1 part to wife, **Barbara**, extx.,
and hrs., and 1 part to father-in-law, **Wm. Langham**,
and hrs.

Test: Henry Spinke, Jude Salten, Edw. Spinke, Wm. Abell.
14. 234.

Davis, Jno., St. Mary's Co.,   23rd Dec., 1716;
29th Mar., 1717.

To youngest son **George** and dau. **Mary**, each ⅓ personal
estate.
"   two child., **Jno.** and **Briscoe**, and their hrs., all land
equally divided between them, excepting ⅓ of dwelling
plantation.
"   wife **Ann**, extx., ⅓ of dwelling plantation during life
and ⅓ personal estate, absolutely.

Test: Peter O'Neale (O'Neall), Alexd. Scott, Peter Harris.
14. 235.

Machetee, Patrick, Charles Co.,   5th Oct., 1716:
26th Mar., 1717.

To sons **Patrick, Edmond** and **James**, dwelling plantation
equally. Son **Edmond** to have northernmost part where
his house is, division to be made by friends Wm. Chandler
and Antho. Neale.
"   godson and grandson **Patrick Machetee**, personalty.
"   wife **Rosomond**, extx., residue of estate and use of dwelling plantation during life, excepting son **Edmond's** part.

Test: Anthony Neale, George Walker, Thos. Webster.
14. 235.

Machetee, Rosamond, Charles Co., 3rd Mar., 1716;
20th Mar., 1717.

To granddau. **Frances,** personalty.

Residue of estate to be divided equally among 7 child., viz.:
Edmond, Patrick, James, Katherine Galahaw, Mary Boswell, Elinor Clements and **Rosomond Clements.**

Ex.: son **James.**

Test: Antho. Neale, Geo. Walker. 14. 236.

Welch, Thos., 22nd Jan., 1716;
29th Mar., 1717.

Testator leaves to Thos. Wheeler's care his two daus., **Elinor** and **Katherine,** with ½ estate for children's use. To Margaret Camel's care his dau. **Ann.** To Mr. Peter Harris's care his son **John,** and personalty for use of sd. son.

'' Peter Harris, ex., personalty.

Dau. **Ann** afsd., residuary legatee.

Test: John Seager, Dennis Mahany, Philip Harney. 14. 237.

Wiseman, John, St. Mary's Co., 26th Jan., 1716;
18th Apr., 1716-7.

To father, **Richard Shirley,** ex., and mother, **Katherine,** his wife, personalty for life.

'' bros. **Robert Wiseman, Richard Shirley,** sister **Catherine Greenwell,** cousin **Francis Miles,** personalty.

Test: Nich. Richardson, Francis Miles, Mary Miles. 14. 238.

Cooper, Thos. (freeholder), St. Mary's Co.,
1st Feb., 1714;
17th Mar., 1714-5.

To sons **Thomas** and **Richard,** exs., jointly, entire estate, real and personal, equally.

Test: Thos. Dillon, Anne Green, James French. 14. 239.

Hambleton, Edward (innholder), Queen Anne's Co.,
2nd Mar., 1713;
10th Dec., 1716.

To 5 child., viz.: **William, Edward, Elizabeth, Margaret** and **Sarah,** entire estate.

Son **Edward** and daus. **Margaret** and **Sarah** to be in care of their uncle, **Walter Quinton,** ex.

Son **Edward** of age at 18, daus. at 16 or marriage.

Test: Mary Allchurch, Chas. Vanderford, Chas. Lemarr.

14. 240.

William, Thos. (nunc.), Queen Anne's Co.,

11th Oct., 1716;
13th Oct., 1716.

To wife, ⅓ of estate.
Edmond Thomas ex. and residuary legatee.
Test: Trustam Thomas.   14. 241.

Wintersell, William,

20th Dec., 1716;
15th Jan., 1716.

To eldest son **William,** 20s.
" son **Thomas,** 12d.
" son **Joshua** and son **Thomas'** eldest son **William,** "Wintersell," between Island Ck. and a branch of Tredhavon
   R., equally. Should either die without male issue, their
   portion to pass to survivor (their widows to have 3rds
   during life).
" dau. **Mary Brown,** and to **Elisha** and **Margaret,** child. of
   dau. **Jane,** personalty.
" youngest son **William** and hrs., dwelling plantation.
Wife **Jane,** extx., to have use of plantation during her widowhood. Should she marry, her thirds only and sd. plantation to pass at once to youngest son **William** afsd.
To daus. **Amelkey, Elinor, Catherine** and **Susanah,** 12 pence
   each.
Test: Denis Hopkins, Jno. Jackson, Faith Jackson.   14. 241.

Smith, Wm., Talbot Co.,

10th Dec., 1716;
5th Feb., 1716.

To John King, Jr., James Harvey, Andrew Skinner and Kath-
   erine Emerson, personalty.
" Thomas Emerson, ex., and James Harvey, residue of estate.
Test: J. Emerson, Mary Thornton, Jane Youons.   14. 243.

Emerson, Anna, Talbot Co.,

11th Dec., 1716;
8th Jan., 1716.

To grandchild., viz.: **Richard Jones, John Randall, Alice** and
   Richard Emerson, personalty. Two last named to be in
   charge of son **Thomas** during their minority.
" son **Redman John Emerson** and son **Thomas'** wife, ——,
   personalty.
Son **Thomas** ex. and residuary legatee.
Test: Maj. **Thomas Emerson,** Joseph Homes, Charles Stevens.
                                                14. 243.

Millington, Ruth (widow), Dorchester Co.,

5th Feb., 1716;
25th Feb., 1716.

To godson Samuel Harper and to James Edgar, John Lunn, Isabel Gray (wife of Jacob Gray), Tryphen Edgar, Dorothy Todd, Rachel Adams, Susanah Cardeau, John Hobson and Elinor Adams, personalty.

Lewis Griffen, Sr., ex., and residuary legatee.

Test: Joseph Andrews, Margery Ruth, Elizabeth Merrydeth.

14. 244.

Dorrington, Wm. (gent.), Dorchester Co.,   19th Feb., 1716;

12th Mar., 1716.

To sister **Anne Hooper** and male hrs., "Harmless," lying near head of Black Water R.

" wife **Mary**, extx., entire personal estate. Should she marry, to pass to son **William** at age of 18 yrs.

Test: John Sare, Thos. Hayward, Jno. Riche.   14. 246.

Hambrooke, John, Dorchester Co.,   4th Jan., 17—;

12th Mar., 1716.

To son-in-law **John Stewart**, personalty at decease of testator's wife.

" sons-in-law **John Stevens** and **Thos. Stewart** and their hrs., all real estate in Dorchester Co. equally at age of 21 yrs., provided they do not turn their mother off.

" servant boy, John Gaudy, and to godson, Wm. Dorrington, personalty.

Wife, **Mary**, extx.

Test: Wm. Dorrington, Christopher King, Mary King.

14. 247.

Fisher, Alexander, Dorchester Co.,   19th Jan., 1716-7;

25th Mar., 1717.

To son **Thomas** and hrs., dwelling plantation, "Tarcell's Neck," and personalty at decease of testator's mother, **Mrs. Eliza: Rawlings.**

" son **Alexander** and hrs., 50 A., "Ellson," and personalty.

" dau. **Elizabeth** and hrs., 63 A., being that part of "Anchor and Hope" which Thos. Newton bought of Robt. Dicks, and personalty.

" unborn child, tract between "Ellson" and "Tarcell's Neck." Should sd. child die during minority and unmarried, sd. land to revert to son **Alexander.**

" brother **Mark**, 50 A. from "Tarcell's Neck" to land of **Charles Pitts.**

Testator directs that his sister, **Sarah Marriott**, shall live
at mansion house where his mother now dwells, so long
as she lives apart from her husband, **Mark Marriott**.

To wife **Mary**, extx., residue of estate, real and personal.

Test: Phillip Phillips, Mary Phillips, Thos. Hopewell.

14. 249.

Bonner, Theodorus (gent.), Talbot Co.,   9th Dec., **1716**;
28th Mar., **1717.**

To son **Theodorus** and hrs., 100 A., ''Brice's Hope,'' in Dorchester Co.

   ''   dau. **Elizabeth** and hrs., 100 A., ''Betty's Lott,'' at head of Little Choptauk R. in Dorchester Co.

   ''   son **William** and hrs., 170 A. of a tract of 300 A. on Pocomoke R., Sommerset Co.; residue of sd. tract to be sold by exs. for benefit of estate.

Wife **Rachel** to have sole management of child. until of age.

Exs.: Wife **Rachell** and friend Walter Quinton, jointly.

Test: Patrick Pursell, Joseph Earle, Jas. Knowles.   14. 251.

Disharoone, Michael, Somerset Co.,   23rd Mar., 1714-5;
30th Aug., 1715.

To 2 sons, **William** and **Michael**, and hrs., real estate equally (eldest to have first choice), and personalty.

   ''   wife **Anne**, extx., dwelling plantation with ⅓ of land during life, and ⅓ personal estate; other ⅔ to child., viz.: **Rachell, Sarah, Mary, Anne, William** and **Michael**, equally. Sons to be of age at 18 yrs.

Overseers: Mathew Dorman and John Rock, Jr.

Test: John Crouch, Jno. Hodgin, **Jno. Disharoone**, Alice Layton.   14. 253.

Powell, William, Somerset Co.,   15th Apr., 1715;
22nd June, 1715.

To son **John** and hrs., dwelling plantation, 200 A. of ''Greenfield'' and 50 A. ''Powell's Addition.'' (For desc. see wil'..)

   ''   son **William** and hrs., ''The Exchange'' and the balance of ''Greenfield.''

   ''   son **Levin** and hrs., ''The Middle'' if not repurchased by John Starrat, and 112 A.., ''Powell's Recovery'' (marsh at seaside).

   ''   sons **John** and **William**, plantation at seaside, being part of ''Powell's Lott.''

   ''   dau. **Margaret**, a double portion of personal estate and certain interest in Powell's Lott marsh left testator by his father, ——.

Wife **Eliza**: extx.

Testator directs that he be buried according to the directions of Quakers.

Test: Jane Calvert, Sarah Peale, John Starrat.   14. 254.

Patton, William, Somerset Co.,   22nd Apr., 1715; 6th July, 1715.

To eld. son **John**, dwelling plantation and adjoining plantation, ——, purchased from Christopher Glass, containing 200 A. He to pay to his bros., **William**, **Thomas**, **Robert** and **James** each 1,500 lbs. tobacco and to his sisters **Mary** and **Sarah** each 500 lbs. tobacco. Portions to be paid each when they arrive at age of 21 yrs. Son **John** afsd. to have possession of sd. house and land at decease of wife, **Elinor**.

> In event of death or marriage of wife, sons to be of age at 18 yrs.

"   son **William**, personalty.

"   wife **Elinor**, extx., 200 A. dwelling plantation and ⅓ personal estate during life. Residue of personal estate to child. equally at age of 21 yrs.

Test: Wm. Robeson, Hannah Robeson, Robt. Perry.   14. 255.

Bowditch, Robert (carpenter), Somerset Co.,   2nd Nov., 1710; 8th July, 1715.

To wife **Anne**, extx., entire estate, real and personal, during life or widowhood, then to pass to 2 daus.-in-law, **Joanna** and **Rebecca Clarke**, and their hrs. Should either die without issue, the survivor to inherit portion of deceased. If they both live, the land to be divided between them, **Rebecca** to have the manor plantation, being the lower end of sd. land.

"   son-in-law **John Cheesman**, and to John Gillis, Sr., personalty.

Test: Jas. Weathertee (Weatherby), **John Cheesman**, Jas. Smith.   14. 257.

Hopkins, Joseph, Kent Co.,   19th Mar., 1714; 16th May, 1717.

To son **Joseph** and hrs., at decease of wife, dwelling plantation, "Chiva Chase." Should he die without issue, to pass to next surviving of blood.

To 2 youngest sons, **Benj.** and **Nathaniel,** and hrs., ''Duck Pye'' and ''Hangman's Folly'' equally at wife's decease. Should both die without issue, to pass to the next surviving of blood.

'' sons **Joseph, Benj.** and **Nathaniel,** ⅔ of personal estate equally.

'' wife **Sarah,** entire real and ⅓ personal estate during life.

Exs.: Wife **Sarah** and Thomas Racten.

Test: Humphrey Younger, James Deocan, James Smeathers.

14. 258.

Bateman, William, Kent Co.,   21st Mar., 1715; 9th Apr., 1716.

To wife **Elizabeth,** extx., entire estate, real and personal.

Test: John Hodges, William Sweatman, Antho. Danes, John Holland.   14. 260.

Briver, William, Kent Co.,   22nd May, 1715; 24th July, 1715.

To child., entire estate, equally.

Edw. Scott, ex., to have charge of sons **Charles** and **Elias.** Robert Dunn to have charge of son **Thomas.**

Mary Scott to have son **Elias** after she marries.

Test: Wm. Mackey, Robt. Dunn, Thomas Hynson.   14. 260.

Candue, Randall (planter), Cecil Co.,   12th Apr., 1698; 13th Mar., 1715.

To wife **Elizabeth,** extx., dwelling plantation during life; at her decease to pass to son **Randall.** Should he die without issue, to pass to Wm. and Elizabeth Marshall and their hrs.

Test: Edw. Beck, Sr., John Beck, Geo. Warner.   14. 261.

Note—''**Randall Candue** being dead without hrs., I make no dispute at all that the land within devised belongs to Eliza: Marshall and her hrs.''

(Signed) Chas. Carroll.

Gwyn, John, Kent Island, Queen Anne's Co.,   15th Dec., 1714;

To son **John** and hrs., 100 A., ''Gunner's Harbor'' on Corsica Creek, Chester R., purchased from Vincent Hemsley.

Wife **Hannah,** extx., to enjoy a share of sd. land during life. At her decease to pass to son **John** afsd. and his hrs. Should he die without issue, to son **James** and hrs. Should he die without issue, to son **Robert** and hrs. Testator

always reserving to his wife her share of sd. land during
her life. Son **Robert** to be of age at 21 and sons **John**
and **James** at 18 yrs.

Overseer: William Kirby.

Test: Wm. Rakes, Jno. Darnall, Wm. Winlock. 14. 262.

Mecay, Alexander,

24th May, 1715;
12th Dec., 1715.

To son **Alex.**, 60 A. beginning at the branch next John Clayton's dwelling and running to the branch on which Phil.
Holaiger lives, and personalty.

" son **Robert,** 60 A. (for description see will), and personalty.

" son **John,** 70 A. (for description see will), and personalty.

" son **George,** residue of real estate, and personalty.

" daus. **Martha, Anne** and **Rosamond Clayton,** personalty.

" **John** (son of Robt. Elexsander), personalty.

" sons **Robt.** and **John,** residue of personal estate for payment of debts.

Ex. unnamed.

Test: Jno. Clayton, Phil. Holeadger, Thos. Clarke. 14. 263.

Stevenson, Edw.,

25th Jan., 1715;
17th Apr., 1716.

To children, male and female, real estate, equally.

Extx.: Wife **Mary.**

Test: Geo. Hitchcock, Thomas Long, Geo. Walker. 14. 265.

Bosley, Walter, Baltimore Co.,

29th July, 1715;
2nd Nov., 1715.

To son **Joseph,** 100 A., "Bosley's Pallace" on n. side Patapsco
R., near Jones Falls, and personalty.

" son **John,** dwelling plantation at wife's decease.

" son **James,** 100 A., "Bosley's Expectation" on Gunpowder R.

" youngest son **William,** 99 A., remainder "Bosley's Expectation."

" son **Charles,** 95 A., part of "Arthur's Choice" on Gunpowder R.

" wife **Mary,** extx., dwelling plantation during life, and
personalty.

Test: Joseph Presbury, Margaret Machentee, Rich. Parker.

14. 266.

Jonsson, Arch., Talbot Co.,

—— —— 1714-5;
19th July, 1715.

To wife **Margaret,** extx., entire estate.

Test: Robt. Levin, Jno. Skinner, Jno. Dennis. 14. 267.

Sandford, Stephen,   27th Dec., 1715;

To Mrs. Eliza: Marsh, personalty.
Thomas Marsh ex. and residuary legatee.
Test: Jno. Carter, Sam Tharley, Charles Stevens.
Mem.—(This will never proved.)   14. 268.

Barton (Bartton), Elizabeth, Charles Co.,   12th Dec., 1716;
9th Apr., 1717.

To grandson and granddau., **Nathan** and **Elizabeth Bartton,**
personalty. Residue of estate equally between them.
Should either die during minority, the survivor to inherit
portion of deceased. Dau.-in-law **Rachel Bartton,** extx.,
to have use of estate during widowhood.
Overseer: Edward Brendner.
Test: Wm. Halthom White, Jas. Parrandie, Jno. Parrandie.
14. 268.

Stevens, Kezia (nunc.),   12th Mar., 1716;

Son **James** left to the care of Ozias Wills, together with his
estate.
To goddau. Anne Wilson and to Elizabeth Wilson, personalty.
Test: John Wilson.   14. 269.

Posey, John, Charles Co.,   21st Mar., 1716;
28th Apr., 1717.

To mother, **Mary Posey,** extx., tract of land, "Shrimp's Neck,"
and dwelling plantation during life. At her decease to
pass to brother **Francis** and hrs.
" bro. **Benjamin** and hrs., 100 A., "Burlains Hill," which is
the plantation now called "Holt's Divising."
" bro. **Francis** and hrs., "St. John's" and personalty.
" bro. **Bolaine** and hrs., "Noddall's Brand."
" sister **Mary,** personalty.
Test: Chas. Musgrove, Timothy Reading, Edw. Evens.
14. 270.

Lawson, Thomas, planter, Charles Co.,   10th Dec., 1716;
12th Mar., 1716.

To wife **Elizabeth,** extx., ⅓ of estate, real and personal.
" son **William,** residue of estate.
Test: Will. Wilkinson, Thos. Beach, Thos. Cooksey.   14. 271.

Mercer, Jacob, A. A. Co.   30th Jan., 1716; 2nd Apr., 1717.

To mother, ——, personalty during life. At her decease to son **John,** and in event of his death to dau. **Elizabeth.**

Residue of estate equally between wife **Mary,** son **John,** and dau. **Elizabeth.** Son to receive his portion at 21 yrs., dau. to receive hers at 16 yrs. or marriage.

Extx.: Wife **Mary.**

Test: Henry Bateman, Richard Loadin.   14. 271.

Pierce, John, Cecil Co.,   12th Dec., 1715; 3rd Jan., 1715.

To friend Patrick Kelly, ex. (husbandman, of Cecil Co.), entire estate, real and personal.

Test: Hans Tillman, Rich. Vanderwerf, Mathew Stacey.   14. 272.

Peirce (Pierce), Thomas, planter, Cecil Co., 2nd Jan., 1707; 28th Feb., 1715.

To wife **Eliza:,** entire estate, real and personal, during life. At her decease to pass to son **Thomas** and hrs., excepting 50 A. and some personalty.

"   son **Thomas,** personalty.

"   son-in-law **Francis Steele** and **Rebecca,** his wife, and their hrs., 50 A. where sd. **Francis** is now seated.

"   **Thomas,** son of **Francis Steele** and **Rebecca,** his wife, grandson **William,** son of **Wm. Bateman** and **Abigail,** his wife, personalty.

Exs.: Wife **Eliza:** and son **Thomas,** jointly.

Test: Jno. Willinger, Jno. Mackinel, Francis Lacon.   14. 274.

Howard, Cornelius, A. A. Co.,   18th Sept., 1715; 19th Mar., 1716.

To son **Charles,** 12d., in full of his part of estate.

"   son **Cornelius** and hrs., 300 A. on "Hockley Creek," "Howard's Hills" and "Howard's Heirship."

"   son **Thomas** and hrs., 250 A. "Roper's Increase" on Patapsco R., Balto. Co., and 250 A., "Howard's Addition."

"   son **John,** £50 and a proportional part of personal estate, also all land lying at Tuckahoe on Choptank R. Personal estate to unmarried children equally. Sons of age at 18 yrs.

Exs.: Sons **Cornelius**, **Thomas** and **John.**
To trustees, bro. **Joseph Howard** and cous. **Jno. Beale**, each
of them 20s. to buy rings.
Test: Sam'l Howard, Jos. Howard, Vachell Denton.   14. 275.

Grey, John, Charles Co., 23rd Apr., 1715; 20th Dec., 1716.

To sons **John**, **Edward**, **Francis** and hrs., 100 A. each where
they now live.
  " sons **Richard** and **William** and their hrs., 398 A., dwelling
plantation, equally between them.
  " son **James**, 1s.
  " Susannah Hergesson, personalty at 16 yrs. of age.
  " sons **John**, **Edward**, **Francis**, **Thomas**, **Richard** and **William**,
residue of personalty equally.
Exs.: Sons **Thos.** and **Rich.** and neighbor Joseph Harrison, Sr.
Test: David Hambleton, Jno. Jerson, Margarett Magreger.

14. 276.

Barton, William, Charles Co., 25th Nov., 1716; 18th Feb., 1716.

To. son **Nathan** and dau. **Elizabeth**, estate equally.
Should wife **Rachell** marry and stepfather not be agree-
able to child., dau. **Elizabeth** to go to godfather. Son
Nathan to go to Francis Bucher. Their expenses to be
paid out of estate.
Ex.: Francis Bucher.
Test: James Boyd, Elizabeth Bucher, James Tinsone. 14. 277.

Dennis, Donnack, planter, Somerset Co., 16th Feb., 1716; 23rd Mar., 1716.

To wife ——, dwelling plantation, "Dennis' Purchase," 300
A., during life; at her decease to son **Donnach** and hrs.,
and personalty.
  " grandson **William** and hrs. (son of **Donnack Dennis, Jr.**),
100 A., part of "Dennis' Purchase."
  " **Theopolus** (son of **Donnach Dennis, Jr.**), personalty.
  " grandson **Donnack** (son of **John Dennis**), 100 A. on Littleton's Creek, s. side of Potomac R.
  " dau. **Elenor**, wife of **Jeremiah Morris**, personalty.
  " son-in-law **Hugh Porter**, to dau. **Margaret**, to son **Henry
Hudson**, 1s. each.
Residue of estate to sons **John** and **Donnack**, equally.
Ex.: son **John.**
Test: **John Dennis, Jr.**, Robt. Weer, Wm. Lane,   14. 278.
Note—23rd Mar., 1716. **Elizabeth Dennis**, widow of testator,
did revoke the within will, and fly to her thirds.

Gyllot, William, Somerset Co.,   21st Jan., 1716;
20th Mar., 1716.

To eldest son **William** and hrs., all lands and plantation, including "Buchaneer Green."

Two sons, **William** and **John,** till age of 18, to care of bro.-in-law **Abraham Tripe.** Son **Abraham** to Richard Chambers till 18 years of age.

To dau. **Mary,** personalty; she to be in care of Olife Chambers.

"   son **George,** personalty.

Bro. **John Phillips,** ex., to have debt that is in hand of Wm. Willson, to pay for nursing of son **George.**

Remainder of personal estate divided among child. afsd.

Test: Jno. Raymond, Sam. Alexander, Rich. Mogua (Mages).

14. 280.

Willis, Thomas, planter, Somerset Co.,
11th Aug., 1715;
21st Mar., 1716-17.

To John Coleburne, ex., and hrs. (planter of Somerset Co.), 150 A., "Amity."

"   wife **Elizabeth** and John Coleburne afsd., residue of estate, equally.

Test: Sam. Mayo, Thos. Layfield, John Townsend.   14. 280.

Marshall, Elizabeth, widow, Coventry Parish, Somerset
Co.,   12th Mar., 1716-7;
21st Mar., 1716-7.

To sons **George, Samuel, Thomas** and **Adrian** and dau. **Adria,** personalty.

Child. **George, Samuel, Adria** and **Thomas** to care of bro. **Randolph Long** until they reach age of 18.

To bro. **Randolph Long,** 700 lbs. tobacco borrowed of bro. **David Long,** to be paid by bro. **Jeffrey Long.**

Youngest son **Adrian** to be free at 18 years.

Ex.: Bro. ——.

Test: Esau Boston, Margaret Taylor, Abigall Biggin.

14. 281.

Lane, Walter, planter, Somerset Co.,   20th Dec., 1715;
21st Mar., 1716-7.

To son **William,** ex., and hrs., dwelling plantation, 200 A, bought from Mark Gendaron.

"   dau. **Mary,** wife of **Wm. Beraus,** and dau. **Joana,** wife of **John Hollum,** 1s. each.

"   wife ——, ⅓ personal estate. Residue to rest of child., equally.

Test: John Townsend, Sarah Townsend, Jane Townsend.

14. 282.

Howkins, Thos., Baltimore Co.,   7th Aug., 1715;
26th Nov., 1715.

To three children, dwelling plantation, 225 A. Part with dwelling to son **Aron.** Next choice to son **Joseph** and last choice to dau. **Ruth.** Should any of afsd. child. die without issue and under age of 21 yrs., the survivors to divide portion of deceased.

" wife **Elizabeth,** extx., personal estate.

Test: **Joseph Hawkins,** Mary Witershell, Ailce Marsh. 14. 283.

Breadey (Bredey), Owen, St. Mary's Co., —— —— ——;
10th Jan., 1716.

To sons **Owen** and **Pott** and **Charles,** personalty.

" **William Malohan,** personalty.

Test: Thomas Sikes, Alex. Clilan.   14. 284.

Note—By codicil dated 7th Dec., 1716, testator leaves dau. **Liza. Malohan** personalty.

Barber, James, planter, Kent Co.,   7th Sept., 1715;
29th Dec., 1715.

To dau. **Sarah** and hrs., 300 A., "Summerly" on King's Ck., Talbot Co.

" dau. **Deborah Gumley,** 200 A., "Plain Dealing," on e. side Chester R., Queen Anne's Co., during life; at her decease to pass to **James,** son of **Deborah Gumley,** and his hrs. Should sd. **James** die without issue, sd. 200 A. to pass to next hr. to sd. **Deborah.**

" youngest dau. **Mary** and hrs., dwelling plantation. Should she die during minority, sd. plantation to pass to dau. **Deborah Gumley** and hrs.

" daus. **Deborah Gumley** and **Mary,** personalty, equally.

Ex.: Friend Daniell Malihan, advised by Henry Hosier and Friends of the monthly meeting.

Test: to be buried in Friends burying place.

Test: Wm. Howard, Joseph Hartlew, Christopher Knight.

14. 285.

Shoklee (Shokley), Rich., carpenter, Somerset Co.,
7th Dec., 1708;
23rd Aug., 1716.

To son **Richard,** 200 A. adjoining land formerly belonging to James Traenes, where he is now seated.

" son **David,** dwelling plantation, 200 A. Should he die without issue, the sd. 200 A. to pass to son **William.**

Handmill to remain on plan. where it now is, for use of testator's wife and children.

To sons **John, David** and **William,** personalty.
" daus. **Elinor** and **Eliza:,** 1s.
" dau. **Mary,** personalty.
" wife **Ann,** extx., dwelling plan. during widowhood.

Test: John Flemming, Thomas Layfield, Wm. Couland.

14. 286.

McRagh, Owen, Somerset Co.,   27th Apr., 1716; 24th Aug., 1716.

To son **William** and hrs., dwell. plan. and personalty. If he should die during minority, to pass to dau. **Mary** and hrs. Son **William** to remain with his uncle **John** to age of 18 yrs.
" son **Robert** and hrs., land that lies in the neck, and personalty. He to be of age at 18 yrs.
" bro. **John,** Margaret Willson and dau. **Mary,** personalty.

Extx.: Wife **Jane.**

Test: John Scott, John Brown, Joseph Bran.   14. 287.

Mem. to will signed by **Jane McRagh** renouncing will and claiming her thirds. Dated 23rd Aug., 1716.

Robinson, William, Somerset Co.,   21st Apr., 1716; 19th Oct., 1716.

To eldest son **Michael** and to son **Joseph** and their hrs., 225 A., being 2 tracts, "Robinson's Purchase" and "Assawamuh." (For desc. and division of sd. tracts, see will.) Also 150 A., part of "Fairhaven."
" two sons, **William** and **Peter,** and their hrs., 450 A. in Sussex Co. on Delaware Bay, being part of two tracts purchased of Robert Bracy. Son **William** to have first choice.
" son **John** and hrs., 250 A. where he now lives, being part of "Cow Quarter," taken up for Ambrose White.
" three eldest sons, **Michael, William** and **John,** personalty.
" two sons afsd., **Peter** and **Joseph,** personalty.
" sons **Thomas** and **Joshua** and to dau. **Mary,** personalty; son **Thomas** to receive his legacy at age of 21, dau. **Mary** at 16 or marriage, son **Joshua** at 16.

Two sons, **Joseph** and **Joshua,** to be of age at 16 should their mother marry again. Should she remain a widow, not to be of age until 21 yrs.

To wife **Mary,** extx., residue of personal estate during life or widowhood. Shd. she marry, her portion to all child. afsd., equally.

Test: Jno. Richards, Ann Fowset, Wm. White.   14. 288.

Stevens, Edward, Somerset Co.,   11th Aug., 1715;
                                                      18th Dec., 1716.

To dau. **Mary Whorton,** the part of dwelling plant. she lives
          on and personalty.
"   dau. **Cattran Dormond,** part of tract bou. of Robert Colt
          (being the under side of Isaac Wheeler's plantation, but
          not to touch sd. land).
"   dau. **Sarah Wheller,** 50 A. of tract bou. of Robt. Colt, be-
          ginning where the 50 A. of Dormond's ends, and per-
          sonalty.
"   dau. **Eliz. Stevens,** 50 A. of afsd. tract, being the upper-
          most part of sd. tract, and personalty.
"   **Tabbither Stevens,** dwell. plant., "Blackshop," after de-
          cease of her mother. Should unborn child be a son, he
          to have sd. dwell. plan. Should the child be a dau., to
          have equal part of sd. plan., **Tabbiter** to have first
          choice. In event of death of either without issue, the
          survivor to have portion of deceased.
"   the public, ½ A. for use of meeting house, where it now
          stands.
Wife —— extx. and residuary legatee.
Test: John Stevens, Robert Malven, Eliz. Ducks, Wm. Noble.
                                                      14. 290.

Pitts, Elizabeth, Somerset Co.,   22nd Apr., 1715;
                                                      25th Aug., 1716.

To son **George,** personalty.
"   eldest dau. **Ann,** personalty, some of which is on **Edw.**
          Stevens place.
"   second dau. **Jane,** personalty.
Exs.: John and Ann Tilman.
Test: Mary Upshur, Robert Mills.   14. 292.
Note—29th Dec., 1715, John Tilman and Ann Tilman by joint
          consent make over administration of above will to **John
          Pitts.**

Elzey, Peter, Somerset Co.,   8th Oct., 1715;
                                                      26th Sept., 1716.

To friend Wm. Wallis of Monokin, Somersett Co., and hrs.,
          50 A., "Chance," on Jenzakin Creek, and also a tract
          joining the sd. 50 A. (for description see will).
"   2 daus., **Frances** and **Elizabeth,** and their hrs., remainder
          of land in St. Peter's neck and 150 A. on Nanticoke R.
          Shd. either die without issue, the survivor to inherit por-
          tion of deceased. Personal estate divided equally bet.
          Frances and **Eliza:,** who are named extxs., jointly.
Test: John Bosman, Sr., John Talbot, Geo. Feabus, Wm.
          Merer.   14. 293.

Crowlie (Crowle), Cornelius,   25th May, 1715;
                                            25th July, 1715.

To daus. **Ellinner** and **Honor,** real estate at decease of wife,
    equally. If eldest dau. should marry before her mother's
    decease, she shall live with her mother or have her portion.
Personal estate to be equally divided between wife —— and
    2 child.
Ex. ——.
Testator directs that property shall never be sold or mort-
    gaged by them or their hrs.
Test: Rich. Green, John Magnell.   14. 294.

Wyatt, John, planter, Kent Co.,   26th Oct., 1711;
                                          19th June, 1716.

To son **John,** ½ of "Buckinham," and, at decease of wife,
    residue of "Buckinham." If son **John** have no issue,
    this tract is to pass to eldest dau. **Anne,** born of test.
    present wife, **Elizabeth,** and her hrs.
"   unborn child, if a son, plantation up the river, part of a
    tract called "Viana"; if a girl, this tract is to go to
    dau. **Rebecca** and hrs.
"   dau. **Rachel,** ½ of "Viana."
"   dau. **Sarah,** 150 A., "Haccots Chance," in Queen Anne's
    Co. on Cabin Branch.
"   wife **Elizabeth,** dwell. plant. and ½ "Buckinham" during
    life.
The property above named, excepting "Haccots Chance,"
    shall be entailed and not be sold, swapped or disposed of,
    but to descend from hr. to hr., and in default of issue
    in child. of wife, **Elizabeth,** then to eldest dau. **Mary**
    Milton and hrs. Should wife require her thirds in lands
    given to children, she is then to have what the law allows
    and no more.
Personal est. to be divided equally bet. **Ann, Johanna, Sarah,**
    and, if unborn child be a boy, dau. **Rebecca** to have a
    child's part with former three; but if a girl, she to have
    that part.
To **Mary Millton,** personalty.
Test: John Woodall, Samuel Wallis, John Kendrickson.
                                          14. 294.

Note—Should wife die before children attain majority, testa-
    tor intrusts them to care of the Friends of this county,
    and desires nothing in this shall be altered.

Bosman (Bozman), John, Somerset Co.,

26th Apr., 1716;
26th Sept., 1716.

To son **William**, tract of land where Geo. Horner now lives.
" son **Thomas** and hrs., plant. formerly owned by bro. **Geo.** at mount of Great Branch (for desc. see will).
" cousin **William Bosman** and male hrs., tract of land on n. side of Goose Creek (for descrip. see will). In default of such hrs., to cousin **George Bosman.**
" 2 daus., **Ann** and **Bridget,** as much land as either of them shall have occasion to use; if either should marry, the other to enjoy sd. privileges alone, until she marry. Also property back of son **John's** land, and personalty.
" wife **Blandina**, extx., dwell. plan., beginning at mouth of branch which divides land of son **George** from sd. plant., and along river to branch wh. divides it from land of son **John** (for desc. see will); at her death to pass to son **Risden** and male issue, failing which, to pass to male issue of following, in order given: dau. **Ann,** dau. **Bridgett** and son **Wm.**
" wife **Blandina,** residue of personal estate during life or widowhood, to be divided at her death bet. 2 sons and 2 daus., viz.: **Thos.** and **Risden** and daus. **Ann** and **Bridget.**
Test: ——.   14. 296.
Note—Wm. Stourten testifies that Mrs. Blandina Bozaman requested him to search among papers of deceased husband in order to find within will.

Grady (Gredy), Owen, Kent Co.,

8th Feb., 1715;
28th Feb., 1715.

To Dennis Collins and his wife, Jane; Charles Collins, son of Dennis; Patrick Niner and Catherine Maeding, personalty.
Mem. of indebtedness of testator: To Thomas Mochon, 742 lbs. tobacco upon Col. Henson's acct., and to Capt. Sparks, 1,700 lbs. Should there be a hogshead to spare on own account, 540 lbs. to be paid to Carpenter Lilleston.
To John Maden, ex., residue of estate.
Test: Jno. Bryning, Wm. Roorock (Rowrock), Dennis Collins.
                                                         14. 298.

Perry, Hugh, Kent Co.,

31st Jan., 1715-6;
20th Feb., 1715.

To James Donovan, personalty.
" son **Samuell,** residue of estate, real and personal. Edw. Skidmore, ex., to have charge of sd. son until he be of age.
Test: Joseph Skidmore, Rebecca Skidmore, James Dunavin.
                                                         14. 298.

Parsons, William, gentleman, Town Point, Cecil Co.,
7th Aug., 1716;
18th Sept., 1716.

To wife **Mary,** ½ dwell. plant. and personalty during life,
and ⅓ personal estate, absolutely.
" son **William** and hrs., tract bou. of Col. Casparus Aug.
Herman. Shd. son **William** die without issue, sd. land to
pass to 2nd son **Jan.**
" son **Jan** and hrs., tract bou. of Ephraim Augustine Herman (son of Casparus Aug. Herman, afsd.) and containing
100 A. Shd. son **Jan** die without issue, his portion to
be equally enjoyed by 3 daus., **Mary, Margaret** and **Catharine** and their hrs. Also, shd. both sons, **William** and
Jan die without issue, their land to be equally divided
among the daus. afsd.
" eldest dau., **Susannah Linton,** personalty under certain
conditions, she having had a portion.
Exs.: Wife **Mary,** assisted by eldest son **William,** when he
arrives at age of 21.
House, now occupied by Jan Parker, left testator by grandfather in Branford, Dorchester, to be sold and proceeds
divided among said five children, viz.: **Wm., Jan, Mary,
Margaret** and **Catharine,** who are residuary legatees of
estate, real and personal.
Test: Henry Jones, Sarah Hues, John Tarvert. 14. 299.

Jennings, Henry, clerk, Rector of Wm. and Mary's Parish,
St. Mary's Co., 13th Mar., 1715-6;
27th Oct., 1716.

Testator directs that debt due Capt. —— Machartie be paid.
To son **Thomas,** ex., personalty.
Residue of estate to be divided into 3 equal portions; one to
wife **Elizabeth,** the other 2 portions to only son, **Thomas.**
Bro.-in-law **John Beale** to serve during minority of son **Thomas.**
Test: Jonathan Coy, Archibold Johnstone, Terren Sweeney.
14. 302.

Note—Deposition mentions Wm. and Terren Sweeny.

Jordan, Thomas, St. Mary's Co., 15th Oct., 1716;
—— Nov., 1716.

To sons **Jesse** and **John,** 50 A. each, and personalty.
" sons **Thomas** and **Jerad,** dwelling plantation, 170 A.; 100
A. to **Thomas** and 70 A. to **Jerard** at their mother's decease, and personalty.
" sons **Samuel** and **Theodor,** personalty value £30.
Wife **Elizabeth** extx.
Test: Alex. Cleland, Thos. Latton (Laton). 14. 303.

Richardson, Nicholas, chirurgan, St. Mary's Co.,

2nd Nov., 1716;
8th Jan., 1716.

To son **Nicholas** and hrs., 150 A., dwell. plan., "Hunting Quarter."

" daus. **Elener** and **Ann**, plantation divided equally.

" dau. **Bridgett Charmes**, personalty.

" son **Nicholas**, personalty; he dying without issue, to 3 daus. afsd.

" wife **Bridgett**, extx., residue of personal estate.

Overseer: Richard Thurley.

Test: Edward Morgan, Mary Morgan, John Gage, Wm. Sanders.
14. 304.

Guyther, Mary, widow, St. Mary's Co., 29th Oct., 1716;

29th Nov., 1716.

To son **Owen** and dau. **Sarah** and hrs., "The Folly," equally.

" daus. **Dorothy** and **Mary** "Barron Neck," equally. Should either die before they are of age, their portion to go to son **Owen** and hrs., or in event of marriage of either of sd. daus. to a landed man, her part to go to son **Owen**.

Cousin **Elinor Keave** to have full liberty to live on any part of sd. land during her life, but not to interfere with sd. child. Personal estate to child. equally, when they become of age.

Ex.: Friend Owen Smithson.

Test: Robt. Rossin, John Baker, Dorothy Leigh.
14. 305.

Halayrd, Edward, St. Mary's Co.,　　28th Oct., 1716;

To godsons Wm. Watts, Christopher Combs, Jacob Williamson, granddau. **Jeane Hebb**, personalty.

Residue of estate, real and personal, to wife ——, son-in-law **Thomas Hebb, Jr.**, and dau. **Frances.**

Test: Geo. Daffan, John Seikes, Wm. Cannady.
14. 306.

Note—Test. proceedings, 1718, give **Jane Hillyard** extx. of **Edward Hillyard**, St. Mary's Co.

English (Engelich), Alex., St. Mary's Co.,

30th Jan., 1716;
5th Feb., 1716.

To Geratt Jordan, money borrowed from sd. Jordan's mother, ——, on testator's account.

" Justinen Jordon, 10s.

" Joseph Gesep, Alex. Chilan, John Lets, Luke Barber, Timothy Crowelly and Eugen Fleirs, personalty.

Ex.: Luke Whiler.

Test: Alex. Chilan, Dolle Leu.
14. **307.**

Mings, Edward, Charles Co.,   10th Mar., 1716;
14th July 1716.

To wife **Mary,** extx., and hrs., "Mingses Chance," residue
of real estate and personalty.

Test: Thos. Smith, Jane Anderson, John King.   14. 308.

Dew, Patrick, Calvert Co.,   17th July, 1716;
8th Feb., 1716-17.

To son **John** and hrs., dwell. plan., "Archers Hays." Should
son **John** die without issue, sd. plan. to pass to eldest dau.
Ann and hrs. In event of death of dau. **Ann** and son **John**
without issue, sd. land to pass to youngest dau. **Rachell**
and hrs.; and at the decease of sd. three children without
issue, land to pass to son-in-law **Richard Leafe** and hrs.

" three child., **John, Ann, Rachell** and son-in-law **Richard
Leafe,** personalty.

Wife **Ann,** extx., to have ⅓ of dwell. plan. during widowhood, with ⅓ of personal estate.

Test: Jos. Smith, Samuel Griffith, Jr., **Rich. Leafe.**   14. 308.

Hunt, John, carpenter, Calvert Co.,   15th Jan., 1715;
15th Jan., 1716.

To eldest bro., **Jobe,** and hrs., 64 A. of "Lordship's Favor."

" youngest bro., **Thomas,** and hrs., 50 A., being part of land
afsd., and next to William Mead.

Ex.: ——.

Test: Thos. Godsgrace Robinson, John Readman, Thos. Morgin.   14. 310.

Corbett, Benonie, Calvert Co.,   12th Nov., 1716;
28th Jan., 1716.

Wife **Margaret,** extx. and sole legatee of estate, real and personal.

Test: Jeremiah Leach, Chas. Somersett, Math. Parette.
14. 310.

Sulivant, Darby, Calvert Co.,   5th Dec., 1716;
2nd Feb., 1716.

To son **Joseph** and hrs., dwelling plantation. Shd. he die
without issue, sd. plan. to pass to son **Jeremiah.** Shd.
he die without issue, to pass to eldest dau. **Elizabeth.**
Shd. she die without issue, to youngest dau. **Ann** and hrs.
Son **Joseph** to be of age at 18.

" daus. **Eliza:** and **Ann,** personalty at day of marriage and
other personalty at age of 14 yrs.

To son **Jeremiah,** certain personalty, to be delivered at ages of 14 and 20 years. Shd. any of afsd. children die before they come to age, their portion to pass to next youngest. Should there be none younger, to next older.

" wife **Elizabeth,** extx., personal estate during life. After her decease the residue of estate not bequeathed to be equally divided among children afsd.

Test: Henry Johnson, Margaret Askew, Thos. Harvey.

14. 311.

In deposition Margaret Askew is called Michael.

Blackburn, Edward, planter, Calvert Co.,

4th Feb., 1717;
20th Mar., 1716-17.

Testator gives his body during sickness to the care of William Richardson and Anne Burton of Calvert Co. At his death to be interred in any proper place on sd. plantation. In consideration of which he appoints the sd. William Richardson and Anne Burton joint executors, and bequeaths to them his entire estate, divided equally.

Test: James Nolson, James Williamson, Katherine Henry.

14. 313.

Leaf, Richard, Calvert Co., 2nd. Dec., 1716;
8th Feb., 1716-17.

To bro. **John Dew** and mother **Ann Dew,** personalty.

" bro. and sisters-in-law, viz.: **John, Ann** and **Rachel Dew** and hrs., real and residue of personal estate, equally, at majority.

Ex.: Father-in-law **Patrick Dew.**

Test: Henry Johnson, Samuel Griffith, Jr., Allen Magdaniel.

14. 314.

Creed, Wm., blacksmith, Calvert Co., 9th Feb., 1716;
14th Mar., 1716.

To granddau. **Eliz. Creed** and hrs. (at decease of testator's wife), dwell. plan., 64 A., and personalty. Shd. sd. **Eliz. Creed** not accept this legacy, she is to have no share in estate.

" granddau. **Elizabeth Williams,** personalty in consideration of testator's indebtedness on father's estate. If not accepted, sd. **Elizabeth Williams** to have no share in estate. Also to gr.-dau. **Elizabeth Williams,** personalty on plan. where Wm. Clark now lives, formerly estate of **Jos. Williams,** deceased.

Friends Col. John Marshall and Mr. John Smith of Cox Town
shall have in their care the legacies for sd. granddaugh-
ters until they arrive at age of 16 or marry.

To wife **Mary**, extx., dwell. plant. for life, and residue of
personalty.

Test: John Brooke, Henry Young, Joseph Williams.   14. 315.

Hall, Elisha, Calvert Co.,   7th May, 1716;
                                              8th Feb., 1716-17.

To son **Richard** and hrs., part ''Hall's Hills,'' about 650 A.
(For desc. see will.)

" son **Elihu** and hrs., part of ''Hall's Hills'' (for desc. see
will), estimated about the same quantity as son **Richard's**
part, also tract of land, ''Hall's Mount,'' and personalty.

" sons afsd. and hrs., land bou. of Joseph Chew, and house
and lot at Marlborough, equally.

" dau. **Sarah,** wife of **Saml. Harrison,** a silver tankard and
personalty.

" wife **Sarah,** personalty, also use of certain personalty during widowhood; at her marriage or death to pass to **Mary
Hall,** eldest dau. of son **Richard Hall.**

" Friends of Western Shore for charity, £5.

Exs.: Wife **Sarah** and sons **Richard** and **Elihu,** the 3 to be
residuary legatees.

Test: John Smith, J. Sheredine, Francis Young, Nich. Sporne
(Snorne).   14. 317.

Crouley, Joseph, Sr., planter, Dorchester Co.,
                                              4th Jan., 1716;
                                              13th Mar., 1716.

To wife **Ann,** extx., dwelling plan., ''Calias,'' during widowhood, then to son **Jacob** and hrs. Shd. she continue a
widow until **Jacob** is 16 yrs. of age, plan. to be equally
divided between them.

" wife entire personal estate during widowhood. Shd. she
marry, her thirds only, and residue to son **Jacob** and hrs.,
to be delivered at age of 16.

" son **Andrew** and hrs., 200 A., ''Loer Landing''; he dying
without issue to pass to son **Jacob.**

" eldest son **John** and hrs., ''Hall's Ridge'' and all land
lying on s. side of sd. ridge. He dying without issue, sd.
land to pass to son **Jacob.**

" dau. **Lucy,** 50 A., ''Chance.''

" youngest son **John** and hrs., 100 A., ''Cowbrook,'' and
land bet. sd. ''Cowbrook'' and Blackwater R. He dying
without issue, sd. land to pass to son **Jacob.**

" daus. **Eliz. Shorter, Mary Robinson, Ruth, Rosannah,
Triphena, Lucy** and **Elinor** and son **Joseph,** 1s. each.

Test: Wm. Evans, Jr., Jno. Cole, Wm. Shorter.   14. 319.

Fray, Wm., planter, Talbot Co.,   25th July, 1716;
    29th Jan., 1716.

To wife **Jane**, extx., dwel. plan., "Chance," and entire estate, real and personal, during life. Personal estate to be disposed of as she thinks fit. Should she die intestate, personal estate to be equally divided among children ——. In event of death of wife before children are of age, son **Charles**, the eldest, shall have them educated. Sons of age 20 yrs., and dau. 16 yrs. or day of marriage.

Test: Rev. Dan. Maynadier, Jno. Bullen, Arthur Connor.

    14. 320.

Harrison, John, A. A. Co.,   17th Jan., 1648-9;
    12th Mar., 1716.

To John Gartrell and William Griffith and Francis Johnston, personalty.

"   James Cruchley, his wife and hrs., 122 A. now in possession of John Gartrell.

"   Silvester Wellch, ex., all that is in his possession belonging to testator, including tobacco consigned to Mycall Yokley, in England.

Test: Henry Ridgeley, Jr., Thos. Godman, John Gartrell (Garterell).   14. 321.

Prise, Edward, planter, Prince George's Co.,
    29th Apr., 1717;
    18th May, 1717.

To Basil Worinall, 100 A., "Litchfield," in Chas. County, on s. side of Wheeler's Branch and adjoining "Planter's Delight."

"   Joseph Nuton, personalty now in possession of Wm. Mattingly and Nicholas Dawson.

"   Andrew Hamilton and James Stodert, personalty.

"   Charles Beall, if testator's wife should die, personalty.

Test: David Patton, James Juers, Chs. Beall, Mark Worinall.

    14. 322.

Note—Test. Proc. mention Basil Warring as admr. on this estate.

Chancy, Geo., Baltimore Co.,   18th Mar., 1715-6;
    5th June, 1717.

To son **George** and hrs., 74 A., "Turkey Neck," s. side of Middle River, and personalty at age of 18 yrs., and to receive his legacy and be at liberty at 16 yrs. of age.

Extx.: Wife **Sarah.**

Test: Joseph Johnson, Wm. Cottann, Wm. Osborn, Wm. Byfoot.

    14. 324.

Merchant, William, planter, Dorchester Co.,

30th Jan., 1711;
23rd Sept., 1717.

To son **Joseph** and hrs., personalty and 50 A., "Merchant's Outlett," and 200 A., "Herriford." He failing issue, to grandson **Thomas Wall** and hrs.

" grandsons **Alexander** and **William Wall** and their hrs., residue of "Herriford" and land called "Slow" equally bet. them; for want of issue in sd. grandsons to pass to rightful hrs.

Son-in-law **Alexander Wall** and **Mary,** his wife, guardians to son **Joseph** until he be 21 yrs. of age.

To son-in-law **John Stanford, Jr.,** 108 A., "Mount Silley," during life; after his decease to granddau. **Margaret Stanford** and hrs.; she lacking issue, to lawful hrs. of **John Stanford,** afsd.

" **Alexander Wall,** ex., residue of personalty.

Test: Av. Smith, Phil. Tedman, Thos. Cook, John Kirke.

14. 325.

Peterson, Harmon, Dorchester Co., 29th Aug., 1717;
23rd Sept., 1717.

To dau. **Rebecka** and son-in-law **James Beswick,** ex., and their hrs., entire estate, real and personal.

Test: John Mondy, Thos. Brannock, Walter Fitchew (Fitzchew). 14. 328.

Crope (Crooper), Thos., planter, Queen Anne's Co.,

6th Jan., 1716;
19th Jan., 1716.

(Crooper written in will signed Tho. Crope, also Cropper.)

To son **Thomas** and hrs., 100 A., part of plantation where Lewis Deford lives.

" son **John** and hrs., 100 A., residue of afsd. plan. Should either of sd. sons die during minority or without issue, sd. land to pass to survivor.

" brother-in-law **Samuel Taylor,** personalty. Residue of personal estate divided equally between sons afsd. William Elbert to have sons apprenticed until they are 21 yrs. of age.

Exs.: Wife **Joan** and William Elbert, jointly.

Test: Nath. Wright, Neb. Taylor, Ishmael Devinish. 14. 328.

Note—On 11th Jan., 1716, **Joan Crooper** assigns all right of executorship to Wm. Elbert.

Wright, Solomon, Queen Anne's Co., 3rd Oct., 1716; 20th Apr., 1717.

To son **Thomas Hynson** and hrs., dwelling plantation, ''Warplesdon,'' and 100 A., ''Solomon's Friendship''; he dying without issue, to son **Solomon** and hrs.

'' sons **Solomon** and **Charles** and their hrs., 440 A., ''The Forrest,'' in Kent Co., equally, son **Solomon** to have first choice. If either die without issue, survivor to inherit portion of deceased.

'' sons **John** and **Edward** and their hrs., 500 A., ''Narbrough,'' on Island Marsh Ck., equally, son **John** to have first choice. If either die without issue, survivor to inherit portion of deceased.

'' son **Hairclough** and hrs., 370 A., ''Range,'' in Kent Co., he to live with son **Charles** as apprentice until 21 yrs. of age.

'' son **Edward** and hrs., 140 A., ''Dispute,'' on s. side of Hambleton's Branch and adjoining ''Fox Hill,'' now in possession of George Vandervourt. To live with son **Thomas Hynson** as an apprentice until 21 yrs. of age.

'' sons **Nathaniel, Solomon** and **Thomas Hynson,** personalty.

'' daus. **Ann** and **Rachell,** personalty, to be paid by ex. at age of 16 yrs. or day of marriage.

Residue of personal estate, except as before devised, divided equally bet. sons **Edward** and **Hairclough** and daus. **Ann** and **Rachell.**

Ex.: Son **Nathaniel.**

Test: Wm. Wrench, Thos. Croper, Chas. Lowder. 14. 330.

Mackall, James, Calvert Co., 26th Dec., 1716; —— Apr., 1717.

To son **James** and hrs., dwell. plant. that was his mother's, and Perry Neck.

'' son **John** and hrs., tract called ''The Schoolhouse,'' bou. of Wm. Brabau.

'' son **Benjamin** and hrs., 100 A., ''Outlet,'' and 30 A. adjoining it called ''Ueubert.''

'' daus. **Mary** and **Dorkass,** and to youngest dau., ——, personalty.

Wife **Ann** extx. and residuary legatee. She to enjoy use of all lands so long as she remains a widow. Shd. she marry, sons to have their land at age of 21.

Overseers: Bro. **Benjamin Mackall** and friend Walter Smith.

Test: D. Mackgill, Wm. Skinner, Thos. Howe. 14. 332.

Armiger, Daniell, Calvert Co., 19th Nov., 1712;
13th Apr., 1717.

To 2nd son **John,** youngest son **Robert** and eldest son **Daniell,**
ex., personalty. Residue of estate divided equally bet. 3
sons afsd. and dau. **Ann Field.**
Test: Henry Austin, Thos. Harvey, Chas. Nalk. 14. 333.

Forster, William, gent., Charles Co., 17th Apr., 1717;
25th May, 1717.

Wife **Ann,** extx., and hrs., 150 A., "St. Edmonds," and residue of estate.
Test: Wm. Howard, Rich. Ashman, John Ashman. 14. 334.

Makey (Macky), James, Charles Co., 8th Feb., 1716:
18th May, 1717.

To wife **Elizabeth,** extx., all real and personal est., including
100 A. at Md. point called "St. Johns." In default of
issue in wife **Elizabeth,** to pass to cousin **Francis,** son of
Francis Meeks, gent., late of Chas. County, deceased.
Test: John King, Thos. Annis. 14. 335.

Moore, Semour, planter (nunc.), Dorchester Co.,
24th Jan., 1716;
25th Jan., 1716.

To John Rider, gentleman, ex., entire estate, real and personal.
Test: Wm. Rawly, John Severerne, Sam. Rawly. 14. 335.

Price, Thos. (nunc), —— Dec., 1715;
1st Feb., 1716.

To dau. **Eliza:,** personalty.
Ex.: Father-in-law **Chas. Jones.**
Test: John Ramsey (about 30 yrs. of age). 14. 336.

Hargess, Thomas, Charles Co., 22nd Jan., 1716:
8th Feb., 1716.

To sons **Thomas, William, Francis** and **Abraham,** "Hargess
Hope," equally divided bet. them.
Ex.: ——.
Test: Wm. Williams, Timothy Carrington, Jno. Martin.
14. 336.

Cantwell, Thos., Charles Co., 19th Jan., 1716;
6th Feb., 1716.

To William Hunter, Edw. Anderson, Wm. Green, Jno. Hause,
Hassey Luckett and Elizabeth Price, personalty.
Mrs. Juliana Price extx. and residuary legatee.
Test: Anth. Neale, Mrs. Mary Semmes. 14. 337.

Davis, Thomas, Charles Co., ——— ——— ———;

14th Mar., 1716.

To son **William,** 150 A. adjoining dwell. plan., he to have privilege to settle on land after he is of age.

"   daus. **Rachell** and **Margaret,** 64 A., "Wanister," Pr. Geo. Co., land to be equally divided between them.

"   unborn child, if a boy, residue of "Hardshift," to be of age at 18. Shd. unborn child be a girl, then sd. land divided bet. 3 daus., **Rachell, Margaret** and **Onor.**

"   wife ——, dwel. plan. during life, excepting ½ the fruit, which goes to son when 18 yrs. of age.

Ex.: ——.

Test: James Hagan, Thos. Hagan, Jonathon Wood.   14. 338.

Cissell (Chissell), James, St. Mary's Co.,

30th Mar., 1717;
22nd Apr., 1717.

To son **James** and hrs., dwel. plan. with 25 A. "Poplar Neck," 50 A. "Broadneck" and personalty.

"   daus. **Mary** and **Ruth** and hrs., the other 50 A. "Broadneck" to be equally divided bet. them. In event of death of either during minority or without issue, the entire 50 A. to pass to survivor and hrs.

"   dau. **Mary,** personalty.

"   three children, **James, Mary** and **Ruth,** residue of estate equally. In event of death of any child during minority, their part to be equally divided among the survivors.

Ex.: Friend Chas. Neale.

Test: John Brown, Margaret Anderson, Clair Moore, James Thompson.   14. 339.

Marritt (Marett), John, cordwinder, St. Mary's Co.,

9th Apr., 1717;
1st May, 1717.

To son **John** and hrs., dwelling plantation and personalty when 21 yrs. of age.

"   dau. **Alice Gibson,** personalty.

"   dau.-in-law **Mary Christian,** Abraham and Absolem Tenison, 1s.

Wife **Frances** extx. and residuary legatee.

Test: John Turner, James Foster, Phillip Herbert.   14. 340.

Mason, Susanna, widow of **Robert Mason,** gent.. St. Mary's Co., 14th Jan., 1716; 13th Feb., 1716.

To son **Mathew** and hrs., tract of 200 A. in Chas. Co., conveyed to testator by Thos. Witcherly, being part of Christian Temple Manor.

" dau. **Mary,** personalty.

" grandson **Robert Mason,** two rings and personalty.

" sons **John** and **Mathew** and daus. **Elizabeth Rogers** and **Susanna Clarke,** residue of estate, equally.

Ex.: Son **John.**

Test: John Greenwell, Catherine Greenwell, **Geo. Clarke,** Edw. Morgan. 14. 341.

Louring (Louering), William, planter, Cecil Co., 23rd Mar., 1716; 28th Mar., 1717.

To John Cox, Wm. Ward, Jr., and Andrew Clements, personalty.

" James Numbers, ⅓ of residue of estate.

Ex.: Peter Numbers.

Test: Rich. Morgans, Alex. Machey. 14. 342.

Canada, Jno., planter, Sassafrax, Cecil Co., 5th Jan., 1716-7; 31st Jan., 1716-7.

To son **Charles** and dau. **Mary,** entire estate, real and personal.

Ex.: Francis Collins.

Test: Margarett Sappington, Peter Wombell, Rowland Jones. 14. 344.

Cooper, Edward, Cecil Co., 16th Mar., 1716-7: 25th Apr., 1717.

To dau. **Mary** and hrs., real and personal estate. In event of death during minority, to pass to wife **Mary** and hrs., and shd. dau. **Mary** afsd. die before she arrives at age, wife to give sister **Margaret Cox** (wife of **Cornelius Cox,** of Alluster, in Warrickshire, in the kingdom of Great Brittain, skinner), or to her hrs., the sum of 40 lbs. Maryland money; and should dau. **Mary** and wife **Mary** both die without hrs., estate, both real and personal, to be enjoyed by sister **Mary** and hrs.

Extx.: Wife **Mary.**

Stephen Knight of Cecil Co. and Andrew Peterson of New Castle Co., Pennsylvania, guardians to dau. during minority.

Test: York Yorkson, Walter Scott, Robert Wood, James Vanbibber. 14. 345.

Lancaster, Henry, planter, Cecil Co.,   9th May, 1717;
    13th May, 1717.

To six children, **Benjamin, William, George, Phillip, Elloner**
and **Catherine,** entire estate, equally.

Ex.: Wm. Sinklar.

Test: Solomon Bowen, Col. Ephraim Augustine Herman.

    14. 346.

Clements, Abraham, planter, Cecil Co.,   27th Mar., 1717;
    4th Apr., 1717.

To uncle **Jacob Clements,** ex., entire estate, real and personal.

Test: Gabriel Pillington, Andrew Clemments, Thos. Markero.

    14. 346.

Rasin, Philip, Kent Co.,   29th Mar., 1717;
    24th May, 1717.

To Samuel Smith, 1,500 lbs. tobacco for building new meeting
house.

  "   three sons and their hrs., all lands lying in Kent Co. on
Jacobs Ck. Son **Philip** to have dwelling house and middle
part of land.

  "   son **Thomas,** that pt. next Wm. Jones; son **John,** pt. next
head of Jacobs Ck. Shd. either son die without issue,
portion of deceased to be divided by survivors. Shd. all
sons die without issue, lands to fall to "daughters-to-be"
and their hrs.

  "   wife **Elizabeth,** use of dwelling plantation during widowhood (shd. she marry, her thirds only); and to wife **Elizabeth,** ⅓ personalty. Residue divided equally among all
children.

Exs.: Wife **Elizabeth** and bro. **Thomas Rasin,** jointly.

Test: Oliver Pamer, Ann Fizhew, Rachel Fizgerrald.   14. 347.

Note—Testator directs that he be buried at Friends' burying
place, Scisell Meeting House.

Pryer, Phillip, Kent Co.,   18th Sept., 1716;
    20th Mar., 1716-17.

To son **Phillip,** dwelling plantation and 100 A., being ½ of
"Hens Roost."

  "   son **Jacob,** the plantation where **John Pryer** now lives
and the remaining part of the land.

Exs.: wife ——, and Roger Hicks. Personal estate to be
equally divided between three children, viz.: **Sarah,
Phillip, Jacob** and unborn child.

Test: John Linkhorn, Geo. Sanders, Phil. Holendger.   14. 349.

Clark, Denes, Kent Co., 11th Dec., 1716; 24th Jan., 1716.

To dau. **Mary Wilde** and hrs., personalty, and all that is left unsold of "Kemp's Beginning" on Mudy Cr. Testator directs wife **Mary** to make over to purchaser the portion of sd. land verbally sold to William Dickus. Shd. sd. Wm. Dickus not buy the land, wife **Mary** is empowered to sell it for the benefit of herself and six youngest child.

" dau. **Rebecca** and hrs., 100 A., "Viana," nr. head of Chester R., and personalty.

" son **William** and hrs., 150 A., upper part of "Viana."

" daus. **Mary** and **Sarah** and hrs., 100 A. each of afsd. tract, "Viana."

" son **Dennis** and hrs., the upper pt. of dwelling plantation. Shd. he die during minority, land to pass to son **John.**

" wife **Mary,** extx., ⅓ pt. of dwelling plantation during life; at her decease to son **John;** also ⅓ personal estate, remaining part to six younger child., equally.

" son **John** and hrs., remaining pt. of dwelling plantation at age of 21 yrs. Shd. he die during minority, his portion to ascend to son **Denis.**

" grandson **John Wilde,** personalty.

Testator states that having purchased 150 A. of Cornelius Comegys, Sr., and not having had the full complement, sd. Cornelius bequeathed to him a piece of the same tract called "The Release," and desired his complement to be made good. Child. not to sell or dispose of lands, but to fall to next heirs.

To Edw. Comegys, 20s. for writing will.

Test: Thos. Mackdaniell, Edw. Comegys, Timoty Mackhone.

14. 350.

Willis, John, cordwinder, Kent Co., 1st Jan., 1706; 11th Feb., 1716.

To bro. **Richard,** dwelling plantation, and personalty which is in the hands of James Murphy, Chas. Ringold, James Meeks, and 5s. in the hands of Francis Meeks, and all other personal estate. Sd. **Richard** to be under care and management of Wm. Hopkins until of age.

Test: Jeremiah Rickan, John Reddish, Wm. Coch. 14. 352.

Beauchamp, Dodgett, planter, parish of Coventry, Somerset Co., —— —— ——; 18th Mar., 1716-7.

To wife ——, extx., use of dwelling plantation during widowhood and until son **Gray** arrives at age of 21 yrs. Shd. she marry, sd. plantation to pass at once to son **Gray** afsd.

" daus. **Hannah, Sarah, Smith** and son **Gray,** personalty.

Overseers: James Curtis and Jeffey Long.

Test: John Heath, James Curtis, Jean Johnson.   14. 353.

Mem.—18th March, 1716-7, **Sarah Beauchamp**, extx., revokes her pt. thereof and flyeth to her thirds.

Mackneal, Hugh, Somerset Co.,   22nd Jan., 1716-7;
14th May, 1717.

To wife **Alice**, ½ estate, real and personal, and ½ dwelling plantation, w. side, including house, during life.

" dau. **Katherine**, extx., residue of estate, also all that remains of her mother's portion at her decease.

Division line to run from Thomas Walston's line.

Test: John Tull, John Threhearne, Robt. Woods.   14. 355.

Muguane (Mugunane), Wm., planter, Annimesex, Somerset Co.,   4th Apr., 1717;
15th May, 1717.

To Margaret Sumner, personalty.

" James (son of Thos. Ward), Mrs. Barns and Stephen (son of John Riggin), personalty.

" John Starling and William Puzey, the debts they owe testator.

" Thomas Ward, ex., residue personal estate, conditionally.

Test: Thos. Stockwell, John Starling, Hannah Starling, Wm. Williams, John Moore.   14. 356.

Wharton, Chas., planter, Somerset Co., 28th Sept., 1716;
15th May, 1717.

To son **William** and hrs., 15 A., dwel. plan., also 100 A. adjoining it and next the river, being ½ of tract bou. by test. called "William's Hope," at decease of his mother **Mary,** and personalty.

" child unborn and hrs., whether male or female, residue of "William's Hope" and personalty.

" wife **Mary**, extx., real estate during life (son **Wm.** to be allowed to build on and improve land), also residue personal estate. Should child. afsd. die without issue, the survivor to enjoy land above given.

Test: Sam Dorman, Wm. Noble, Wm. Paine.   14. 357.

Long, David, Somerset Co.,   26th Nov., 1716;
18th Mar., 1716-17.

To bros. **John, Dan.** and **Randolph,** and to sister **Ann Wood,** personalty.

To bro. **Jeoffry**, ex., and hrs., all real estate and remainder
of personal estate. Shd. he have another son, testator desires he be named "**David**" and at bro. **Jeoffry's** decease
land to pass to his son. Should bro. **Jeoffry** have no son
named "**David,**" land to pass to **Jeoffry**, son of **Jeoffry**
and **Mary Long**.

Test: Wm. Lidster, Edw. Stockdall, John Benson. 14. 358.

Beauchamp, Thos., Somerset Co.,   2nd Jan., 1716-7;
                                          18th Mar., 1716-7.

To son **Isaac** and hrs., a certain part of dwelling plantation
"Contention" (for description see will).

"   son **John** and hrs., the lower part of sd. land, with that
which was bought of **Jno. Beauchamp**, and personalty.

"   dau. **Hannah Williams** and hrs., 12 pence and personalty
to be her full portion of estate.

"   daus. **Sarah, Elizabeth, Margaret** and **Mary**, and wife
Sarah, extx., personalty.

Residue of estate, real and personal, to be equally divided
between sons **Isaac** and **John** and daus. **Sarah, Elizabeth,
Margarett** and **Mary** and hrs. (Land at Marumscolt to
be sold for debt.)

Overseers: James Curtis and son-in-law **Thomas Williams, Jr.**

Test: James Curtis, John Benson, London Wallstorne. 14. 359.

Note—18th Mar., 1716-17, **Sarah Beauchamp** renounces will
and demands her thirds.

Morees, Morris, planter, Somerset Co.,   7th Nov., 1716;
                                        15th Jan., 1716.

To John Ireland, John Mercy, John Carter, Thos. Higman and
Robert Twilly, personalty.

"   Robert Giraus, ex., and hrs., 100 A., land on s. side of
Broad Creek, in Somerset Co., and residue of estate.

Test: James Giraus, Mary Giraus, James Caldwell, John Ireland.   14. 361.

Dohaty, James, Somerset Co.,   —— ——, 1716;
                                         8th Mar., 1716.

To dau. **Mary** and hrs., personalty.

"   dau. **Rose** and hrs., 75 A. of "Long Ridge" and personalty.

"   daus. **Sarah, Elizabeth, Janet** and their hrs., personalty.

"   dau. **Katharine** and hrs., the remainder of "Long Ridge"
and personalty.

"   wife **Janett**, the residue of estate, with all the rights,
benefits and privileges.

Ex.: Capt. William Planner and Thos. William, Jr.; they to
have care of children until of age.

Test: Wm. Planner, Wm. Dixon, Thos. Williams, Jr. 14. 363.

Maddux, Lazarus, Somerset Co.,   18th Jan., 1716;
     19th Mar., 1716.

To sons **Thos., Lazarus** and **Daniel,** 900 A. on s. side of Mano-
     kin River, divided as follows:

"   **Thos.** and hrs., 300 A. on Woolf Trap Creek (for descrip-
     tion see will), and personalty on west side of sd. ck.

"   **Lazarus,** 300 A. on west side of sd. creek (for description
     see will), and personalty.

"   **Daniell** and hrs., residue of above mentioned 900 A.,
     being dwelling plantation, also personalty. Should sons
     Lazarus and **Daniell** die without issue or intestate, then
     the survivor shall enjoy both tracts of land. Neither of
     the three sons, viz.: **Thos., Lazarus** and **Daniell,** have
     right to dispose of property nor sell, but to each other.

"   sons **Alex.** and **William,** personalty and 700 A., "White
     Field," equally between them. Should either die with-
     out issue or intestate, portion of deceased to pass to sur-
     vivor.

"   daus. **Mary, Sarah, Elinor** and **Elizabeth,** personalty.

"   wife ——, extx., dwelling plantation during widowhood
     and ⅓ of personal estate, the remainder to be equally
     divided between above mentioned children.

Test: Francis Lord, James Willis, Wm. Henderson, Marcy
     Fountaine.   14. 364.

Carlsly, Peter, planter, Somerset Co.,
     13th Jan., 1716;
     19th Mar., 1716-7.

To sons **Peter, Richard, William, Sam'l** and **Robert,** all real
     estate, equally. Sons shall not sell property except to
     one another. Should their mother marry, sons to be free
     at age of 18 yrs., and if she remain a widow sons shall
     remain with her until of full age according to law.

"   wife **Elizabeth,** extx., dwelling plantation with 50 A.
     during life, and personal estate; residue to be equally
     divided among five child. afsd.

Test: Thos. Woods, Jacob Adams, John Outten.   14. 366.

Ducks, John, planter, Somerset Co.,   7th Jan., 1716;
     19th Mar., 1716-7.

To sons **John** and **Robert,** 1s. each.

"   daus. **Grace** and **Rachel,** 1s. each.

"   wife **Ann,** extx., and hrs., 100 A., "Sunken Ground,"
     and residue of personal estate.

Test: Thos. Maddux, John Outtèn, Wm. Conner.   14. 367.

Maddux (Madux), Alex., Somerset Co., 10th Apr., 1717;
14th May, 1717,

To son **Lazarus**, dwel. plant., 225 A., to live upon and to
have use of a part during his mother's life; wife **Mary**
not to be debarred of the manor plan. and what privileges she thinks fit to take in and enjoy. At her decease
the afsd. 225 A. to go to son **Lazarus** and hrs.
"   sons **Thos., Alex.** and **Nathaniel**, 12 pence each.
"   daus. **Mary, Elizabeth** and **Ann**, 12 pence each.
"   wife **Mary**, extx., residue of personal estate.   At her
decease to pass to son **Lazarus** and hrs.
Test: Luke Johnson, Thos. Marshall (Marchell), Anthony
Seady, Thos. Savage.   14. 368.

Hayman, James, planter, Somerset Co.,
13th Feb., 1716-7;
14th May, 1717.

To sons **Henry, James** and **John**, ''Hopewell,'' equally, provided they pay other 2 sons, **Chas.** and **Isaac**, fifteen hundred lbs. of tobacco each at the age of 21 yrs.
Wife **Sarah**, extx., she to divide estate equally among children
when of age, sons at 18 yrs. and daus. at 16 yrs.
Test: Mathew Dorman, Henry Dorman, Abraham Heath.
14. 369.

Veze (Veazey), Nathaniell,   16th Oct., 1710;
13th Feb., 1716-7.

To son **Nathaniell** and hrs., 200 A., dwel. plant., ''Burmadus
Hund.''
"   son **Chas.** and hrs., 90 A., ''Could Harbor,'' adjoining sd.
plan. and left to testator by Thos. Purnell.
"   son **William** and hrs., 50 A. on s. side of Pocomoke R.,
at Matypynie Landing.
Sons **Nathaniell** and **Chas.** to pay to their two bros., **George**
and **John**, 2,000 lbs. tobacco each when at age 21 yrs.
Three sons, **Wm., Geo.** and **John**, to remain with mother
until 21 yrs. of age.
To wife **Elizabeth**, extx., entire personal estate.
Test: Wm. Henderson, Robt. Watson, Wm. Aydelett. 14. 370.

Walton, John, Somerset Co.,   1st May, 1716;
5th Feb., 1716-7.

To eldest son **Jno.** and hrs., dwelling plantation (for description see will).

To son **Wm.** and hrs., remainder of land on w. and s. w. side of certain bounds. Shd. either sd. sons **Jno.** or **Wm.** die without issue, their share to pass to survivor. Not to sell until 3rd generation, except to each other.

" eldest dau. **Elizabeth**, daus. **Sarah, Rebecca** and **Mary** and youngest dau. **Hannah**, personalty.

Residue of estate equally bet. 7 child. afsd. when of age. Sons of age at 18 yrs., daus. at 16 yrs.

Wife —— extx.

Test: Rich. Holland, John Holland, **Wm. Walton.**   14. 371.

Note—Extx. applies for her thirds.

Tompson (Thompson), Joseph, Dorchester Co.,
26th Aug., 1717;
4th Sept., 1717.

To son **Joseph,** 102 A., "Thompson's Addition."

" Enoch Barkleton, 100 A., part of "Thompson's Addition," after he pays exs. 900 lbs. of tobacco.

" 6 children, viz.: sons **Joseph** and **John,** daus. **Frances, Ann, Elizabeth** and **Sarah,** personal estate.

Exs.: Wife **Elizabeth** and bro. **Chas.**, jointly.

Test: Chas. Marin, Isaac Marrett, Mark Marrett.   14. 373.

Davis, Rich., Dorchester Co.,
8th Jan., 1716;
7th Oct., 1717.

To Margaret Branock, personalty in Henry Ellit's possession.

" Moses Lecompte, Sr., ex., and hrs., tract of land on Taylor's Island called "Pardonaram."

Test: John Lecompte, Mary Lecompte, Joseph Lecompte.
14. 374.

Wall, Joseph, Dorchester Co.,
—— —— ——;
17th Oct., 1717.

To unborn child, one seat of land and personalty; to be of age at 17 yrs., male or female.

" wife **Rachel,** extx., residue of estate, real and personal.

Test: Pettygrew Solsbury (Soldesbury), John Lowder, Mark Fisher.   14. 375.

Crowley, Daniell, planter, Talbot Co., 28th Sept., 1717;
28th Nov., 1717.

To eldest dau. **Elinor** and hrs., 80 A. on Island Creek, "Hyerdier Lloyd" (formerly in poss. of Richard More and, "for want of hrs. did return to the Lord of the soil," and purchased of Charles Carroll, agt. for Lord Baltimore). Sd. dau. **Elinor** to pay to second dau., **Elizabeth**, £15 at age of 18 yrs. or on day of marriage. Shd. **Elinor** die without issue, **Elizabeth** to inherit sd. land; she failing issue, land to pass to wife's eldest son, **Wm. Jones**, and to remain unto the male hrs. of the Jones family for ever.

To wife **Elinor**, extx., personal estate. Shd. she die before afsd. daus. attain their majority, daus. to be under direction of Wm. Cary.

" Mr. Thomas Huttson, personalty.

Test: Andrew Renells, Margaret Booth, George Johnson.

14. 376.

Pitt, John, merchant, Talbot Co., 21st Oct., 1717; 14th Nov., 1717.

To dau. **Elizabeth Sherwood**, personalty; she and her husband, **John Sherwood**, to be content therewith, in consideration of the estate settled on grandson **James Berry**.

" dau. **Susannah** (wife of **Daniell Powell**), personalty; to have no further interest in estate, in consideration of the estate already given to sd. **Daniell Powell**.

" grandson **Howell Powell**, personalty.

" grandson **John Powell**, 500 A. of a tract of 1,500 A. called "Colerain," on Tuckahoe Creek, and personalty.

" grandson **James Berry**, dwelling plantation after decease of testator's wife. He to live with her if he chooses, and may build on the uncultivated part of sd. plan.; also residuary legatee of est., real and personal, and in event of wife's death, ex. of estate.

" wife **Rebecca**, extx., dwelling plantation for life unless she marry, when dwel. plan. shall pass in 6 mos. to grandson **James Berry**, and water mill for life. Also to her and her heirs, that part of Henry Hossier's estate which belonged to her when she was his widow, and personalty.

" the monthly meeting of Quakers of Talbot Co., £5. Shd. any differences arise bet. extx. and legatees, testator directs that the Monthly Meeting appoint 2, 4 or 6 of its male members, who shall have absolute authority to settle such differences; any beneficiary not abiding by their decisions to forfeit all benefits from testator's est.

Test: Robt. Walker, William Harrell, William Dobson, Thomas Anderson, James Townsend. 14. 377.

Wilson, Josiah, gent., Pr. Geo. Co.,   11th Nov., 1717;
                                                  5th Dec., 1717.

To brother **William Kid** and hrs., 24 A., ''Refuge,'' also the
adjoining tract, 84 A., ''Kid's Levell,'' and 59 A. called
''Island Plains,'' which adjoins ''Kid's Levell.''

''   son **Josiah** and hrs., 500 A., ''Ozburn's Lott,'' in Balto.
Co., east side Bush River, also ½ of 380 A. called ''Buttington'' and 3 lots in Marlborough, one being part of one
of the southernmost lots on the market-place; also a lot
on e. side of Mr. William Head's lot and a lot on the south
side of the meeting lot, and personalty.

''   son **Lingen** and hrs., 500 A., ''Lingans Adventure,'' in
Balto. Co., on s. side of Gunpowder R., and 450 A., ''Back
Lingan,'' in same county, and personalty.

''   son **Janus** and hrs., 250 A., ''The Ridge,'' at head of
Hunting Creek, 90 A., ''The Angles,'' at head of same
creek, 200 A., ''George's Desire,'' and 42 A., ''Addition,''
joining ''The Ridge,'' also a slip of land in Annapolis,
being part of a lot sold to Patrick Ogilby, and one lot
of land and house in Mount Calvert, Pr. Geo. Co., formerly
taken up and built on by Henry Boteler; one other lot
and house in Mount Calvert, purchased of Christopher
Beam, now deceased, also warehouse on waterside at
Mt. Calvert, and personalty.

''   son **Joseph** and hrs., 150 A., ''Cockalds Point,'' on s. side
of west branch of Patuxent River; 20 A., ''Beams Landing,'' and the adjoining tract of land; also 43 A. of the
same ''Beams Landing'' with the appurtenances thereto,
and 100 A., ''Brook Hill,'' on n. side Charles Branch in
Pr. Geo. Co.; also 200 A. of adj. tract, ''Kingsale,'' and
personalty.

''   son **Joshua** and hrs., tract of land and houses in Mt.
Calvert purchased of Thomas Emos; 247 A. and 132 A.,
part of Mt. Calvert manor purchased of John Deakins;
also a tract purchased of Christopher Beam on s. side of
Charles Branch cont. 18 A., and personalty.

''   dau. **Martha** and hrs., 206 A., ''Indian Gyant's Sepulcher,''
in Charles County, purchased of Walter Beam, and personalty.

''   Mrs. Catherine Boteler, personalty.

Residue of personalty to be divided among the 6 child. afsd.,
first division when son **Lingan** attains the age of 16.
Son **Josiah** to have first choice, and then son **Lingan.**
The Justices of Pr. Geo. County Court, with Mr. Edward
Boteler and Mr. Thomas Lingan in Calvert County to
assist at division. Should any of five sons afsd. die before age of 18, his share of est. to be equally divided
among all surviving child. Dau. **Martha** of age at 16.

Exs.: Sons **Josiah** and **Lingan,** jointly. They to maintain child. at schools and provide a competent support till they come of age. Servants Walter Thompson, John Hastins, John Smith, Izia Bonnell and George Noble to be disposed of by exs. for own benefit till their time of servitude expires.

Test: Jos. Belt, Rich. Pile, Robt. Hall.   14. 381.

Comerford, Elizabeth, Queen Anne's Co.,
                     21st Nov., 1717;
                     10th Dec., 1717.

To husband **George Comerford,** £100 ster. and 10 thousand-weight of tobacco, being gifts to testatrix of her father, **Maj. John Hawkins,** also care of testator's child. until they become of legal age. He to have their estate in his possession until their marriage, and also testatrix's thirds.

Test: Edw. Smith, Mary Smith, Domnick Martin.   14. 385.

Rose, Rich., Prince Geo. Co.,   30th Apr., 1716;
                       29th June, 1717.

To friend Sam. Plummer and hrs., plan. and tract, "Rose's Purchase," and personalty.

Thos. Plummer, Sr., ex. and residuary legatee.

Test: John Evans, John Turner, Sol. Turner.   14. 385.

Baron (Barron), Robt., clerk, St. Mary's Co.,
                     10th Aug., 1717;
                     1st Oct., 1717.

To child., viz.: **Benj., Martha** and **Bridget,** ⅔ of estate to be divided into four equal parts, two parts to son **Benj.** and the other two parts to two daus. afsd.

" wife **Mary,** extx., residue of estate.

Test: Ferrin Sweeny, Alex. Edmonds, John Donaldson, Mathew Toddadill.   14. 386.

Steele, John, planter, A. A. Co.,   30th Aug., 1717;
                       2nd Oct., 1717.

To 3 child., **John, Mary** and **William,** estate equally, at majority.

Ex.: John Chew.

Test: Neh. Birckhead, Jr., John Tucker, **Mary Steele.** 14. 387.

Wheatley, John, St. Mary's Co.,   25th Apr., 1717;
                       8th Aug., 1717.

To son **James,** 500 lbs. tobacco.

" son **John** and hrs., 110 A., "Wheatley's Meadows," and 50 A., "Hiccory Plaines."

To son **Joseph** and hrs., 114 A., "Umtiguint."

" wife **Elizabeth**, extx., dwelling plantation with tract of land belonging thereto during life; at her decease to pass to sons **Thomas** and **Francis** and their hrs., equally divided bet. them. If wife shd. marry, sons **Thomas** and **Francis** to be of age at 18; if she remains a widow, to be under her tuition until 21 yrs. of age.

Also to wife **Elizabeth**, ½ of personal estate, the other half to be equally divided amongst 5 daus., viz.: **Winifride, Anne, Elizabeth, Susannah** and **Mary,** at age of 16 or day of marriage.

Test: Wm. Hoard, Susannah Norrice, John Norrice, Henry Spinke.   14. 388.

Fletchell, Thos., planter, Prince Geo. Co.,
17th July, 1717;
2nd Aug., 1717.

To son **Thos.** and hrs., 300 A., being half of "Widows Mite," when he arrives at age of 21 yrs., and the remaining 300 acres at decease of wife.

" dau. **Elizabeth** and hrs., 150 A., "Lancaster," on Broad Ck., also tract of land in Piscattaway, Pr. Geo. Co., called "Containing," and personalty.

Extx. to sell all real estate not before mentioned for the payment of debts, the money remaining to be equally divided between wife and two child.

To wife **Anne,** extx., dwelling plantation and so much land adj. to make up 300 acres; at her decease to pass to son **Thos.** and hrs.

Test: John Bradford, James Riggs, Wm. Renshaw.   14. 389.

Batie, John, A. A. Co.,   30th Jan., 1709;
19th June, 1717.

To grandson **William Young, Jr.,** and hrs., land bought of Clement Hill and land bought of Col. Henry Darnell.

" wife **Sarah,** extx., entire personal est. during life; at her decease to be equally divided among three daus., viz.: **Mary Young, Eliz. Stoddart** and **Rebecca Bishop.**

Test: Josiah Towgood, Sarah Hardick, Edward Evans, Abraham Birkhead.   14. 391.

Mercer. Jacob, parish of Sainte ——, A. A. Co.,
30th Jan., 1716;
2nd Apr., 1717.

To mother ——, personalty during life; at her decease to
pass to son **John.** Shd. he die, to pass to dau. **Elizabeth.**
Residue of estate equally divided bet. wife **Mary,** extx.,
son **John** and dau. **Elizabeth.** Son to be of age at 18
yrs., but not to receive his portion until 21 yrs. of age;
dau. **Elizabeth** to have her portion at 16 yrs. of age or
day of marriage.
Test: Honeri Bateman, Rich Loador (Loaden). 14. 392.

Powell, George, Queen Anne's Co., 2nd Sept., 1717;
28th Nov., 1717.

To son **John,** personalty.
" son **Thomas,** personalty and 1,000 lbs. of tobacco when
at age of 21 yrs.
" son **James** and hrs., part of "Partnership" cont. 250 A.,
personalty and 1,000 lbs. of tobacco when at age of
21 yrs.
" 3 daus., **Mary Burross, Eliz. Long** and **Jane Jones,** 1
shilling each.
" daus. **Judith** and hrs., and **Rachell,** personalty.
" granddau. **Anne Powell,** personalty, to be delivered to
her father.
" wife **Anne,** extx., dwelling plantation during life, excepting that part where son **John** now lives. At her
decease entire tract to be divided equally bet. sons
John and **Thomas** and hrs. Son **John** and hrs. to have
part on which he now lives. Son **Thomas,** dwel. plan.
Wife **Anne,** residuary legatee of personal estate.
Test: John White, Henry Rawlings, Augustine Thompson.
14. 393.

Kirby, Wm., Kent Island, Queen Anne's Co.,
7th May, 1716;
3rd Oct., 1717.

To sons **Walter** and **James** and hrs., two tracts, "Allen's
Deceit" and "Kirby's Addition," to be equally divided
bet. them at age of 18 yrs., **Walter** to have first choice.
Shd. either of sd. sons die without issue, their share of
land to pass to survivor and his hrs. Sons to be of age
at 18 yrs.
" son **Walter,** personalty.

Residue of est., after wife's thirds are deducted, to be divided
equally among child. **Walter, James, Sarah** and **Mary**
and their hrs.

Wife **Anne** extx.

Test: Wm. Rakes, Wm. White, Rich. Houlding.   14. 394.

Mitford (Mittford), Wm., Talbot Co.,   8th Oct., 1716; 26th Jan., 1716.

Test: leaves all accounts and other writings into hands of
Foster Turbutt, ex., to raise the sum of £30 Ster. as a
legacy to sister **Mary Mitford,** in North Allerton, in
Yorkshire.

"   Wookman Gibson, personalty.

"   College of Virginia, £90 currency.

Test: Nich. Lurtey, Rich. Borden, Jno. Smallshaw.   14. 395.

Cromwell, Rich., Baltimore Co.,   12th Aug., 1717; 23rd Sept., 1717.

To cousin **Joshua Cromwell**, £10 and personalty.

"   Margaret Rathenbury, personalty; at her decease to pass
to her dau. Hannah.

"   **Edith** (dau. of **Richard Gist,** and to **Zippora**, his wife),
personalty.

"   cousin **Richard Gist**, £30 and personalty.

"   mother-in-law —— Bosson, bro.-in-law **James Phillips** and
cousin **Thomas Cromwell,** each a gold ring.

"   Isaac Larogne, £10.

"   **Nicholas Besson,** personalty.

"   eldest son **Richard,** 1s. and no more. Exs. to maintain
sd. son, provided he will remain with them. Shd. estate
pass to **Edith Gist,** she and her hrs. to maintain sd. son.

"   wife **Elizabeth,** use of estate during widowhood; shd. she
marry, her thirds only.

"   son **John,** entire estate at decease of his mother. Shd.
he die without issue, sd. estate, both real and personal,
to **Edith Gist** afsd.

Exs.: Wife **Elizabeth** and son **John,** jointly.

Test: Wm. Cromwell, James Jackson, Jabes Marray.   14. 396.

Harris, Edw., planter, Queen Anne's Co., 22nd Sept., 1716; 18th May, 1717.

To son **Edward** and male hrs., "Ditteridge" on Wye R. and
dwel. plan. Land not to be sold nor any lease or mortgage placed on it except for the space of one yr. Should
Edward die without male hrs., then to pass to son **Thos.**
and male hrs., and to be possessed by them as above ex-
pressed.

Testator having bequeathed sd. plan. to son **Edward,** he (son **Edward**) shall purchase for son **Thos.** 150 A. of good plantation land in Queen Anne's Co., and to be made over to sd. **Thos.** and hrs.

Residue of estate to be equally divided among wife and child. Sons to receive their portions at age of 21 yrs. and daus. at age 16 or day of marriage.

Exs.: Wife **Elizabeth** and son **Edward.**

Testator recommends to his exs. the advice of Doctor Thos. Godman, William Cammell and Horton Knatchbull. Dr. Godman (being godfather to son **Thos.**) to see to his education.

Test: Rich. Cooke, Thos. Comerford, Thos. Morton, Horton Knatchbull, Harklus Cooke. 14. 398.

Johnston, Robt., planter, Prince George's Co.,
14th May, 1717;
6th July, 1717.

To sons **Joseph** and **Benj.** and hrs., 100 A., "Poor Man's Industry," on Tinkers Branch in Piskathaway, equally.
" dau. **Elizabeth,** personalty.
" wife **Elizabeth,** extx., dwelling plantation during life, at her decease to pass to son **James** and hrs., and residue of personal estate, absolutely.

Test: Isabella Dickinson, Anne Johnston, Rupert Butler.
14. 400.

Robins, Henry, Prince George's Co., 29th July, 1717;
5th Oct., 1717.

To Thos. Robins, elder (planter), of Pr. Geo. Co., 1 hand mill, personalty. He to dispose of goods to relatives of testator.
" sister **Margaret** and bro. **James,** personalty.

Ex.: ——.

Test: Dave. Hopper, David Parsons, John Queen, Alex. Parsons. 14. 402.

Mansell, Robt., taylor, St. Mary's Co., 16th Apr., 1716;
5th Oct., 1717.

To Mr. Daniell Magill, 500 lbs. tobacco.
" joint exs., Joseph Edwards, St. Mary's Co. and **Mr.** William Young of Prince Geo., and to Mr. Dan'l Magill, personalty.
" cous. **Robt.** Mansell and his sister **Grace,** of Hatherly in Devonshire, residue of estate.

Test: Chas. Wane, Francis Ratcliffe. 14. 403.

Shaw, Thos., Somerset Co.,   22nd Dec., 1716;
24th June, 1717.

To Thos. Hudson, personalty and use of a house to preach in during his life.

"   wife **Mary**, extx., use of dwelling plantation and real estate for life. At her death to pass to grandson **Wm. Robinson** and hrs.; also residue of personal est., absolutely.

Test: John Janes, Geo. Martin and Margaret Bryan.   14. 404.

McClester, Margret, widow, Somerset Co.,
28th Nov., 1715;
21st June, 1717.

To sons **John, Neal** and **Joseph** and dau. **Martha** and hrs., 20s. each.

"   son **Daniell**, ex., residue of personal estate.

Test: Rich. Samuell, Peter Samuell, Charity Harvey.   14. 405.

Worthington, Saml., Somerset Co.,   15th May, 1717;
19th June, 1717.

To wife ——, extx., entire estate.

"   John Banister, of Liverpole, personalty.

Test: Arnold Elzey, William Stoughton, Sarah Elzey.   14. 406.

(Test: Proc. V. 23, folio 285, show **Alice Worthington** extx. of above will.)

Highway, Jacob,   29th Mar., 1717;
—— —— ——.

To sisters **Elizabeth Adkins** and **Hanah Higheway**, and bro. **Robert Adkins** and **Jas. Highway**, personalty.

"   **Robert Adkins**, residue of estate.

Ex.: ——.

Test: James Machon, Deborah Machon, Moses Duskey.
14. 407.

(Test. pro. 23 f. 285, Robt. Adkins admin. filed bond 21st June, 1717.)

Henry, John, Pocomoke, Somerset Co.,   1st Oct., 1715;
20th June, 1717.

To bro. **Hugh** and sisters **Jannet** and **Helen**, £15 ster., to be pd. to Rev. Alex. Sinclaire, in Plumked St., Dublin; if he be dead, to the Rev. Messrs. Francis Iredale or Cragehead, in Cable St., Dublin.

"   Alex. Sinclaire, if living, 20s. to purchase a ring.

To son **John** and hrs., ½ "Buckland," on St. Martin's R.,
division to be brother —— King's line. (For desc. see
will.) Also to son **John** and his male hrs., ½ of store-
house and lot at Snowhill, and 100 A. of a tract called
"Pershoar" on Whorekill Creek (for desc. see will); and
if son **Robert** disturb him or his male hrs., then to son
John and male hrs. other half of "Buckland" also at
decease of wife, and ⅓ personal est.

" son **Robert Jenkins** and hrs., two tracts of land on Morat-
tock R. in N. C., one cont. 930 A. and the other 640 A.;
also dwel. plan., 400 A., "Mary's Lot," and 50 A.,
"Henry's Addition," adj.; also a tract of 150 A. lying
above Snow Hill called "Joshemon," another called
"Providence," cont. 200 A. at Dividing Creek; also the
southernmost half of "Buckland," under afsd. condition;
½ of lot and store at Snow Hill, also a tract on Pocomoke,
wherein Tho. Ellis now lives, called "Necessity," and
also all other real est. not herein mentioned, and ⅔ of
personal est. at decease of wife.

Wife **Mary**, extx., to have use of entire est. during life.

Sons to have an education such as their genius inclines them
to. Test: desires bro. **Robt. King** and Epr. Eilson to be
counsellors to wife. Shd. either die before sd. sons become of age, desires neighbor Robt. Mills to join with
survivor and also Rev. Mr. John Hampton.

Test: Jonathan Noble, Robt. Harris, Eliz. Dinaly.   14. 408.

Paul, Chas., Sr., planter, Dorchester Co.,
9th Feb., 1716;
11th June, 1717.

To three youngest child., viz.: **Chas., Geo.** and **Jacob,** dwel.
plan., "Stanaway's Lucky Chance," and 16 A. lying in
the same neck, equally divided between them when the
youngest son **Jacob** arrives at age 21 yrs. Should any
of them wish to be disinherited, then his other two bros.
shall pay to him 2,000 lbs. of tobacco, they to hold all sd.
land. Shd. two of them be disposed as afsd., the like
method shall be followed, but no stranger to buy, inherit
or hold sd. land.

" son **Robert,** 50 A. on his grandfather **Hopkins'** island,
given by sd. grandfather, **Robt. Hopkins,** to his dau.
Sarah, wife of testator, and 1s.

" son **William** and daus. **Sarah Groase, Elizabeth, Ann** and
Mary, 1s. each.

" wife **Sarah,** extx., real and personal estate during life.
Should wife marry, child. to enjoy and have the benefit
of their labor at 16 yrs. of age.

Test: Josiah Wroughton, Robt. Johnson, Jr., Michell Todd.
14. 410.

Early, John, Dorchester Co.,   24th Nov., 1717;
                                                11th June, 1717.

To wife **Eliz.**, extx., entire est., real and personal, for life.

" **Rich. Woodland** and hrs., grandson of testator's wife,
   dwel. plan. and tract "Northampton," also adj. tract
   "Early's Chance," and personalty.

" **Rich. Woodland** (son-in-law of testator's wife), during
   life, test. share of a tract which they hold in co-partner-
   ship; at his death to his son, **Wm. Woodland,** and personalty.

" **Wm. Woodland** and his sister, **Eliz. Woodland,** personalty.

" **John Woodland** (grandson of test.'s wife), personalty.

Elizabeth Woodland and her sister, **Mary Woodland,** residuary
   legatees of personal estate.

To neighbor Michael Todd, cordwinder or shoemaker, personalty.

Test: Rich. Deah, Margaret Todd, Michael Todd.   14. 411.

Kirwan (Carrawen), Matthew, Dorchester Co.,
                                                4th Jan., 1716;
                                                17th June, 1717.

To two sons **John** and **Matthew** and male hrs., all real estate.
   For want of such issue, estate to pass to daus. **Jane** and
   Mary and their hrs.

" wife ——, extx., use of entire estate during widowhood.
   Shd. she marry, her thirds.

Test: Wm. Cooke, Edw. Elliott.   14. 413.

(Test. pro. v. 23, f. 279, **Mary Kirwan,** extx. of above will,
   files bond.)

Lake, Robert, blacksmith, Dorchester Co.,
                                                27th Jan., 1716;
                                                14th Aug., 1717.

To wife **Jane,** extx., ½ real and ⅔ personal estate.

" dau. **Mary,** ½ real and ⅓ personal estate. Shd. sd. dau.
   die without issue, her portion to revert to wife. Shd.
   wife be now with child, estate bequeathed to dau. **Mary**
   afsd. to be divided equally bet. 2 child.

Test: Tobias Pollard, John Peopell, John Bramble, Jr.
                                                14. 413.

Busick, Rebecca, Little Choptank, Dorchester Co.,

14th June, 1700;

14th June, 1717.

To son **James** and hrs., dwel. plan. 50 A., "Ellsing," and 50 A., "Gadumne," on Little Choptank R., after decease of husband, **James Busick.** Should child (unborn) be a male, then the land to be equally divided between two sons, with the exception of dwell. mansion, bequeathed wholly to sd. son **James.** Should he die without issue and no male hr. appear, then lands to remain to dau. **Ann** and hrs.

" dau. **Ann,** 200 lbs. tobacco, to be pd. to her at marriage by son **James,** and other personalty.

Exs.: Wm. Douse and Edw. Tench, after decease of husband.

Test: Thos. Howell, Wm. Michen, Wm. Douse, Jno. Kirke.

14. 415.

Note—Testatrix is spoken of in the test. as **Rebecca Busick,** alias **Rebecca Peterson.**

Vaughan, Wm., planter, Dorchester Co., 13th Mar., 1717;

11th June, 1717.

To wife **Prudence,** extx., entire estate, including "Exchange." Shd. there not be enough to pay debts, extx. to sell 100 A. of easternmost end of "Exchange."

Test: Graves Jarrard, John Judrell, Geo. Haa. 14. 416.

Hackett, Thos., Sr., blacksmith, Dorchester Co.,

9th June, 1716;

12th Nov., 1716.

To wife **Eliz.** and hrs., 103 A., part of "Neighborly Kindness," and personalty.

" sons **Oliver** and **Thos.** and hrs., residue of real estate equally divided bet. them, and personalty.

" grandson **Theophilius,** son of **Oliver Hackett,** and to grand-daus. **Litia,** dau. of **Thos. Hackett,** and **Elizabeth,** dau. of **Oliver Hackett,** personalty.

Exs.: Wife **Eliz.** and son **Oliver,** jointly.

Test: Rich Webster, Chas. Deane, John Gray. 14. 417.

Note—12th Nov., 1716, Oliver Hackett renounces ex.

Harrison, Marmaduke,   14th May, 1717;
                                                  13th Aug., 1717.
To Thomas Ewbanks, Sr., ex., entire estate.
Test: Elizabeth Williams, Dennis Hopkins, Thos. Ewbanks, Jr.
                                                  14. 419.

Cox, John, planter, Talbot Co.,   3rd June, 1716;
                                                  17th Aug., 1717.
To son **Jeffrey** and hrs., "Spring Close."
Wife **Rebecca** extx.
Test: Abraham Beesley, Alex. Jeames, **Joseph Cox.**   14. 420.

Sands, Robert, planter, Talbot Co.,   20th Feb., 1716;
                                                  30th July, 1717.
To eldest son **Robert** and hrs., 100 A., being part of "Sand's
    His Lot."
  "   son **Thomas** and hrs., 100 A., "Fishbourn's Landing,"
    conditionally. Shd. son **Thomas** die without issue, sd. land
    to pass to dau. **Elizabeth** and hrs., with restrictions as
    imposed on son **Thomas.**
  "   dau. **Judith,** 50 A., remaining part of "Sands His Lot."
    Shd. she die without issue, land to pass to dau. **Sarah**
    and hrs.
  "   dau. **Mary** and hrs., 50 A., "Barron Spot," adj. plan.
    of Mich. Cummins. Shd. she die without issue, sd. land
    to pass to dau. **Susannah.** Land not to be sold except
    to sons **Robt.** or **Thos.,** and they having bought it shall
    not sell again.
  "   wife **Sarah,** ⅓ personal estate absolutely, also 50 A.
    "Chance," for life. Shd. son **Robt.** not live with wife
    during her widowhood, he to build dwell. house on
    "Chance," and this land at her decease to be equally
    divided between sons **Robt.** and **Thomas.** Son **Thos.** to
    have half joining "Fishbourn's Landing."
Residue of personal estate to be divided equally among
    children.
Exs.: Wife **Sarah** and son **Robt.,** jointly.
Test: M. T. Ward, John Leeds, Mich. Cumming, Eliz. Roberts.
                                                  14. 421.

Waple, Osmond, gent., Charles Co.,   10th Dec., 1717;
                                                  28th Dec., 1717.
To cousin **Sarah Waple,** 200 A., "Neck Pastime," for the use
    of her son **John** and his hrs.
  "   Ann Gooman and hrs., 100 A. and 2 tobacco houses,
    "Healy's Plantation."
  "   Robt. Hanson, £20.

To Col. Phillip Hoskine, residue of estate, real and personal, for the use of child. by his late wife Ann.

" wife **Elizabeth**, ⅓ of estate.

Exs.: Phil. Hoskine and Robt. Hanson, jointly.

Test: John Morton, Jeffrey Evins, James Russell.   14. 423.

Foester, Ann, widow, Charles Co.,   10th Oct., 1717;
                                              13th Dec., 1717.

To son **John Ashman** and to dau. **Mary**, wife of **Richard Ankrum**, 150 A., "St. Edmonds," lying at Portobacco and formerly in poss. of **Wm. Foester**, testator's deceased husband, to be equally divided bet. them. Son **John** lacking issue, land to pass to the hrs. of dau. **Mary** afsd.

" son **Richard Ashman**, personalty.

" granddau. **Ann Ollover**, personalty.

" James Penny, personalty, and to the rest —— of grandchild., personalty. The legacies to child. of **Mary Ankrum** being delivered from plant. at Portobacco.

Residue of estate to be divided equally among test. 3 sons, **John** and **Rich. Ashman** and **Rich. Ankrum**, who are named as exs.

Test: Walter Story, Wm. Puttneck, Charity Thompson.

14. 424.

Test. directs that whatever is due to **Henry Hardy**, a legatee under will of her former husband, **Henry Hardy**, shall remain in hands of her son **Rich. Ashman** till sent for.

Hugh, Even, Charles Co.,   22nd Oct., 1717;
                                         6th Dec., 1717.

To John (son of Peter Harrow) and to Jane Shiler, personalty.

" bro.-in-law **Josias Mankin** and Peter Harrow, exs., residue of estate, real and personal.

Test: John Wilkenson, Henry Hew.   14. 426.

Note—Mem to above will states that testator Even Hugh paid for the accounts of the est. of Thos. Hawes, 2,250 lbs. tobacco.

Smith, Samuel, Charles Co.,   18th Oct., ——;
                                         12th Nov., 1717.

To friend Mary, dau. of Bowling Speak, £4.

Exs.: Richard Odeton and John Stapleton.

Test: Jonathan Wood, Elizabeth Barman.   14. 426.

Pickett, Mathew, Talbot Co.,   19th Oct., 1717;
                                                          9th Nov., 1717.

To daus. **Mary** and **Elizabeth,** personalty, to be pd. them at
   age of 20 by ex. Samuel Dickison, who is to have charge
   of them.

Test: James Dickinson, Magnus Spence.   14. 427.

Guithins (Guitthins), Morris, gent., Talbot Co.,
                                                          29th Oct., 1717;
                                                          9th Dec., 1717.

To grandson Morris **Guithins,** £28 in hands of John Lovlidge
   when at age, and 13,500 lbs. tobacco due to testator by
   bond from son **Benjamin Guithins,** late deceased.
"   son **Edward Hardin** and to Wm. Burton, personalty.
John Stubbs to be free after serving two yrs.
To wife **Mary,** residue of estate, real and personal.
Exs.: Wife **Mary,** John Lovelidge and son **Edward Harden.**
Test: Anthony Evans, Rebecka Burton, Abrm. Taylor.

                                                          14. 428.

Thompson, William, tailor, Talbot Co.,   5th Dec., 1717;
                                                          7th Jan., 1717.

To son **Thomas** and hrs., land on n. side Deep Branch, after
   decease of his mother **Mary;** also 8 A., "Stoneload Living," near Courtgill, in the parish of Orton, Westmore-
   land, England, at decease of his grandmother, **Jennet
   Thomson.**
"   son **Richard** and hrs., land on s. side Deep Branch, after
   decease of his mother **Mary.**
Two-thirds of personal estate to be divided equally among
   4 child., viz.: **Thos., Richard, Mary** and **Sarah.**
To wife **Mary,** ⅓ real estate during life, and ⅓ personal
   estate. She to have use of entire estate so long as she
   remains a widow. Shd. she marry, 4 friends of the
   Monthly Meeting, viz.: Thomas Bynard, Richard Webb,
   Jonathan Taylor and James Willson, Jr., are to take bond
   for payment of child.'s estate when of age. Sons to be of
   age at 18, to have estate at age of 21; daus. at age of 18.
   Shd. wife die during widowhood, the 4 friends afsd. to
   admin. estate.
Exs.: Wife **Mary** and son **Thomas,** jointly.
Test: Wm. Godfrey, Dr. Paul Ronge, Alex. Cruickshank, Walter Riddley.   14. 430.

Note—Testator directs that he be buried at Tuckahoe Meeting House, Talbot Co.

Gill, Stephen, Jr., planter, Balitmore Co.,

23rd Sept., 1717;
18th Nov., 1717.

To friend Darbey Lane and hrs., 100 A. of land with "Garrison Plan." (which testator's father bought of Tho. Randall) and personalty.

" uncle **Peter Bond** and hrs., one part of "Millstones," lying at Guins Falls and 100 A. adjoining Guins Falls, to be laid out according to **Peter Bond's** desire.

" mother **Jane Gill**, 100 A. with dwel. plan. purchased by testator's father of Geo. Valentine; at her decease to pass to testator's uncle, **Steven Gill**, and hrs.

" uncle **Steven Gill** and hrs., residue of est., real and personal, except bequest to Darbey Lane.

Ex.: ——.

Test: Thos. Randall, Edw. Osbourne, Matthew Organ, Dennis Newman. 14. 432.

Sutton, Robt., planter, Talbot Co.,   15th Apr., 1717;
15th May, 1717.

Ex.: James Morgan, to have the charge and bringing up of testator's godchild, Elizabeth Mason, to age of 16 yrs.

Test: John Morgan, Thos. Jolle, James Dobson. 14. 434.

Writson, John, Talbot Co.,   15th Mar., 1716-7;
16th July, 1717.

To son **John** and hrs., part of "Lucky" and "Clay's Neck."

" son **Francis** and hrs., "Jorden Folly" and "Gauskins Point."

" wife **Mary**, extx., personal estate and "Reviving Spring" on Chester R., which is either to be equally divided among 5 child., viz.: **Margaret, Mary, Deborah, Catherine** and **Thomas,** or to be sold and the proceeds to be equally divided among child. afsd.

Test: Wm. Whittaker, John Kersey, John Reynolds, Wm. Colly. 14. 435.

Harris, Isaac, Kent Island, Queen Anne's Co.,

—— —— ——;
1st June, 1717.

To son **Isaac** and hrs., "Claxton" and personalty. Should he die without issue, sd. land to pass to dau. **Rhoda** and hrs.

" son **Workman** and hrs., dwel. plan. when he arrives at age of 21 yrs., and personalty.

" daus. **Mary** and **Ann,** personalty. Residue of personalty to be divided among three daus. afsd.

Wife **Rhoda** extx., to be advised by testator's friend **and** father-in-law, **Benj. Ball.**

Test: Wm. Brown, Edw. Hambleton, John Hawkins, Jr.

14. 437.

Faulkinn, Peter, Queen Anne's Co.,   17th Aug., 1717; 23rd Nov., 1717.

To sons **Wm., John** and **Valentine** and their hrs., personalty.
"   grandson **Wm. Goldsborgh,** daus. **Margaret Goldsborgh** and **Mary Burn** and their hrs., personalty.
"   wife **Mary** and son **Peter,** residue of personal est., and to be joint exs. Three sons afsd. to stay with their mother until 21 yrs.; dau. **Ann** to remain with her mother until 18 yrs. or marriage.

Test: Jno. Emory, Chas. Lemar, Martha Paxton.   14. 438.

Lashly, John, Prince Geo.'s Co.,   21st Nov., 1717; 11th Dec., 1717.

Testator directs that after payment of debts, residue of est. be divided equally bet. wife and six child. (unnamed). Should any child. die before they arrive at 21 yrs., estate to be equally divided between the survivors. Should wife **Eals** marry, then sons to be at liberty at 18 yrs. of age, but should she remain a widow, then they are to remain with their mother until 21 yrs.

Ex.: Joseph Belt.

Test: Christopher Thomson, Thos. Orton, Edw. Dawson.

14. 440.

Meed, Francis, A. A. Co.,   4th Jan., 1716; 6th Aug., 1717.

To sons **Wm., John, Benjamin** and their hrs., land at head of Magothy R. equally divided. **Benjamin** to have his part adj. his dwel. house. **Wm.** to have next choice.
"   sons **Wm.** and **John,** personalty after decease of their mother.
"   son **Benjamin,** personalty.
"   John and James Beard, personalty, to be pd. them at age of 18 by son **William.**
"   dau. **Susannah Long,** personalty.
"   son-in-law **Thos. Dawson,** personalty.
"   granddau. **Hannah Crans,** personalty at age of 14.
"   dau.-in-law **Mary Wright,** 5s.
"   3 sons, viz.: **William, John** and **Benjamin,** residue of estate. Est. not to be divided until decease of wife, unless she be willing.

Exs.: Wife **Ann** and son **William,** jointly.

Test: Capt. Phil. Jones, Thos. Buckinham, Jno. Hammond.

14. 441.

Capell, Isabell,

10th Sept., 1717;
22nd Dec., 1717.

To grandson **Jacob Holand** and hrs., 50 A., part of tract ''Friendship,'' and personalty.

" granddau. **Isabelle Price** and grandson **Thomas Tucker,** personalty.

" dau. **Mary Price,** extx., and hrs., residue of estate, real and personal.

Test: William Foard, Robt. Gott. 14. 442.

Gant, James, Brittain's Bay, St. Mary's Co.,

10th May, 1717;
4th Aug., 1717.

To son **John** and hrs., 100 A. on s. e. side of Brittain's Bay, near Wm. Davis's house, and personalty at 21 yrs. of age.

" son **Mathew** and hrs., 100 A., ''Drydocking'' in the forest of Brittain's Bay, at head of St. Lawrence R., and personalty at 21 yrs. of age.

" daus. **Anne, Eliz.** and **Mary,** personalty at 20 yrs. of age or marriage.

" wife **Mary,** dwelling plantation, being part of ''Revell,'' during life; at her decease to pass to son **Matthew** and hrs., wife residuary legatee.

Test: Nicholas Mills, John Medley, Thos. Walker, Henry Spinke. 14. 444.

Sanders, Robt., Charles Co.,

22nd Jan., 1717;
4th Feb., 1717.

To Ann Coulson, widow, two sets of bills of exchange for £14 ster., drawn by Capt. John Morecraft of Liverpool, mariner, consigned to John Crosby, merchant, in Liverpool, and the money Capt. John Gardiner, Capt. John Ball and Stephen M. Robinson owe testator.

" bro. **Mathew** and father **Mathew,** Henry Ward, sister **Margaret Ward** and to bro. **John (Sanders),** personalty.

" Capt. Samuell Bowman's cabin boy, 100 lbs. tobacco.

" Anthony Smith, 16d.

" Wm., son of Mary Johns (an orphan bound to Wm. Sanders), 20s. when of age.

" Mary, dau. of Geo. Ares, 20s. when at age of 16 yrs.

To Elizabeth and Chas. Camill, personalty, they to live with
Francis Robinson and Wm. Sanders. Should they not be
willing to live with them during minority, their portion
to be equally divided between executors.

Exs.: Francis Robinson and Wm. Sanders, jointly.

Test: Stephen Robinson, Dan. Hopper, Calri: Brown.   14. 445.

Manning, Joseph, Charles Co.,   14th Jan., 1717; 4th Feb., 1717.

To dau. **Esther Mathews**, 100 A., ''Mannings Discovery,'' to
her and the male heirs of herself and present husband,
Thomas Mathews, who shall be born after the date
hereof, and personalty.

''   son **John** and hrs., ex., residue of estate, real and personal.

Test: John Hayes, Dunkin Cambell, Wm. Herald.   14. 447.

Raggs, John, Queen Anne's Co.,   11th Jan., 1717; 22nd June, 1717.

To dau. **Frances**, personalty.

Wife **Sarah** extx. and residuary legatee.

Test: Mary Jones, Thos. Jones, John Joanes.   14. 448.

Moore, Richard, planter, Queen Anne's Co., 10th Mar., 1715; 29th Mar., 1717.

To sons **Norest, Richard** and **Charles** and daus. **Juliana, Rebecca** and **Hannah**, personalty.

''   wife **Edith**, extx., dwel. plan., 220 A., ''Confusion,'' during widowhood, and no longer; then to be equally divided
between three sons afsd., eld. son **Norest** to take his
choice. Should sons die without issue, their share to pass
to survivor or survivors; also personal est. during widowhood.

Test: Rich. Powell, Edw. Wright, Sol. Wright.   14. 449.

Macklin, Robert, Queen Anne's Co.,   11th Nov., 1716; 28th Jan., 1717.

To daus. **Elizabeth** and **Mary** and hrs., estate, real and personal, equally, at age of 18 yrs. or marriage. Estate to
be under the care and possession of their mother, **Elizabeth**, until they come to the above age or marry.

Extx.: Wife **Elizabeth.**

Test: Robt. Phillips, Thos. Phillips.   14. 450.

Beckwith, Henry, Sr., planter, Dorchester Co.,
17th Aug., 1717;
27th Oct., 1717.

To son **Nehemiah**, ex., and hrs., "Berry's Chance" and "Willmot's Choice" on Little Choptank R.

Test: Wm. Ellis, Clare Mackell, Judith Griffin.　　14. 451.

Stanford, Mary, Dorchester Co.,　　15th Apr., 1717;
13th Nov., 1717.

Ex. friend Rich. Pritchett to have the charge of testator's child., ——, until they arrive at age.

Test: Anthony Rawlings, William Stephens, Andrew Smith.
14. 452.

Lowe, Henry, Sr., gent., St. Mary's Co., 25th Oct., 1717;
6th Nov., 1717.

To son **Henry, Jr.**, and hrs., tract where he now lives, 1,300 A.
" son **Bennett** and hrs., tract where he now lives.
" son **Thos.** and hrs., old plan. in the Freshes.
" son **Nicolas** and hrs., dwel. plan., with all lands belonging thereto.
" daus. **Ann, Elizabeth** and **Henrietta Maria** and their hrs., "Golden Grove" equally among them.
" dau. **Dorothy** and hrs., "New Design" in the Freshes.
" dau. **Mary** and hrs., "Woods Quarter."
" son **Henry** and hrs., "Green Oak" and £300.
" son **Bennett** and hrs., all lands in Balto. Co. held between Mr. Darnall and testator, and £200.
" dau. **Susanna Maria**, wife of **Chas. Diggs**, £100 in full of her portion of estate. Residue of personal estate in England and in this province equally divided between child. (with the exception of dau. **Susanna Maria Diggs**).

Ex.: Sons **Henry** and **Bennett**.

Test: Samuel Grasty, Rich. Brooks, Michall Jenefer. 14. 453.

Bork, Cislye,　　6th Oct., 1717;
13th Nov., 1717.

To son **Edward Alford**, personalty; he dying without issue, certain legacies to return to **Eliz.** and **Ann.**
" daus. **Elizabeth** and **Ann Alford** and dau. **Rachel**, personalty. Residue of estate to be equally divided among son **Edward** and daus. **Elizabeth** and **Ann**, who are named exs.

Test: James Kidder, John Clark, Elizabeth Higan.　　14. 455.

Note: 13th Nov., 1717, **Elizabeth Alford** and **Ann Alford** make over all rights of executorship to their bro., **Edward Alford.**

Test: Isaac Nicolls, Wm. Evans, Jr.

Millmon, Thos., Dorchester Co.,   16th May, 1717;
    10th Nov., 1717.

To wife **Mary,** entire estate, real and personal, during life, to
    pass after decease with exception of following legacies,
    to son **Nicholas,** ex.

"   daus. **Elizabeth Pain, Bridget Baylor** and **Charity Han-
    cock,** 12 pence each to be pd. by ex.

Test: Isaac Nicols, Jno. Monatt, Rosehana Haley.   14. 456.

Dickinson, Edward, Calvert Co.,   10th Nov., 1717;
    14th Dec., 1717.

Testator directs that 100 a. lying next to "Scotland" be sold
    for benefit of estate.

To brother **John** and hrs., all other lands.

"   sister **Katherine Bowles,** rent of dwelling plantation for
    five yrs.

"   **David Bowles** and hrs., personalty.

"   sister **Sarah** and hrs., personalty.

"   Isaac and Mary Walley, personalty.

Test. desires that Jasper Floyd shall live with Mary Creed
    until he is of age.

Bro. **John** ex. and residuary leg. of estate, real and personal.

Test: James Pull or Pell, Jonahan Hollyday, Thos. Glover.

    14. 458.

Rankin, John, planter, A. A. Co.,   26th Dec., 1716;
    1st Dec., 1717.

To Sam. Culy, personalty.

"   wife **Elizabeth,** entire estate, with exception of the above
    mentioned legacy.

Ex.: Richard Bond.

Test: John Orrell, Robt. Lazenby, Mary Castle.   14. 461.

Miller, John, planter, St. Mary's Co.   15th Feb., 1717;
    17th Feb., 1717.

To dau. **Rebecca** and hrs., 2 tracts of 180 A. in St. Mary's
    hundred, bou. of George Thompson, "Farnham" and
    "Chelsey."

"   dau. **Priscilla** (wife of **Wm. Hebb**) and hrs., land in Pop-
    lar Hill hundred, "Forest of Dane," and a tract in St.
    George's, "Gardiner's Purchase."

"   grandson **John** (son of **Wm. Hebb**), "Strife," bou. of
    John Batson.

Wife **Ann** extx.

Test: Wm. Healder, Timothy Jolle, Wm. Asquith.   14. 462.

Taylor, Thos., St. Mary's Co.,   23rd July, 1717 ;
13th Nov., 1717.

To son **Ignacius**, personalty. To be of age at 16 yrs., he being
10 yrs. of age on 7th April next.

"   Rich. Mogg, personalty.

"   dau. **Grace**, personalty, she being 14 yrs. of age on 30th
March next.

"   wife **Ann**, extx., residue of estate.

In event of death of wife before son and dau. attain their
age, testator's brother, **James Taylor**, to care for them.

Test: Rich. Moy, Chas. Coalman, Wm. Johnson.   14. 463.

Ashcom, Winifred, spinster, St. Mary's Co.,
21st Oct., 1717 ;
27th Mar., 1718.

To mother **Martha Dansey**, widow, and hrs., personalty.

"   niece **Mary Ashcom Greenfield** and hrs., £50 due to testator from **Robt. Dansey**, and personalty.

"   niece **Elizabeth Greenfield** and hrs., £50 and personalty.

"   niece **Martha Ashcom** and hrs., dau. of bro. **Chas.**, personalty. Should she die without issue, to pass to niece
Elizabeth Greenfield and hrs. Shd. all afsd. nieces die
without issue, sd. bequests to pass to heirs at law.

Mother **Martha Dansey**, extx., residuary leg.

Test: Mary Johnson, Capt. Tho. Truman Greenfield.   14. 464.

Fisher, Abraham, A. A. Co.,   27th Dec., 1717 ;
21st Jan., 1717.

To Joseph Whips Standforth and to Elizabeth Standforth, the
son and dau. of John Standforth, personalty.

John Standforth ex. and residuary legatee.

Test: Henry Hall, Isaac Nicholan, Philothea Standforth.
14. 466.

Spinke, Edw., St. Mary's Co.,   18th Nov., 1717 ;
1st Dec., 1717.

To bro. **Henry** and hrs., 25 A. near dwelling plantation of
testator, also nr. dwelling house of Annastatia Langham.
(For description see will.)

Test. establishes a line and bequeaths all land on n. side of
it to dau. **Elizabeth** and hrs., and remaining part to son
William and hrs.

To daus. **Margaret** and **Mary** and their hrs., "Hicors Hallows"
(bou. of bro. **Henry**), equally bet. them. Residue of estate divided equally among child.

Exs.: Two bros., **Henry** and **Francis**, jointly.

Test: Francis Nevitt, John Poulton, Wm. Abell.   14. 467.

Reeder (Reedar), Rich., ——— ——— ———;
5th Mar., 1717-8.

To bro. **Benj.**, 1s.

" wife **Elizabeth**, extx., dwelling plantation left by testator's father, **Seimon Reeder.** At her decease to pass to dau. **Elizabeth.** Shd. sd. dau. die without issue, then to pass to John Blockars and hrs. Personal est. to wife and dau. **Elizabeth**, divided as the law directs.

Test: Thos. Boult, Geo. Hoskins, William Olman.   14. 469.

Gardiner, John, gent., St. Mary's Co.,   13th Oct., 1717;
9th Dec., 1717.

To sons **John** and **Clement** and hrs., "Hillaley," son **John** to have 100 A. more than son **Clement.** Should sons **John** and **Clement** die without issue, the sd. tract "Hillaley" to pass to two sons **Rich.** and **Wilfraid** and hrs.

" son **John**, personalty.

" Charles Smith, John Hayes and Edw. Hall and their hrs., 2 tracts, "Gardiner's Grove" and "Addition of Gardiner's Grove." There being no patent granted for sd. tracts, testator directs wife **Mary** to obtain patent for them in her own name for use of sd. Smith, Hayes and Hall.

" wife **Mary**, extx., personalty, ½ dwel. plan., "Cannon Neck," during life. The sd. tract of land, "Cannon Neck," to be equally divided at her decease between two sons, **Rich.** and **Willfraid**, and hrs.

Residue of personal estate divided between wife and child., 4 sons, **John, Clement, Rich.** and **Willfraid**, and 5 daus., **Susannah, Elizabeth, Mary, Ann** and **Henrietta Maria;** wife to accept afsd. legacies in lieu of her thirds.

Test: Thos. Williams, John Reid, John Atkinson, Dorothy Smith.   14. 470.

Coursey, Wm., Queen Anne's Co.,   29th May, 1714;
3rd. Feb., 1717.

To wife **Elizabeth**, extx., dwelling plan. and tract called "Cheston," also 800 A. of adj. tract called "Coursey Upon Wye," lying on west side of Carrolls Cove, during life. At her death afsd. lands, with appurtenances thereto, to pass to kinsman **Wm. Coursey** and hrs. (son of **Henry Coursey**). The remaining part of "Coursey on Wye" and a tract called "Long Week," on e. side of sd. Carroll's Cove, cont. in all 1,000 A., also 200 A., "Hawkins Pharsalia," on fork of Tuckahoe, and remaining part of "Whitefield" in Kent Co., at head of Langford Bay, cont. 300 A., to wife **Elizabeth** and her hrs., with personal estate of testator.

Test: Jacob Covington, Wm. Turbett, Elizabeth Bennett, Jane Evans.   14. 472.

Hitchcock, John,   16th Feb., 1717;   24th Mar., 1717.

To wife ——, ⅓ of estate, real and personal.
"   dau. **Sarah,** residue of estate.

Ex.: ——.

Friend and kinsman **John Punning, Jr.,** to be guardian to child **Sarah.**

Test: Edw. Spencer, James Numbers, Cornelius Poulson.

                 14. 474.

Note—Test. directs that he be buried on dwel. plantation.

Wellman, Michael, planter, St. Mary's Co.,   18th Apr., 1715;   19th Apr., 1718.

To son **Joseph** and hrs., dwel. plan., "Siles Chance," and personalty.
"   wife **Martha,** ⅓ personal estate. Residue of est. to be divided equally among testator's 5 child., ——.

Exs.: **Thos.** and **Joseph Wellman,** jointly.

Test: Anthony Brocklehorst, Chas. Waldron, Grace Watkins, Jno. Watkins.   14. 474.

Hoskins, Col. Phillip, Charles Co.,   20th June, 1714;   3rd Apr., 1718.

To son **William** and hrs., 100 A. bou. of Thos. Love, personalty and former gifts confirmed.
"   son **Phillip** and hrs., 50 A., "Friendship," and personalty on son **William's** plantation. Certain personalty to be sold and proceeds divided among all child. equally.
"   every grandchild (both sons and daus.), personalty.
"   son **Oswald** and hrs., 178 A., dwelling plantation and his pt. of personal estate.
"   son **Bennett,** 200 A. bought of Garrett Sinett, and 187 A., "Hoskins' Lot," and share of personal estate.
"   son **Ballard,** 190½ A. bou. of James Mackey, nr. China Moxson Cr., 100 A., "St. John's," and 100 A. adj. "St. John's, lying bet. the two Bever Dams, and share of personal estate.
"   daus. **Mary, Ann** and **Martha,** personalty.

Shd. any of sd. child. die during minority, estate bequeathed to child. of former wife to be divided among them; and estate given to child. of last wife, **Ann,** divided among them.

To wife **Ann,** extx., residue of personal estate during life; at her decease to be divided among child. testator had by sd. wife **Ann.** She to settle a plantation for each son, and neither the child. testator had by former wife nor child. present wife had by her former husband to have any part of estate more than is justly due them. Testator desires to be buried in Portobacco Church.

Overseers: Wm. Hoskins, Thos. Stone and Joseph Harrison.

Test: Archibald Johnson, Jane Booth, Sarah Mudd.   14. 475.

Test. speaks of Jane Hamilton, late called Jane Booth. 3rd Apr., 1718. Caveat filed by son **William.**

Dorsey, Nicholas, Baltimore Co., 16th Sept., 1717; 13th Feb., 1717-8.

To 4 sons, **Thos., Nicholas, Benjamin** and **Edward,** and hrs., personalty at age of 21 yrs. Sons to have liberty to choose guardians at 18 yrs. Should any of sd. sons die before of age, their portion to be divided among survivors.

" son **Thos.** and hrs., 50 A. of ''Long Reach,'' near Patuxent.

" son **Nicholas** and hrs., 50 A. of ''Long Reach.''

" son **Benja.** and hrs., dwelling plantation at decease of wife.

Wife **Frances** extx. and residuary legatee.

Test: Henry Ridgely, John Dorsey, son of E. Dorsey, Josh Dorsey, Timothy Regan, Thomas Smith, John Dorsey.

14. 478.

Cusack, George, St. Mary's Co., 15th July, 1717;

To son **Michall** and dau. **Mary** and hrs., entire estate between them equally.

Ex.: Henry Wharton.

Testator directs that child. be brought up Roman Catholics.

Test: Elizabeth Doyne, Thos. Smith.   14. 481.

Rumsey, Charles, Cecil Co., 3rd Dec., 1706; 6th Nov., 1717.

To eldest son **Charles** and male hrs., dwel. plan. with 150 A. on n. side of the Neck at age of 21 yrs., or at death or marriage of his mother, and personalty.

" 2nd son **William** and male hrs., 150 A. on south side of plantation, and personalty.

To youngest son **Edward** and male hrs., 100 A., "The Adventure," on Back Cr. at age of 21 yrs., and personalty.

Sons **Charles, William** and **Edward** to receive est. at 21 yrs. Should any of sd. sons die without male issue, their estate to pass to eld. bro. then living, or his male issue. In event of there being no male issue of sd. sons, their estate to be divided among all daus. —— of testator and their issue, male or female.

To wife **Katherine,** use of entire personal estate for payment of legacies, debts and for care of children until of age at 21 yrs., and ⅓ of rents and profits of lands, tenements and real estate during widowhood. Shd. she marry before son **Edward** afsd. reaches 21 yrs., personal est. to be divided among all child. of testator (sons and daughters). Shd. she not marry, to be divided at her decease as afsd.

Exs.: Wife **Katharine** and two sons, **Chas.** and **Wm.**

Test: Obadiah Hoult, Wm. Dover, John South. Rich. Hunter.

14. 482.

Butterworth, Michaell, St. Mary's Co., 1st Feb., 1717; 5th Feb., 1717-8.

To wife **Jane,** real and personal estate during life. At her decease personal estate to be equally divided between Wm. Pritchard, the dau. of Wm. and Mary Pritchard, and the other half for Thos. Jordan, the son of Gerrard and Rebecca Jordan, to be delivered them at their marriage, if it be after decease of testator's wife.

" Thos. Jordan, dwelling plantation. Should sd. Thos. Jordan die during minority, dwel. plan. to pass to afsd. Jane Pritchard and hrs.

Exs.: Wm. Pritchard and Gerard Jordan. Should they refuse the managing of personal estate as testator desires them, neither they nor their hrs. shall claim any rights or title in estate, real or personal.

Test: Thos. Alman, Wm. Sandys, Wm. Douglass. 14. 484.

Brooke, Leonard, gent., St. Mary's Co., 1st Nov., 1716; 2nd Apr., 1718.

To dau. **Elinor** and hrs., "Hardshift."

" dau. **Jane** and hrs., "Haphazard," always providing that 150 A. of sd. land be excepted for use of the plan. now thereon, and sd. plan. for the use of two daus., **Jane** and **Ann,** and their hrs.

" dau. **Ann** and hrs., tract of land lying in fork of the creek that runs to Col. Henry Lowe's landing.

" son **Charles** and hrs., residue of real estate and personalty. Residue of personal estate to four child. afsd. and delivered to them as they arrive at maturity.

Shd. any of afsd. child. die during minority and without issue, their share in est. to pass to survivors. Shd. all afsd. child. die before attaining majority or without issue, estate, real and personal, to be equally divided bet. cousins **Richard** and **Leonard Brooke.**

Exs.: Bro.-in-law **Raphael Neale** and cousin **Richard Brooke.**

Test: Chas. Hutton, Thos. Ashton, Thos. Dillon.   14. 486.

Tarent, Leonard, of Essex Co., Va.,   4th June, 1718;
                                                7th June, 1718.

To wife **Mary,** dwelling plantation, 100 A., ——, personalty and residue of personal estate (excepting mchd. in store and outstanding debts), to be accepted by her in lieu of dower rights. Also £50 and the debt due from her father, **Robert Brooks.**

Exs. empowered to sell 300 A. nr. the "Range" for benefit of personal estate, and to conclude purchase of 1,600 A., "The Grove," Cecil Co., at mouth of Sassafrass R., with Mr. James Harris, atty. for Mr. George Warner, mercht., London, sd. estate to be purchased for son **Leonard** at price of £600, exs. being empowered to pay £700 if necessary. Shd. purchase not be consummated, afsd. 300 A. to son **Leonard,** personalty and £500 at age of 21.

To 2 daus., **Mary** and ——, residue of estate equally at age of 18 or day of marriage.

Son and his interest to care of wife **Mary** during her widowhood.

To friends Paul Machoo and William Upshaw, exs., books.

Test: Col. Richard Tilghman, John Lawson, Robert Grove.

                                                        14. 487.

Read, William, St. Mary's Co.,   18th Mar., 1717-8;
                                            22nd Apr., 1718.

To son **John,** north pt. of land ——.

" son **William,** south pt. of land ——. Sons not to sell land nor rent for longer than 3 yrs. at a time, their sisters to have refusal of it.

" wife **Ann,** extx., certain personalty during life; at her decease to son **John,** and residue of estate divided equally with children ——.

Test: Robert Scot, John Read, James Meakin.   14. 489.

Heathman (Hathman), Allexander, St. Mary's Co.,
4th Feb., 1717-8;
25th Feb., 1717-8.

To wife **Frances,** extx., personalty during life; at her decease
to 5 child., viz.: **Mary, Thomas, Margaret, Anne** and **John,**
equally, and residue of estate, absolutely.

Test: James Thompson, Richd. Morgans.   14. 491.

Critchet, Frances (alias **Watkins**), St. Mary's Co.,
31st Mar., 1718;
7th Apr., 1718.

(Will starts: I, Frances Watkens, als Critchet, signed Frances
Critchet.)

To husband **William Critchett** and hrs., dwelling plantation,
300 A., "The Ripe," and personalty.

" 2 godchild., James, son of Henry Horn, and Ann, dau of
John Woodward, residue of real estate.

Test: Samll. Grasty, Margrett Morgan.   14. 492.

Sampson, Jeremiah, St. Mary's Parish, London, Rother-
hith, in County of Surry, mariner,   18th Sept., 1717;
2nd Feb., 1717.

To Henry Sampson (who now lives with testator), £20 to
place him as apprentice to trade of own choosing.

" dau. **Mary,** wife of **John May,** silversmith, £50.

Dau. **Sarah** extx. and residuary legatee.

Test: Joshua Bangs, Mary Butcher.   14. 493.

Olandman (O'Landman), Denum,   ·15th Feb., 1716-7;
24th Aug., 1717.

To wife **Mary,** entire personal estate, provided she does not
give testator's 3 child. away. Shd. she do so, to give to
each certain personalty.

" brother **William Bouland,** 100 A., "Atland."

Test: Richard Hall, Wm. Lanman, Jane Megrath (Jean Magraugh).   14. 495.

Booker, Martha, widow, Charles Co.,   8th Apr., 1718;
21st Apr., 1718.

To Elizabeth Noble, **Ann Booker,** Rebecca Dunington, Elizabeth Whartown and **George,** son of **Henry Britt,** personalty.

" Francis Dunington, personalty, with proviso that he put
his dau. Rebecca at school for 2 yrs.

To son **William Barker**, dwelling plantation, 100 A., "Stepney," being that testatrix had from his father, **John
Barker**, and residue of estate. Rents of land afsd. to be
used for his schooling; to be for himself at age of 18,
but not to sell anything without consent of his uncle.
Henry Britt, or receive estate until of age at 21 yrs. Shd.
sd. son **William** die during minority, the 100 A., "Stepney," to Mary Godfry and personal estate to be equally
divided bet. **Richard** and **George**, sons of **Henry Britt**, and
Elizabeth Noble and Rebecca and Ann, daus. of Francis
Dunington.

Ex.: **Henry Britt.**

Test: Gil. Fyffe, **Sarah Britt**, John Smith.   14. 496.

Hawton, John, blacksmith, Charles Co., 26th Dec., 1717; 23rd Jan.. 1717.

To 2 bros., **Joseph** and **Benja.**, and their hrs., land devised
testator by grandfather ——.

"   grandmother **Mrs. Lydia Yates**, bro. **Joseph** afsd., Judith
O'Caime and Mrs. Sarah Maddox, personalty.

"   John Maddox, ex., a servt. boy Richard Smoot, with what
estate of the Smoots now in testator's hands, until sd.
boy comes of age.

"   4 bros., ——, residue of estate.

Test: Sam. Hanson, Jno. Owens, Richd. Smoot.   14. 498.

Norton, Andrew, planter, Charles Co., formerly of Fairfield Stope Parish, So. Britain, 10th Aug., 1712; 1st Aug., 1717.

To son **Cornelius**, ex., and hrs., all estate lying in **Fairfield**
afsd. purchased of one Burk by testator's father and conveyed by him to testator, the conveyances being left in
hands of kinsman **Wm. Morwood**, of Burbige Green, near
Buxton, in Darbyshire; also residue of estate, real and
personal, in South Britain, Maryland, or elsewhere, and
personalty.

"   Ann Cope and goddaughter Ann, dau. of Rebecca **Duplex**,
personalty.

Test. appoints father-in-law **Cornelius White**, gent., of Charles
Co., guardian and trustee for son during minority, he being
7 yrs. old 2nd of Feb. last. In case of decease of sd.
guardian, test. appoints his brother-in-law, **Luke Barber**,
to act in his place.

Test. describes himself as eld. son and heir of **Andrew Norton, Sr.,** yeoman, of Fairfield afsd., and states that it has been 13 yrs. since his leaving Cheshire and arrival in this province. He directs that he be buried in the garden of his dwel. place, as near as may be to his late wife.

Test: Rich. Jenkin, Charles Jones, Rebecca Duplex, **Luke Barber.** 14. 500.

Note—In probate on this will Rebecca Duplex has become Rebecca Cumberbitch.

Fordman, Benj., gent., Annapolis, 11th Aug., 1716; 24th Apr., 1718.

To youngest child., **Rich.** and **Sarah,** £25 each.

" 8 child., viz.: **Benj., John, Joseph, James, Richard, Margaret, Lydia** and **Sarah,** residue of estate, real and personal. Shd. any child. die before attaining majority or without issue, their share to be divided among survivors.

Ex.: James Purrock of Phila., shipwright.

Test: Edward Roberts, John Cadwallader, Edward Jones.
14. 502.

Martin, John, Baltimore Co., 21st Apr., 1718; 12th May, 1718.

Test: directs that his wife **Eleanor** shall have power to administer on personal estate; if she refuses, desires John Buck to do so.

Test: Benj. Howard, Thos. Fairbrother. 14. 503.

Beall, Ninian, Prince George's Co., 15th Jan., 1717; 28th Feb., 1717.

To son **Geo.** and hrs., 480 A., "Rock of Dumbarton," on Rock Creek, and personalty.

" son **Charles** and hrs., 1,000 A., "Dunn Back," on Wattes Creek, s. side Gr. Choptank, and personalty.

" granddau. **Mary Beall** and hrs. (dau. of son **Ninian,** deceased), after payment of legacies, ½ of personal est., also that part of "Bacon Hall" lying on s. side of road to "Mt. Calvert," and to have her share at marriage.

" grandson **Samuel Beall,** ex., and hrs., water mill on Collington Branch and remaining part of "Bacon Hall," providing that at 21 yrs. he makes over to afsd. **Mary Beall** a tract of land called "Sams Beginning" on s. side of sd. road to "Mt. Calvert." Shd. he die before he be of age to convey land afsd., then the entire tract of "Bacon Hall" is bequeathed to sd. granddau. **Mary Beall.**

To son-in-law **Andrew Hambleton**, personalty.

" son-in-law **Joseph Belt** and hrs., 245 A., "Good Luck," he to allow to heirs of testator 4,000 lbs. tobacco.

Two grandchildren of deceased son **Ninian** to be cared for and educated.

Test. directs that a tract of 400 A., "The Recovery," in the Freshes of Patuxent R., at head of Weston Branch, and adj. land bequeathed to **Joseph Belt**, be sold for payment of debts.

Sons **Charles, Joseph Belt** and **Geo.** to aid executor until he arrives at age of 21 yrs.

Test: John Busey, Rebecca Getward, Ed. Willet.   14. 504.

Jobson, John, Cecil Co.,   30th Dec., 1713;

To son **John** and hrs., land bou. of Cornelius Tobey.

" son **Philip** and hrs., land bou. of Quinton Crafford.

" son **Michael** and hrs., 100 A. bou. of Henry Penington.

" dau.-in-law **Mary Holyday**, personalty.

" wife **Easter**, extx., ⅓ of entire estate.

Residue of personal est. to be equally divided among 3 sons afsd. at 18 yrs. of age.

Test: Wm. Freeman, Benj. Hazlehurst, Jacob Colke (Caulk).

    14. 507.

Ferrill, Mathew, Charles Co.,   12th Feb., 1717-8;
                                 29th Mar., 1717.

To wife **Fran.**, extx., entire est., real and personal.

Test: Thomas Stone, John Barker, John Smith.   14. 508.

Smith, Wm., Charles Co.,   7th Feb., 1717;
                                 12th Mar., 1717.

To eldest son **Wm.**, £30.

" son **Elias**, 100 A. adj. land of Rich. Estey's.

" wife **Priscilla**, extx., dwelling plantation ——. Residue of personal estate to be divided between wife **Priscilla** and her children as law directs.

Test: Thos. Crabb, Jno. Anderson, Wm. Smith, Jno. Barneby.

    14. 509.

Brett, Wm., Charles Co., 12th Feb., 1717;
8th Mar., 1717.

To **Eliza: Nobell,** 300 lbs. tobacco.

"   Henry, the younger son of Mary Harper, otherwise called Henry Brett, 100 A., "Chosen," and 150 A., "Findone," he to be put at school at age of 7 for 7 yrs., schooling paid from rent of land——; also residue of personalty and to be of age at 18 yrs. Shd. he die during minority, sd. lands and personalty to pass to three children of testator's sister **Martha,** viz.: **Geo., Wm.** and **Eliz. Barker.**

Ex.: George Brett, or Britt.

Test: **Henry Brett,** Eliz. Wharton, Margaret Hutchison.

14. 509.

Hawkins, Eliz., widow, Charles Co., 12th June, 1716;
14th June, 1717.

To three grandchildren, **Francis, Eliz.** and **Mary Wine** (son and daus. of **Henry Wine,** late of Gr. Britain, deceased), each £10.

"   dau. **Eliz. Lewis,** wife of —— **Lewis,** of Gr. Britain, 5s.

"   granddaus. **Eliz.** and **Martha Keech,** personalty. Shd. either of sd. granddaus. die before reaching age of 16 or without issue, their interest in certain personalty to pass to survivor. Shd. both die, to son **Henry Holland Hawkins** and hrs.

"   grandson **Henry Holland Hawkins,** son of H. H. H. afsd., personalty.

"   granddau. **Eliz. Hawkins** and hrs., 500 A., "Jamaica," in Pr. Geo. Co., and personalty.

"   grandson **John Hawkins,** personalty.

"   Richard Tubman, son of Rev. Geo. Tubman, personalty.

"   kinswoman **Eliz. Middleton** (wife of **Wm. Middleton**), personalty.

"   son **Henry Holland Hawkins,** ex., residue of estate, real and personal, for life; at his death to be divided equally among his children. Shd. he die before any of his child. attain age of 21 yrs., estate to be put in hands of Michael and John Martin for use of child. of sd. son. Shd. any child of his be of age at his death, estate to be put in hands of that child during minority of others, or be divided as before directed.

Test: Martha Stone, Wm. Howard. 14. 510.

Gray, Andrew, Dorchester Co.,   29th Jan., 1705;
                                                 21st Mar., 1717.

To son **Thos.** and hrs., dwel. plan., ——, 225 A.

" son **John** and hrs., the plan. whereon son **Thos.** now lives,
with 225 A. adj. Shd. son **Thos.** not have given poss. of
this estate to son **John** within two yrs. after decease of
testator, son **John** to have dwel. plan. with 225 A., and
son **Thos.** to have the plan. where he now lives, with 225 A.

" Wm. Thornton and Eliz., his wife, the plan. they now live
on, with 50 A., during their lives.

" wife **Eliz.** and son **John,** who are made exs. jointly, personalty.

Test: Geo. Kirby, Wm. Thornton, John Kirk, Tho. Taylor.

14. 512.

Wetharell, Wm.,   14th Dec., 1717;
                                                 11th Jan., 1717.

To wife **Eliza:,** dwel. plan. for life; at her decease to pass to
sons **John** and **Edward.**

Residue of estate to sons afsd. **John** to be in the charge of
Edward Billiter, **Edward** in the charge of Wm. Perry, they
to be of age at 18 yrs. Dau. **Grace** to be with wife until
16 yrs. of age.

Exs.: Wife **Eliza:** and Edward Billiter, jointly.

Test: James Kidder, Amos Gottrell, Basoll Rose, James Carter.

14. 514.

Note—11th Jan., 1717, Ed. Billiter renounces executorship
of above will of **Wm. Wetherell** unto **Eliz:,** widow of
deceased.

Plunket (Plinket), Thos., Prince George's Co.,
                                                 5th Oct., 1716;
                                                 17th July, 1717.

To godson Ed. Brawner, goddaus. Violetta Harrison, **Frances
Barnes** and Sarah Coffer, personalty, and to godson and
servant Henry Barnes, personalty at 20 yrs. of age, to
which age sd. Henry is to be maintained.

" goddau. Henrietta Barnes and hrs., water mill at Mattawoman; she dying without issue, to pass to godson Thos.
Barnes. Also to sd. Henrietta, servant tailor, Thos. Lloyd.

" Anne and Benj., dau. and son of friend Henry Barnes;
Barbara Barnes, Thos. Coffer and Mary his wife, Rev. Wm.
Maconachie, Rev. John Fraser, Eliz. Clements, Benj. Hen-
son, Jacob, Charles, Francis and Joseph Clements and
Alex. Contee, mourning rings.

To godson Thomas Barnes at 18 yrs., ex. and residuary legatee,
and his hrs., all lands in Charles or Pr. Geo. Co., also mill
adjoining dwelling house. He dying without issue, to
pass to Benjamin Barnes and hrs., and in turn to Anne
Barnes and hrs.
Test: Lawrence Anderson, Mary Anderson, Eleanor Sanders.
14. 516.

Semms (Sims), Marmaduke, Newport, Charles Co., 11th May, 1717; 29th July, 1717.

To eldest dau. **Ruth** and hrs., tract of land in Pr. Geo. Co. at
hd. of Broad Creek, and personalty. She to receive same
at age of 16 or marriage.
" son **Francis** and dau. **Eleanor** and child unborn, dwel. plan.
to be equally divided among them. In case any of sd.
child. die without issue, sd. plantation to be divided between surviving two.
" son **Francis,** personalty at age of 18.
" dau. **Eleanor,** personalty at age of 16.
" James Haddock, personalty.
" wife **Eliz.,** extx., residue of personal est.
Trustees: Wm. Borman, Wm. Clarkson.
Test: Wm. Ash, Jon Higton, Jr., Geo. Brett.   14. 518.

Rookwood, Edw.,   13th Feb., 1717;
——— ——— ———.

To dau. **Mary Sanders,** personalty.
" children of wife **Mary,** 12 pence each.
Ex.: Son **Thomas.**
Test: Wm. Wilson, Edw. Askins, Eliza Coome.   14. 519.

Pery, Thomas, Charles Co.,   ——— ——— ———;
——— ——— ———.

To sons **John, Thomas, William, Hugh** and **Samuel** at 18 yrs.,
and to daus. **Mary** and **Anne,** personalty.
Wife **Mary** extx.
Test: Wm. Brett, Anne Harryson.   14. 519.
Note—Both witnesses dead, **Mary Pery,** extx., filed bond 29th
Apr., 1718.

Crumpton (Crumptin), Francis, Charles Co., 13th Nov., 1717; 13th Feb.,1717-8.

To wife **Johanna,** extx., entire estate, real and personal.
Test: Rev. Wm. Machonchie, John Suttle, Mary Dawson.
14. 520.

Rogers, John, gent., Charles Co.,   4th Nov., 1717;
                                         13th Jan., 1717.

To wife **Eliza:**, extx., dwel. plan. ——, for life, and personalty.
"   son **Richard,** personalty when of age, and 10,000 lbs. of
tobacco to be sold during his minority for his education,
remainder to be paid him at majority.
"   son **John,** interest poss. by test. in right of his (**John's**)
mother, deceased, to part of estate of **Charity Courts,** in
hands of his uncle, **John Courts** (to be administered), and
personalty to be pd. when he comes of age; also testator's interest in tract of land in Pr. Geo. Co., called
"Clean Drinking," and any estate falling to testator
by death of any of his uncles or relations.
"   son **Roadham,** dwel. plan. at decease of his mother, and
personalty, also land testator had with his mother.
"   Rev. Wm. Maconchie, for the church, personalty.
"   Alex. Contee, **John Courts,** Robert and Sam. Hanson,
neighbor Mary Theobalds and to Johanna Price, personalty.
Test. directs that his servant, Wm. Sympson, be discharged
from service on 25th Dec. next.
Shd. son **Richard** die before he is of age, bequests made to
him to pass to sons **John** and **Roadham,** or survivor. Shd.
son **Roadham** die before he is of age, lands bequeathed
him to pass to son **Rich.,** and in case of his death, to son
John. In case of son **John's** death without issue, to pass
to nearest of blood.
Residue of estate to be divided equally among wife and 3
child. and unborn child.
Wife to have charge of child. during their minority. Shd.
she marry, **Alex. Contee** to have care of **Rich.** and **John.**
Test: Jno. Hanson, Jno. Chunn, Rich. Bell   14, 521.

Shakley (Shekertie), John,   2nd Feb., 1717-8;
                                       28th Apr., 1718.

To sons **Edward, Michael** and **Francis,** 12 pence each.
"   son **Benjamin,** ½ of personal estate, and shd. he live to
age of 18 yrs. or have issue, dwel. plan. cont. 100 A.,
"Jugothorp." Shd. son **Benjamin** die before 18 yrs. of
age or have no issue, sd. plan. to pass at wife's decease
to son **Francis.**
"   daus. **Sarah Taylor, Mary Eadkin, Tabithey Kersey** and
Elizabeth, 12 pence each.
"   wife **Mary,** extx., personal estate and use of dwel. plan.
"Jugothorp" during life, she to have labor of son **Francis**
until Christmas next.
Test: Jessie Doyne, Thomas Davis, Judith Gray.   14. 523.

Hogin, Jno., 16th Nov., 1717;
6th Dec., 1717.

To Wm. Kibble, ex., the care of sons **Richard** and **John** and
dau. **Esther** until they are 16 yrs. old. Dau. **Margaret** to
be at own disposing.

Test: John Magee, Isaac Stevens. 14. 524.

Arthur, Alex., Prince George's Co., 14th May, 1717;
22nd Feb., 1717-8.

To wife **Mary,** extx., and hrs., entire estate, real and personal.

Test: Thos. Fletchall, Jno. Allison, Thos. Clark. 14. 525.

Note—An endorsement on this will shows a sale of land by
John Bradford, gent., Pr. Geo. Co., to William Head, of
same county, signed by John Bradford, Jr.

Reaves, John, planter, Prince George's Co.,
2nd Apr., 1718;
5th Apr., 1718.

To dau. **Ellinor,** personalty, she to be of age at 16 yrs.; testator further directs that his three sons, **John, Thomas**
and **Daniel,** be of age at 18 yrs.

Residue of estate to four child. afsd.

Robt. Tyler, ex., to have care of child. should testator not
have designated to whom they are to go.

Test: Rich. Duckett, Mark Brown, Wm. Fowler. 14. 526.

Taylor, Dorothy, Dorchester Co., 20th Apr., 1717;
13th Mar., 1717.

To son **Thomas** and hrs., all lands, lots and possessions in
Philadelphia.

" son **William,** daus. **Frances Bartwith, Eliza:** and **Elinor,**
and granddau. **Eliza Bartwith,** personalty.

Daus. **Eliz.** and **Elinor** and son **Wm.,** exs., jointly.

Estate not to be divided until son **Wm.** comes to age of 21 yrs.

To John Flower, 6 shillings.

Test: John Flowers, Phillodelphy Williams, Mary Eccleston.
14. 527.

Note—13th May, 1717, **Eliz., Elinor** and **Wm. Taylor** renounce
executorship of above will to their bro., **Thos. Taylor.**

Test: Nich. Lowe, Nich. Lockerman. 14. 527.

Ray, John, 24th Mar., 1718;
12th Apr., 1718.

To **John** (son of **Wm. Ray, Jr.**), ½ of real estate; other half
of real estate to Geo., son of John Riddell.

Both beneficiaries afsd. to be of age at 18.

Exs.: Wm. Waford and **James Ray.**

Test: John Halsall, Wm. Aford, Edward Phillips, Mary Ann Johnson, Ruth Halsall, Jane Vinnicom.   14. 528.

Bruff, Thomas, Dorchester Co.,   28th Dec., 1717; 13th Jan., 1718.

To wife **Katherine**, extx., dwelling house in Cambridge, with lands belonging thereto, during life; at her decease to pass to dau. **Margaret** and hrs., and in succession to son **Richard**; also tract known as "Cottman's Swamp" during life; at her decease 100 A. of sd. land to sd. dau. **Margaret** and remainder to son **Richard** afsd. and hrs.

" wife **Katherine**, personal estate during life; at her decease to be divided equally between dau. **Margaret** and son **Richard.**

Brother **Richard Bruff** to have charge of son **Richard** until he arrives at age of 21.

Test: Rich. Webster, James Cullen, Wm. Cullen.   14. 529.

Smith, John, gent., Calvert Co.,   7th Dec., 1715; 19th Mar., 1717.

To son **Samuel**, personalty.

Real estate to be divided among four sons, viz.: **James, John, Benjamin** and **Basill.** Shd. unborn child be a boy, the land to be equally divided bet. five sons.

To dau. **Mary**, unborn child, sons-in-law **Michll.** and **Thos. Taney,** and dau.-in-law **Dorothy Smith**, personalty.

" wife **Dorothy**, extx., ½ personal estate.

Residue of estate to be equally divided among child., viz.: **Elizabeth, Martha, Anne, Eleanor, James, John, Benjamin, Basill, Mary** and unborn child.

Test: Roger Brooke, John Rouse, Geo. Lines.   14. 530.

Note—In codicil to above will, dated 21st Dec., 1717, testator leaves certain personalty to son **Roger.**

Test. to codicil: Jno. Brooke, Wm. Biddle.

Johns, Rich., of the Clifts., Calvert Co.,   15th June, 1717; 14th Jan., 1717-8.

To grandson **Richard** and hrs. (eldest son of deceased son **Abraham**), two tracts made over to testator by Wm. Billingley, being 136 A., "Billingsiey's Swamp," and 150 A., "Friendship Rectifyed"; also 160 A., "Fellowship," bou. of Wm. Dorrumple, and all three tracts lying bet. the "Clifts" and the branches of Battle Creek.

To grandson **Abraham** and hrs. (youngest son of deceased son **Abraham**), two tracts bou. of Wm. Williams, Sr. and Jr., "Chance," cont. 108 A., the other adj. "Dodson's Desire," cont. 100 A., also "The Purchase," bou. of **Thomas Johns**, these three tracts being in Calvert Co. and cont. 308 A.

Testator states that having made over by deed of gift to the hrs. of his deceased son, **Aquilla**, part of a tract called "Letchworth's Chance," cont. 400 A., it passed to **Richard**, eldest son of sd. **Aquila**.

To grandson **Aquila** and hrs. (youngest son of deceased son **Aquila**), a tract bou. of John Edmonson, 600 A., "Cold Spring," in freshes of Gr. Choptank R.

" son **Richard** and hrs. (having already made over to him by deed of gift the plan. where he dwells, being 300 A. of "Letchworth's Chance" afsd.), 300 A., "Fuller."

" son **Kensey** and hrs. (having already made over to him part of tract called "Meares," cont. 200 A., and also 100 A. adj., being part of a tract testator now lives on called "Angellica"), 100 A. of "Angellica" adj. part already given him, also 157½ A., "White's Rest," bou. of James Bechamp, and 50 A., "Chance," bou. of Wm. Griffen and his wife.

" son **Isaac** and hrs. (having already given him two tracts, 100 A., "Batchelors Fortune," and 112 A., "Johns Addition"), remaining part of dwel. plan., "Angellica."

" granddau. **Rebecca Johns**, personalty.

" son-in-law **Robt. Roberts** and hrs., 200 A. the s. side of "Grey's Chance" on the Clifts, being the plan. where he now dwells, and acquit him of all indebtedness to estate.

" dau.-in-law **Eliza: Cole**, Quakers on Western Shore, Sarah Day, Job Hunt and his brother Thos., personalty.

Residue of personal est. to be divided into 10 equal parts and allotted as follows:

2 pts. to child. of deceased son **Abraham**, as eldest son.

1 pt. to be equally divided among child. of deceased son **Aquila**.

1 pt. each to sons **Richard**, **Kensey** and **Isaac**.

1 pt. each to daus. **Priscilla Roberts** and **Margaret Hopkins**.

The remaining 2 pts. to dau. **Eliza: Troth**, she not having had a full portion with her other sisters.

Exs.: Sons **Richard**, **Kensey** and **Isaac**, jointly.

Test: Geo. Harris, Jno. Wilkinson, Elizabeth Giles, Eliz. Wilkinson, Anne Harris.　　　　　　　　　　14. 532.

Note—Codicil to above will dated 15th day of 6th month, 1717,
directs that crop of tobacco now growing on all plans.
be sent to England and sold there to cover indebtedness
of testator to certain persons there.

Test. to codicil: Geo. Harris, Jno. Wilkinson, Eliz. Giles.

Hawkins, John, Queen Anne's Co.,   23rd Apr., 1717;
26th Sept., 1717.

To eldest son **John**, £100 ster., also £100 to be pd. by bill of
exchange to discharge his mortgage to Rich. Bennett, Esq.
Having made advances to sd. son in money and tobacco,
he is to be discharged to them, providing he shall not
bring any manner of account against estate.

" dau. **Eliza: Marsh**, £100 ster., also 10,000 lbs. tobacco, and
the advances made to late husband, **Mr. Thomas Marsh,**
are discharged.

" granddau. **Sarah Marsh**, £60 and personalty to be pd. her
at marriage. Shd. she die before, the £60 to be divided
among the rest of her sisters, children of sd. **Thos.** and
Eliz. Marsh.

" grandson **John** and hrs. (eldest son of son **John**), "Barron Neck," lying on Double Creek, £60 and personalty to
be pd. him when he comes of age.

" other grandson **Ermault** and hrs., remaining part of "Tullye's Delight" not already settled on son **John**, also plan.
lying at Bever Marsh on Tuckahoe Branch, and personalty
to be pd. him when he comes of age.

" **Michael** (son of nephew **Wm. Turbutt**) and to **Marion**
(dau. of nephew **Foster Turbutt**), all remaining part of
tract called "Jaspars Lott" on Red Lion Branch to be
divided bet. them. Shd. both of them die before they are
of age to enjoy sd. land, it is to pass to son **Ernault;** also
to each of them, as they arrive at age, £30.

" nephew **Samuel Turbutt**, the £18 pd. for him to Charles
Carroll.

" Abraham Sherrine, land where he now lives, during life.

" John Lurkey, old servant John Creamer, Jane, widow of
Robt. Clouthier, and to vestrymen of St. Paul's parish,
personalty.

" bro. **Col. Wm. Cousey** and to sisters **Sarah Covington** and
Eliza: Coursey, one mourning ring each.

Test. directs that shd. son **Ernault** die before his wife **Elizabeth,** she is to enjoy the lands conveyed to testator by
Chas. Vandeford on Coursey's Creek, during her life.

To son **Ernault**, ex., and hrs., residue of estate, real and personal, he to consult with Rev. Chis. Wilkinson about tombstone for deceased.

Test: Arthur Emory, Anne Emory, Nath. Tucker, Sarah Tucker. 14. 535.

Howard, Chas., planter, A. A. Co., 19th Jan., 1717; 21st Feb., 1717.

To brother **Thomas** and hrs., ½ 600 A., "Freebornes Progress," Balto. Co., conveyed to test. by Rich. Freeborne, residue of tract having been conveyed to brother **Cornelius** by deed of gift, provided sd. **Thos.** when at age shall ratify disposition of 50 A. on Patapsco R. given him by his father ——, should extx. sell same.

" wife **Mary**, extx., and son **Benjamin**, personal estate equally, extx. to sell "Roger's Increase" on Patapsco R., Balto. Co.

Test: Jno. Beale, Jno. Cunningham, Sam'l Howard, James Howard. 14. 538.

Yeate, George, Baltimore Co., 13th Sept., 1717; 18th Nov., 1717.

To 4 sons, **George, Joshua, Samuel** and **Benjamin,** and their hrs., dwelling plantation "Yeates Contrivance," equal division to be made by Jno. and Richard Warfield when son **Geo.** attains age of 21 yrs. Eldest son to have first choice. Shd. any of sons die before age of 21, the division to be made among survivors.

" son **Geo.**, dau. **Eleanor**, bro. **John Yeate** and **Eliz.**, his wife, personalty.

" friend Ed. Teall, personalty and half the produce of Brickyard until eldest son comes to age. Sd. Ed. Teall to have oversight of plantation and to sell tract called "Forbearance."

" wife ——, £5.

Residue of personal estate to be divided equally among four sons afsd. and three daus., viz.: **Eleanor, Mary** and **Rachael.**

Exs.: Wife —— and Ed. Teall, jointly.

Test: Wm. Hamilton, Samuel Taylor, Jos. Harp. 14. 540.

Dukes, Henry, Baltimore Co., 18th Feb., 1712; 17th Mar., 1717.

To wife **Susanna**, extx., and hrs., dwel. plan. 38 A., "Westminster," in Patapsco Neck, and all other estate, real and personal.

Test: Nich. Rogers, Abraham Shavers, Philip Pisto, Mary Linch (Lynch). 14. 541.

Smith, Thomas, Baltimore Co.,   23rd Jan., 1717;
                                                      17th Mar., 1717.

To wife **Alice,** extx., use of all land during her life; at her
    decease to pass to son **Thomas** and hrs. Shd. he have no
    issue, sd. land is bequeathed to eldest dau. —— and her
    hrs.; she failing issue, to pass to each of child. ——, in
    turn.

Test: John Watts, Edw. Watts, Sam. Hinton.   14. 542.

Howard, Wm., Baltimore Co.,   8th Jan., 1710;
                                                      5th Mar., 1717.

To Henry Munday and hrs., 100 A., ''Howard Forest,'' Balto.
    Co., bet. lands of John Webster and Isaac Butterworth,
    and personalty. To Samuel (son of John Webster, Sr.),
    personalty.
'' wife **Marthe** extx., and hrs., residue of estate, real and
    personal.

Test: Aquila Paca, Thos. Bond, Henry Munday.   14. 543.

Barrett, John, Baltimore Co.,   21st June, 1717;
                                                      24th Mar., 1717.

Testator directs that two tracts joining on Gunpowder Falls,
    viz.: ''Barretts Delight'' and ''Barretts Addition,'' be
    sold for payment of debts.
To grandson **Nich. Corbin** (eld. son of **Edw. Corbin**) at decease
    of wife, dwel. plan. and ½ the land.
'' John Royston, residue of land, to be laid out on ''Little
    Run.''
'' James Wells and John (son of Alex. Keith), personalty.
'' wife **Alice,** extx., use of dwel. plan. for life, and residue
    of personal estate.

Test: Alex. Keith, Kath. Lindall, Moses Edwards.   14. 544.

                                                      21st Sept., 1717.

Caveat entered by Mr. John Bond not to grant administration
    on estate of **Geo. Berry,** since **Simon Pierson** has with
    Mary Berry wasted the estate afsd.
''I hereby resign all rights to administration of estate of
    my late husband to **Simon Pierson,** my father, principal
    cred. of my late husband.''
                    (Signed) **Mary Berry.** 10th Sept., 1717.

Wit.: Geo. Middleton.   14. 545.

Bowles, Mary, widow, Kent Co.,   12th Jan., 1715;
                                                      20th Nov., 1717.

To grandson **Isaac Bowles** and grandchild. **Geo.** and **Mary**
    Hastins, personalty.

Exs.: Michael Hackett and Simon Wilmore, jointly.

In consideration of the use of certain personalty, the afsd.
Geo. Hastins is to pay to exs. 500 lbs. tobacco yearly,
to be applied to education and use of sd. **Isaac Bowles**
during his minority.
Test: Edw. Worrell, Sam. Parsons. 14. 546.

Clouds, Nich., Queen Anne's Co., 4th Sept., 1717; 1st Nov., 1717.

To son **Rich.** and hrs., ½ dwel. plan., and residue at decease
of wife.
" son **Benj.** and hrs., "Plain Dealing" and "Charles Lott"
in Kent Co.
" dau. **Notlear** and hrs., "Killkenny."
" dau. **Mary** and hrs., "Clouds Hermitage."
" dau. **Sarah** and hrs., "Mothers Delight," the rent to be
pd. her mother until she is of age or marries.
" wife **Sarah**, extx., dwel. plan. ——, for life, and "Foole
Play"; she to make over what is clear according to bond
to Wm. Hollingsworth and renew warrant in own right.
Personal est. divided bet. wife and her two daus., **Mary**
and **Sarah,** and residue of real estate between 2 sons,
Rich. and **Benj.** and their hrs.
Test: Marmaduke Coulton, Chas. Maloyd, Albert Johnson.
14. 547.

Sheeld, Catherine, Kent Island, Queen Anne's Co., 2nd June, 1717; 20th July, 1717.

To husband **Edmond Sheeld,** use of entire estate until son
Leonard Maiton is 21 yrs. of age, he to have two years'
schooling and be in charge of husband.
" 2 daus., **Mary** and **Susanna Maiton,** personalty; to be in
charge of husband until 16 yrs. of age.
Test: Wm. Rakes, Joseph Carpender, Mary More. 14. 548.

Colt, Dorothy, Queen Anne's Co., 12th Oct., 1717; 20th Jan., 1717.

To Wm. (son of Col. Rich. Tilghman) and hrs., all real estate;
but shd. **Mr. Robt. Dulton-Colt** desire it, he is to have
use of same during his life; at his decease to pass to sd.
William Tilghman.
" Mary and Henrietta Maria Tilghman, personalty.
" Anna Maria (dau. of Col. Rich. Tilghman afsd.), residue
of personal estate.
Ex.: Friend Col. Richard Tilghman.
Test: Sam. Earle, Thos. Ringgold, John Lawson. 14. 548.

Hall, Edward, planter, Talbot Co.,   9th Sept., 1716;
                                                5th Mar., 1717.

To wife **Sarah,** extx., entire estate, real and personal. Shd.
    she die before dau. **Mary** is of age, she may dispose of her.
Test: Arthur Rigby, Morrice Orem, Jno. Bradshaw.   14. 549.

Johnson, Robert, Jr., Somerset Co.,   27th Jan., 1717;
                                                28th Feb., 1717.

To son **Arthur** and hrs., two tracts, ''The Hope,'' and per-
    sonalty.
"   sons **Robert, Leonard** and **Peter,** personalty.
"   dau. **Mary Goding,** personalty.
Son **Arthur** afsd., residuary legatee, to be of age at 16 yrs.
    Shd. he die before that age, his share of personal estate
    to be divided equally among other four child.
Exs.: Friends John Purnall and Wm. Richardson, jointly.
Test: John Cornwell, Hannah Richardson, James Woods.
                                                14. 550.
Mem. to the effect that John Purnall relinquishes executorship.

Sherwood, Philip, Talbot Co.,   14th Jan., 1717-8;
                                                11th Feb., 1717.

To sister **Catherine** (wife of **Ralph Rice**), personalty.
"   wife **Frances,** extx., residue of personal estate and dwell-
    ing plantation ''Sherwood Neck''; ½ absolutely, other ½
    during life; at her decease to pass to **Daniel Sherwood, Jr.,**
    and hrs. (son of bro. **Daniel**).
Test: M. T. Ward, Wm. Hambleton, Jr., Alexander Swinger,
    Francis Sherwood.   14. 552.

Scott, Sophia, Talbot Co.,   16th Nov., 1717;
                                                14th Jan., 1717.

To niece **Elizabeth Jones** and hrs., pt. of tract containing 45
    A. joining ''Edmonton'' on north, also ''North Bendon
    and Todd,'' 100 A. on Great Duck Cr. in Newcastle Co.,
    Pa. (being pt. of a tract left by testator's father —— to
    Hannah Baxter and herself), and personalty.
"   sister **Elizabeth Evans,** residue of dwelling plantation on
    St. Michael's R., also certain personalty during life, to
    pass at her decease to niece **Eliz. Jones** afsd.
"   nephew **John Evans,** Alex. Raye, John (son of John Sut-
    ton), John Sutton, Margaret Collins, godson Thomas Bruff,
    niece **Sophia** (wife of **Isaac Abrahams**), Anne (dau. of
    James Dawson), Elizabeth (dau. of Michael Russell),
    Elizabeth (wife of John Davis), Anne (wife of Thos.
    Hopkins), Sara Davison, James Kelly, Rebecca Russell and
    Richard Hamon of Queen Anne's Co., personalty.

To **Lewis Jones,** personalty which had belonged to nephew **Joseph Evans.**

" Anne, Sophia, Richard, Jacob Gibson, Jr., Elizabeth Dawson and Benjamin Kininmont, personalty.

" St. Michael's Parish Church, £10 towards furnishing communion table.

Sister **Eliza: Evans** and niece **Eliz. Jones** joint extxs. and residuary legatees.

Test: Juliana Horney, Thos. Neale, Thos. Hopkins, Sr.

14. 553.

Luddingham (Luddenham), John, Talbot Co.,
6th Jan., 1717;
28th Jan., 1717.

To wife **Mary,** dwelling plantation ——, with 100 A. adjoining, during life; to bequeath same to whichever child she pleases.

" eldest son **Edward** and hrs., 50 A. adj. land bequeathed his mother.

" son **John** and hrs., 50 A. Residue of real estate, about 130 A., equally divided among younger son **Isaac** and daus. **Mary, Rebecca** and **Ann** and their hrs.

Extx.: Wife **Mary,** assisted by her bro., **Henry Henrix.**

Test: Derby Mackmahan, Mark Williams, Marmaduke Story.

14. 555.

Palmer, Jacob, planter, (nunc.), Talbot Co.,
16th Feb., 1717;
17th Feb., 1717.

To John Fellows, care of children and land.

Test: Henry Henrix, William Owens, planters of Talbot Co.

14. 556.

Hall, Robert, planter, Talbot Co.,
19th June, 1717;
29th Oct., 1717.

To son **William,** 500 A., "Hall's Harbour," at head of Chester R., and personalty.

" son **Edward,** pt. of "Parker's Thicket" on w. side of branch, 35 A. "Limbrick" (which contains 70 A.), and 5 A., part of "Bartaran," formerly belonging to Kininmonts.

" son **Robert,** residue of "Parker's Thicket" on e. side of branch, and other half of "Limbrick."

" son **Thomas,** 70 A., part of "Daniels Addition," formerly belonging to John Merricks.

Residue of personal estate to be divided among three sons, **Edward, Robert** and **Thomas**, at age of 21. Shd. any of them die leaving neither wife nor child, his share to be divided among surviving two.

To wife **Ann**, extx., ⅓ estate, real and personal, children to remain in her care during minority.

Test: Rich. Barron, Lewey Jones, Joseph Bell.   14. 556.

Skinner, Andrew, gent., Talbot Co.,   ———— ———— ————;
28th July, 1717.

To two sons, **Richard** and **Andrew**, and hrs., all lands lying bet. St. Michael R. and Bare Poynt or Leeds Creek. (For descrip. see will.)

" four daus., viz.: **Anne, Elizabeth, Dorothy** and **Mary**, and hrs., residue of real estate.

" wife **Elizabeth**, extx., use of land given sons afsd. until they attain age of 21 and use of land given daus. until dau. **Anne** attains age of 18.

Test: Sol. Birckhead, Mary Feddeman, Jno. Whaley, Phil. Feddeman.   14. 557.

Note—Test. speaks of Sol. Birckhead and Mary, his wife.

Jones, Jane (Jenere), (St. Michael's R.), Talbot Co.,
18th Aug., 1713; 11th Feb., 1717.

To grandson **John Carselake** and hrs., 100 A. in two tracts, 50 A. ''Doughtyes Hope'' and 50 A. ''Doughtyes Lott.'' Shd. he die without issue, sd. land to pass to his bro. **Edward** and hrs. The sd. **John** to pay to his sister **Jane Shropshill** 4,000 lbs. tobacco to buy a piece of land.

" grandson **Edward Carselake** and hrs., 180 A., ''Jane's Armour,'' on William's Branch at head of Wye R., Queen Anne's Co. Shd. he die without issue, sd. land to pass to his sister **Jane.**

" **Robert Carselake** and to his son **Benjamin**, personalty.

" granddau. **Jane** and to **Robert Carselake's** wife, personalty.

" Edward Cassaway, weaver, personalty. Residue of personal estate to be divided equally among 3 grandchild., **John** and **Edward Carselake** and **Jane Shropshill**, who are appointed exs.

Test: Christo. Higgs, Alex. Kininmont, James Kelly.

14. 559.

Harrison, Robert, Second Creek, Talbot Co.,
22nd. Dec., 1717;
11th Feb., 1717-8.

To 2 grandsons, **James** and **John Harrison,** sons of son **James,** deceased, and their hrs., part of 2 tracts, ''Prouses Point'' and ''Haphazard.'' (For desc. see will.)

'' son **Robert,** ''Crooked Intention'' and 50 A. adj. it, being part of ''Haphazard.'' Shd. son **Robert** die without issue, sd. land to pass to son **Joseph.**

'' son **John,** dwel. plan. ——, and residue of real estate. Should he die without issue, these lands to pass to son **William;** should both **John** and **Wm.** die without issue, to pass to son **Benjamin** and hrs.

Personal estate to be divided among child., viz.: **John, Robert, William, Joseph, Benjamin, Alice, Sarah** and **Abigail.** Son **James** and **Francis Jones** having already had their portions are excluded.

Wife **Alice,** with sons **John** and **William,** joint exs.

Test: Wm. Hambleton, Sr., Wm. Hambleton, Jr., Jos. Dawson.
14. 560.

Mullikin (Mullakin), John, Jr., Talbot Co.,
4th Sept., 1716;
9th Dec., 1717.

To dau. **Sarah,** pt. of a tract, ''Ridley,'' formerly belonging to wife's father, **John Mitchell,** deceased. Shd. dau. **Sarah** die without issue, sd. land to pass to wife **Alice;** she failing issue, to pass to child. of **John Mullakin, Sr.,** and **Sarah,** his wife (father and mother of testator).

Wife **Alice** extx. and residuary legatee.

Test: Abraham Taylor, Magnis Spence and Jane Spence.
14. 561.

Fairbank (Farebank), David, Talbot Co.,
28th Feb., 1717;
25th Mar., 1718.

To bro. **John** and hrs., ''Belfast,'' on condition that he pay to exs. 4,500 lbs. tobacco. Shd. he not pay tobacco, sd. land to be divided equally bet. testator's 2 daus., **Mary Ann** and **Eliza:.**

'' kinsman **Samuel Ireland,** personalty.

Exs.: Philip Casey and Peter Sanders.

Test: Sam. Ireland, Ann Ireland, John Stevens.
14. 563.

Watts, Ann, Sr., Talbot Co.,   22nd Mar., 1718;
                                                12th Apr., 1718.

To bro. **John Mullakin,** ex., care of sons **Peter** and **George**
until they are 18 yrs. of age. Shd. sd. bro. and his wife
die before their time is expired, sons may choose to which
of child. of sd. **John** they shall go.

"   bro. **John,** a servant, Wm. Poor, until he come to age
of 21.

"   bro. **Richard Homes,** an orphan girl, Sarah Summers, to
clear **John Mullakin** of his bond.

Test: Jno. Vale, **Joanna Mullakin,** Jenny Dillgha.   14. 564.

Dawaoughte (Dawaoughate), Charles, Dorchester Co.,
                                                11th Nov., 1717;
                                                14th Dec., 1717.

To **Charles** (young. son of **Geo. Dawaoughate**), "Birchley,"
on Cinkkeeias Ck., Dorchester Co.

"   Edward Newton, ex., and Roger Woolford, personalty on
land of Benj. Woodard.

"   cousin **John Dawaoughate,** Walter Stevens, Thomas Brannock and **Ann Dawaoughte,** personalty.

Test: Ed. Pool (Poole), Wm. Brion, Jos. Kennerly.   14. 565.

Noells (Nowell), John, Dorchester Co.,
                                                31st Mar., 1717;
                                                12th Mar., 1717-8.

To 2 daus., **Eliz.** and **Anne,** and their hrs., 3 tracts equally,
viz.: "Norwell's Pocaty," "Margaret's Fancy" and
"Howards Chance." Testator desires that his father
may live on any part of the afsd.

"   wife **Eleanor,** extx., entire personal estate during life;
at her decease to be divided bet. two daus. afsd.

Test: Jno. Lecompt, **Bazell Noell,** Gary Powell.   14. 566.

Vicars, John, planter, Dorchester Co.,   8th Jan., 1717-8;
                                                10th Feb., 1717.

To only son **John** and hrs., entire real estate and personalty,
including a mare bou. of Henry Branklin.

"   dau. **Eliza:** and nephews **William, Thomas** and **John Abbott,**
personalty.

"   wife **Rachel,** extx., residue of estate.

Test: Thos. Howell, Jno. Miller, Jno. Trego.   14. 567

Roach, John, Sr., Annamessex, Somerset Co.,
8th Feb., 1708-9;
17th Mar., 1717.
To eld. son **John** and hrs. (at decease of wife), 150 A., dwelling plantation, "Make Peace," with 50 A. adj. out of tract called "Exchange."
" son **Nathaniel**, 200 A., "Bald Ridge."
" son **Michael** and hrs., 150 A., residue of "Exchange."
" son **Samuel** and hrs., 150 A., "Cabin Swamp." Marshland to be divided among 4 sons afsd.
" wife **Sarah**, extx., personal estate during widowhood. Shd. she marry, to be divided among 7 daus., viz.: **Sarah, Mary, Eliza, Abigal, Arabella, Rebecca** and **Hannah**.
Test: J. West, John West, Jr., Stephen Horsey, Thos. West.

14. 568.

Knox, Alexander, planter, Somerset Co.,
2nd Jan., 1716-7;
22nd Mar., 1717-8.
To John Gibbon, tobacco due him from testator.
" Maj. Arnold Elzey, ex., tract on Nanticoke R. and residue of estate.
Test: Wm. Caldwells, Wm. Barens, Wm. Turpin, Risdon Bozman. 14. 569.

Gray, Miles, Somerset Co., 20th Sept., 1717;
21st Nov., 1717.
To son **Jno. Gray**, 1s.
" son-in-law **William Turpin**, "Furn's Choice" and 60 A., "Peach," during life; at his decease to pass to his son **John** and male hrs. Sd. land not to be mortgaged, sold or leased during his life; also 50 A., "Flent," to afsd. **Wm. Turpin.**
" godson John Teack, two tracts, higher and lower "Harnack." Wife of testator and son **Wm. Turpin** to have certain privileges during their lives.
" granddau. **Sarah Beachamp** and Richard ——, personalty.
" wife ——, extx., personal estate during life; at her decease to pass to **Mary Turpin** and Sarah Covelan and their hrs.
Test: Lazarus Maddux, Jno. Fountaine (Fantain), Geo. Bozman, Alex. Maddux. 14. 570.

Bray, Edward, of Pocomoke, Somerset Co.,
5th May, 1716;
28th Feb., 1717.

Testator desires that 62 A. be made over to his bros., **John** and **Archibald White**, by his sister **Mary Bray**, in accordance with will of testator's father.
" bros. **John** and **Archibald White** and to **William** (son of sd. **Archibald**), personalty.
" sister **Martha Bray**, all personalty left testator by his father, **Pierce Bray**, above legacies excepted.
" sister **Mary Bray**, extx., real estate.
Test: David Ritchie, Henry Scholfield, James Bratten, Jr.
14. 571.

Moor, John, Sr., Parish of Coventry, Somerset Co.,
31st Dec., 1716;
20th Mar., 1717.

To sons **John** and **Thomas**, land equally. Son **Thos.'s** share to be dwelling plantation ——, at decease of his mother, and personalty.
" dau. **Sarah**, personalty.
" wife **Anne**, extx., use of lands during life.
Test: Randolph Mitchell, Sr., John White, Jr., Mary Mitchell.
14. 572.

Smith, George, Somerset Co.,
14th Apr., 1717;
21st Aug., 1717.

To wife **Sarah**, extx., ⅓ entire estate.
" son **George** and hrs., dwelling plantation, 200 A., "Bacon Quarter."
" dau. **Rebecca**, £5.
" three child., viz.: **George, Archibald, Rebecca** and to unborn child, equally, residue of estate.
Shd. wife marry, sons to be of age at 18 yrs., otherwise at 21 yrs.
Test: Jeremiah Right, James Smith, Rachel Walton.   14. 573.

Cobb, Samuel, Somerset Co.,
18th Nov., 1716;
21st Sept., 1717.

To eld. son **John**, 1s.
" sons **Nathaniel** and **Joseph**, personalty.
" eld. dau. **Margaret** and 2nd dau. **Assibeth**, 1 shilling each.
" 3rd dau. **Sarah Tengell**, personalty at decease of wife.
" wife **Mary**, extx., residue of personal estate during widowhood. Shd. she marry, to be divided among 3 young. **sons, Wm., Jos.** and **Nathaniel**, they to be of age at 20 yrs.

Test: Rich. Holland, Alisha Walton, John Holland.   14. 574.

Note—19th Sept., 1717. Mary Cobb makes over her rights as
    extx. in above will to her son-in-law, **Samuel Tingle**.
Test: **Jos. Wyatt.**

Porter, Hugh, Somerset Co.,   28th May, 1709;
     23rd Aug., 1717.

To eld. son **John** and dau. **Mary**, 12 pence each.
" son **Hugh** and hrs., dwelling plantation ——, at decease
    or remarriage of wife **Katharine**; also 50 A., "Coventry,"
    w. side Herring Ck., and personalty. Shd. he die during
    minority and without issue, dwel. plan. to pass to son
    Joshua.
" sons **William** and **Joshua** and hrs., 200 A., "Metten,"
    being land where Thomas Peale lives.
" son **Francis** and hrs., 100 A., "Clemfast." Shd. he die
    during minority and without issue, sd. land to son **William**
    and hrs.
" grandson **Daniell Donnohon**, personalty at age of 16.
" wife **Katharine**, extx., personalty.
Residue of estate equally divided bet. wife **Katharine** and
    child. **Hugh, Rachel, William, Joshua, Francis** and **Eliza-
    beth**. Sons to receive their share at age of 21, daus. at
    16 yrs.
Test: Thos. Hearne, Rebekah Townsend, Donnock Dennis, Jr.
     14. 576.

Russell, Michael, gent., Talbot Co.,   13th Dec., 1716;
     10th Nov., 1717.

To wife **Rebecca**, dwelling plantation during life at her de-
    cease to pass to son **William** and hrs. Shd. wife be living
    when son Wm. attains age of 21, he may seat on end of
    plantation where John Davis now lives.
" son **William**, personalty.
" son **Thomas** and hrs., 200 A., pt. out of "Huntington"
    and pt. out of "Huntington Grange" adjoining.
" 3 daus., **Sarah, Eliza** and **Mary**, and their hrs., equally,
    remaining pt. of "Huntington" and "Huntington's Ad-
    dition" adj., and 12 A. bought of Henry Parker. All lands
    to be used by wife for maintenance and education of
    child. during their minority.
" Rich. Bruff, Francis Armstrong, Benjamin Kininmont,
    Nicho. Deverex and Mr. Sutton, personalty.
" wife **Rebecca**, ⅓ personal estate, other 2 pts. to be divided
    equally among child.
Exs.: Wife **Rebecca** and son **William**, jointly.

Overseers: Rich. Bruff, Thos. Skantlebury, James Dawson, Francis Armstrong.

Test: Sophia Scott (widow), Jos. Evens (Evans), Marmaduke Harrison. 14. 577.

Note—Depositions in this will are interesting.

Truett, James, Sr., Somerset Co.,   18th Mar., 1715; 30th May, 1718.

To wife **Sarah**, personalty.

" 2 eld. daus., **Sarah Mumford** and **Mary Collings,** 12 pence each.

" dau. **Tabitha Kellum,** personalty.

Residue of estate to be divided equally among five sons, ——, and youngest dau. ——.

Ex.: Son **James**, he to keep young. sons of testator on plantation until they come to age of 18.

Test: Rich. Pennywell, Jno. Webb. 14. 581.

Nowell, James, Dorchester Co.,   16th Mar., 1717; 11th June, 1718.

To 2 sons, **James** and **Bazell,** and their hrs., two tracts on Susquehannah R., "Baturcius Point" and "Pery-Neck," also land ——, on Patuxent R.

" wife **Margaret,** dau.-in-law **Elianor Nowell** and son **James,** personalty, division to be made by John Harwood, ex.

Test: Jno. Lecompt, David Melmill, Jno. Davis, Jno. Pullin.

14. 582.

Dickenson, John, Talbot Co.,   7th Oct., 1714; 29th Apr., 1718.

To wife **Rebecca,** dwelling plantation, "Ridle," during life; at her decease to son **John** and hrs.

" son **Charles** and hrs., 150 A., pt. of a tract bought of Wm. Edmondson and lying in Dorchester Co., he to choose which pt. he shall have.

" son **John** and dau. **Sedney (Sidney)** and their hrs., remaining part of afsd. land, ——, to be divided equally bet. them.

" dau. **Mary Kersey,** silver marked M. D.

Wife **Rebecca** extx. and residuary legatee.

Test: Wm. Thomas, Silvester Abbot, Anne Thomas, Peter Sharpe. 14. 582.

Lord, James, planter, Talbot Co.,   7th Jan., 1717;
     12th May, 1718.

To son **John** and hrs., 100 A., part of "Taylor's Ridge," at head of St. Michael's Cr. Shd. sd. son die without issue, land to revert to dau. **Mary** and her hrs. She failing issue, to pass to son **James** and hrs.; he failing issue, to next of kin.

"   wife **Judith,** extx., 100 A., dwelling plantation, "Lord's Chance," and tract, "Shore Ditch," during life; at her decease both tracts to pass to son **James** and hrs. Shd. he die without issue, to revert to dau. **Rosanna;** she failing issue, to next of kin. Also to wife, personalty, a certain part of which at her decease is to pass to dau.-in-law **Elizabeth Martin** and rest divided among four child., viz.: **John, Mary, Rosanna** and **James.**

Shd. wife **Judith** die before son John is of age, son-in-law **Thos. Martin** to take all child. and their estate into his custody until son **John** afsd. comes of age.

Test: Abr. Taylor, Jno. Blamer, Wm. Ladoh.   14. 584.

Porter, Francis, St. Michael's R.,   18th Apr., 1718;
     27th May, 1718.

To 2 eld. sons, **James** and **Francis,** and their hrs., "Emerby's Square" equally bet. them, son **James** to have first choice. Sons **James** and **Francis** afsd. to pay to sons **John** and **Joseph** each 2,000 lbs. tobacco a year for 2 yrs.

"   bros. **John** and **Lawrence Porter,** and to **Peter Colke** and dau.-in-law **Sarah Colke** and cousin **John Camper** at 21 yrs. of age, personalty.

Exs.: Sons **James** and **Francis,** jointly.

Test: Thos. Studham, Chas. Spencer, Jno. Arnelt.   14. 586.

Hopkins, Robert, Talbot Co.,   13th May, 1718;
     17th June, 1718.

To wife **Elizabeth,** extx., "Turkey Park" during widowhood and until son **Robert** arrives at age of 18.

"   wife and four child. (unnamed), personalty. Sons to have their portion at 18 yrs., daus. at 16 yrs. Shd. any of them die before they come to afsd. ages, their portion to pass to survivors.

Overseers: Brothers **James** and **Joseph Hopkins.**

Test: **Dennis Hopkins,** John Willson, Geo. Powers.   14. 587.

Wise, Anthony, gentleman, Talbot Co., 15th May, 1718;

To eldest son **John** and hrs., dwelling plantation and lands
adj., also 300 A., "Davis' Pharsalia," at head of Chester
R., adj. s. side of Vanderford's branch, and personalty.

" 2 youngest sons, **Christopher** and **Samuel,** and hrs., two
tracts joining and lying in Tuckahoe, 200 A., "Dunsmore
Heath," and 120 A., "Frampton" (Framtum), equally
bet. them, and personalty.

" sons afsd., residue of personal estate, they to be kept
at school for 5 or 6 yrs.

" mother **Abigail Wise,** 500 lbs. tobacco yearly during life.

Testator directs that Daniel Peck be kept at school one year.

Exs.: John Sprignall, Thos. Voss and son **John** afsd.

Test: Geo. Powers, Jas. Robson, Stephen Esgate, Jas. Cundon,
Jno. Sutton.   14. 588.

Start, John, planter, Talbot Co.,   20th Aug., 1717;
                                            17th June, 1718.

To eldest son **John,** dwelling plantation and land belonging
to it.

" 2nd son **Ephraim,** plantation where John Skinner now
lives and land belonging to it bou. of Edwd. Lloyd.

" 3rd and 4th sons (unnamed), entire personal estate equally
bet. them at age of 21 yrs.

Ex.: Charles Stevens, to have oversight of children.

Test: John King, Jr., Joseph King, John Pruitt.   14. 589.

Note—Codicil to above will names Col. Edward Lloyd as
joint ex. to above will with Charles Stevens.

Test. to codicil: John King, Jr., Hororah Hews, **Elizabeth
Start.**

Miller, Robert, Talbot Co.,   4th Apr., 1718;

To son **William,** all real estate.

" 2 children (unnamed), residue of estate.

Three children afsd. left in care of Thomas Brown, ex.

Test: Terrence Connolly, Wm. Goforth.   14. 591.

Evins, Elizabeth (widow of **Griffith Evins**), Talbot Co.,
                                            28th Apr., 1718;
                                            22nd May, 1718.

To son **Curtis** at 18 yrs. of age and hrs., entire estate, real and
personal.

Ex.: Cousin **John Trevilion, Jr.,** who is to have guardianship
and tuition of son afsd., to bring him up in the Protestant
faith and administer estate of testator's deceased husband.

Test: Peter Sharp, Mary Alexander, Alice Foster.   14. 592.

Willson, James, Queen Anne's Co.,   8th Jan., 1716;
    12th Feb., 1716.

To granddau. **Margaret Willson** and grandson **James Willson,** to dau. **Mary Lawrence** and grandson **Henry Lawrence,** personalty at decease of wife.

"   son **William** and hrs., all real estate.

"   **Richard Lawrence,** personalty.

"   wife **Margaret,** extx., residue of personal estate.

Test: Nich. Clouds, Rich. Ponder, Wm. Mountsier.   14. 593.

Chaires, John, Sr., gent., Queen Anne's Co.,
    16th Sept., 1717;
    5th June, 1718.

To son **John,** part of "Lentley" lying on n. side of branch.

"   son **Joseph,** part of "Lentley" lying on s. side of branch.

"   son **Thomas,** "Batchellor's Adventure."

"   son **James,** "Chairs Addition."

"   dau. **Hannah Ellis,** personalty. Personal estate to be equally divided between the rest of child.

"   wife **Catherine,** use of dwelling plantation ——, during her widowhood. Ex. jointly with son **John.** Child. to remain with exs. until they arrive at age of 21 yrs. or marry.

Test: Ephraim Winn, Edward Wright, Patrick Bryon. 14. 594.

Nickolson, John, Queen Anne's Co.,   2nd day xes.;
    26th Mar., 1718.

To wife **Frances,** use of dwelling plantation during life; at her decease to pass to son **John** and hrs.

"   sons **Thomas** and **Patrick** and daus. **Mary Boltick** and **Susannah,** personalty.

Wife **Frances** extx. and residuary legatee.

Test: Rich. Chapman, Anne Chapman, Mary Sharin.   14. 595.

Monroe, Duncan, Queen Anne's Co.,   23rd Jan., 1717;
    17th Mar., 1717.

To son **John** and two daus., **Margaret Berrey** and **Elizabeth,** dwelling plantation ——, equally. Shd. any of them die without issue, their portion to go to dau. **Catharine** and hrs. Sd. **Catharine** to live with wife until she arrives at age of 16 yrs.

Hannah Tulley to serve wife till she is 18 yrs. of age.

3 child. afsd., **John, Margaret Berrey** and **Elizabeth,** to pay to dau. **Catharine** 2,000 lbs. tobacco when she arrives at age of 16 yrs.

To **Rachel Everitt,** personalty.

Testator directs that his five child., viz.: **John, Elizabeth, Catharine, Hannah Tulley** and **Jane Everett**, make a crop of corn and tobacco under care of **James Berry**, produce to be sold for benefit of estate.

Residue of personal estate to be divided equally between wife and child. Son **John** to remain with wife till he arrives at age of 21 yrs.

Wife **Sarah** extx.

Test: Solomon Clayton, Thos. Carman, Eliz. Wood.   14. 595.

Hamon (Hammon), Richard, weaver, Queen Anne's Co.,
27th Jan., 1717;
20th Mar., 1718.

To son **John** and hrs. (at decease of his mother), 150 A., "Forcett's Plains," on Wye R.

" son **Walter** and hrs. (at decease of his mother), two lots on s. side of cove running through town and purchased of Mr. Wm. Coursey at the time of laying out of Queen's town.

" son **Richard** and hrs. (at decease of his mother), dwelling house with one lot. Shd. sd. **Richard** die before he comes of age, sd. house and lot to pass to son **Thomas** and hrs., being house and lot purchased of Samuel Hunter, Innholder in Queen's Town.

" 3 younger sons, **Thomas, James** and **William**, and 2 daus., **Anne** and **Jean**, entire personal estate, excepting their mother's thirds, equally, at age or marriage. Sons of age at 18 yrs.

Exs.: Wife **Anne** and son **John**, jointly, they to enjoy estate until afsd. child. come of age or marry.

Test. desires to be buried by side of deceased dau. **Elizabeth.**

Test: Jos. Earle, Patrick Sexton, Roger Murphy.   14. 597.

Williams, Henry, planter, Queen Anne's Co.,
5th Nov., 1717:
20th Mar., 1717-8.

To wife **Eleanor**, extx., use of dwelling plantation ——, and water mill during her widowhood.

" 3 sons, viz.: **Isaac, Abraham** and **Henry**, and their hrs., dwelling plantation ——, and water mill equally. Shd. any die without issue, their portion to pass to survivors, and if all of 3 sons die without issue, to pass to other 2 sons, viz.: **Henry Price (Williams)** and **George**, and their hrs.

" 2 sons, **Henry Price** and **George**, and hrs., 200 A., "Chestnut Meadow," equally.

" dau. **Mary**, personalty.

Residue of personal estate to 5 sons afsd. Shd. any die without issue, their portion to be divided among survivors. Child. to care of wife **Eleanor** during her widowhood. Overseers: Brother **Matthew Williams** and Thomas Lewis. Test: Edwd. Wright, Wm. Wrench, Peter Wild. 14. 598.

Downs, John, planter, Baltimore Co.,   1st Apr., 1718; 3rd June, 1718.

To Rose Trotten and hrs., ⅓ of estate and personalty.
  ''   son-in-law **Simon Cannon** and dau.-in-law **Elizabeth Cannon,** personalty, they to be of age at decease of testator.
  ''   sons-in-law **Thomas** and **Christopher Durbin,** personalty, to be of age at 18 yrs.
  ''   dau. **Kedimoth** and hrs., residue of estate, real and personal. Shd. she die without issue, her portion to pass to John Eager and hrs.
Exs.: John Eager and Luke Trotten, jointly.
Test: Edward Macham (Mahy), Rich. Gott, Susanna Shavers.
             14. 599.

King, Henry, planter, Baltimore Co.,   18th Jan., 1717; 30th Apr., 1718.

To son **William** and hrs., dwelling plantation, 200 A., ''Todd's Plaines.''
  ''   dau. **Mary** and hrs., other plantation, ''Kingsberry,'' with the addition to it cont. 130 A.
  ''   son and dau. afsd., residue of estate, real and personal, including the great still, which is not to be moved nor sold.
Exs.: William Tibbs and John Willmott, Jr., jointly, and guardians of child. during minority.
Test: Nich. Rogers, Thos. Sheredine, Sam. Macwell, Wm. Reeves.   14. 600.

Bond, Peter, Baltimore Co.,   28th Feb., 1717-8; 16th June, 1718.

To son **Richard,** dwelling plantation ——, and ½ tract of land belonging to it.
  ''   son **William** and hrs., the other half of afsd. tract, and personalty.
  ''   son **Thomas** and hrs., plantation on Garrison Ridge and personalty.
  ''   son **Peter** and hrs., ½ of ''Bond's Pleasant Hills'' and personalty.
  ''   son **John** and hrs., ½ of sd. tract, ''Bond's Pleasant Hills,'' and personalty.
  ''   son **Benjamin** and hrs., 100 A. bequeathed testator by Stephen Gill, Jr., and personalty.

Residue of personal estate divided equally among child.

Wife —— extx.

Test: Jos. Parkinson, Thos. Guine, Wm. Hamilton.   14. 602.

Wilkinson, William, Baltimore Co.,   21st Apr., 1718;
16th June, 1718.

To son **Robert** and hrs., dwelling plantation ——, and all land on both sides of Humphrey's Ck. to which testator has any title or claim.

" daus. **Jane Corbin, Ann, Phillisanah** and **Sophia** and their hrs., "Cumberland"; eldest dau. to have first choice.

" wife **Tamar,** extx., Edward Corbin, daus. **Ann, Phillisanah** and **Sophia,** personal estate equally.

Test: Pearsivall Sheppard, John Craggs, Jos. Dermitt, Saml. Hinton.   14. 603.

Kemble, William, Baltimore Co.,   6th Dec., 1717;
3rd June, 1718.

To wife **Mary,** dwelling plantation, "Joneses Addition," and personal estate.

Test: Edwd. Hall, Aquila Hall, Peter Bonney.   14. 604.

Hall, John, planter, Baltimore Co.,   24th Jan., 1717-8;
7th July, 1718

To mother **Jane Novell,** personalty in care of uncle **John Rawlins.**

Test: Jeremy Downes, Chas. Baker, Caleb Howitt (Hewitt).
14. 605.

Shaw, James, cooper, Prince George's Co.,
13th Apr., 1718;
27th June, 1718.

To two elder sons, **William** and **Christopher,** £5 and personalty. Sd. sons are committed to care of uncle **Christopher Thompson** during their minority, to be educated and brought up in the principles of the Reformed Protestant religion.

" youngest son **James,** £5 and personalty, he to be in care of his mother.

" wife **Margaret,** extx., residue of personal estate, whether here, in Great Britain or elsewhere.

Test: Wm. Young, Robt. Oram, John Reid.   14. 606.

Burke, John, Prince George's Co.,   2nd Jan., 1717;
2nd May, 1718.

To wife **Mary,** extx., and hrs., "Good Luck."

Test: Thos. Stump, John Rodgers, Thos. Fletchall, Robt. Cooke.   14. 608.

Dorset, John, planter, Prince George's Co.,
22nd Feb., 1717;
18th June, 1718.

To nephew **Thomas Webster** and hrs., all land purchased by testator.

" sisters **Ann** and **Mary,** personalty at decease of testator's mother.

" nephew **John Bowers** and hrs., sister **Eliz. Bowers,** bro.-in-law **John Bowers** and mother ——, extx., personalty.

Test: Jos. Noble, Wm. Austin, Thos. Windser. 14. 608.

Davis, Thomas,
13th Jan., 1717;
20th Jan., 1717.

To friend William Hunter, £6.

" William Chandler, ex., Margaret Dorrington and Thomas Webster, personalty.

Residue of personal estate disposed of in charity at direction of Mr. Wm. Hunter.

Test: John Ensey, Margaret Dorrington. 14. 610.

Hoskins, Ann, Charles Co.,
6th May, 1718;
9th May, 1718.

Testator directs that personalty left her by her late husband ——, be divided among her child. as will directs, and appoints as exs. her sons **Oswald** and **Bennett Hoskins,** to whose care she leaves her three other child. ——.

Overseers: William Chandler, bro. **William Thompson,** son-in-law **Mr. Craycroft** and Mr. Brooke.

Test: John Wilkinson, Rodger Elletson, Wm. Hunter.
14. 611.

Gardner, Joseph, Charles Co.,
9th Mar., 1717;
10th June, 1718.

To wife **Elizabeth,** extx., during life, 100 A. lying on Dressing Branch, part of a tract of 300 A., also personal estate during life; at her decease to be divided among child. as she shall think best.

" sons **Biningman** and **Samuel,** 100 A. each of afsd. tract.

" son **Ralph,** 54 A. on Dressing Branch.

" son **Luke,** 100 A. afsd. at decease of wife.

Test: Owen Read, Bowling Speake, John Glaze, Samuel Smith.
14. 611.

Young, George, Calvert Co.,   2nd Apr., 1718;
7th June, 1718.

To eldest son **William,** ex., and hrs., pt. of "Young's Attempt" where he now lives, joining land bought by him of Matthew Garner, "Happata Venture."

" next 2 sons, **John** and **Francis,** and their hrs., residue of real estate equally.

" wife **Elizabeth,** her thirds.

" **Mary Young,** widow of son **Benjamin,** £10.

Personal estate to be equally divided among nine children now living, viz.: **William, Henry, John** and **Francis, Sarah Smith, Anne Demillion, Mary Bennett, Grace Miller** and **Ellinor Hillarey.** To the four child. of son **George,** deceased, his proportionate part equally divided among them, and to the 3 sons of dau. **Elizabeth Swan,** deceased, her proportionate part; sd. sons, viz.: **George** and **James Swan,** to receive same at 21 yrs. of age, and the daus., ——, of the afsd. **George Young** to receive theirs at 16 or day of marriage.

Test: James Ayling, Thos. Bradley, Nich. Sporne.   14. 613.

Note—Nich. Sporne deceased at date of probate.

Boteler, Edward, gentleman, Calvert Co.,
9th Mar., 1717;
9th May, 1718.

To 2 daus., **Martha and Elizabeth,** and their hrs., 2 houses and lots in lower Marlborough equally between them, and personalty.

3 child., **Edward, Martha** and **Elizabeth,** residuary legatees, of personal estate.

Ex.: Bro.-in-law **Thomas Lingan.**

Test: Rich. Stallings, **Alice Boteler,** John Dorrumple.   14. 615.

Woodward, Thomas, Poplar Hill Hundred, St. Mary's Co.,
27th Apr., 1718;
—— —— ——.

To dau. **Johanna,** ½ of real estate.

" dau. **Mary,** residue of real estate. Lands bequeathed daus. afsd. to be entailed.

Wife **Rachel** extx.

Test: John Hammond, Samuel Johnson, Barbara Mosly.

14. 616.

Gulick, Nicholas, St. Mary's Co., 9th Apr., 1718; 27th May, 1718.

To friend John Leck, ex., and hrs., all land on Eastern Shore, on or near Chester R., left testator by John Lundy (excepting 100 A. already given to Bernard Howard).

Test: Jas. Worrick, Mary Howard, Mildred Thompson, Henry Spinke. 14. 617.

Mezick, Julin, planter, Somerset Co., 6th Jan., 1715-6; 28th June, 1718.

To eldest son **Nehemiah,** personalty.

" 3 sons, **John, Jacob** and **Joshua,** 1s. each.

" 6 children of wife, viz.: **Joseph, Isaac, Benjamin, Julin, Sarah** and **Mary Mezick,** residue of personalty.

Wife **Priscilla** extx. Should she desire to dispose of any of her child., son **Isaac** to be placed with brother **Roger Nicholson.** Boys, viz.: **Joseph, Isaac, Benj.** and **Julin,** to remain with wife until 21 yrs. of age if she remain a widow; to be of age at 18, otherwise.

Test: Francis Langcake, David Evans. 14. 618.

Wale, Edward, Somerset Co., 21st Apr., 1718; 18th June, 1718.

To eldest son **John** and hrs., plantation where he now lives, with 200 A. (For desc. see will.)

" son **Nathaniel** and hrs., all the rest of land, 205 A., lying bet. bro. **Rackliff's** line and certain other bounds.

" son **Elias** and hrs., dwelling plantation, 370 A.

" 3 sons afsd. and their hrs., 225 A., "Cay's Folley," equally.

" daus. **Eliza: Turvile, Bridgett Franklin** and to **Rachel Ratcliffe,** personalty.

" wife **Eliz.,** ⅓ dwelling plan. during life and ⅓ personalty absolutely.

Exs.: Sons **Nathaniel** and **Elias,** jointly. Residue of personalty to all child. afsd.

Test: Edwd. Cropper, Wm. Bowin, Jr., Rich. Holland. 14. 620.

Reavell (Revell), Randall, yeoman, Somerset Co., 13th Apr., 1717; 18th June, 1718.

To daus. **Sarah Bosman** and **Alice,** personalty and 12 pence.

" 3 sons, exs. jointly, **Charles, Randall** and **William,** and their hrs., all land equally. Shd. any of them die without issue, portion of deceased to be divided between survivors.

To 3 sons an equal privilege of the Marsh. Dwelling plantation to son **Randall**, the plantation joining **Mr.** Gray's to son **Charles**, and ''Raccoon Point'' to son **William**. Also to 3 sons afsd. and to dau. **Mary**, certain personalty, to be divided among the four when son **William** comes to age of 18 yrs., at which time he and son **Randall** are to be free.

The four child., viz.: **Charles, Randall, William** and **Mary,** are to make over to Job Shary an Indian girl, **Bess.** William Wheatly to have no share in estate.

Exs.: Sons **Chas., Randall** and **William,** jointly.

Overseers: Capt. Plantmer, Job Shary.

Test: John Gibbins, Job Shary, John Benton (Benson).

Cod. dated 7th May, 1717, states that shd. testator have hereafter any interest in any other land, he desires that it be divided bet. 3 sons afsd. Daus. **Sarah, Alice** and **Mary** and their hrs. to have no interest in such land.

Same testes. 14. 622.

Longue, John, planter, Somerset Co., 6th Nov., 1712; 16th June, 1718.

To eldest son **Samuel**, 100 A., dwelling plantation, and personalty.

'' sons **John** and **William** and dau. **Ann,** personalty.

'' wife **Ann**, extx., use of entire estate during widowhood. Shd. she marry, sons to be of age at 15 yrs.

Residue of estate equally to 4 child., viz.: **Ann, Samuel, John** and **William.**

Thomas Adams and Jeffrey Long to be guardians to child. at decease of wife.

Test: Thos. Adams, Jeffrey Longue, Esau Boston, Daniel Longue, John Taylor. 14. 625.

Webb, Henry, planter, Somerset Co., 2nd Dec., 1717; 22nd May, 1718.

To wife **Esther**, extx., personal estate until dau. **Comfort** arrives at age of 16, then a child's portion; the rest divided equally among daus. **Elizabeth, Mary, Esther, Sophia, Tabitha** and **Comfort.** Also to wife afsd., 75 A. on St. Martin's R., bou. of John Cornwell, till dau. **Comfort** is 16; then her thirds.

'' son **William** and hrs., 75 A., bou. of John Cornwell joining William Stevenson's, and personalty. Shd. he die without issue, sd. land to pass to dau. **Mary.**

Test: John Sturgess, Hutten Hill, Jas. Woods. 14. 625.

Strutton, George, gentleman, Cecil Co., 12th June, 1718;
12th Aug., 1718.

To dau. **Mary,** at marriage, £30.

" son-in-law **Cornelius Tobin,** ex. (husband of dau. **Elinor**), and hrs., residue of estate, both real and personal.

Test: Michael Howard, Derby Duscol, Ishll. Bateman.

14. 627.

Price, Mary, widow, A. A. Co., 8th May, 1718;
5th June, 1718.

Money in hands of Francis Waston, merch., London, be applied by exs. to purchase of land for use of sons **John** and **Thomas.**

To sons **Thomas** and **Benjamin,** personalty.

" daus. **Rachel** and **Hannah** and granddau. **Mary Carr,** personalty.

" friend Edward Parish, Sr., claims against estate of testator's mother, **Isabel Caple.**

" following sons and daus., viz.: **Stephen, Mordecai, Leah Forde** and **Elizabeth Carr,** 5s. each.

Residue of estate to daus. **Mary** and **Sarah,** equally.

Exs.: Son **Stephen** and son-in-law **Thomas Carr,** jointly.

Test: Thos. Crutchly, Jacob Holland, Wm. Tipton. 14. 628.

Kent, Absalom, planter, Calvert Co., 3rd June, 1718;
28th July, 1718.

To sons **William** and **Henry,** personalty; to be of age at 18.

" daus. **Priscilla Wilson** and **Mary,** personalty at decease of testator, and **Grace,** personalty at 16 or marriage.

" wife **Mary,** extx., residue of personal estate.

Test: Rich. Stallings, George Larrance (Laurance). 14. 629.

Ennalls, Thomas, Dorchester Co., 7th May, 1718;
13th Aug., 1718.

To nephew **William** (son of bro. **Joseph,** dec'd) and male hrs., 1,479 A., "North Yarmouth," w. side Transquaking R.; 50 A., "The Addition to Cool Spring," e. side sd. R. ad. West Marsh Range at mouth of sd. R.; "Ennals Reserve," on n. side sd. R. Also to **William** the elder and male hrs., son of bro. **Joseph** afsd., lots Nos. 5-8, 46 and 47 in Vienna, and personalty at Vienna and interest (during their lives) in a lease of 200 A., pt. of Manor of Nanticoyne; also all silver plate and household furniture at Transquaking (wife **Elizabeth** to have use of same during life.

To nephew **John** (son of bro. **John**, dec'd) and male hrs., 446 A., "Ennals Inheritance." He lacking such issue, to his bro. **William** and male hrs.; he lacking such issue, to **Thomas** (son of bro. **Joseph** afsd.).

" nephew **William** (son of bro. **John**, dec'd) and male hrs., pt. of "Beaver Dam" (for desc. see will); he lacking such issue, to **Henry** and hrs. (son of bro. **Joseph** afsd.).

" sister **Mary Foster** during life, pt. of "Ennalls Purchase" on w. side Ennall's Ck., s. side Choptank R. (for desc. see will); at her decease to pass to her son **John** and hrs., she and they paying yearly annuity of 16s. to **William Ennalls.**

" Wm. Fookes and hrs., 100 A. of sd. tract, he paying to sd. **Wm.** and hrs. forever a yearly rent of 4s.

" 3 nephews (sons of bro. **Joseph** afsd.), viz.: **William, Thomas** and **Joseph,** and their male hrs., "East Marsh Range."

" nephew **Henry** (son of bro. **Joseph** afsd.) and male hrs., n. w. pt. of tract, "Beaver Dam," from line of plantation where Peter Minner lived (for desc. see will); he lacking such issue, to male hrs. of his bro. **Thomas.**

" nephew **Joseph** (son of bro. **Joseph** afsd.), pt. of tract "Ennall's Outlet," bounded on s. with Richard Mitchell's bank, and adj. on n. land herein conveyed to Thos. Canner.

" Thomas Canner and hrs., 103 A., pt. of "Ennalls Outlet" (for desc. see will).

" Thomas Hayward and hrs., 50 A., pt. of "Ennals Purchase" (plantation where Andrew Willis lived), at head of Shoal Ck., and on branch lying bet. Wm. Jones' and sd. Andrew Willis' (for desc. see will).

" Philip Feddeman, 100 A., pt. of "Ennals Purchase" (for desc. see will) during life; at his decease to his son Richard.

" nephew **Thomas** (son of bro. **Henry**) and male hrs., remaining pt. of "Ennall's Purchase"; he lacking such issue, to male hrs. of his bro. **Bartholomew.** Also all houses and lands in Cambridge.

" nephew **Thomas** (son of bro. **Joseph** afsd.) and male hrs., "Cow Garden."

" James Woolefood, Sr., and hrs., a tract, ——, at head of Jenkins Ck., s. side Choptank R., and 50 A., "Rotterdam," adj. sd. land.

" **Bartholomew,** son of **Henry Ennals** and male hrs., "The Woodyard" on e. side Jenckins Ck. (Bou. of Wm. Dorrington.)

To wife **Elizabeth** and hrs., Lots 23 and 24 in Vienna (bou. of Richard Acworth of Sommerset Co.), with buildings, etc., and use of ''North Yarmouth'' during life.

" nephew **Bartholomew** (son of bro. **Joseph** afsd.) and male hrs., remaining pt. of ''Ennals Outlet.''

" **Sarah Ennals,** personalty and £60 due from Thomas Lingham.

" **Sarah** (dau. of **Roger Woolford**), personalty.

" bro. **Henry,** 50s. for ring.

" **Bartholomew,** son of bro. **Henry,** personalty.

" Francis Hayward, Sr., Thomas Hayward, Henry, Jr. (son of Henry Hooper), bro.-in-law **Maj. Roger Woolford** and his wife, 25s. each for rings.

" sister **Mary Foster,** 5s. for ring.

" **Sarah, Ann, Rebecca** and **Phoebe,** daus. of sd. sister, £5 each.

" ten nephews, viz.: **Thomas, Henry, Bartholomew** and **Joseph** (sons of bro. **Henry**), **Bartholomew, Thomas, Joseph** and **Henry** (sons of bro. **Joseph,** dec'd), **John** and **William** (sons of bro. **John**), £10 each at age of 18 yrs.

Residue of personal estate to wife **Elizabeth** and nephew **William** (son of bro. **Joseph** afsd.), equally.

Test: John and Thos. Hayward, John Price, Margaret Eccleston. 14. 631.

Codicil: 6 July, 1718, to John (son of John Pitt, gent.), 10 A. of ''Ennalls Lott.''

Clark, John, planter, Kent Co.,   2nd Mar., 1713; 29th June, 1718.

To John Reed of Kent Co. and Robert Randall, personalty.

Ex.: Richard Campbell.

Test: Sam. Exell, Mary Bowles, Sarah Exell. 14. 637.

Plesto, Edward, carpenter, Kent Co.,   15th Dec., ——; 18th June, 1718.

To Col. Thomas Smith and Martha, his wife; Edward Scott and Martha, his wife; Edward Wornel and Sarah, his wife; Daniel Farrels and Agnes, his wife; Thomas Piner, John Tilden, John Woodel and Martha, his wife, and John Willson's wife ——, personalty.

" Thomas Lee, **Dorothy** (dau. of bro. **John**), all of Grt. Britain, £10 each.

" sister **Catharine Eats,** of Gt. Britain, and hrs., plantation bou. of Col. Richard Tilghman, and residue of personal estate.

Exs.: Col. Thomas Smith and William Thomas.

Test: John Willson, Joseph Cox, Col. Edward Scott. 14. 638.

Goldsberry, John, planter, St. Mary's Co.,

—— —— ——;
29th Mar., 1718.

To son **Robert,** lease of 60 A. and personalty.
" son **William,** personalty.
" **Margaret Goldsberry,** grandson **Edward Goldsberry** and **John** (son of **William Goldsberry**), personalty.
Residue of estate to sons **Robert** and **William,** equally.
Test: Thos. Blackman, Thos. Thornley, **Margaret Goldsberry** (Gouldsberry).   14. 640.

Burroughs, John, planter, St. Mary's Co.,

13th Mar., 1715-6;
5th Dec., 1717.

To wife **Mary,** ⅓ of personal estate absolutely, and dwelling plantation during life; at her decease to eldest son **John.**
" eldest son **John,** personalty and tract where he now lives, excepting that pt. conveyed by deed of gift to dau. **Margaret Cartwright.**
Lands conveyed to youngest son **Richard** and to dau. **Margaret** afsd. by deed of gift confirmed.
To dau. **Sarah Carter** during life, n. pt. of dwelling plantation. Residue of personal estate divided among 6 child., ——.
Test: **John Cartwright,** William Hulse, Samuel Johnson.
14. 641.

Langham, William, Brittain's Bay, St. Mary's Co.,

2nd Oct., 1717;
—— Nov., 1717.

To bro.-in-law **Anthony Browne** and **William,** his son; bros.-in-law **Richard Walker** and **Nicholas Miles,** James Thompson, Richard Phinice and Edward Spinke, personalty.
" wife **Annastatia,** extx., residue of personal estate.
Test: Henry Spinke, Wm. Abell, Elizabeth Spinke.   14. 643.

Arnold, Ralph,   26th Nov., 1717;
15th Sept., 1718.

To housekeeper Jane Ginkens, personalty.
Ex.: John Gibb.
Test: Frances Nichelston, Jean Ginkins, John Gibbs. 14. 644.

Cole, Edward, St. Mary's Co.,   16th Apr., 1717;
20th Dec., 1717.

To wife **Elizabeth,** personalty at "Maiden Bower" and her thirds.
"   son **Edward,** 1s., he having rec'd share of estate. Goods from Capt. John Hyde, consigned to testator, and merchandise left in store to be disposed of by son **Edward** for benefit of estate.
Residue of estate divided equally among six child., viz.: **Elizabeth Heard, Robert, Honour Spalding, Ruth Mattinly, Susanna Jenkins** and **Mary Jenkins.**
Exs.: Wife **Elizabeth** and son **Robert,** jointly.
Test: Clement Gardiner, Joseph Power, James Thompson.

14. 644.

Coode, John, St. Mary's Co.,   20th Apr., 1718;
29th Apr., 1718.

To eldest son **Thomas** and hrs., personalty and 192 A. upon Mattapany R., St. Clements Hundred. Shd. sd. son die without issue, to pass to youngest son **William** and hrs.; he dying without issue, sd. land to be divided among 3 daus., viz.: **Jane, Susannah** and **Ann.**
"   second son **John** and hrs., personalty and 300 A., "Crosshall" or "Dinard's Point"; he dying without issue, to pass to son **Wm.** afsd., and he dying without issue, to pass to three daughters afsd.
"   King and Queen Parish for a glebe, in consideration of 10,000 lbs. tobacco received by testator, land bou. of Samuel Cooksey.
"   James Lewis and hrs., "Frogg Hall," provided he pays to exs. 7,500 lbs. tobacco according to bond.
"   eldest dau. **Jane,** and daus. **Susannah** and **Ann,** personalty.
"   son **William** afsd., personalty.
"   wife **Ann,** extx., her thirds and residue of personal estate during life; at her decease to child. afsd., equally.
Overseers: Bro. **William** and Mathew Mason.
Test: John Hoskins, Daniel Kelly, John Barnes, Daniel Henly.

14. 646.

Mason, John, St. Mary's Co.,   30th Sept., 1717;
29th Oct., 1717.

To sister **Susannah Clarke** and her husband, **George,** personalty, provided they care for sister **Mary (Mason).**
"   sisters **Elizabeth Rogers** and **Susannah Clarke** and their hrs., "Mason's Purchase," being pt. of tract formerly called "Cooke's Folly," divided as they see fit.

To nephew **Robert Mason**, personalty, including ½ the stock
on plantation "Dunbar and Bloonsberry." £50 to be
pd. him by Tobias Bowles, merchant, of Deale, Kent, and
expended in his education, also all other lands in Md.
or elsewhere; he not to sell either lands or negroes until
he is 25 yrs. of age. Shd. he die before attaining age of
18, portion bequeathed him to revert to bro. **Mathew** and
hrs., sd. bro. to pay to nephew **Rodham Rogers** £25, and £25
eldest child of sister **Clarke** afsd.

To Mrs. Ann Waughop, £5 and personalty.

"   John Greenwill, full balance of accts.

"   sisters, each 20s. for mourning rings.

"   **Stratford**, bro. to **Robert Mason**, personalty.

Bro. **Mathew** ex. and residuary legatee, he to possess nephew
Robert (his son) in the lands, stock and negroes at age
of 18.

Test: Geo. Gillespie, Tho. Waughop, Robt. Mosley, Jas. Croxon.

Codicil: 21 Oct., 1717, to Mrs. Eliza: Smith, personalty.

Test: William Sweale, Ka. Daliner.   14. 648.

Truman, Thomas, Prince George's Co., 15th Sept., 1717;
14th Jan., 1717.

To mother **Mrs. Jane Taney**, personalty for maintenance during her life.

"   eldest son **Henry** and hrs., dwelling plantation ——, at
decease of his mother; he to enjoy two-thirds of sd. plantation at age of 21 yrs., and personalty.

"   son **James**, land bou. from bro. **Edward**, "Thomas and
Anthony's Choice" (not yet made over according to law);
also personalty at decease of mother afsd.

"   dau. **Jane** and unborn child, personalty.

"   nephew **Thomas Truman**, personalty. Shd. he die during
minority, sd. bequest to his next of kin; shd. there be
none, then to proper heirs of testator.

"   wife **Sarah**, extx., residue of personal estate during widowhood. Shd. she marry, her thirds only.

Test: Truman Greenfield, Philip Willisey.   14. 649.

Codicil: 15th Sept., 1717. Bro. **Edward** to be discharged of
debt to testator, providing he makes over "Thomas and
Anthony's Choice" to son **James** afsd. at once.

Cooper, Christina Barbara, widow, St. Mary's City,
5th Oct., 1717;
23rd Oct., 1717.

To son **Nicholas Guyther**, grandchild. **Richard Beard, Mary
Leigh** and dau. **Ann Beckwith**, personalty.

Residue of estate to daus. **Dorothy Leigh** and **Ann Beckwith**,
equally.

Exs.: Son-in-law **John Leigh** and dau. **Ann Beckwith.**
Test: Elizabeth Williams, Elizabeth Potter. 14. 651.

Walker, Richard, planter, St. Mary's Co.,
10th Oct., 1717;
7th Nov., 1717.

To son **James** and hrs., land on s. side branch ———, and personalty.

" dau. **Mary** and hrs., land on n. side sd. branch, and personalty. Shd. either die during minority or without issue, survivor to inherit portion of deceased. Shd. both die during minority or without issue, dau.'s portion to pass to nephew **Thomas Walker,** the part on s. side to pass to nephew **Thomas** (son of **Thomas**).

" nephew **Richard Walker** and hrs., "Berry."

" wife **Ann,** extx., residue of personal estate.
Test: Peter Browne, Anthony Browne, Thos. Dillon. 14. 652.

Smith, Peter, Sr., carpenter, St. Mary's Co.,
30th Dec., 1717;
8th Jan., 1717.

To son **Peter,** 130 A., "Dansburry Hill," personalty, and after legacies are pd., ⅓ personal estate.

" daus. **Sarah Howard, Mary Johnson** and grandchild **Joseph,** personalty.

" daus. **Elizabeth** and **Susannah,** residue of personal estate equally, and shd. son afsd. die during minority or without issue, his estate, real and personal, to pass to sd. daus.

" dau. **Susannah** afsd., dwelling plantation at decease of wife.

" wife **Dorothy,** personalty and use of dwelling plantation during life. No part of her estate to be claimed by ex. as belonging to testator, she having relinquished her dower rights.

Ex.: Robert Ford, Sr.
Test: John Ford, Rebeckah Allen, Thos. Dillon. 14. 653.

Payne, Charles, Brittain's Bay, St. Mary's Co.,
11th Dec., 1717;
7th Jan., 1717-8.

To son **Peter** and hrs., 75 A., "Howard's Gift," where Joh Drury now lives (pt. of "Howard's Mount").

" son **Charles** and hrs., 100 A., dwelling plantation, "The Fox."

To son **Leonard** and hrs., 50 A., "Strife," where James Warrick now lives. Sons **Peter** and **Charles** not to sell or dispose of any of their lands. Shd. either die without issue,
their portion to pass to dau. **Mary**; shd. both sd. sons die
without issue, portion of one of them to pass to son
Leonard. Shd. all child. die without issue, son **Peter's**
portion to **Henry** (son of bro. **Thomas**), son **Charles'**
portion to **Charles** (son of bro. **Thomas** afsd.), son **Leonard's** portion to **James** (son of bro. **Thomas** afsd.).
"   dau. **Mary**, bro. **Ezekiel** and **Mary**, dau. of bro.-in-law
Alexander Heathman, personalty.

Residue of personal estate to child. equally.

Sons **Charles** and **Leonard** to care of bro. **Thomas,** and son
Peter and dau. **Mary** to care of bro.-in-law **John Meekin.**
Sons to be of age at 18, dau. at 16.

Exs.: Bro. **Thomas** and bro.-in-law **John Meekin,** jointly.

Test: Jas. Warrick, John Drury, Henry Spinke.   14. 655.

Mackall, Mary, Calvert Co.,   25th Jan., 1715;
                                     15th May, 1718.

To son **John** and his wife, **Susannah**; son **James** and his wife,
Ann; daus. **Ann** and **Elizabeth Skinner**, personalty.
"   **Mary** (dau. of **James Mackall**) and **Mary** (dau. of **Wm.
Skinner**), £3 and personalty each at 21 yrs. or marriage.
"   **Ann** (dau. of **Robt. Skinner**), personalty.

Son **Benjamin** ex. and residuary legatee.

Test: Jonathan Cay, Tho. Howe.   14. 657.

Barton, William, gent., Charles Co.,   5th Sept., 1717;
                                              22nd Sept., 1717.

To   grandsons **Barton Smoot, Barton Warren** and **William
Smoot**, granddaus. **Rachell** (wife of **Mathew Stone**), **Ann
Smoot, Mary Hungerford, Eliza:** (wife of **Charles Phil-
pott**), **Eliza** (wife of **John Neale**), personalty.
"   3 youngest child. of dau. **Margaret Miller**, half residue of
estate, and to **Thomas** and **Barton** (sons of grandson **Barton Smoot**), the other half.

Exs.: Dau. **Margaret Miller** and grandson **Barton Smoot,**
jointly.

Test: Wm. Howard, John Jones, Jno. Willard.   14. 658.

Ewebank, Richard, Kent Co.,   13th Apr., 1718;
                                     26th Apr., 1718.

To son **Richard**, entire estate; to be in care of testator's
father, **Thomas Ewebank**, ex., and receive estate at 21
yrs. of age.

Test: Marke Williams, Walter Crump, Marmaduke Story.

                                                 14. 659.

James, John, St. Leonard's Ck., Calvert Co.,
19th Oct., 1717;
5th July, 1718.

To son **John** and hrs., dwelling and lot, at age of 21 yrs. Shd. sd. son die during minority, to wife **Hannah** and hrs. Shd. she marry, son **John** to be for himself at 16 yrs.
" dau. **Mary**, personalty.
" wife **Hannah**, extx., and hrs., residue of estate, real and personal.

Test: John Johnson, Elizabeth Turner, Tho. Howe. 14. 660.

Harding, Thomas, planter, Kent Co., 23rd Apr., 1718;
24th May, 1718.

To Edward Davis, ex., and hrs., entire estate.
Test: George Harrison, Thomas Welding (Welden). 14. 660.

Harbert, William, gent., Charles Co., 9th May, 1715;
26th July, 1718.

To dau. **Anne** (wife of **George Dent**), 500 A., part of "Clarke's Purchase," during life; after her decease to granddau. **Rebeckah Dent** and unborn child of dau. **Anne** afsd.
" **Jno.** and hrs. (son of **John Douglass**, dec'd), 150 A., "Harbert's Chance," and personalty.
Personal estate to wife **Sarah** and **George Dent**, joint exs., equally.

Test: Sam. Hanson, Jno. Payne, Elizabeth Dollar. 14. 661.

Harbert, Sarah, widow, Charles Co., 8th July, 1718;
26th July, 1718.

To son **Joseph Douglas** and hrs., dwelling plantation and 200 A., "The Hills."
" grandsons **Thomas, Benjamin,** and **Joseph Douglas** and **Douglas Giffard**, personalty.
" granddaus. **Eliz. Howard** and **Mary Douglass**, personalty.
Son **Joseph** afsd., ex. and residuary legatee.

Test: Col. Walter Story, Tho. Harriss, Sam. Hanson. 14. 662.

Ransom, George, planter, Prince George's Co.,
5th Dec., 1717;
18th Jan., 1717.

To James (son of Sarah Taneyhill) and hrs., 30 A. on the River out of "The Wedge," a 20-ft. dwelling to be built on same out of personal etate.
" Sarah Taneyhill and her son James, personalty.
" eldest son **George, Jr.**, personalty.
" dau. **Elizabeth Harris**, land on which her husband has built, with land bet. prongs of Patuxent branch (pt. of "The Wedge"), and personalty.

To four sons, **William, Richard, Ignatius** and **Joseph**, residue
of estate, real and personal, divided equally; son **William**,
ex., to have first choice of land.

Test: John Orme, Moses Orme, Robt. Orme.   14. 663.

Mills, John, Prince George's Co.,   21st Oct., 1717; 25th Jan., 1717.

To son **William**, ex., and hrs., 50 A., being upper pt. of tract
bou. of John Tait, and 40 A. bou. of Richard Edwards.

"   son **Robert** and hrs., lower 50 A. of tract bou. of John
Tait, and personalty; to be free at decease of testator.

"   son **Richard**, personalty.

"   son **John**, 5s.

"   daus. **Ellinor, Seliner** and **Mary Travis**, granddau. **Elizabeth Travis** and grandsons **John** and **William Mills Travis**,
personalty.

Residue of personal estate to wife and child. equally, excepting son **John**.

Test: Benjamin Brassoure, Thos. Willson, Jr., Thos. Brassure,
Nathaniel Wickham, Sr., Chas. Hyatt, Sam. Bresshear, Sr.
    14. 664.

Coleman, Richard, planter, Charles Co., 19th May, 1718; 27th June, 1718.

To Elizabeth Osborne (wife of Thomas Osborne, smith), personalty.

"   Thomas Mitchell and Archibald Johnstone, joint exs., residue of estate, equally.

Test: Joseph Clemment, Rhafele Clement.   14. 666.

Dashiell, Robert, Somerset Co.,   15th Jan., 1717-8; —— Aug., 1718.

To eldest son **Hast** and hrs., dwelling plantation, 300 A.,
Johnson's Lot," also 50 A., "Greenwidge," and personalty.

"   2 sons, **Robert** and **James**, and their hrs., 300 A., "Longhill," n. side Lipkin Ck.; son **Robt.** to have upper pt.
where Eliza: Collier now lives, son **James** the lower pt.,
from Dancing Branch downwards (for desc. see will), and
personalty.

"   son **Mathias**, 100 A., "Gorden's Delight," and personalty.

"   sons **Mathias** and **William**, personalty divided bet. them
when son William attains age of 16.

Sons **Hast** and **Robert** each to pay to son **William**, when he
attains age of 18, 20,000 lbs. tobacco.

To daus. **Elizabeth** and **Rebeckah,** personalty.

" wife **Sarah,** extx., ⅓ of personal estate, the other ⅔ to child. equally.

Son **Hast** to be of age at 18 and in care of bro. **Thomas;** son **Robert** of age at 16 yrs. and in care of bro. **George;** son **James** of age at 18 and in care of cousin **James Dashiell;** son **Mathias** of age at 18 yrs. and in care of cousin **George Dashiell;** son **William** of age at 18 yrs. and in care of John Irving.

Test: William Round, Alex. Carlyle, **George Dashiell.** 14. 666.

Note—16th July, 1718. "Within named **Sarah Dashiell** flyeth to her thirds."

Chew, Samuel, merchant, A. A. Co., 16th July, 1718; 31st Oct., 1718.

To son **Samuel** and male hrs., 600 A., "Ayres," at Herring Bay, and 300 A., "Chews' Right."

" grandson **Samuel** and hrs. (son of son **John**), testator's share in "Wells Hill," "West Wells" and "Little Wells," which testator and Nehemiah Birckhead lately bou. of George Wells, all lying at or near Herring Bay.

" son **Nathaniel,** 318 A., lately bou. of Jas. Heath, being pt. of 3 tracts, "Burrage," "Burrage Blossom" and "Burrage's End," lying w. of Herring Ck.; also tract lately bou. of Nathaniel Rigbye, adj. above lands, and where son **Nathaniel** now lives, also personalty and £200.

" grandchild., viz.: **Samuel, Ann, Sarah** and **Mary** (child. of son **John,** dec'd), £1,200 divided equally among them or the survivors, to be pd. as follows: to **Samuel** at 21 yrs. and to granddaus. at 18 yrs.

" grandchild.-in-law **Cassandra** and **Elizabeth** (daus. of **Philip Coale** and **Cassandra,** his wife), £100, equally divided.

" cousin **Benjamin** (son of **Wm. Chew**), personalty.

" friends on the Western Shore, £20.

Son **Samuel** ex. and residuary legatee.

Test: Robert Sollers, John Scriven, **Benj. Chew,** Katharine Johnson. 14. 669.

Phillpott, Edward, Charles Co., 19th Aug., 1718; 28th Oct., 1718.

To son **Edward** and hrs., tract of land in Charles Co., adj. 300 A. sold by James Walker to father **Edward Phillpott** (for desc. see will).

To sons **John, Edward** and **Charles** and their hrs., 60 A., "Timber Neck," jointly, they to hold sd. land and to dispose of no timber without consent of all parties; also personalty.

" son **Charles** and hrs., remainder of land on n. side of Hospital Run.

" daus. **Eleanor** and **Mary**, and to granddau. **Susanna Musgrave** (at age of 16 or marriage), personalty.

" wife **Eleanor**, dwelling plantation ——, adjoining that of Capt. Jno. Fendall's (for desc. see will), and ⅓ of residue of personal estate; other ⅔ to child. afsd., equally.

Exs.: Wife **Eleanor** and son **John**, jointly.

Overseers: Capt. Jno. Fendall, Samuel Hanson.

Test: John Fendall, Sarah Smoot, Sam. Hanson.   14. 672.

Hammon, Edward, Sr., gent., Somerset Co.,
17th July, 1718;
4th Sept., 1718.

To Hester (dau. of Catherine Diall), Oliver Griffin, Anne Griffin, Catherine Diall, grandsons **John** and **Edward** (sons of son **Edward**), **William Bowen** and Hannah (dau. of Denis Diall), personalty.

" dau. **Mary Bowen**, 1s.

Residue of estate to Anne and Oliver Griffin, equally.

Exs.: Dennis Driskell and Anne Griffin, jointly.

Test: John Truitt, John Jones, Benj. Burton.   14. 674.

Hellin, David, Patuxent R., Calvert Co.,   15th July, 1717;
8th Sept., 1718.

To **James Hellin**, £5.

" son **John** and hrs., ½ tract bou. of Geo. Harris and Samuel Wallis called "Hooper's Neck" (plantation where he is now seated), and personalty.

" son **Peter** and hrs., other half of tract afsd. Shd. son **David** prefer this land he is to have it, son **Peter** taking quarter bequeathed **David**.

" son **David** and hrs., all tracts of land where quarter now is, viz.: one pt. formerly Wm. Turner's, one pt. formerly Geo. Busey's and one pt. land of Jno. Turners, bou. of widow Turner.

" son **Richard**, dwelling plantation after decease of his mother. Shd. she marry again, to have ⅓ pt. of sd. land, other ⅔ to son **Richard** when he comes of age.

" dau. **Penelope**, £50 and personalty.

" wife **Susanna**, ⅓ personal estate, residue to sons **David, Peter** and **Richard** afsd., equally.

Exs.: Wife **Susanna** and son **David,** jointly.
Test: Math. Dorman, Ann Garner, Sarah Howe, Tho. Howe.
14. 676.

Aldridge (Aldeir), Thomas, A. A. Co.,   7th Oct., 1718;
22nd Nov., 1718.

To son **Thomas,** 100 A., "Murphes Choyce," Baltimore Co.,
with personalty belonging to sd. land.
" dau. **Sarah Merraday,** 20s.
" wife **Rebekah,** extx., residue of personal estate.
Test: Jno. Hammond, Matthew Talbott, Wm. Barnet. 14. 678.

Watkins. Mary,   16th Nov., 1716;
3rd May, 1718.

Two sons, **Thomas** and **John,** to be free at decease of testator.
To dau. **Clare,** extx. (wife of **Jno. Norris**), for maintenance of
son **Basiel,** entire personal estate.
Test: Wm. Worrell, Wm. Jones, Rich. Wells.   14. 678.

Peirpoint, Amos., planter, A. A. Co.,   1st June, 1718;
24th June, 1718.

To bro. **Alexander Warfield,** ex., entire estate. Shd. any place
of public worship be built near heads of Severn and
South Rivers, ex. to pay £5 towards builidng thereof.
John Rawlings to have benefit of orchard on his dwelling
plantation for 7 yrs., then to return it to bro. **Alexander
Warfield** afsd.
Test: **Jno. Warfield,** Thos. Davis, Edward Benson.   14. 680.

Wilkinson. William, Jr. (nunc.),   28th Mar., 1715;
31st Mar., 1715.

To bro. **Robert,** land given testator by his mother ——.
Test: Edward Mahun, Mary Lynch, **Wm. Wilkinson** and
Tamor, his wife.
Note—"Requested to be recorded by James Wilkinson, ex."

Hall, Mary, widow, Talbot Co.,   20th June, 1718;
8th Sept., 1718.

To Hannah, extx. (dau. of John Oldham), and hrs., 71 A.,
"Glaids Addition," on n. side Tredhaven Ck.
Test: Rich. Townson, Amos Law, Robt. Sinckleare, Jas. San-
ford.   14. 681.

Moss, Robert, A. A. Co.,   22nd Apr., 1718;
—— ——.

To bros. **Edmund** and **Thomas** and Ralph Moss (son of Ailee
Coley), personalty at age of 18 yrs.
" John Nickolson, ex., residue of estate in Maryland.
Test: Will. Worthington, John Gray, Zachariah Gray. 14. 682.

Maudsley (Mondsley), James, planter, Hunger R., Dorchester Co.,   25th Sept., 1715;
3rd Mar., 1715-6.
To wife **Mary,** extx., entire estate.
Test: Capt. John Keen (Keene), Elenor Jones.   14. 683.

Beswick, Thomas, smith, Talbot Co.,   18th Aug., 1718;
15th Sept., 1718.
To Rebeckah Cromwell, extx., widow, entire estate in Oxford,
with all money due testator, and after decease of wife
Silley, plantation on n. side Cabin Ck., Dorchester Co. (pt.
of "Gutriges Choice"), with all personal estate.
Test: Nich. Lowe, John Robinson, John Padinson.   14. 684.

Davis, Thomas, St. Mary's Co.,   19th Jan., 1711;
31st July, 1718.
To son **Samuel,** 1s.
"   wife **Mary,** extx., entire estate.
Test: Sebastion Thompson, Archabel Pike, Margaret Tompson,
Mildred Pike, James Tompson.   14. 685.

Manders, Cecisley, widow, Kent Island, Queen Anne's Co.,
24th July, 1717;
27th May, 1718.
To 2 daus., **Amy Folson** and **Hannah Orsborne,** personalty.
"   son **Joseph Sudler,** ex., personal estate.
Test: Peter Denney, Sarah Denney, Valentine Carter. 14. 686.

Dason, John, Dorchester Co.,   26th Nov., 1713;
8th June, 1715.
To son **John,** 150 A., "Mount Pleasure," where he now lives
and dwelling plantation, "Barter," at decease of wife
——.
"   grandson **John Croney** and dau. **Mary,** personalty.
Test: Wm. Angley, **Daniel Croney,** Steven Ileharty. 14. 687.

Blunt, Robert, Kent Island, Queen Anne's Co.,
7th May, 1718;
8th Aug., 1718.
To wife **Elizabeth,** extx., use of dwelling plantation ——,
during widowhood, care of child. during minority. Shd.
she marry, 2 eldest sons to select someone as guardian
for them all; also ⅓ real estate during life and ⅓ personal estate, absolutely.
"   sons **Richard, Robert** and **Samuel** and their hrs., "Great
Neck" equally, at legal age. Shd. either die during
minority and without issue, the portion of dec'd to pass
to young. son **Benjamin.**

To son **Benjamin**, personalty and £18 in hands of John Midford, mcht., in London.

Test: Val. Carter, Thos. Goodman, Phil. Connor.   14. 687.

Barwell (Barwill), Justinian, A. A. Co.,   26th Nov., 1717; 21st May, 1718.

To son **John** and hrs., "Barwell's Hope," and residue of land at wife's decease. Shd. sd. son die without issue, his portion to pass to son **Justinian**; he failing issue, to pass to son **Richard** and hrs.

" sons **Justinian** and **Richard**, ½ of personal estate equally. Child. of age at 18 yrs.

" wife **Penelope**, extx., use of lands during life, and ½ personal estate, absolutely.

Test: Tho. Tucker, Thomas Cruchley, Jane Pratt, Catharine Crad.   14. 689.

Note—pp. 690-699 omitted.

Grundy, Margaret, Queen Anne's Co.,   1st Apr., 1709; 20th Aug., 1718.

To son **James Pemberton** and hrs., personalty and "Kingsall" and "Kingsale's Addition"; he dying without issue, sd. lands to pass to son **Benjamin Pemberton**; he failing issue, to revert to hrs. of son **John Pemberton**.

" son **Benjamin** and hrs., dwelling plantation, 870 A., pt. of "Partnership"; he dying without issue, sd. lands to pass to hrs. of son **James** afsd.; he failing issue, to hrs. of son **John** afsd. Also to son **Benj.** a lot at Kingstowne, Talbot Co., and personalty.

" 2 sons, **James** and **Benjamin Pemberton** afsd., residue of estate, equally.

Ex.: Henry Hosier of Chester R., Kent Co., and Howell Powell of Gr. Choptank R., Talbot Co., to have care of son **Benjamin** until age of 18 yrs.

Testator desires to be buried at Friends Meeting House, Tuckahoe.

Test: Tho. Fisher, Sarah Fisher, Tho. Bullin.   14. 700.

Long, John, planter, Talbot Co.,   8th Sept., 1712; 5th Sept., 1718.

To 2 sons, **William** and **Thomas**, at age of 21 yrs., plantation on Bulling brook Ck., pt. of two tracts, "Parkers Point" and "Enlargement."

" son **William** and bro. **Thomas**, personalty.

" wife **Sarah**, use of plantation until sons afsd. attain age of 21 yrs. and residue of estate, real and personal.

Exs.: Wife **Sarah** and father-in-law **Nicholas Lowe** of Talbot
Co., gent.
Test: Griffith Evans, Wm. Sanders, Wm. Rich.   **14. 702.**
Note—John Pattison of Talbot Co., planter, having inter-
married with executrix of above will, caused the same to
be proved by above test.

Ransom, William, Prince George's Co.,   15th July, 1718; 9th Aug., 1718.
To sister **Eliz. Harris**, personalty.
" bros. **George, Richard, Ignatius** and **Joseph** and sister
Eliza: Harris, residue of estate, real and personal, equally.
Ex.: **William Harris.**
Test: John Orme, Moses Orme, Aron Orme, Leonard Hollyday.
     14. 704.

Kennett (Kennitt), John, Somerset Co., 24th Apr., 1718; 1st Aug., 1718.
To mother ——, personalty during life; at her decease to
child. of following persons: **Wm. Kennett**, John Tull and
Richard Webb, viz.: **Samuel**, son of bro. **William**, Eliza-
beth and John, child. of John Tull, and Richard, son of
Richard Webb.
" bro. **William** and hrs., ex., 80 A., and personalty.
Test: John Turville, George Taylor, Elizabeth Latcham.
     14. 705.

Miller, George, planter, A. A. Co.,   10th Apr., 1718; 10th May, 1718.
To sons **George, Thomas, Joseph** and **William** and their hrs.,
each 100 A. of tract "Georges Park," Baltimore Co., son
George to have first choice. Shd. any of sons die without
issue, his pt. to fall to next bro.
" sons **George** and **Thomas**, personalty.
" wife **Eliza:**, use of dwelling plantation and residue of
personal estate during widowhood; at her decease dwelling plantation to pass to dau. **Eliza:**. Shd. wife marry,
dau. **Eliz.** to possess same at age of 16, or day of wife's
marriage. Shd. dau **Eliza:** die without issue, sd. land
to pass to dau. **Sarah** and hrs.
Test: John Hardin, Phillip Tennerly, George Man.   **14. 706.**

Sparrow, Solomon, A. A. Co.,   17th Apr., 1718; 18th July, 1718.
To wife **Sarah**, extx., and hrs., dwelling plantation, 100 A.,
"The Angles," 150 A., first purchase out of Ann Arundle
Manor, and 100 A., being 2nd purchase out of sd. Manor,
absolutely. Also residue of all land during life; at her
decease to pass as follows:

To kinswoman **Cassandra Smith** and hrs., 50 A., being other part of 2nd purchase out of A. A. Manor.

" Sarah (wife of Richard Gott), 50 A. of "Sparrows Nest" on n. side Patapsco R.

" **Solomon Sparrow** and hrs., 45 A., "Loyds Point," and 55 A. adj. out of "Sparrows Nest" afsd.

" Richard Galloway, Jr., and Sophia, his wife, during their lives, residue of "Sparrows Nest."

Shd. they leave no issue, sd. land to pass to Daniel and hrs., son of Wm. and Margaret Richardson.

To Elizabeth (wife of John Wooden, Sr.), £30.

" Richard Galloway, Sr., £10.

Test: Benj. Lawrence, Rachel Lawrence, Mary Price, Jr., Wm. Browne. 14 707.

Meare, Abraham, planter,   22nd Dec., 1716; 19th Sept., 1718.

To son **James** and hrs., plantation where mother —— now lives and land on w. side of branch, at 20 yrs. of age.

" 2 sons, **William** and **Isaac**, dwelling plantation to them and their hrs. or to the longest survivor.

Bro. and sister, **Francis** and **Mary Neighbor**, to live on land on w. side of branch for term of 20 yrs.

To wife **Martha**, extx., use of dwelling plantation ——, during life.

Test: Eliza: Sury, Alexander Hurrell, Joseph Owen, Jr. 14. 709.

Wellman, Michael, carpenter, A. A. Co., 13th Apr., 1718; 13th May, 1718.

To wife **Eliza:**, extx., entire estate during life; at her decease to 2 bros., **Thomas** and **Joseph** and their hrs.

Test: Wm. Mills, Rich. Mills, Wm. Smith. 14. 710.

Warfield, Benjamin, A. A. Co., 22nd Mar., 1717; 24th June, 1718.

To son **Joshua** and hrs., dwelling plantation —— and 240 A. of "Warfield's Range," near falls of Patuxent R.

" dau. **Elizabeth** and hrs., ½ of "Winkapin Neck." Shd. either child die without issue, the survivor to inherit all afsd. land. Shd. both die without issue, testator's share of "Winkapin Neck" to be divided among 3 daus. of bro. **Richard**, viz.: **Ruth, Rachel** and **Lydia**, and their hrs., and 240 A. of "Warfield's Forrest" to be divided bet. 2 daus. of bro. **Alexander**, viz.: **Rachel** and **Sarah**, and their hrs.

To bro. **Richard** and hrs., ½ of "Benjamin's Discovery," other ½ to be disposed of by exs. for education of children.

"   Mary Yate, personalty at age of 16.

Exs.: Wife **Elizabeth** and bros. **Richard** and **Alexander.**

Test: Caleb Dorsey, Dr. John Rattenbury, Robt. Ridgely.

14. 711.

Meekins,.Richard, Dorchester Co.,   9th June, 1718; 11th Nov., 1718.

To son **Abraham** and hrs., 50 A., "Meekin's Chance."

"   son **Richard,** personalty.

"   wife **Sarah,** dwelling plantation 99 A., "Meekins' Hope," during life; at her decease to son **Richard** and hrs. He dying without issue, to son **William** and hrs., also ⅓ of personal estate absolutely. The residue to child. equally.

Exs.: Wife **Sarah** and son **John.**

Test: John Meekins, Elizabeth Ferguson, Hannah Kyard.

14. 712

Harde, William, Charles Co.,   4th Jan., 1717; 12th Aug., 1718.

To son **George,** 1s.

"   son **William** and dau. **Elizabeth,** personalty.

"   son **Ignatius,** 50 A. dwelling plantation ———, at decease of wife **Elizabeth,** extx.

"   son **John,** 50 A., "Dividing Run," and personalty.

"   daus. **Mary Wheatley** and **Martha Cohow,** 1s. each.

Test: Bowling Speake, Owen Reed, John Stapleton.   14. 714.

Cusack, George, St. Mary's Co.,   15th Jan., 1717; 5th Mar., 1717-8.

To son **Michael** and dau. **Mary,** entire estate equally.

Ex.: Henry Wharton. Child. to be brought up **Roman** Catholics.

Test: Ethelbert Doyne, Jno. Smith.   14. 715.

Valentine, George, Annapolis, A. A. Co.,

18th Sept., 1718; 2nd Oct., 1718.

To **Elizabeth** and hrs. (dau. of Mrs. Elinor Clinton), 100 A., "Girl's Portion," Baltimore Co.

"   **Elinor** and hrs. (dau. of Elinor Clinton afsd.), 200 A., "Bole Venture," A. A. Co., bou. of Richard Cattleing.

Mrs. Elinor Clinton, extx. and residuary legatee of estate, is
instructed to sell house, built by testator on ground said
to belong to Col. Francis Nicholson, former Governor,
for benefit of estate.

Test: John Beale, Samuel Dorsey, W. Burford.   14. 716.

Collson, Ann, Charles Co.,   30th July, 1718; 28th Aug., 1718.

To Isabella Dryden, Elizabeth Trimble, Faith Alavery, Mary
Davis, personalty.
" son **George,** residue of estate, real and personal.

Ex.: Joseph Harrison.

Test: Robt. Bennett, John Cook (Cooke).   14. 717.

Note—Book 14, f. 681, 12th Nov., 1718, Joseph Harrison refuses to act as ex. of above will.

Test: Rich. Bell.

Westall, George, planter, Baltimore Co., 23rd June, 1718; 6th Oct., 1718.

To 2 sons, **George** and **Richard,** and their hrs., 365 A., dwelling plantation, "Jackson's Venture," equally, son **George**
to have first choice. Neither to disturb wife **Ann** on sd.
plantation during her life.
" cousin **Thomas Bayly** and bro. **John,** personalty.
" wife **Ann,** extx., residue of personal estate divided with
children. Child. to be of age and receive their portions
at 18 yrs.

Test: Joseph Bourton, John Westall, John Risteau.   14. 718.

Jackson, James, planter, Baltimore Co., 26th Aug., 1717; 31st Oct., 1718.

To Thomas Prestwood, personalty at age of 21.
" wife **Sarah,** personal estate during widowhood; at day
of marriage ½ of sd. estate to pass to James Wood.

Ex.: ——.

Test: John Wood, John Risteau.   14. 719.

Frith, Henry, Talbot Co.,   21st June, 1718; 30th Dec., 1718.

Lots and house nr. Pitts Bridge to be disposed of by exs.

To wife **Rebecca,** estate during life; at her decease to be disposed of among her child. ——, as she thinks best.

Exs.: Wife **Rebecca** and Dennis Hopkins.

Test: W. Clayland, George Skannahone, Andrew Robson.   14. 721.

Banks, William, Second Ck., Talbot Co.,   29th Oct., 1717;
                                                25th Nov., 1718.

To sister **Elizabeth Edwards** and hrs., 200 A., "Banks Fork,"
    in the forks of White Marsh, Dorchester Co.
"   dau. **Elizabeth,** 400 A., "Hadden," nr. White Tree Branch.
"   sister **Mary Wilson,** 200 A., "Pockhiccory Ridge," nr.
    other side of sd. branch, Choptank R.
"   cousin **Edward Starky,** personalty.
Wife **Bridget** extx.
Test: John Hunt, John Blamer, Wm. Hambleton, Sr. 14. 721.

Howell, William, Prince George's Co.,   30th Dec., 1718;
                                              27th Jan., 1718.

To Margaret and Mary Thacker, personalty.
"   wife **Christian,** "who ran away," 2 s. and 6 p. for gloves;
    and she having been absent 5 or 6 yrs., testator renounces
    her from having any other share of personal estate.
"   Samuel Thacker, ex., entire estate, real and personal.
Test: Francis Tolson, Jacob Jackson, Jane Jackson. 14. 723.

Wells, Thomas, Sr., planter, Prince George's Co.,
                                              26th Sept., 1718;
                                              5th Jan., 1718.

To wife **Frances,** dwelling plantation, ——, "Strife," and adj.
    tract "Something," in all 218 A., during life; at her decease
    to four sons, **Thomas, Robert, Nathan** and **Joseph.** Shd.
    all of sd. sons, **Thomas, Nathan** and **Robert,** die without
    issue, lands to descend to son **Joseph;** shd. he die without
    issue, to 4 daus. equally, viz.: **Frances, Mary, Sarah**
    and **Elizabeth,** and their hrs. To sd. daus., personalty.
"   son **George,** 5s.
"   wife **Frances,** extx., and hrs., house and lot in Queen Ann's
    Town and residue of estate.
Test: Richard Duckett, Wm. John Black, Thomas Howell.
                                                      14. 724.

Beswick, Thomas, Talbot Co.,   14th Oct., 1718;
                                    23rd Dec., 1718.

To son **William** and hrs., 150 A., pt. of "Normington," and
    personalty.
"   son **George** and hrs., ½ "Christopher's Lott" and ½
    dwelling plantation, "Stevens Plains," bou. of Charles
    Stevens, to touch Mr. Clayland's land (for desc. see will),
    and personalty.
"   son **Richard** and hrs., upper ½ "Christopher's Lott" and
    "Stevens Plains."

To son **Robert** and hrs., 111 A. of "Harris' Lott" and personalty. Sons not to sell land, but shd. any of them die without issue, land to pass to next heir of name of Beswick.

" daus. **Eunice** and **Martha** and to Charity Jones and 2 daus. of Ferdinand, personalty.

" six child., viz.: **William, Eunice, Richard, George, Martha** and **Robert,** residue personal estate, equally.

Exs.: John and James Pemberton, of Queen Ann's Co.

Test: Ferd Callaghanes, Jon. Robinson, Mary Robinson.

14. 726.

Earle, Anne,   4th Apr., 1709 ;
                                                    8th Oct., 1709.

To son **Carpenter** and hrs., 400 A., being testator's pt. of "Carpenter's Point," Cecil Co.; he dying without issue, to dau. **Elizabeth** and hrs.; she dying without issue, to son **James;** he dying without issue, to Carpenter and Mary Lillistone and their hrs.

" dau. **Elizabeth** and hrs., personalty left testator by sister **Jane Coursey.**

" cousin **Elizabeth** (dau. of bro. **John Coursey**), sister-in-law **Sarah Denny,** Geofrey Mathew Shaw, Rhodah Threisby, bros. **John** and **James Coursey,** personalty.

Test: Richard Tilghman, **James Coursey,** Carpt. Lillistone, **Chas. Denny.**   14. 727.

Note—Entire will is freely given consent of **Michael Earle,** husband of testatrix.

Lewis (Levis), Glode, Sr., Dorchester Co.,
                                                    2nd May, 1716 ;
                                                    11th Nov., 1718.

To sons **John, Glode, Thomas, Abraham** and **William** and daus. **Sarah Myrsby, Elizabeth, Anne Aron** and **Jane,** each 1s.

" wife **Ann,** extx., residue personal estate.

Test: John Meekins, Sr., John Meekins, Jr.   14. 730.

Dawson, Anne, widow, Dorchester Co., 16th July, 1717 ;
                                                    14th Nov., 1718.

To son **Jonas** and daus. **Mary Oulford** and **Margaret Cronean,** personalty.

" son **John,** ex., and dau. **Eisbel,** residue of personalty, equally.

Dau. **Isabel** to receive her portion at age of 18 or marriage.

Overseers: John Needle and Thos. Berry.

Test: Grace Williamson, John Holland, John Needells. 14. 731.

Hall, Edward, St. Mary's Co.,   13th Oct., 1718;
                                                    5th Nov., 1718.

To **Abraham** (son of **Thomas Hall**), ½ real estate.
"   **James** (son of **John Hall**), the other ½. Land not being
      pd. for, the fathers of sd. child. to pay remaining pt. due
      mother ——.
"   **William** and **Mary** (son and dau. of Thomas King), sister
      Mary, bro. **Thomas, John Hall,** Thomas King, **Thomas Hall,**
      Susan, wife of Charles King, ex., and Anne (dau. of
      Charles King), Hugh Hopewell and James Baker, per-
      sonalty.

Test: John King, Elizabeth Fisher, Eliz. King, Hugh Hope-
      well.   14. 732.

Reagan, Philip, St. Mary's Co.,   14th Feb., 1718;
                                                    15th Nov., 1718.

To Thomas Webster, personalty.
"   Jenny Horn, extx., residue of estate.

Test: Frances Hopewell, Thos. Welch, Mary Yates.   14. 733.

Taylor, Henry, New Town Hundred, St. Mary's Co.,
                                                    8th Nov., 1718;
                                                    26th Nov., 1718.

To son-in-law **James Delicourt,** ex., interest in plantation for
      10 yrs., at end of which time lease of sd. plantation to
      youngest son **James.**
"   son **John,** 1s.
"   son **James** and dau. **Rachel,** personalty.
3 youngest child., viz., son **James** and daus. **Rachel** and **Grace,**
      residuary legatees, and to be in care of afsd. **Delicourt**
      until daus. are 16 and son **James** 18 yrs. of age.

Test: Dan'l Smith, Thos. Cambell, Jas. Plomfeilde. 14. 733.

Brisco, John, St. Michael's Hundred, St. Mary's Co.,
                                                    9th May, 1718;
                                                    11th Nov., 1718.

To son **Thomas,** land he now lives on.
"   sons **John** and **James,** dwelling plantation ——, equally.
"   dau. **Mary,** tract in the forest ——.
"   dau. **Anna,** "Underwood's Choice."
"   wife **Anne,** ⅓ personal estate, residue to 3 child., **John**
      James and **Anna,** equally.
Exs.: Wife **Anne,** sons **Thomas** and **John.**

Test: Jas. Edmonds, Bryan Dulsey (Dussey).   14. 735.

Irvine, George, 13th Oct., 1718; ——— ——— ———.

To Rev. Mr. Jonathan Cay, Mrs. Mary Barron, 2 daus. (unnamed) of Robt. Barron, dec'd, and George Gillispy, personalty (now at St. Mary's).

Horse (if found) to be sold and glass purchased for windows
of glebe house of testator's present parish.

To mother **Margaret Thompson,** extx., residue of personal
estate.

Overseers: George Gillespie, Rev. Jonathan Cay.

Test: Danll. Ray, Robt. Crane, Wm. Thomas, Jno. Green.

14. 735.

Talbott (Tabott), Edward, A. A. Co.,
5th of 1st month, 1718;
3rd July, 1718.

To wife **Elizabeth,** extx., ⅓ of "The Vineyard" (cont. 1,000
A.), Balto. Co., during life, and ⅓ personal estate, absolutely.

" son **John** and hrs., ⅓ of afsd. tract, and personalty.

" 2 sons, **Edward** and **Richard,** and their hrs., ⅓ of sd. tract
and at decease of wife the ⅓ bequeathed her divided
equally. Shd. one of the 3 sons afsd. die during minority
and without issue, portion of deceased to unborn child
if a son, if a dau. to surviving sons equally.

" bro. **John,** dwelling plantation on delivery of bills of
exchange for £160 within 4 mos. after decease of testator.
Shd. bro. **John** refuse to accept lands on these terms, sd.
lands to be sold and included in personal estate.

" dau. **Elizabeth,** personalty.

" following child., **Edward, Richard, Sarah, Mary** and unborn child, £30 and personalty. Daus. of age at 16 or
marriage; sons at 18 yrs.

" 7 child. afsd., residue of personal estate.

Test: Joseph Allean, Lewcresia Day, James Elderton.

14. 736.

Drayden, Isabella, Charles Co., 19th Mar., 1718-9;
1st July, 1719.

To dau. **Susanna Yopp** and William, son of Thomas King, personalty.

" son **Mathew Breeding (Breed),** residue of personal estate
at age of 18.

Extx.: Dau. **Susanna Yopp,** who is to give her bro., **Mathew
Breed,** 1 yr. schooling.

Test: John Beale, **Roger Yopp,** Elizabeth Trimbell. 15. 1.

Marriott, John, planter, A. A. Co.,   20th Aug., 1716;
                                               10th Mar., 1718.

To son **Joseph,** ''Cawdwell,'' where he now lives.
"   son **Emanuel,** 100 A., ''Heriford,'' where he is now seated,
     and dwelling plantation ——.
"son **John,** residue of ''Heriford'' and 100 A., ''Brooks-
     bey's Point.''
"   2 sons, **Augustine** and **Silvanus,** residue of ''Brooksbey's
     Point,'' also 250 A., ''Shepard's Forrest,'' and personalty.
"   John Riggs, 50 A., residue of ''Shepard's Forrest.''
"   Henry Sewell and Wm. Stephens, each 40s.
"   dau. **Anne Gambrell,** £5 and personal estate she is now
     possessed of.
"   dau. **Sarah,** £30.
"   5 sons afsd., residue of personal estate, equally.
Exs.: Sons **Joseph** and **Augustine.**
Test: Peter Porter, Wm. Stevens, Edw. Benson.   15. 1.

Hood, Thos., A. A Co.,   31st Jan., 1718-9;
                                        17th Mar., 1718.

To son **William,** entire estate; to be in care of ex. until of
     age at 18 yrs.
Ex.: Son-in-law **Fardinands Battee.**
Overseers: John Talbott and John Watkins.
Test: Richd. Wigg, John Wooden, P. Thomas.   15. 3.

Tood, Richard, Westminster Parish, A. A. Co.,
                                        10th Oct., 1718;
                                        10th Mar., 1718.

To eldest son **Richd.,** 50 A., ''Whealler's Chance,'' and 75 A.,
     pt. of ''Young Richd.,'' being 2 tracts bou. of **Tytus**
     Peninton. He dying without issue, to son **Lance.**
"   son **Lance,** dwelling plantation ——, at decease of **wife.**
     Shd. sd. son die without issue, to pass to nearest of blood.
"   dau. **Eliza,** silver poringer and £20.
"   dau. **Mary,** £12.
Residue of personal estate to sons **Richard** and **Lance** and
     youngest dau. **Anne.**
* Extx.: Wife **Margaret.**
Test: John Lamb, John Conaway, Saladine Eagle.   15. 4.

———
* Note—10th March, widow claims her thirds.

Martin, James, planter, Charles Co.,   18th Jan., 1711-2; 10th Mar., 1718.

To wife **Eliza,** extx., dwelling plantation ——, during life; at her decease to sons **William** and **James** equally. Son **William** to have first choice. Sons not to dispose of lands unless to each other.

"   son **James,** personalty. Shd. wife **Eliza.** marry, son **James** to be of age at 21 yrs.

"   4 child., **William, Anne, Margaret** and **James** (at wife's decease), residue of personal estate. Shd. any of afsd. child. die before the others, his pt. to be equally divided amongst survivors.

Test: Henry Brett, Thos. Evans, Edwd. Skellden.   15. 6.

Compton (Campton), John, Charles Co.,   29th May, 1713; 5th Mar., 1718.

To eldest son **John,** ⅔ of patten's land, lying both in Charles and St. Mary's Counties, and ⅔ of personal estate.

"   son **Mathew,** ⅓ real and ⅓ personal estate; at decease of sd. sons lands to pass to next heir of them both.

Exs.: Sons afsd.

Test: Philips Briscoe, Sr., John Farfax, Susanna Briscoe.   15. 8.

Hebb, William, St. Mary's Co.,   2nd Oct., 1718; 9th Jan., 1718-9.

To son **William,** dwelling plantation ——, also leased lands and personalty.

"   son **Mathew,** "Small Hogs" at decease of father ——, and personalty. Sons afsd. of age and receive their estates at 20 yrs.

Shd. wife **Priscilla** marry again, to return with husband to her own land, bro. **Thos.** to take 2 sons and their estate and keep them on new dwelling plantation till of age afsd.

Extx.: Wife **Perseller.**

To bro. **Thos.,** overseer, 500 lbs. of tobacco yearly.

Test: Fran. Hopewell, Thomas Hebb, Jr., Susanna Coleman.   15. 10.

Charles Co., **Cathrine Harrison,** relict and widow of **Joseph Harrison,** of Charles Co., gent., dec'd, intestate, renounces right to administer on estate of afsd. **Joseph Harrison.** 12th Feb., 1718.

A. Contee, Richd. Bell.   15. 13.

Fielder (Filder), William, St. Mary's Co.,

                 18th Dec., 1718;
                 24th Jan., 1718-9.

To son **William** and dau. **Mary Lee,** 1s. each.
"   wife **Barbary,** extx., residue of estate.
Test: Richd. Gyles, Darby Carter, John Harwood.   15. 14.

Holbrock (Holbrook), Thomas, gent., Somerset Co.,

                 1st Dec., 1717;
                 24th Nov., 1718.

To son **Thomas,** dwelling plantation ——, on s. side of **Wicka-**
    comoco R.
"   daus. **Martha Brown** and **Sarah Write,** 1s. each.
"   grandsons **Thos. Brown** and **Thos. Wright,** 1 dollar each.
"   son **Thomas,** ex., residue of personal estate.
Test: Joseph Austen, Wm. Harris, Anne Aveten.   15. 15.
Test. shows that at date of probate Joseph Austen and Anne
    Aveten are dec'd.

Larey (Lary), Danll., planter, Allhalloes Parish, Somerset
    Co.,   22nd June, 1718;
                 20th Nov., 1718.

To daus. **Willmoth** and **Mary,** son **Joshua** and William Elliott,
    personalty.
"   daus. **Willmoth,** or **Welmoth,** and **Mary,** extxs., residue of
    estate.
Test: Wm. Tazewell, Francis Allen, Mary Allen.   15. 17.

Bedder, William, Sr., Somerset Co.,   20th Sept., 1718;
                 12th Nov., 1718.

To sons **William** and **Richard,** daus. **Elizabeth Williams** and
    Mary Evans, and son-in-law **Nathan'll Williams,** per-
    sonalty.
"   4 child., viz.: **William, Richard, Elizabeth Williams** and
    Mary Evans, residue of estate, equally.
Exs.: Sons **William** and **Richard.**
Test: Henry Alexander, John Ridgby, Thos. Purnell.   15. 18.

Willson, Alexr., Somerset Co.,   17th Sept., 1716;
                 25th Nov., 1718.

To wife **Jone,** ⅓ of estate.
"   sons **Francis** and **James** and dau. **Anne,** equal parts of
    estate.
"   sons **Francis, Alexr.,** ex., and **James,** personalty.
Test: Eliza: Handy, Willm. Handy, Geo. Full, Willm. Mills.

                                   15. 21.

White, Stevens, of Pocomoke, Somerset Co.,
8th Oct., 1718;
8th Dec., 1718.

To son **William,** personalty, including silver tankard marked
W. W., and ⅔ of personal estate, including ⅔ of debts due
testator. Shd. son die during minority or without issue,
his portion to be divided among **John** (son of bro. ——,
dec'd), **Rose** and **Sarah,** daus. of bro. ——, cousin **Rose**
Drummond and rest of child. of testator's three sisters.
" child. of 3 child., **Tabitha, Precella, Sassiah,** 20s. each.
" wife **Kathrine,** ⅓ personal estate absolutely, and ⅓ real
estate during life.

Exs.: Wife **Kathrine,** Tho. Howard, Col. Wm. Whittington.

Overseers: Bro. **John Watts** and Robert Nane (Naire).

Test: Isaac Piper, Robt. Nairne, Robt. Nairne, Jr. (also
Nearne). 15. 22

Note—8th Dec., 1718. Mrs. Cathrine White renounces as extx.

Round, Willm., marriner, Somerset Co., 12th Jan., 1716-7;
26th Feb., 1718-9.

Testator directs 500 A., "Conveniency," be sold for benefit
of estate.

To son **Edward,** all he has in his poss. at decease of testator,
"Aminedown," testator's share of "Mulberry Grove,"
150 A., "Conveniency," at back of Ephraim Heather's
plantation, house and lot in Snowhill Town, also plate,
not belonging to wife **Mary** at marriage.
" sons **Edwd.** and **James,** lands at seaside Poccomoke,
equally.
" son **James,** house and lot in Greenhill Town, No. 3.

Wife **Mary,** sons **Edwd.** and **James,** exs. and residuary legatees.

Test: Jno. McClester, Neale McClester, Cha. McClester.
15. 25.

26th Feb., 1718-9. **Mary Round** claims her thirds and renounces ex. to **Edward Round.**

Bratten (Brattan), John, Somerset Co., 4th Aug., 1718:
20th Feb., 1718-9.

To son **Saml.,** plantation and personalty.

Wife **Eliza:** extx.

Test: Benj. Scholfield, **Quantan Brattan,** Hugh Nilson (Nelson). 15. 29.

Note—Widow, **Eliza Bratten,** claims her thirds.

Moncester (Mankester), Wm., Charles Co.,

24th Feb., 1718-9;
17th Mar., 1718.

To son **James,** dwelling plantation, 98 A., ''Mankester's Craft.''

''   sons **James** and **William** and daus. **Prudence** and **Mary,** personal estate equally.

Son **James** and dau. **Prudence** to be in care of John Sudfif.
Son **William** and dau. **Mary** to be in care of John Craxson.
Sons to be of age and receive their portion at 18, daus. at 16.

Exs.: Thos. King and Jon. Cooper.

Test: Dan. Jenifer, Mary Ratfif (Ratclief), Eliza: Monkester.
Two last testes. are described as being about 15 yrs.

15. 30.

Neale, James, Jr., Charles Co.,   28th Feb., 1718-9;
13th Mar., 1719.

Testator directs that ½ the profit from his plantation for the year be given to the poor, at direction of Mr. Willm. Hunter, the other half to the Roman Catholic Church.

To widow Ash, John Lancaster, George Newman and bro. **Roswell,** personalty.

Bro. **Raphael** ex. and residuary legatee.

Test: Cuthbert Tompson, John Smith.   15. 32.

Busey, Paul, planter, Prince George's Co.,

24th Sept., 1718;
1st Nov., 1718.

To wife **Sarah,** ''Chas. Hill Land'' and ''Touloon'' during life; at her decease to six sons, viz.: **Paul, John, Chas., Samll., Edwd.** and **Joshua,** equally, the eldest to have first choice. Also residue of personal estate to wife during life; at her decease to be divided equally among all child., both sons and daus. ——.

Exs.: Wife **Sarah,** son **Paul** and bro. **Chas.**

Test: Thos. Blacklock, Benj. Berry, Sr., Edwd. Mobberley.

15. 35.

Miller, George, Prince George's Co.,   —— —— ——;
15th Nov., 1718.

To grandchild **Mary Miller,** 1s.

''   son **Adam,** after decease of wife, personalty and dwelling plantation, 60 A., ——, until grandchild **George Holsill** comes to age of 21 yrs., at which time sd. grandchild is to possess plantation afsd.

To son **Adam,** 440 A. adjoining dwelling plantation, being tract where he now lives.

" grandchild. **George** and **John Holsill, Jr.,** personalty.

" dau. **Ruth Holsill,** 50 A. belonging to plantation where she now lives, and personalty.

" wife **Ruth,** use of dwelling plantation with personalty during widowhood. Shd. she marry, dower rights only. At her decease personal estate to son **Adam** and dau. **Ruth** equally.

Test: John Henrick, John Tatam, Cha. Bullett. 15. 38.

Jones, Morgan, carpenter, of Herring Ck., A. A. Co., 18th Feb., 1717;

To son **William,** 50 A., ——, northern half of tract which belonged to Jenerate Sulivann, divided from the bay to head.

" son **Morgan,** the s. part of afsd. land.

" son **John,** Eglul Island and personalty.

" daus. **Jane** and **Blanch,** personalty.

Son **Morgan** ex. and residuary legatee. 15. 40.

Deposition of **Wm. Jones,** described as eldest son of testator, age about 23.

Deposition of John Standforth, age about 52 yrs. 8th Dec., 1718.

Fisher, William, phisitian, A. A. Co., 26th Mar., 1718; 21st Apr., 1719.

To son ——, dau. **Isabelle** and wife ——, ⅓ personal estate each. Entire real estate to son ——.

Exs.: Maj. John Smith, of Calvert, and Willm. Smith, of Pr. Geo., latter to be guardian of dau. **Isabella** until she attains age of 16 or marries.

Test: Thos. Walker, Chas. Brown, Richd. Hayward (Haywood). 15. 43.

Note—15th April, 1719. John Smith renounces as ex. of will of **Doctor Wm. Fisher.**

Jones, John, of Mattapany, Somerset Co., 29th Mar., 1718; 6th Apr., 1719.

To son **John,** 100 A., "Warsester," and personalty, and handmill after his mother's decease.

" daus. **Grace** and **Eliza:,** personalty.

" son **Giles,** daus. **Mary Walton, Margarett Oydolett, Sarah Walton** and **Sabro Outen,** 12d. each.

Wife —— extx. and residuary legatee.

Test: Ardis Lemmen, Nathll. Brumbill, Christopher Pardice. 15. 46.

Cox, Phillip, Harris Hundred, St. Mary's Co.,
11th Apr., 1714;
20th Mar., 1718-9.

To daus. **Eliza:**, at age of 16, and **Jeane Manghoin,** personalty.
Wife **Mary** extx. and residuary legatee.
Test: Willm. Watts, Anne Watts.   15. 48.

Johnson, Steven, carpenter and cooper, Prince George's
    Co.,
25th Dec., 1718;
20th Mar., 1718-9.

To sons **Jacob** and **Micael,** dwelling plantation ——, equally,
"   son **John,** personalty.
"   son **Andrew** and dau. **Elinor,** after wife's thirds are de-
    ducted, residue of personal estate.
Sons of age at 21 yrs., daus. at 16 or marriage.
Extx.: Wife **Elizabeth.**
Test: James Beal, Thomas Graifan, William Scott.   15. 49.

Clark, William, planter, A. A. Co.,   15th Dec., 1716;
16th Apr., 1718.

To dau. **Elsey,** Thos. Kitely and grandson **John Clark Greace,**
    personalty.
"   daus. **Eliza:** and **Elsey,** residue of estate equally. Thos.
    Kitely to live on dau. **Elsey's** land during his life, and to
    have her in his care till age of 18.
40 A., "Brushey Neck," s. side Maggety R., to be sold for
    benefit of estate.
To Elizabeth Wormesly, her lifetime in the "Great Neck."
Exs.: Thos. Kiteley of Balto. Co., planter, and John Greace
    (Grace), A. A. Co., planter.
Test: Richd. Womsley (Wamsley), Sarah Kitely, Pa. Neale.
15. 51.

In depositions Sarah Wamsley is also spoken of as one of
    other evidences. 3rd Apr., 1718: Exs. resign to Amos
    Garrett, of Annapolis.
Test: Wm. Mead.
Deborah Rawlings, widow of **Richard Rawlings,** dec'd. of A.
    A. Co., assigns adm. of estate to Amos Garrett, of Annap-
    olis. 6th Apr., 1719.
Test: Jos. Young, Amos Woodward.   15. 54.

Gant, Eliza:, Prince George's Co.,   14th Nov., 1717;
9th Mar., 1718.

To mother, **Anne White,** extx., entire estate.
Test: Jon. Smith, John Townley, Phillip Dorsey.   15. 54.

Aisquith, Willm., St. Mary's Co.,   25th July, 1700;
                                              1st Apr., 1719.

To dau. **Eliza,** 220 A., "Well Close," on Patuxent R., above
    Joseph Edlos' quarter, and personalty.
    "   son **Thos.,** 200 A., "Hunting Neck," bou. of Thos. Hat-
    ton, and pt. of mill on sd. land, bou. of Jno. Price, and
    personalty.
    "   son **William,** 100 A., "Hickory Hills," joining "Chan-
    cellar's Manor"; 120 A., "Beaver Dam," and personalty.
    "   youngest son **George,** dwelling plantation ——, after his
    mother's decease.
    "   dau. **Frances,** wife of **Thos. Loker,** personalty.
    "   4 child., viz.: **Eliza:, Thos., William** and **George,** person-
    alty at age of 18.
Tract ——, Gunpowder R., Balto. Co., to be sold to purchase
    servts.
Wife —— extx. and residuary legatee, to expend 1 hhd. of
    tobacco in gloves for neighbors and friends.
Overseer: Thomas Grunwin, to render account of debt and
    clerk's fees necessary.
Test: Nich. Richardson, Gilbert Tervervild (Terbifield), Roger
    Tolles, Abraham Rhodes.   15. 55.

Turlo (Turloe), William, Queen Anne's Co.,
                                              2nd Feb., 1716;
                                              8th Apr., 1719.

£100 for erection of a church at head of Wedge R., on s. side
    of a branch running up to Wedge Mill and nr. old church.
To Wm. and Eliza: Dawson and Mary Allens, personalty.
    "   Ralph Dawson, dwelling plantation ——, and personalty.
    "   goddau. Eliza: Emerson, £100 and personalty.
    "   sister ——, £10 yearly, during life.
Maj. Thomas Emerson ex. and residuary legatee.
Test: Val. Carter, Thos. Price, Margarett Smith, Arthur Emory,
    Edmd. Thomas.   15. 59.

Arland, William, Queen Anne's Co.,   26th —ber, 1718;
                                          15th Apr., 1719.

To Edward Jones, Sr., ex., ½ of testator's share in estate of
    father **Ralph Arland,** and the right to administer on sd.
    estate.
    "   Edward, son of Edward Jones, Sr., remaining half of
    share in sd. estate.
Test: Geo. Holliday, John Rozier, Thos. Parrare, Den. Sulli-
    vane.   15. 61.

King, Juliana, Queen Anne's Co.,   18th Sept., 1718:
                                            26th Feb., 1719.

To eldest dau. **Sarah** and dau. **Sophia,** personalty and residue
    of estate, with exception of legacy to granddau. **Anne
    Merredith,** which she is to receive at age of 16 or mar-
    riage.

William and Eliza: Turbot to have care of child. until age
    of 16 or day of marriage.

Ex.: Bro. **Arthur Emory.**

Test: Willm. Merredith (Merideth), James Cross, Thos. Jones.
                                                    15. 63.

Fellengame (Fillengame), Richard, Kent Co.,
                                            13th Jan., 1717:
                                            17th Mar., 1718.

To wife ——, extx., use of entire estate during widowhood,
    then to 3 child., **Richard, John** and **Sarah,** equally.

"   son **Richard,** 50 A., ——.

Test: Wm. Croree, Thos. Joce.   15. 65.

Spinke, Henry, planter, St. Mary's Co.,   6th Jan., 1718-9:
                                            ——— ——— ———.

To son **Clement,** pt. of "Gilmort's Fields," beginning about
    the middle of gr. marsh next Court House (for desc. see
    will); 100 A., "Spinkies Rest," in forest by John Heard's,
    69 A., "The Adjoyner," and personalty.

"   Ann Grasty, a pt. of afsd. "Gilmort Hills," providing
    her huband, Samll. Grasty, shall take no care or notice
    of her. Shd. sd. Samll. die, to sd. Anne during widowhood,
    and personalty.

"   son **Henry,** residue of "Gillmorts Hill," including that
    pt. bequeathed Anne Grasty afsd.; 290 A., ——, in the
    forest next to Walter Davises, and personalty.

"   dau. **Leocresia,** 50 A., "The Branch," and personalty.

"   daus. **Henrieta** and **Monica,** personalty.

"   2 nieces, **Margarett** and **Mary,** 119 A., "Hickory Hollow."

"   Thos. Walker, about 50 A. conveyed to father, **Henry
    Spinke,** dec'd, by John Shirclef, Jr., dec'd.

"   bro. **Francis,** ex., about 14 A., "Dividing Hills," pt. of
    which tract was sold to Jno. Cissell and pt. to Thos.
    Walker.

Personalty divided among all child. Sons to receive portions
    at 21, daus. at 18.

To Scieatie, last assistant living at Clem Town, 500 lbs.
    tobacco. Shd. there be liberty to rebuild St. Ignatius
    Chappell, 1,000 lbs. towards the work; otherwise 200 lbs.
    tobacco for pailing a graveyard for own family.

To 5 child. afsd., residue of estate.

Test: Wm. Yeates, David Castlea, Robt. Salleman, James Thompson.   15. 66.

Spink, Francis, St. Mary's Co., 30th Jan., 1718-9; 4th Mar., 1718.

To dau. **Cathrine,** land on s. side of line established by testator (see will), being pt. of ''Farney Hill,'' and personalty.

" dau. **Teclo,** pt. of afsd. tract (for desc. see will), and personalty.

" unborn child, residue of afsd. tract and ''Devidiug Values.''

" children afsd., residue of estate.

Extx.: Wife **Eliner.**

Test: Jno. Farr, Wm. Yates (Yeates), Chas. Neale.   15. 71.

Lawton (Laton, Latton), Thos., St. Mary's Co.,

—— —— ——; 4th Mar., 1718.

To sons **Jno., Thos.** and **Joseph,** daus. **Mary** and **Anne,** personalty.

" servt. Aaron Nesley, liberty to enstock children, and personalty when at liberty.

Extx.: Wife **Jemine.** Should she marry again, sons to be free at 18; if she remains a widow, to be free at age of 21.

Test: Alex. Clealeand, Luke Wheeler.   15. 74.

Doagan, Jno., St. Mary's Co., 11th Dec., 1718; 5th Mar., 1718-9.

To dau. **Mary,** personality.

" 3 sons, **William, Jno.** and **Thos.,** and dau. **Mary,** residue of personal estate equally.

Sons to remain with ex. until 21 yrs., dau. until 16 yrs. of age.

Ex.: Jno. Heard.

Test: Jno. Love, Jno. Jarbo, Wm. Heard.   15. 76.

Jessup (Jesup), Joseph, St. Mary's Co., 26th Dec., 1717; 4th Mar., 1718.

To wife **Mary,** extx., entire estate.

Test: Gerard Slye, Alex. Clealeand.   15. 77.

Lord, Edwd., St. Mary's Co., 31st Dec., 1718; 4th Mar., 1718.

To James Swan, ex., entire estate.

Test: Thos. Chambers, Eliza: Farmeorth (Farmleorch). 15. 78.

Lloyd, Edward, Talbot Co.,   15th Mar., 1718;
8th Apr., 1719.

To wife **Sarah,** dwelling plantation ——, and land belonging thereto during life (excepting plantation Four Hundred Acres), at her decease to son **Philemon.**

" son **Edward,** "Thrimby Grange," "Marsgate," "Nathaniell's Point" and "Roadway," with all other lands in White House Neck, or Woolman's Neck, lying **w.** of "Thrimby Grange."

" dau. **Rebecca,** 400 A., "Darland," at hd. of Wye R., 1,000 A., "Lloyd Town," at hd. of Chester R.

" son **James,** "Darby," at mouth of Langford's Bay, Chester R., and tract adj., lately bou. of Joseph Milby.

" son **Richard,** 3 tracts at head of St. Michael's R., nr. Jno. King's, being forest plantation, and "Stock Range," at Davis's Bridge.

" **Philemon** afsd., residue of real estate.

£50 towards building a church in St. Michl. Parish, n. side of St. Michl. R., at Dundee.

To each bro. and sister ——, a mourning ring, value 20s.

" wife **Sarah,** extx., personalty and ¼ of plate, remaining ¾ to 5 child. afsd., equally, and to divide with afsd. child. residue of personal estate.

" overseers, Robert Gouldesborough and bro.-in-law **Matthew Tilgman Ward,** £10 each.

Test: Hen. Nicholes, Edward Brinkworth, Thos. Crouch, Thos. Lindy (Linday).   15. 80.

Pigman, John, Prince George's Co.,   10th Oct., 1712;
27th Oct., 1712.

To wife **Sarah,** extx., dwelling plantation ——, during life.

" youngest son **Mason** and hrs., 50 A. adj. and sd. plantation at decease of his mother. Shd. sd. son die during minority and without issue, his portion to pass to testator's other child. by present wife.

" dau. **Mary Mason** and hrs., 37 A., ——, where Anthony Long lives.

" eldest son **John,** 50 A. adj. tract bequeathed dau. **Mary.** Shd. son **John** die during minority or without issue, sd. 50 A. to dau. **Mary** and hrs.

" daus. **Elizabeth, Grace, Catherine** and **Ann,** personalty.

Test: Fran. Clarvo, Robt. Wade, William Hunter.   15. 83.

Smith, John,   15th Apr., 1710;
                                      28th Mar., 1718.

     To bro. **John Sumerland,** bro. **James,** sister **Margaret Summerlin** and sister **Mary,** personalty.

     `` Hannah Gauslin, 4s.

     Ex.: ——.

     Test: Thos. Johnson, Rachel Roberson, Jasper Wood.   15. 85.

Payne, Isaak, St. Mary's Co.,   14th Mar., 1712-3;
                                      28th Mar., 1713.

     To son **Thomas** and hrs., dwelling plantation ——; he dying without issue, to 2 daus., **Hannah** and **Sarah,** and their hrs.; also personalty. Son to be of age at 18.

     `` 2 daus., **Hannah** and **Sarah** afsd., and their hrs., tract in Courseys Neck, "Riders" and "Broadneck," equally. Shd. either die without issue, portion of deceased to survivor; shd. both die without issue, to pass to son **Thomas.**

     `` 3 child. afsd., residue of personal estate. Dau. **Hannah** to care of son **Thomas** so long as she is lame and unmarried.

     Ex.: Richd. Griffen.

     Test: Wm. Johnson, John Langley, John Mackintosh, Wm. Nouland.   15. 86.

Lee, Samuel, planter, St. George's Hundred, St. Mary's
     Co.,   16th Nov., 1706;
                                      29th Apr., 1713.

     To wife ——, ⅛ personal estate.

     `` son **Luke,** ex., residue of personal estate.

     Overseer: Thos. Griffen. In event of his death, Richard Griffen to act.

     Test: Jon. Miller, Wm. Johnson, Anne Miller, Rebecca Miller.   15. 89.

Adderton, Jeremiah, gent., St. Mary's Co.,
                                 11th Apr., 1713;
                                 19th May, 1713.

     To wife **Mary,** extx., ⅓ personal estate.

     `` unborn child at age, £50.

     `` son **James,** residue of estate.

     Test: Jno. Seager, Henry Jeniugs.   15. 90.

Smith, Philomon, A. A. Co.,   6th Mar., 1712-3;
                                     27th Mar., 1713.

     To wife **Anne,** extx., entire estate.

     Test: Wm. Rowles, Sarah Maynard, Eliza Cronch.   15. 92.

Williams, Thomas,   1st Mar., 1712-3;
                                         —— —— ——.

To son **Thomas Short,** personalty.
" son **John,** personalty and plantation ——, at end of 5 yrs.;
    until then to be in care of his bro., **Thomas Short.**
" Jane Ellis, extx., dwelling plantation, "William's Folly."
Test: Thos. Burch, Robt. Mahaine, Robt. Saint Clare.   15. 93.

Mark, John, planter, Baltimore Co.,   21st May, 1711:
                                           17th Nov., 1712.

To Dorothy and hrs. (dau. of George and Jane Hall), entire
    personal estate.
Ex.: Landlord Martin Taylor.
Test: Jeremiah Downes, Jno. Rawlings and Dorothy, his wife.
                                                    15. 95.

Hadder, Woring, planter, Somerset Co.,   8th Jan., 1718;
                                              6th Apr., 1719.

To son **Woring,** plantation ——, and 100 A.
" son **Anthony,** 100 A., ——.
" dau. **Mary,** 1s.
" sons **Woring** and **Anthony** and dau. **Sarah,** residue of estate
    at decease of wife ——.
Exs.: Wife —— and son **Woring.**
Test: John Bassett, Thos. Nathaniell Williams, Robert Hodge
    (Hogg).   15. 97.

Marrett, William, planter, Dorchester Co.,
                                               5th Mar., 1718-9;
                                               9th Apr., 1719.

To eldest son **John** and son **William,** use of personalty until
    21 yrs. of age.
" wife **Philies,** extx., residue of estate.
Test: Isaac Nicols, Jno. Dawson, Jno. Richardson, Denis
    Mackartey.   15. 99.

Sparrow, Thos., Road R., A. A. Co.,   10th June, 1713;
                                           12th May, 1719.

To sons **Solomon** and **John** and their hrs., "Crany Island."
    North Carolina.
" son **Kensey** and hrs., 145 A., part of "Sparrows Rest,"
    Road R., bou. of Mary Francis, sold by testator's father
    ——, to Thos. Francis. Sd. son not to sell land. Should
    he die during minority, sd. land to pass to unborn child,
    if a son, otherwise to son **Solomon;** and shd. he die during
    minority, to son **Thomas.**

To son **Kensey** and unborn child (if a son), land on Dere-
ham's Ck. in Pamplicoe, North Carolina. Shd. unborn
child be a dau., sd. lands to son **Kensey.**
" daus. **Eliza:, Matilda** and unborn child (if a dau.), land
on Dividing Ck. in Pamplicoe, N. C., equally.
Residue of personal estate to child., equally.
To sons **Thomas, Solomon, John** and **Kensey** and unborn
child (if a son), all rights and interests in any lands
hereafter descending to testator.
" son **Solomon** and hrs., ground in Rathtown, Pamplicoe,
being front of Simond Alderson's, and bou. of him.
" son **John,** lot adj. sd. front.
" son **Kensey,** lot adj. afsd. lot.
" son **Thomas,** personalty.
Exs.: Wife **Anne** and bro.-in-law **Capt. Richard Jones.**
Test: Jno. Taylor, Henry Mace, Danl. Fowler, Ann Fowler.

15. 101.

Yopp, Charles,   5th Jan., 1717;
21st Apr., 1719.

To father **Roger Yopp,** personalty.
Testator directs that legacies left in his hands by his grand-
father, **Jno. Alward,** be delivered to **Sarah** and **Jane Yopp**
and Dorothy Brown.
To wife ——, extx., residue of estate.
Test: Stephen Mankin, Jno. Goley, Margaret Mankin.

15. 105.

Jenkins, Thomas, wheelwright, Talbot Co.,
22nd Apr., 1719;
19th May, 1719.

To eldest son **Mattheu,** young. son **Walter,** and dau. **Margaret
Barrett,** personalty.
" 2 sons, **Mattheu** and **Walter,** exs., residue of personal
estate.
Son-in-law **Thomas Barrett** to have charge of son **Walter** until
16 yrs. of age.
Test: Wm. Thomas, **Thomas Barnett, Sen.,** Howell Powell.

15. 106.

Taylor, James, Talbot Co.,   8th Nov., 1718;
19th May, 1719.

To sons **James** and **Thomas** and their hrs., dwelling plantation ——, equally, division to be made when eldest son
James is 21 yrs. of age.
" son **Joseph,** 100 A., "Taylor's Chance," Tuckahoe, at
age of 21.

To dau. **Elizabeth,** personalty at age of 16 or marriage.
" wife **Isabel,** extx., ⅓ of estate; residue to child. equally.
Shd. afsd. child. die during minority or without issue,
survivors to divide portion of dec'd.
Overseer: Thomas Adkinson.
Test: Dens. Hopkins, John Tate, Catharine Harris.   15. 109.

Browne, John, St. George's Parish, Spesutie Hund., Baltimore Co.,   14th Jan., 1715;
16th May, 1716.
To son **Thomas** and hrs., dwelling plantation, 500 A., "Cheinton."
" son **Augustus,** 150 A., "Cooks Cove," Swann Ck., and
118 A., "Hopp," lying bet. the lands of Capt. Thos.
Stockett and "Bourn," the rights to sd. land to be made
over to son **Augustus** by Antho. Drew and Margaret, his
wife. Shd. son **Augustus** die without issue, sd. lands to
pass to son **Gabriel** and hrs.
" son **Gabriel** and hrs., 400 A., "Brown's Entrance,"
Swann Ck.
" wife **Eliza:,** extx., ⅓ of estate; residue of personal estate
to 3 child. afsd. Son **Thomas** to pay to his two bros. £20
each at age of 21 yrs.
Child. not to sell any pt. of estates till of age at 21 yrs.
Test: John Stokes, Hez. Haynes, Garrett Garretson.   15. 111.

Lowe, Anne, late of St. Mary's Co., now of Prince George's
Co.,   14th June, 1718;
23rd May, 1718.
To bro. **Nicholas Lowe,** 500 A., pt. of "Golden Grove" (cont.
1,500 A.), Dorset Co.
" sister **Jane** (wife of **Mr. James Bowles**), 25s. for mourning ring.
" sister **Dorothy,** £100 and personalty at age of 16 or marriage.
" **Mildred** (wife of Denis Mehony), of St. Mary's Co., £5.
" sisters **Susanna Maria Diggs, Elizabeth** and **Mary,** bros.
Henry, Bennett and **Nicho.,** godson **Henry Diggs** (2nd son
of sister **Susanna Maria Diggs,** afsd.), residue of estate,
equally.
Testatrix desires to be buried according to rites of Roman
Catholic Church.
Exs.: Bros. **Henry** and **Bennett.**
Test: Luke Gardiner, Benj. Wheeler, Eliza: Wheeler.   15. 115.

Robins, Thomas, carpenter, Prince George's Co.,
22nd Feb., 1718;
4th Apr., 1719.

To dau. **Elizabeth** and to each boy ——, personalty when they attain legal age.

Exs.: Wife —— and bro. **James.**

Test: John Halkmer, Robt. Clyd.

Note—7th March, 1718. **Elinor** and **James Robins,** within named exs., relinquish adm. of sd. will, and surrender same to testator's greatest creditor.

Test: Robt. Clyd, John Queen.   15. 117.

Webb, Richard, planter, Talbot Co.,   6th Jan., 1718;
16th June, 1719.

To Tuckahow Meeting, £10 or personalty.

" wife **Rebecca,** extx., entire estate, real and personal, during life, testator's mother, **Eliza: Meares,** to have maintenance out of estate. Should wife marry contrary to advice of Quakers, to have her thirds only, the residue to **James, Richard** and **Park Webb** (sons of bro. **John**) and Rebecca Carwick, equally. Shd. wife afsd. remain a Quaker, at her decease the entire estate to be divided among the four above named, or to their guardians to be delivered to them as they come of age or marriage.

" nephew **Richard** afsd. and hrs., dwelling plantation, 150 A., "Highfields Addition," and the adj. 130 A., "Barrys Range." Shd. he die without issue, then to **James Webb;** he dying without issue, to **Park Webb.** Shd. all three die without issue, the above lands to their next heirs.

Testator desires John Stephens, of Talbot Co., to take all goods belonging to Francis Wason & Co., merchants, in London, and dispose of them for their best advantage.

Test: Thomas Berry, Richard Dudley, Thos. Dudley, George Bowes.   15. 119.

Turbervile, Gilbert, St. Mary's Co.,   1st Dec., 1718:
15th June, 1719.

To St. Innigoes Church, £10.

" **Margaret Cavinaugh** and John Bemberige, 10s. each.

" grandson **William Cavinaugh,** entire personal estate.

Vitus Harbert ex. and guardian to grandchild. **William** and **Margaret Cavinaugh** afsd.; after his decease, William Tompson to act.

Test: Robt. Haking (Hackins), Henry Chandler, Francis Moacrinick.   15. 122.

Turner, Edward, Sr., planter, Talbot Co.,

29th May, 1716;
16th June, 1719.

To grandson **Thomas Spurier,** 40 A., ——, adj. portion bequeathed son **Joseph.**

" 5 sons, **William, Edward, Thomas, John** and **Joseph,** residue of lands, in all about 400 A. Son **Joseph** to have dwelling house and orchard. None of them to sell lands, excepting to each other.

" wife **Anne,** use of plantation ——, during life, and entire personal estate absolutely.

Exs.: 2 eldest sons, **William** and **Edward.**

Test: Eliza: Rassom (Russam), Mary Turner, Geo. Bowes.

15. 124.

Kendeloe, Thomas, St. Mary's Co.,   18th May, 1719;
2nd June, 1719.

To godson Thomas Addersson, 1s.

" John, ex., Thomas and Joanna Jeane, entire estate.

Test: Richd. Gattes, Jno. Bullock, James Vowles.   15. 127.

Smith, William, planter, A. A. Co.,   21st Mar., 1718-9;
18th June, 1718.

To dau. **Eliza:,** £100 at marriage. Sh. Dr. Wm. Fisher die, not having pd. testator for 100 A., "Turkey Hill," then sd. land to dau. **Eliza:** at day of marriage in lieu of the £100 bequeathed her, and personalty. Shd. dau. afsd. die before marriage, or leave no issue, sd. money or land to wife **Anne** during life; at her decease to bro. **Henry Atwood.**

" dau. **Mary Knight** and James Henson, personalty.

" wife **Anne,** residue of personal estate during life; at her decease to bro. **Henry** afsd.

Exs.: Wife **Anne** and bro. **Henry Atwood.**

Test: Francis Crandle (Candle), Ester Crandle, Wm. Fish.

15. 129.

King, John,   18th Feb., 1718;
23rd May, 1719.

To bro.-in-law **Hugh Hopewell,** personalty.

" child. **Hugh** and **Jane,** residue of estate, equally, at age of 21 or marriage.

Hugh Hopewell ex. and guardian to child. afsd.; at his decease, **Charles** and **Edward King** to act.

Test: Robt. Clarke, Sr., Jno. Winsett, Peter Jarboo (Jarboe).

15. 133.

Harwood, Jno., A. A. Co.,

19th Dec., 1713;
16th July, 1719.

To wife **Mary**, extx., entire estate.

Test: Phillip Jones, Thos. Rockhould, Andrew Johnson, Mary
Climps. 15. 135.

Note—Within named **Mary**, now wife of Edwd. Comegies,
makes oath that she knows of no later will than above.

Husband, William, Cecil Co.,

25th Mar., 1717;
8th May, 1717.

To sons **William** and **Thomas**, dwelling plantation, cont. 2
tracts, "Stillington" and "Chaunce" (160 A. and 65 A.),
conveyed by Mr. Edw. Warner, of London, and personalty
and the new house, to contain certain personalty, including some belonging to child. of **Thos. Scorry**, until son
Wm. arrives at age of 21.

" son **Thomas**, personalty.

" son **James**, 200 A., "Scanterbury."

" sons **William** and **Thomas** and dau. **Hannah**, exs., residue
of personal estate, equally. Shd. son **William** die without
issue, his portion to pass to son **Thomas**. Should they both
die without issue, their portions to 2 grandsons, **Thos.
Scurre** and **Jno. Husband.**

Test: Thos. Marcer, Cathrine Dawson, Benj. Pearce. 15. 137.

Head, William, Prince George's Co.,

14th June, 1718;
5th June, 1719.

To son **Bigger** and daus. **Mary, Ann** and **Katherine**, personalty.

" dau. **Charity** and hrs., "William and Ann" and land bou.
of Rich. Weaver, cont. in all 232 A. Shd. she die without
issue, to dau. **Mary** and hrs.

" unborn child, 412 A., "Red House." Shd. sd. child die
without issue, to daus. **Ann** and **Katherine**, equally.

" wife **Ann**, extx., unborn child —— and dau. **Charity**, residue of estate..

Test: Levin Covington, Weldon Jefferson, Jno. Wall, Jas.
Gibson.

Note—Codicil, 1st Sept., 1718. Tract in Calvert Co. sold to
John Mortemore and not made over to him, testator directs his extx. to make over to hrs. of sd. Mortemore.

Test: Weldon Jefferson, Robt. Hall, Jno. Wall. 15. 140.

Blangey, Jacob, Kent Island, Queen Anne's Co.,
1st Mar., 1715-6;
1st June, 1719.

To sons **Lewis** and **Jacob** and their hrs., dwelling plantation "Cilley," equally, at age of 21. Shd. either die without issue, portion of deceased to survivor. Shd. both afsd. sons die without issue, sd. land to sons **Charles Merriken** and **John Wells.**

" 2 sons, **Charles Merriken** and **John Wells,** and their hrs., 550 A., "Upper Deal," equally, at age of 21. Shd. either of sd. younger sons die without issue, survivor to inherit portion of deceased. Shd. both die without issue, "Upper Deal" afsd. to sons **Lewis** and **Jacob** and their hrs.

" Nathaniel Connor and godsons Charles Griffins and William Rakes, Jr., personalty.

" wife **Elizabeth,** extx., entire personal estate for maintenance of child., viz.: **Lewis, Jacob, Charles Merriken, John Wells, Mary** and **Elizabeth,** each to have 2 or 3 yrs. schooling. Sons of age at 18, daus at 16 or marriage.

Test: Wm. Rakes, Timothy Macartley, John Boucher. 15. 143.

Watts, Peter, gent., St. Mary's Co.,
12th Mar., 1718;
27th July, 1719.

To grandson **Thomas** and hrs. (son of **Thomas Waughap),** two tracts, "Bennets Delight" and "Jenifer's Gift," at decease of wife ——. Shd. sd. grandson die without issue, lands to pass to **James** and hrs. (son of **James Watts);** shd. he die without issue, sd. lands to pass to next male hr. of dau. **Mary Waughap,** and she lacking such issue, to revert to rightful hrs. of testator.

" 2 granddaus., **Elizabeth Waughop** and **Hannah Clarke,** 1 pistole each, to be sent to Annapolis for purchase of rings.

" wife ——, extx., use of dwelling plantation and estate during life. Shd. sd. wife be disturbed in possession of same (inasmuch as sd. plantation belonged to former wife ——), to have use of other two tracts during life, she being an aged woman; the personalty on sd. tracts at her decease to sons-in-law **Thos. Waughop** and **George Clark,** trustees, equally, for use of grandchild ——.

" wife ——, £20 and use of mother's great ring during life; at her decease to return to dau. **Waughop.**

Test: Maj. **Wm. Watts,** Archbald Johnstone, **George Clarke,** Richard Forrest. 15. 147.

Note—Codicil: To bro. **Stephen Watts,** Richard Forrest and Maj. **Wm. Watts,** personalty.

Bell, Adam, St. Mary's Co.,   21st Nov., 1718;
                                                          30th Dec., 1718.

To wife **Ann,** extx., estate real and personal, during life.
   Shd. she not accept the same, then ⅓ personal estate
   absolutely; also "Paradise," up the River, St. Mary's Co.
"   sister **Margaret Hackney** and hrs., dwelling plantation,
   "St. Richard's Mannor."
"   cousin **Margaret Hunter** (dau. to sister **Margaret** afsd.),
   part of "Hampstead," nr. Chesapeack Bay.
"   nephew **Richard,** son to **Richard Hopewell, Sr.** (bro. of
   testator's wife), and godson Adam King, personalty.
"   cousin **Thomas Hunter,** 1s.
"   cousin **John Critchett** and hrs., "Scotch-Mans Wonder"
   and "Shirley's Point."
Samuel Grasty to live on plantation during life.
Test: John Seager, Charles King, Samuel Grasty.   15. 152.

Paul, Jacob (late of Boston, New England), Dorchester
   Co.,   28th July, 1719;
                                                          22nd Aug., 1719.

To son ——, 10 A., pt. of "Gahead."
"   2 bros., **Joseph** and **Peter,** exs., and their hrs., residue of
   "Gahead" and 100 A., "Pawquapsie," equally, and personalty; also tract "Tuscatacat," they to pay bal. of the
   price of sd. land to Isaac Pamatuck, also to John Ottis
   £5, and other debts.
"   John Petuxet, personalty, including a gold ring and wages
   due from Capt. John Motton.
"   sister **Martha,** £10.
"   landlady Dorcas ——, personalty.
Test: John Lawson, Govert. Lockerman, Sarah Lockerman,
   Mary Eccleston.   15. 155.

Smyth, Thomas, Kent Co.,   30th June, 1718;
                                                          4th Aug., 1719.

To son **Thomas** and hrs., dwelling plantation, being pt. of
   "Trumping," "Smyths Meadow" (excepting pt. hereafter
   bequeathed), "Ratcliff Cross," "The Addition" on s.
   side of Davies' Ck., and "Smyths Venture," on both
   sides afsd. ck.; also lot in New Yarmouth, on Grasin Ck.,
   adjoining Mr. Tovey's.
"   dau. **Martha** and hrs., land bou. of Mr. Neatkin, being
   a pt. of "Hinchingham," and "Smyth's Desert," excepting 100 A. joining where John Griffith is now seated,
   which 100 A. testator bequeaths to sd. John Griffith and
   Mary, his wife, during their lives.

To son **Thomas** and dau. **Martha,** pew in St. Paul's, Kent Co.
" Jane Coursey, pt. of "Smyth's Meadows" (for desc. see will), during life; shd. she have child., to them and their issue. When all are extinct sd. land to revert to son **Thomas** afsd. and hrs. Sd. Jane to pay Proprietary Rent and other charges.
" George Hanson, 600 lbs. tobacco for like sum had of Maj. Pott on his acc't.
" John Griffith, tobacco due testator.
" wife **Martha**, extx., dwelling plantation ——, and "Smyth's Meadow" during life, or half "Ratcliff Cross" during life. She to make a choice when son arrives at age of 18; and ⅓ personal estate.
Plantation, 150 A., Langford's Bay, being pt. of "The Plaines," for use of a free school in the Parish of St. Paul's, Kent Co. When no schoolmaster lives on it, wife to let any poor man or men live thereon till a schoolmaster comes; after wife's decease son **Thomas** to do same; after decease of both, the Vestry to do same forever.
Overseers: Thomas Bordley, James Harris and Col. Edward Scott.
Test: Wm. Granges, Josiah Lanham, David Read.   15. 159.

Medford, Thomas, planter, Kent Co.,   15th Sept., 1718;
24th June, 1719.
To son **Thomas** and hrs., 200 A. with dwelling plantation ——.
" 3 sons, **Bullwin, Maccall** and **George,** and their hrs., residue of above tract, with 50 A., "Magyes Joynter," equally. Sons not to sell lands excepting to each other.
" dau. **Rachell,** tobacco sent to England by Capt. Landon and consigned to Thomas Bond, mcht., in London.
" wife **Rachel**, extx., use of dwelling plantation, and, with child., residuary legatee of personal estate.
Test: Abraham Redgrave, Sr., Richard Hennard, James Course, Jr.   15. 166.

16th Dec., 1718.
Elizabeth Griffith, wife of **Samuel Griffith,** dec'd, being part admin. of will of afsd. dec'd, makes son **Samuel** lawful hr. of her part of husband's will.
Test: Tho. Smith, Joseph Smith, Joseph Smith, Jr.   15. 169.

Deed of Gift from **Elizabeth Griffith,** Calvert Co.,
17th Dec., 1718;
—— —— ——.

Son **Samuel** to pay following gifts after decease of **Elizabeth Griffith:**

To Elizabeth Miles, Mary Bowers, Sarah Devall, Rebecca Mobley and Rachel Giles, personalty.

Note—Signed **Samuel Griffith,** obliges himself and hrs. to comply with above gifts.

Test: Tho. Smith, Joseph Smith, Joseph Smith, Jr.   15. 170.

Sedwicks, Elisha, Calvert Co.,   13th May, 1719;
                                                                              26th June, 1719.

Wife **Grace,** extx., sole legatee.

                                                                                      15. 171.

Hamilton, Andrew, Prince George's Co., 23rd Oct., 1718;
                                                                    24th June, 1719.

To wife **Mary,** extx., ⅓ estate, real and personal, during life, residue to child —— and unborn child ——. Division to be made by James Stoddert and Thomas Addison, overseers.

Test: Hon. Thos. Addison, Jos. Belt, Henry Crampton, Ann Renshaw.   **15. 172.**

Bowen, David, Calvert Co.,   4th May, 1717;
                                                                              27th June, 1719.

To wife **Elizabeth,** extx., personal estate absolutely, and dwelling plantation, 300 A., "Norton," on Battle Ck. during life; at her decease to lawful hrs. of testator.

Test: John Derrumple, Jno. Brooke, Alphonso Cosden, James Deavour, Sarah Brook.   15. 175.

Brook, Richard, St. Mary's Co.   5th Dec., 1718;
                                                                      3rd Aug., 1719.

To wife —— and 2 child., ——, entire personal estate.

" 2 sons, **Richard** and **Baker,** pt. of Dellebrook Mannor, wife —— to have use of dwelling plantation —— during life.

" child. of uncle, **Leonard Brook,** dec'd, any interest testator may have in land of sd. uncle, in Mannor of Dellebrooke or elsewhere (excepting "Hardship," on n. side of branch running from Charles Ashcombs to ext. line of Mannor), to be holden of them and their hrs.

Bro. **Leonard** ex. on behalf of 2 child., and wife —— extx. in her own part.

Test: Robert Elliot, William Cabinet, John Farnile.   15. 178.

Chiseldyne, Kenelm, St. Mary's Co.,   4th Jan., 1717-8;
                                            29th Jan., 1717;
                                            29th May, 1719;
                                            5th June, 1719.

 To wife **Mary,** extx., her thirds.
  " younger son **Cyrenius,** 20,000 lbs. tobacco for purchase of
   land.
  " godson Kenelm Bolt, personalty, to be applied in his education.
  " James Robertson and Joseph Owen, personalty.
  " 3 child., ——, residue of estate, equally.
 Overseers: Bros.-in-law **T. Truman Greenfield** and **Hen. Peregrine Jowles,** and guardians to child.
 Test: Wm. Groome, Thos. Boult (Bolt), Wm. Hooke.
 Note—Codicil, 23rd Jan.: To niece **Mary Hay,** 1,000 lbs. tobacco yearly until her marriage.
 Test: Wm. Coode, Thos. Boult.   15. 181.

Bickerdike, Richard (nunc.), Annapolis, A. A. Co.,
                                            30th Aug., 1719;
                                            30th Sept., 1719.

 To wife ——, extx., use of estate during life; at her decease
  to child ——.
 Test: Thomas Williams.   15. 185.

Reed, Walter, Somerset Co.,   29th Dec., 1716;
                                    6th Apr., 1719.

 100 A., "Taunton," to be sold for benefit of estate.
 To son **Walter,** dau. **Mary** and dau. —— of dau. **Elizabeth,**
  dec'd, personalty at decease of wife.
  " wife ——, extx., residue of estate.
 Test: Jno. Purnell, Francis Harper, Jonathan Hutson, **Pearce**
  Reed.   15. 186.
 Note—3rd Aug., 1719. Within named extx., **Easter Reed,** being
  unable, on account of age and infirmities, to execute above
  will, resigns same to son, **Pierce Reed.**

Brown, John, Somerset Co.,   6th Oct., 1718;
                                   17th June, 1719.

 To dau. **Elizabeth,** personalty; to be in care of William Colbrune. Son **Tarell** to care of John Fountain until of age.
  " son **Alexander,** £5; to be in care of Nicholas (son of **Mary**
   Fountain).
  " son **George,** £10; to be in care of Mary Fountain, Sr.
  " 4 child. afsd., residue of estate. Should any of them die
   during minority, survivors to inherit portion of deceased;
   shd. all 4 die, estate to Nicholas, John and William, sons
   of Mary Fountain, extx.
 Test: Mary Fountain, James Cambell, John Smith. 15. 190.

Fall, Abraham, tanner, Somerset Co.,　　16th Apr., 1718;
　　　　　　　　　　　　　　　　　　3rd July, 1719.

To son **John,** 100 A., ——, on Green Branch, and personalty.
" son **Abraham,** 150 A., —— plantation, and personalty.
" dau. **Mary,** personalty at age of 15.
" wife **Mary,** extx., residue of personal estate.
Test: Nath. Rackliff, Jr., John Turvile, William Collings.
　　　　　　　　　　　　　　　　　　　　15. 193.

Taylor, Abraham, Baltimore Co.,　　—— ——, 1717;
　　　　　　　　　　　　　　　　　6th Aug., 1719.

To son **John,** ex., and hrs., 100 A., "Ayes' Addition."
" sons **Abraham** and **John** and dau. **Lettice Dottrage,** personal estate, equally.
Test: Henry Wetherall, Andr. Durgee, Josiah Tompson, Zachariah Keadle.　　　　　　　　　　15. 196.

Barron, John, planter, Charles Co.,　　14th Sept., 1718;
　　　　　　　　　　　　　　　　　　19th Aug., 1719.

To sons **John** and **Thomas,** personalty at age of 21.
" son-in-law **John Watters,** personalty.
" wife **Ann,** extx., residue of estate.
Test: John Manning, Adam Clinkscales.　　　　15. 198.

Boye, Jane, widow, Charles Co.,　　28th July, 1719;
　　　　　　　　　　　　　　　　　21st Sept., 1719.

To dau. **Elizabeth,** personalty at age of 18 or day of marriage.
" 5 sons, **Pigeon, John, Thomas, Abraham** and **Bowman,** residue of personal estate. Shd. any of sd. sons die before age of 18, their portion to pass to dau. **Elizabeth.** Shd. sd. dau. die before age of 18 or marriage, her portion to be divided among survivors.
Ex.: Son **Pigeon.**
Test: Thos. Evans, Anne Evans.　　　　　　15. 200.

Dare, William, Sr., Cecil Co.,　　18th Mar., 1718-9;
　　　　　　　　　　　　　　　　13th Aug., 1719.

To son **William,** personalty and debts due from Robert Smith and **William Dare,** of West Jersey.
" granddau. **Margaret Larramore,** personalty at day of marriage.
" dau. **Mary Thompson,** extx., use of dwelling plantation —— until son **William** shall put plantation where he now lives in good repair to amount expended by **John Thompson** on dwell. plant. afsd., and residue of personal estate.
Test: Francis Mauldin, John Manly, Easter Davis, Nicholas Hyland, Wm. Warram.　　　　　　15. 203.

Smith, John, blacksmith, Pr. Geo. Co.,   8th July, 1718;
                                            10th Aug., 1719.

To wife **Elizabeth,** extx., entire estate during widowhood;
  at her marriage to 2 child., **John** and **Margaret.**

"   dau. **Mary Townley,** 1s. Neither she nor her husband,
  Jno. Townley, to have any further share in estate.

Test: P. Dorey, William Welch.   15. 205.

Smith, Renatus, Queen Anne's Co.,   2nd Apr., 1719;
                                       16th June, 1719.

To Deborah Brown, pt. of "Bramton" (for desc. see will),
  and personalty.

"   dau. **Mary,** all lands not otherwise bequeathed; sd. lands
  not to be sold by Richard Cole nor Mary, his wife.

"   Ann Butler and hrs., 300 A., "Winnfield," in Tulley's
  Neck, formerly owned by Robt. Smith.

"   Solomon, Jr., and hrs. (son of Solomon and Rachel Clayton), 100 A. adj. sd. Clayton's plantation, formerly belonging to Robt. Smith (made over to testator by act of
  assembly).

"   Solomon Clayton, ex., use of dwelling plantation for 1 yr.
  and 1 day.

Test: William Shepard, Ann Marshall, Martha Collins.

                                            15. 207.

Eareckson, Charles, Kent Island, Queen Anne's Co.,
                                            30th Dec., 1718;
                                            27th May, 1719.

To 3 sons, **Mathew, John** and **Benjamin,** real estate, equally.
  Sons not to dispose of lands, except to each other.

"   wife **Elizabeth,** extx., use of dwelling plantation ——
  during life.

Test: John Hutchins, Thomas Williams, Geo. Comerford.

                                            15. 209.

Gardiner, James, innholder, Prince George's Co.,
                                            27th Sept., 1717;
                                            10th Oct., 1719.

To wife **Mary,** entire estate.

Ex.: Phillip Lee, of afsd. Co., mercht. Shd. he refuse, John
  White of same Co.

Test: Wm. Turner, Sam'll Heighe, John Ansloe.   15. 211.

Jones, Jonathan, A. A. Co., 2nd Oct., 1719; 5th Nov., 1719.

To son **Thomas** and hrs., dwelling plantation, being pt. of "Paschall's Purchase." He dying without issue, to pass to issue of following: Dau. **Mary,** son **John,** son **Lewis;** these all failing issue, to hr. at law.

" 3 sons afsd., **John, Lewis** and **Jonathan,** and their hrs., 100 A., "Quick Sale." No land to be sold so long as any of testator's posterity be alive.

" dau. **Mary,** £10 at age of 16 or marriage.

" wife **Mary,** extx., £10; she and child. afsd. residuary legatees of personal estate.

Overseer: Alexander Rosenquist.

Test: Henry Hall, John Gray, William Roberts, Francis Taylor.
15. 214.

Pearce, Williams, A. A. Co., 12th Sept., 1719; 19th Oct., 1719.

To 2 sons, **William** and **John,** and their hrs., real estate, equally. Shd. either son die before division leaving issue, sd. hrs. to have an equal right with surviving son. Sons to be for themselves at 16 yrs.

Wife **Elizabeth,** extx., to bring up child. and give them, at age of 21, their lawful share of personal estate.

Overseers: Nephews **Thomas** and **William Tipton.**

Test: Rev. Henry Hall, John Stevens, Susanna Wanill.
15. 217.

Stevens, Sarah, Talbot Co., 18th of 4th mo., June, 1719; 21st Sept., 1719.

To dau. **Magdalen Maud,** £30.

" dau. **Sarah Webb** and son **John** and wife, 4 granddaus. (unnamed), granddau. **Sarah Webb** and grandson **Thomas Stevens,** personalty.

" **Elizabeth** (widow of **Wm. Stevens**), £10.

Son **John** and dau. **Sarah Webb** exs. and resid. legatees.

Test: Henry King, John Mears, William Warner. 15. 220.

Tiler, Thomas, Talbot Co., 28th July, 1719; 7th Aug., 1719.

To son **Jonathan** and hrs., entire real estate and personalty.

" dau. **Martha,** personalty.

Son and dau. afsd., residuary legatees of personal estate, and in care of Edward Turner. Son to have schooling and be of age at 21.

Ex.: Edward Turner. In event of his death, Richard Cribb to act.

Test: John Hammitt, Thomas Buckingham, Katharine Buckingham.   15. 223.

Wilmote, John, Sr., Baltimore Co.,   15th Sept., 1719;
                                             5th Nov., 1719.

To wife **Jane** (or **Jean**), dwelling plantation ——, during life;
  at her decease to grandson **John Wilmote** and hrs.; he
  failing issue, to grandson **Richard Wilmote.**
  "   wife **Jane** and sons **John** and **John Ashman,** personal es-
       tate, equally.
  "   servant Thomas Bevans, 1 year of his time.
  "   grandson **John Wilmote,** personalty; he being but a child,
       choice to be made for him by ex.
Ex.: Son **John.** Shd. he die, son-in-law **John Ashman.**
Test: George Walker, John Brooks, Rebecca Tayler.   15. 226.

Barratt, Edward, —— Co.,   26th Aug., 1719;
                                          1st Sept., 1719.

To relation **John Barratt,** ex., the care of wife —— and 2
  child., **John** and **Peter,** until they arrive at age of 21.
Test: Peter Garratt, Joseph Stratfoord, Richard Poore.
                                                      15. 230.

Hutchings, Frances, St. Mary's Co.,   1st June, 1719;
                                             25th Sept., 1719.

To sister **Katharine Hassell,** personalty and land bequeathed
  testatrix by will of father —— (with consent of bro.
  Robt., sd. land not being divided).
  "   bro. **William,** personalty.
  "   bro. **Robert,** ex., personalty in possession of Jonathan
       Gurr and 14s. in Wm. Ennises hands.
Test: William Wilkeson, Jr., Robt. Clark, Jr., Richard Os-
  berne.   15. 231.

King, Henry, tailor, Talbot Co.,   21st Feb., 1718;
                                             12th Dec., 1719.

To Joseph and hrs. (son of Peter and Sarah Webb), "Kings
  Misfortune," Dorchest Co.
  "   Sarah Webb, Jr., personalty.
  "   Sarah Webb, Sr., extx., and hrs., "Barnstaple," in Dor-
       chester Co., "Phillip's Range" and "Lawyers Discovery."
       Shd. it be necessary, sd. Sarah Webb to sell some or any
       part of above land for payment of debts; also to her, en-
       tire personal estate.
Test: Henry MaGowen, Edward Davis, Barbara Burroughs.
                                                      15. 234.

Gittings, Mary, Talbot Co., 20th Oct., 1718;
18th Aug., 1719.

To dau. **Sarah Lovdy,** personalty.

" son **Edward Harding,** ex., residue of estate, real and personal.

Test: Andr. Alden, Sarah Hurlock, John Kenedy. 15. 236.

Forrester, Peter, A. A. Co., 26th Nov., 1719;
14th Dec., 1719.

To John Rooxbey, personalty when free.

Wife **Mary,** extx., residuary legatee.

Test: Daniel Machee, John Elder. 15. 239.

Preston, John, planter, A. A. Co., 19th Aug., 1719;
18th Dec., 1719.

To son **William** and dau. **Margaret Childe,** 5s.

" dau. **Elizabeth Trott** and hrs., dwelling plantation, "Bersheba." Shd. she die without issue, sd. plantation to pass to son **William** and dau. **Margaret Childe,** equally.

Ex.: Son-in-law **Thomas Trott.**

Test: Henry Childe, Jr., John Brown, Wm. Ludwigg, Mary Skinbnor. 15. 241.

Ogilvie, Patrick, Boston, N. E., mercht., Annapolis,
3rd May, 1714;
14th Oct., 1719.

To mother, **Anna Tyry,** in North Brittain, £20.

" each bro. and sister ——, now living, 12d.

" wife **Margaret,** extx., and hrs., residue of estate, real and personal. Shd. sd. wife now be with child, testator directs that sd. child shall receive at 21 yrs. one portion of estate, real and personal.

Testator states that being employed by and concerned in disposal of a cargo of merch's. in N. E., but rendered incapable of pursuing the sd. voyage, he empowers friend John Weakfild to act in sd. venture, and confirms to him for his own use all profits, commissions, etc.

Test: Benjamin Fordham, Lydia Fordham, W. FitzRedmond. 15. 243.

Lowe, Elizabeth, widow, Talbot Co., 20th June, 1719;
11th Nov., 1719.

To son **Nicholas** and male hrs., "Anderton" and "Anderton's Addition," on Treadhaven Ck. He dying without such issue. sd. tracts to the male hrs. of son **Vincent;** both afsd. sons lacking male issue, then in succession to the female hrs. of sd. sons. Shd. sons die without issue, sd. tracts to revert to dau. **Mary Bozman** and hrs. Also to son **Nicholas** and hrs., Hunting Ck. mill; he dying without issue, to son **Vincent.**

To son **Vincent** and hrs., "Lower Plantation," now in tenure of David Mills and William Mathews. Sd. son dying without issue, to dau. **Dorothy Harrison** and hrs. Also "Tack's Point," excepting 1 lot in Oxford (bet. lot where Judith Robinson dwelt and John Oldham's lot), which is bequeathed to David and hrs., son of David Robinson.

" dau. **Sarah Pattison,** 100 A. of "Anderton" convenient to her now dwelling plantation during life; at her decease to her son **William Long** and hrs. He dying without issue, to her son **Thomas Long.** Shd. both afsd. grandsons die without issue, sd. land to revert to son **Nicholas** and hrs.

" dau. **Elizabeth Combs** and hrs., residue of "Todcaster." She dying without issue, to pass to dau. **Prudence Price,** having already given her the other pt. of "Todcaster."

" grandson **William Combs** and hrs., land on Choptank R. and Island Ck., where Elinor Cranley and Darby Barrett now dwell.

" dau.-in-law **Judith Robinson,** "Long Point," joining "Anderton," during life; at her decease to her son **Edward Combs** and hrs.

" grandson **John Glen** and hrs., tract on Treadhaven Ck., ——, adj. "East Otwell," bou. by testator's father, **Edward Rowe,** of Nicholas Hackett, dec'd.

" each of daus., viz.; **Elizabeth Wood** and **Dorothy Harrison,** £15.

" sons **Nicholas** and **Vincent,** residue of personal estate. Son **Nicholas** to have water mill in Dorchester Co., at head of Hunting Creek, and tankards engraved with coat of arms of dec'd husband, **Nicholas Lowe.**

Exs.: Son **Nicholas** and friend David Robinson.

Test: Anne Mathews, Solomon Robinson, William Woods, Foster Turbutt.   15. 248.

Bond, Richard, Calvert Co.,   7th day, 6th mo., 1719;
                                       16th Nov., 1719.

To son **Richard** and hrs., land ——, conveyed by Elisha Hall and Sarah, his wife.

" son **Benson** and hrs., land ——, conveyed by Benj. Hall and Mary, his wife.

" son **Thomas** and hrs., land ——, bou. of John Smith, of Coxtown, and Dorothy, his wife.

" son **John,** land on e. side of Ridge path, conveyed by Sabrett Sollers and Thos. Holdsworth, except that pt. of "Holdsworth" on e. side main Branch, which is bequeathed to Sabrett Sollers and his hrs.

To son **Phinehas,** 2 shares of personal estate. Shd. any of sons die without issue, portion of dec'd to pass to son **Phinehas.**

" 5 child., viz.: **Richard, Sarah, Benson, Thomas** and **John,** residue of personal estate.

Extx.: Wife **Elizabeth.**

Test: Richard Stallings, Mary Chew, Elizabeth Restell.

15. 254.

Glanvill, William, Kent Co., 22nd Jan., 1718; 17th Oct., 1719.

To son **William** and hrs., 100 A., ——, at mouth of Langford's Bay. He dying without issue, to 2 daus., **Rachel** and **Martha,** and their hrs., equally.

" son **John** and hrs., 196 A. on bayside ——. He dying without issue, to sons **William, Nathaniel** and **Stephen,** equally. Shd. all sons die without issue, sd. lands to revert to daus. afsd. Son **John** to pay to sons **Nathaniel** and **Stephen,** at age of 21, 2,000 lbs. tobacco each.

" sons **Nathaniel** and **Stephen** and hrs., 200 A., ——, bou. of Wm. Blay, equally. Shd. both sons die without issue, sd. land to daus. afsd.; also dwelling house and other houses and lots in Chestertown, equally.

" wife **Mary,** ⅓ personal estate, residue to afsd. six child., equally. Shd. all 6 child. die without issue, real estate to revert to cousin **Sarah** (dau. of **James Smith**).

Ex.: Son-in-law **Thomas Piner.**

Test: David Macbride, Saml. Smith, Sarah Smith. 15. 257.

Sullivane, Denis, Kent Co., 6th Nov., 1719; 18th Nov., 1719.

To wife **Agnes,** extx., "Jones Fancy," s. side Chester R., Queen Ann's Co., she to pay debts of testator. Shd. **wife Agnes** fail to do so, sd. plantation to be sold for payment of same.

" Mary Burk, £30.

" David Kimball, 3 yrs. schooling and personalty, provided he stays with testator's wife till 21 yrs. of age.

Test: Wm. Comyers, Sr., Timothy Kesey, John Withington, John Macnemara. 15. 261.

Note—John Wetherington deposes that abt. the 6th day of Nov. last Dennis Sulivant signed, pub. and declared a will, and testes. to same were William Comyers, Timothy Kesey, John Machemara, with deponent. Sullivants bequeathed his plantation in Queen Ann's Co. to wife **Agnes** and hrs. She to pay his debts. If she thought not fit to pay same, plantation to be sold to pay debts. Sworn 28th March, 1720.

Hall, Robert, gent., Prince George's Co.,   4th Dec., 1719;
17th Dec., 1719.

To wife **Elizabeth,** ⅓ estate.
"   Benjamin Allen, £30.
"   Josiah Wilson, personalty.
"   serv't Richard Chubbard, his freedom and personalty.
James Haddock and Weldon Jefferson exs. and residuary
legatees.
Test: Anne Head, Mary Head, Bigger Head.   15. 263.

Hemsley, Philemon, Queen Anne's Co.,   14th Apr., 1719;
7th Nov., 1719;
10th Nov., 1719.

To child. **William** and **Anne,** certain negroes and residue of
estate on Eastern Shore.
"   wife **Mary,** certain negroes and residue of personal estate
on Western Shore, with debts due on Eastern Shore to
estate of Col. John Contee, of Charles Co., dec'd, viz.: from
Philemon Lloyd, John Bozman, ex., and Thomas Kellton,
of Cecil Co. Also share from cargoes held in partnership
with Jonathan Forward, mercht., of London, with management of same. Sd. bequests in lieu of any claim against
estate on Eastern Shore.
Debts contracted by testator concerning estate on Eastern
Shore to be pd. by exs. appointed for management of estate
on that Shore, viz.: Robert Noble and son **William.** All
rest and residue of debts, due in England or on Western
Shore relating to wife's dealings when in England or
concerning her proper estate, or that of Col, John Contee,
be pd. by extx. for her estate on Western Shore, viz.: wife
Mary. Shd. she refuse executorship and legacies, Thomas
Boardley, Esq., to act in her place.
Son to be of age at 18.
Test: Rich. Cotton, Geo. Constable, David Lindsay, Mary
Owens.   15. 266.

Note—Codicil, date afsd. To dau. **Anne,** pt. of "Towten-
fields" at hd. of Choptank R., Queen Ann's Co., bou. of
Renatus Smith, and formerly laid out for Col. **Vincent
Lowe.**

Cross, Elinor, A. A. Co.,   23rd Oct., 1719;
2nd Nov., 1719.

To dau.-in-law **Mary Cross,** extx., and hrs., "Ferry Point" on
Baldwin's Ck. (for desc. see will), dwelling house and
personal estate.

To sons **Joshua** and **Thomas Cross**, residue of ''Beard's Dock.'' Shd. son **Thomas** die without issue, his portion to pass to Jacob, son of John Lusby. Shd. **Joshua** afsd. die without issue, his portion to Jacob Lusby afsd.

'' dau. **Priscilla Fowler**, personalty.

Debts contracted with Saml. Young and Joseph Hill to be satisfied out of rents.

Test: Saml. Warner, Stephen West, Jane Sardy, Elizabeth West. 15. 273.

Rose, Mary, Chaptico Hundred, St. Mary's Co.,
10th Mar., 1716-7 ;
18th Dec., 1719.

To grandson **John Johnson Sothoron**, ex., 200 A., dwelling plantation ——, during term of lease.

'' grandsons **Harman Clarke** and **Samuel, Richard** and **Benjamin Sothoron**, at age of 18, and granddaus. **Ann** and **Mary Sothoron** at marriage and dau. **Mary Clarke**, personalty.

'' dau. **Mary Birch,** 3 dollars, ''current money of this province.''

Test: Sam. Williamson, Michael Brantson, John Brantson. 15. 276.

Clark, Thomas (nunc.), St. Mary's Co., 6th Nov., 1719 ;
10th Nov., 1719.

To wife **Mary,** what she had at marriage and use of real estate during widowhood. Shd. she marry, sd. lands to bro. **John.**

'' William Gardiner, personalty.

'' chapel at Mrs. Jean Doyne's. (Legacy not indicated.)

Test: John Clark, about 30 yrs. old. 15. 280.

Jackson, Barbara, widow, Queen Anne's Co.,
3rd Feb., 1717-8 ;
28th Jan., 1719.

To son **George,** 1s., and to his son **Thomas,** personalty.

'' dau. **Elizabeth Jonings,** 1s., and her son **John** and her dau. **Barbara,** personalty.

'' dau. **Barbara Hyett** and her sons **Thomas** and **Henry Richardson** and her dau. **Barbara Hyett,** personalty.

'' 2 sons, **Francis** and **Joseph,** exs. residue of personal estate, equally. Son **Francis** to have first choice and 2,000 lbs. tobacco out of his bro. **Joseph's** part.

Test: Tho. Townson, Jacob Ratliff, Tho. Jones. 15. 281.

Hissett, Elinor, Kent Co.,   20th Jan., 1719-20;
                                                  5th Feb., 1719.

To son **Philip,** daus. **Rose, Johanna** and **Elinor; Ann Hissetts;**
   Thomas Butler and Thomas (son of Ann Bush), personalty.
Exs.: Richard Holmstead and Thomas Hunter.
Test: Anne Bush, Richd. Holmstead, T. Hunter.   15. 283.

Hissett, Philip, Kent Co.,   23rd Sept., 1713;
                                                  5th Feb., 1719.

To wife **Elinor,** entire personal estate.
   "   son **Philip,** 100 A., ''Downdale,'' after death of wife
        Elinor. He to be of age at 16.
   "   dau. **Elinor,** ''Strickland's Rest'' after death of her
        mother, **Elinor.** She to be of age at 16. Shd. she die
        without issue, sd. land to pass to next hr. of blood. Shd.
        son **Philip, Jr.,** afsd. die without issue, his portion to
        pass to **Johanna Hissett.**
   "   daus. **Jane** and **Elizabeth,** 1s. each.
Test: Richard Holmstead, Margaret Flanesey.   15. 285.
Note—5th Feb., 1719. Richd. Holmstead deposes that he did
   write a will at request of above **Philip Hissett** on the back
   of a deed of sale made from Eliza: Beven to sd. **Philip
   Hissett,** dated as above, which sd. will by bad usage is
   almost unintelligible, but corresponding word for word
   with above copy.

Chiley, Samuel, Calvert Co.,   10th Oct., 1719;
                                                  1st Feb., 1719.

To **Mary** and hrs. (dau. of **Thomas Marshall** and **Margaret,**
   his wife), dwelling plantation ——, being pt. of ''The
   Defence.'' She dying without issue, sd. plantation to
   Thomas and hrs. (younger son of the afsd. **Thomas** and
   Margaret Marshall).
   "   Elizabeth Bowen, personalty.
Ex.: Son-in-law **Thomas Marshall.**
Test: Thomas Joys, Deborah Cody, **Margaret Marshall,** Robt.
   Wood.   15. 286.

Johns, Richard, Calvert Co.,   6th day, 5th mo., 1719;
                                                  14th Dec., 1719.

To wife **Priscilla,** extx., 1 pt. of dwelling plantation, ''Triller,''
   during life; at her decease to eldest son **Richard** and hrs.,
   he to possess the other pt. of sd. tract when of age, and
   personalty.
   "   son **Abraham** and hrs., pt. of ''Letchworths Chance,''
        cont. 300 A.
   "   Friends of the Western Shore, £3.

Wife and child. residuary legatees of personal estate.
Sons to be of age at 18.
Testator desires to be buried at The Clifts burying ground
by father ——.
Test: George Harris, Joseph Harris, Isaac Johns. 15. 288.

Berry, Benjamin, Prince George's Co., 7th Nov., 1719;
10th Feb., 1719.

To wife **Mary**, extx., ⅕ of personal estate (excepting tobacco
consigned to Mr. Hunt, merch't, in London), absolutely,
and dwelling plantation during life.
" eldest son **Benjamin** and hrs., dwelling plantation ——,
at decease of wife. Shd. sd. son die before his mother,
sd. plantation —— to pass in succession to following:
Son **Jeremiah**, dau. **Mary** and dau. **Verlinda**; also to son
Benj. and hrs., 800 A., "Thompson's Choice" Baltimore
Co., pt. of "Long Lane" (pt. east of plantation where
Geo. Bankes now lives) and "The Chance."
" 2 sons, **Benjamin** and **Jeremiah**, and their hrs., lot No. 14
in Marlborough Town, equally, and personalty.
" **Thomas** (son of Benj. Long, dec'd), 50 A., pt. of "Charles
and Benjamin," next to the line separating Charles Bell's
land from testator's, conditionally ——.
" dau. **Verlinda** and hrs., 140 A., "Charles and Benjamin,"
adj. 50 A. bequeathed Thomas Long, and personalty.
" son **Jeremiah** and hrs., remaining pt., 900 A., of "Charles
and Benjamin," also 340 A., pt. of "The Levell."
" Capt. Thomas Claggett and hrs. (at request of son-in-law
Richard Keene), 70 A., pt. of "Long Lane."
" eldest dau. **Mary** and hrs., "Evan's Range" and personalty, 5 yrs. after decease of testator.
" Baruch Williams and hrs., 200 A., part of "The Levell's."
Son **Jeremiah** to be for himself at 18 yrs.

Residue of personal estate divided among 4 child. afsd.; dau
Mary to receive hers at age of 16 or day of marriage;
son **Benjamin** at expiration of 5 yrs.; shd. he die before
that time, his personal estate to be divided among surviving child. of testator. Son **Jeremiah** to receive his
portion at age of 21, or sooner if he seats his land; shd.
he die during minority, his portion of real and personal
estate to testator's surviving child. Shd. wife **Mary** die
before child. arrive at ages afsd., son **Benjamin** to take
charge of them and their estates.
Overseers: Samuel Magruder, Thomas Hillary, Edward Willett,
John Cleggatt.
Test: John Clegatt, Charles Beavan, John Adams. 15. 289.

Jeanes, Joseph, Prince George's Co.,   14th Jan., 1719-20;
                                              19th Feb., 1719.

To sons **Joseph, Edward** and **William,** daus. **Mary** and **Ann,**
  personalty.
Sons to be of age at 18.
Wife **Elizabeth** extx. and residuary legatee.
Test: Francis Tolson, Edward Hollingsworth, Joseph Woodro.
                                                    15. 295.

Lee, Winifred (nunc.), Charles Co.,   7th Dec., 1719;
                                             ⸺ ⸺ ⸺.

Child. (unnamed) to care of Thomas Jameson, who is to receive personal estate of testator and her husband, and
  retain same until child. are of age to receive their portions. Child. to be brought up Roman Catholics (courts
  allowing).
Test: Ann Heathcot.   15. 297.

Brett, Henry, Charles Co.,   ⸺ ⸺ ⸺;
                                          8th Dec., 1719.

To Ann Booker and Elizabeth Noble, personalty.
  "   son **Richard,** "The World's End," "The Addition" and
      personalty at death or marriage of his mother ⸺.
  "   son **George,** "Southrich," "Bretts Addition," and per-
      sonalty.
  "   wife ⸺, extx., her thirds. Residue of estate to child.
      ⸺, equally. Sons afsd. to receive each 3 yrs. schooling.
Bro. **George** guardian to child.
Test: Thos. Price, Margaret Blackester, Francis Dunnington, Jr.
                                                    15. 297.

Harrison, William, planter, Talbot Co.,   22nd Jan., 1719:
                                              2nd Feb., 1719.

To wife **Frances,** "Rowclift," bou. of Walter Proctor, during
  life. Shd. sd. wife be now with child, to pass at her decease to sd. child; and to sd. child, if a son, 116 A., "Popler Levell," at Bever Dams (bou. of Richard Turner).
  Also to wife **Frances,** ⅓ personal estate.
  "   dau. **Rachel** and hrs., 200 A. of "Fearborrough" in the
      fork of Tuckaho, Queen Ann's Co., to adj. land of Charles
      Channer and Richard Bennet, Esq.
  "   dau. **Elizabeth** and hrs., 200 A. of same tract, adj. pt.
      bequeathed dau. **Rachel.**
  "   dau. **Ann** and hrs., 200 A. of same tract, adj. pt. be-
      queathed dau. **Elizabeth.**
  "   cousin **Jeremiah Jadwin, Jr.,** and hrs., 200 A. of same tract,
      adj. pt. bequeathed dau. **Ann.**
  "   John Keeas, planter, of Kent Co., 125 A., ⸺, in Kent
      Co. (bou. of Wm. Barker), he to pay exs. £20 and 3,500
      lbs. tobacco before 10th Apr. next.

To son **William** and hrs., residue of lands.

"   4 child., viz.: **William, Rachel, Elizabeth** and **Ann,** ⅔ personal estate, equally.

Exs.: Wife **Frances** and son **William.**

Test: Samuel Dickinson, Charles Hill, Judith Dickinson, Peter Sharp.   15. 299.

White, Richard, Talbot Co.,   13th July, 1719;
                                                              23rd Feb., 1719.

To 2 sons, **William** and **James**, entire real estate, equally. Son **James** to have dwelling plantation ——.

"   2 daus., **Elizabeth** (wife of **William Aires**) and **Mary** (wife of **Benjamin Ballock**), 1s each.

"   grandson **James** (son of dau. **Mary** afsd.), personalty.

Exs.: Wife **Elizabeth** and sons **William** and **James.**

Test: John Barnyeatt, Wm. Foreman, Terence Connelly.

                                                              15. 302.

Luke, Isaac, planter, —— Co.,   29th Aug., 1718;
                                                              10th Dec., 1719.

To dau. **Amy** and hrs., 200 A., ——, in Northampton Co., Charek Neck, on n. side Honggos Ck., and personalty at age of 16.

"   wife **Mary**, extx., residue of personal estate.

Test: Nath'll Rackliffe, Jr., John Turville, John Peety.

                                                              15. 304.

Kellam, John, Sr., Somerset Co.,   30th Sept., 1719;
                                                              15th Mar., 1719-20.

To son **John** and hrs., 600 A. dwelling plantation ——, bou. of Joseph and James Gray.

"   grandson **John** (son of son **William**), 150 A., pt. of "Kellams Choice" (the e. pt. of sd. tract), provided sd. grandson or his hrs. shall not possess any of afsd. tract of 600 A. bou. of Joseph and James Gray.

"   dau. **Mary**, personalty.

"   5 daus., **Sarah Nicholson, Charity Johnson, Anne Coard, Eliza: Marron, Catherine Taylor,** 5s. each.

"   son **John**, ex., res. of estate, including 300A., remaining pt. of "Kellams Choice." Shd. son **John** die without issue, sd. land to grandson **Joshua** and hrs.

Test: John Gunby, John Benson, Alice Jones.   15. 306.

Kirk, John, planter, Annamessex Hundred, Somerset Co.,
                                                              18th Oct., 1718;
                                                              15th Mar., 1719-20.

To John Gunby and John Kellam and to grandson **Wm. Beaven.** 1s. each, which shall debar them and their heirs from all claim against estate.

To wife **Bridget,** extx., and dau. **Sarah,** entire personal estate, equally, at day of dau.'s marriage. Wife to enjoy lands till dau.'s marriage and afterwards the ½ thereof during life; to pass at her decease to dau. **Sarah.** Shd. sd. dau. die without issue, her portion of personal and real estate to wife **Bridget,** absolutely.

Test: Antho. Bell, Thos. Bell, John Benson.   15. 308.

Richie, David, Somerset Co.,   8th Dec., 1719;
                                            17th Mar., 1719-20.

To Robert Nairne, Jr., and his bro., James Nearne, entire estate.

Test: David Dreadin, Thos. Benston, Edw. Peacocke. 15. 311.

Sanders, Mathew, Sr., Charles Co.,   19th Dec., 1719;
                                            20th Feb., 1719-20.

To grandson **Robt. Roberson** and hrs., 100 A., dwelling plantation, "Prickard." Shd. he die without issue, sd. plantation to pass to 2 sons, **John** and **William.**
  "   son **John** and hrs., 30 A., "Sander's Folly."
  "   eldest son **Mathew,** half a crown and personalty.
  "   dau. **Margt. Ward** and hrs., 83 A., ——, whereon they now live.

Wife **Elinor** extx. and residuary legatee.

Test: **James Ward,** Richard Houldin, James Simson. 15. 313.

Short, George, planter, Charles Co.,   17th Oct., 1718;
                                            4th Mar., 1719.

To wife **Anne,** extx., dwelling plantation ——, and personal estate during life; at her decease to be divided bet. son **Daniel** and dau. **Eliza: Dent.**
  "   son **Daniel** and hrs., 60 A., "Smith's Purchase"; he dying without issue, to dau. **Elizabeth Dent** and hrs.
  "   son **George** and dau. **Elizabeth Dent,** 50 A., "Simpson's Supply" during their lives; after their decease to grandson **George Short** and hrs. Shd. he die without issue, to dau. **Elizabeth** afsd., absolutely.

Test: John Bucknam, John Cadell, Susanah Bucknam. 15. 315.

Dawson, John, gent., St. Michael's Parish, Talbot Co.,
                                            20th Nov., 1719;
                                            22nd Mar., 1719-20.

To wife **Anne,** extx., dwelling plantation ——, with ½ land adj., and personalty during life.
  "   son **John,** entire real estate (pt. bequeathed wife during her life excepted), and personalty. Shd. son **John** die without issue, entire estate to wife **Anne** and hrs. Shd. she die without issue, sister **Susanah** and hrs. to have ½ dwelling plantation ——.

Overseers: Jacob Gibson, Sr., Woolman Gibson.

Test: Lewis Jones, Jacob Gibson, Woolman Gibson.   15. 318.

Note—Vide further probate, Lib. 20, page 172, anno 1731.

Jones, Samuel, Somerset Co.,　　　　11th Oct., 1719.
　　　　　　　　　　　　　　　　　1st Mar., 1719-20.

To son **Lewis** and hrs., land at Rock Ck. ——, now in his possession, also 300 A. of Marsh.

" 　son **Roland,** 150 A. belonging to dwelling plantation ——,
with 30 A. of that at Rock Ck. during life; at his decease
to son **Lewis** and his son **John** and hrs., and personalty.

" 　son **John** £100. Shd. he die without issue, to son **Lewis.**

" 　**Catherine** (dau. of son **Lewis**), personalty, and servant
Anne English ½ yr. of her time.

" 　dau. **Mary,** 1 piece of gold.

Son **Lewis** ex. and residuary legatee.

Test: William Polke, Charles Williams, Wm. Pollett.   15. 321.

Reves (Rives), Thomas, planter, St. Mary's Co.,
　　　　　　　　　　　　　　　　8th Dec., ——;
　　　　　　　　　　　　　　　　7th June, 1719.

To son **Ubgate,** ex., and hrs., dwelling plantation ——, personalty and proper share of personal estate.

" 　son **Thomas** and hrs., 100 A., "Walles," personalty and
equal share of personal estate with rest of children.

" 　son **William** and hrs., 100 A., "Leeth."

" 　dau. **Anne Hoskins** and grandson **Thomas** (son of son
Ubgate), personalty.

" 　wife **Mary,** use of dwelling plantation ——, during widowhood.

Test: John Hoskins, Saml. Maddox, Jr., John Ireland.

　　　　　　　　　　　　　　　　　　　　15. 323.

Nicholson. William, mercht., A. A. Co., 25th Sept., 1719;
　　　　　　　　　　　　　　　　19th Oct., 1719.

To son **William** and hrs., 1,000 A., "Poplar Neck," Baltimore
Co., and 2 lots in Londontown, A. A. Co., bou. of Thos.
Holland and Mahittable Pairpoint.

" 　son **Joseph** and hrs., 3 tracts, viz.: 298 A., "Batchelors
Delight," 702 A., "Clerk's Directions," in A. A. Co., and
400 A., "Lockwood's Adventure," in Baltimore Co.; and
also 1 lot in Londontown, taken up by Capt. Richard
Jones, dec'd.

" 　sons **Benjamin, Samuel and Edward** and their hrs., testator's pt. of Nicholson's Manor, Baltimore Co., cont.
4,200 A.

Friends James Monat, Stephen Warman, James Nicholson and Jno. Beale, exs. of estate in Maryland, or any two of them, are empowered to make over in fee to purchasers, following tracts, viz.: part of ''Covell's Troubles,'' ''Rockey Point,'' pt. of ''Covells Cove,'' ''Turkey Island,'' pt. of ''Michells Chance,'' ''Puddington,'' pt. of ''Puddington Harbor,'' ''Elk Thickett,'' ''Williams Addition'' and ''Poplar Neck,'' all in A. A. Co., to be sold with personalty thereon for benefit of personal estate.

To son **Benjamin** and hrs., 1 lot in London Town, next lot now belonging to Turner Wooten (originally taken up by Capt. Edward Burgess).

''   servt. James Nicholson, £5 and personalty formerly belong. to Samuel Burgess.

''   sons afsd., entire personal estate, equally. Plate to be sold by exs. in Md. Money from personal estate and lands directed to be sold to be remitted by exs. in Md. to Wm. Hunt, mercht., in London, for use of sd. children. Child. left to the care of sisters **Mrs. Elinor Foster, Mrs. Anne Nicholson** and **Mrs. Eliza: Nicholson** till of age. In case of death of any two of sd. sisters, Wm. Hunt to have care and tuition of sd. child.

Sisters afsd. and Wm. Hunt, exs. of estate in Great Brittain.

Exs. in Maryland: James Monat, James Nicholson, Stephen Warman, John Beale.

Test: John Arnold, Wm. Simme, Marg. Kinnerstone.   15. 325.

Conyer, Henry, planter, Dorchester Co.,   9th Mar., 1718-9;
                                          22nd June, 1719.

To wife **Sarah** and her child. by testator, if any, entire estate, and for want of such issue, dwelling plantation, 150 A., ''Sarah's Delight,'' to be divided equally bet. wife ——, Isaac Anderson and Katherine (dau. of Daniel Crowen by his 1st wife). Wife **Sarah**, extx., to have 58 A., ——, with improvements on it, and to make over to Lewiston Abitt and hrs., accord. to bond, the ½ of 400 A., ''Hills Neck,'' Talbot Co., bou. of Edward Hill (for desc. see will).

Test: James Anderson, Miles Johnins, Margt. Anderson.

                                                    15. 330.

Cullein, James, Dorchester Co.,   20th Oct., 1719;
                                           4th Apr., 1720.

To mother ——, 300 A., ''Bells Gift,'' Patuxent R., Pr. Geo. Co.
Test: John Cullen, **William Cullin,** Thos. Reed.   15. 332.

Hart, Arthur, planter, Dorchester Co., 11th Jan., 1719-20;
8th Mar., 1719.

To son **Robt.,** "Hog Quarter" and lower pt. of "Hart's Content" on s. e. side of Jacob Pateson's path (for desc. see will), to be in custody of son **Richard** and wife **Elinor** (during her widowhood) until appearance of son **Robt.** afsd. Shd. son **Robt.** not personally appear, sd. lands to pass to **Arthur** (son of son **Richard**).

"   wife **Elinor,** use of dwelling plantation during widowhood. Shd. she marry again, dower rights only.

"   grandson **Arthur** afsd. and hrs., residue of "Hart's Content" on n. side of afsd. path, leading to plantation called Jacob Pattesons', now in possession of James Insly.

"   goddau. **Mary Macmillington, Jr.,** and dau. **Mercy,** 100 A. "Vale of Misery," equally.

"   dau. **Mercy,** personalty at day of marriage.

Shd. any of above beneficiaries die without issue, their portions to revert to next surviving hr.

To 2 servts., John Joanes and John Haper, and to **Mary Macmillington, Sr.,** dau. of wife **Elinor,** personalty.

Testator desires to be buried on s. side of grave of wife **Mary,** mother of son **Richd.**

Child. afsd. and **Mary Macmillington, Jr.,** residuary legatees of personal estate.

Exs.: Son **Richard** and wife **Elinor.**

Test: James Insley, **Mary Macmillington, Sr.,** Michael Todd.

Note—1st Mar., 1719-20. Within named **Elinor Hart** renounces extx. to stepson **Richard.**

Test: Mary Robertson, Michel Todd.   15. 334.

Fenwick, John, —— Co.,   20th Mar., 1720;
28th May, 1720.

To priest, £12.

"   cousin **John Fenwick** and hrs., dwelling plantation, 350 A., ——, providing that he gives plantation where he now lives to cousins **Cuthbert** and **Ignatius Fenwick** and their hrs., equally. **John** and **Cuthbert** afsd. to give 200 A. in "Beaver Dam Mannor" to cousins **Richard** and **Enoch Fenwick** and their hrs., equally. (For further conditions see will.)

"   5 cousins afsd., exs. (as tho' they had but one mother), residue of estate, real and personal.

Test: Robert Clark, Jr., Charles Joy, Peter Joy, Jr.   15. 339.

Foreman, Robert, —— Co.,   22nd Sept., 1711;
                                           15th Mar., 1719-20.

To son **Robert,** 50 A., "Susetren," pt. of a tract of 200 A.
" youngest son **Charles,** son **William** and son **John,** each
   50 A. of afsd. tract.
" youngest dau. **Elizabeth,** personalty.
" daus. **Milderatt Hendrickson** and **Mary Fanning,** 1s. each.
" son **Arthur,** 100 A., "Calead," where he is now seated,
   being the upper pt. of "Blackletakes Hermitage."
" wife **Margt.,** use of dwelling plantation —— during
   widowhood for maintenance of child., and residue of estate
   absolutely. Shd. any of 4 youngest child. die without
   issue, their portions to be divided among survivors of the
   4. Dau. **Elizabeth** then to have equal pt. of sd. land.
Exs.: Wife **Margt.** and son **Arthur.**
Test: Tho. Winn, Michael Haskell.   15. 341.

Ellis, John, Kent Co.,   1st Feb., 1719;
                                         17th Mar., 1719-20.

To son **Benja.** and hrs., 300 A. at Little Duck Ck., Pennsylvania, bou. of Wm. Nileson.
" son **William** and hrs., 500 A., ——, Kent Co., bou. of
   Arthur Miller, and 100 A., dwelling plantation ——.
" godson Abraham Cockerel and hrs., 200 A. adj. 100 A. dev.
   to son **Wm.,** and out of same tract.
" dau. **Jane Borrock** and hrs., 400 A., being residue of dwelling plantation, and personalty.
" Elizabeth Cockerel, a life interest in land bequeathed
   Abraham Cockerel afsd.
Son William ex. and residuary legatee.
Test: George Glives, Anne Kineday, John Florety.   15. 343.

Jones, William, planter, Kent Co.,   10th Dec., 1719;
                                            8th Mar., 1719.

To wife **Anne,** use of dwelling plantation ——, and personalty
   during widowhood. Shd. she marry, dower rights only.
" son **William,** ½ of land lying next the neck ——.
" son **Benjamin,** other half of sd. tract. Sd. sons to share
   equally in personalty bequeathed wife, at her decease or
   marriage.
" daus. **Mary** and **Elizabeth,** personalty.
" dau. **Rachel,** one equal share of personalty with her
   brothers afsd. Sons to live with bro. **Peter** until of age.
Exs.: Bro. Peter and James Willson, Jr.
Test: Gidian Pearce, Anne Pearce, George Dunekin.   15. 346.

Joanes, Robert, Kent Co.,   25th Oct., 1719;
                                            9th Mar., 1719.

To eldest son **John,** personalty.

To 2 sons, **John** and **Robert**, personalty. Sd. sons to be brought up by ex. until 21 yrs. of age.

Residue of personal estate to all child. ——, equally.

Ex.: William Comeges.

Test: Jervis Spencer, Charles Garfoot, William Boots. 15. 349.

Hyland, Nicholas, Cecil Co., 18th Jan., 1717-8;
12th Mar., 1719;
29th ——, 1720.

To wife **Mellice**, extx., and 2 sons **Nicho.** and **John,** entire estate. Son **Nicholas** and hrs. to have the land on Elk. R., son **John** the tract from John Butterums, up Susquehanna R.

Education of sons to be charge of wife. To be brought up in faith of Church of England.

Test: James Robinson, Isaac Hargrave, Andrew Rosenquist, Richard Kempton, William Warum and Francis Mauldin.

15. 350.

Bavington (Banington), John, Sr., planter, Cecil Co.,
5th Mar., 1718;
27th Aug., 1719.

To wife **Mary**, extx., and hrs., entire estate, excepting as follows:

" 2 sons, **William** and **John,** and their hrs., 100 A., "The Addition," equally.

" sons **Hugh, Jona.** and **Thomas** and daus. **Mary, Roseman** and **Elizabeth,** personalty. Son **Jona.** to live with his uncle, **Jonathan Beck,** if they both live until sd. son arrives at age of 18. Shd. sd. uncle die before that time, son afsd. to live with his mother again.

Sons **Hugh, Jona.** and **Thomas** to be free at age of 18. Daus. **Roseman** and **Elizabeth** at age of 15.

Exs.: Wife **Mary** and sons **William** and **John.**

Overseer: Bro.-in-law **Jona. Beck.**

Test: Edw. Boaston (Beason), Timothy March, Frances Steel.

15. 352.

Kirby, William, plasterer, St. Mary's Co.,
29th May, 1710;
13th Apr., 1720.

To 2 sons, **Thomas** and **William,** and their male hrs., lands entailed for them (son **Thomas** to have 1st choice), and personal estate, equally.

" grandchild **William Adams,** personalty.

" dau. **Jane Adams,** 2s. 6d.

Ex.: ——.

Test: Taren Sweeney, Stephen Milbourn, Sarah Milbourn.

15. 356.

APPENDIX

The following wills have been taken from sources other than the will books at the Land Office in Annapolis, as may be seen by the references.

As these wills would be chronologically out of place in the body of this volume, yet are of much importance, it is thought best to add them as an appendix.

From Land Office
Annapolis, Md.

Brandt, Marcus, late of town of St. Michaells, and Island of Barbadoes, —— —— ——;

23rd July, 1705.

To bro. **Charles,** £20 and personalty.

" sisters **Margaret Manzey** and **Mary Lattemore,** £20.

" cousin **Rebekah Dunckly,** £10.

" godson **Bassill Dunckly,** £15

" godson Richard Farroll, £5.

" Mme. Frances Collins, widdow, her sister Mrs. Margarett Tyrwhit, widdow, Frances Collins, Charles Tyrwhitt and Frances, his wife, Mrs. Elizabeth Beachfield, her sister Anne Tyrwhitt, spinster, Mrs. ——, wife of John Jordan, her dau., Mrs. Elizabeth Mills, Isaiah Davis, personalty.

" Mary, spinster, dau. of Anne Morgan (since married) 4 yrs. schooling.

To the poor decayed housekeepers of St. Michaell Town, £5.

Bro. **Randolph** ex. and residuary legatee.

To overseers Capt. John Barry, John Jordan and **Mr. Bassill Dunckly, Sr.,** personalty.

Test: Matthew Conihane, George Tyrwhitt, Isaiah Davis.

C. No. 2, 34.

Note: Testator desires to be buried at the e. end of St. Michaell's church yard, in the grave with Uncle **Jacob.**

From Testamentary Proceedings
Land Office, Annapolis, Md.

Brome, John, of Calvert Towne, Calvert Co.,

5th Feb., 1687;
18th Mar., 1689.

To eldest son **John,** 550 A., "Stonesby," nr. Muffetts Island, and personalty.

" dau. **Martha,** 600 A., "Hamsted," nr. freshes of Choptank.

" youngest dau. **Heneretta,** 1,000 A., "Bromes Bloome," Baltimore Co.

" godson Henry Truman, Jr., personalty on plantation of Edward Harlock, other side of Battle Ck.

Shd. any of afsd. child. die during minority and unmarried, survivors to divide portion of dec'd. Sons to be of age at 21, daus. at 18 or marriage.

To friends Henry Freeman and his wife ——, and their son Henry, Cecil Butler, Heenry Farnly and George Curiven, each a gold ring.

" wife **Winifred Margaret,** extx., use of estate during minority of child. and 600 A., "Island Neck," n. side Patuxent R., bou. of Nicholas Sporne; personalty, some of which was bou. of John Willymott, and residue of personal estate divided with 3 child. afsd.

Test. states that at date of drawing will he is starting for England.

Test: Cecill Butler, Henry Trueman, Henry Fernley, John Ledyatt, Thomas Barnett.   16. 1.

Denine, Henry, Calvert Co.,   19th Feb., 1689;
—— —— 1690.

To wife **Elizabeth,** extx., entire personal estate and ½ real estate.

" Jeremy Eldridge, personalty and other ½ realty.

Test: Charles Wheeler, Stephen Ansbee (Onsbee), Jacob Williams, Elizab. Onsbee.   16. 5.

Hopewell, Hugh, Sr., Calvert Co.,   23rd May, 1687;
20th Feb., 1688.

To daus. **Mary** (wife of **John Keene**), **Agnes, Ann** and **Susanna,** sons **Hugh** and **Richard,** personalty.

" wife **Ann,** extx., entire real estate and residue of personalty.

Test: James Harper, Harry Fitzharbert, Charles Jones. 16. 7.

Martin, William, of the Clifts, Calvert Co.,

23rd Sept., 1689;
21st Aug., 1690.

To dau. **Elizabeth,** 100 A., ''Thabush Manning,'' bou. of John Manning, and personalty at age of 16 or marriage, and ½ personal estate. Shd. sd. dau. die during minority, sd. lands to pass to next of kin after decease of wife.

'' sons-in-law **Thomas, John, George, William** and **Samuel Abbott,** personalty.

'' wife **Isabell,** extx., ½ of personal estate.

Test: Samuel Holdsworth, **Ja. Martin,** Thomas How. 16. 8.

Deposition shows at date of probate extx. **Isabella** to be wife of John Holdsworth.

Simpson, Jeremiah, Calvert Co., 29th Sept., 1690;
12th Mar., 1690-1.

To eldest son **Jeremiah** and 2nd son **John,** real estate equally, son **Jeremiah** to have first choice. Shd. either of afsd. sons die without issue, portion of dec'd to pass to younger son **Thomas.**

'' younger son **Thomas,** Charles Coleman during his servitude.

'' sons afsd., personalty and residue of personal estate equally.

'' wife ——, extx., interest in ⅓ real estate during life.

Test: William Brooke, John Skippers, Isaac Baker. 16. 27.

Dep. of extx. (**Ann Simpson**) shows 4 small child. at date of probate.

Abington, Andrew, 29th Oct., 1691;
9th Nov., 1691.

To son **John,** land —— bou. of Richard Keen.

'' wife **Ann,** extx., and rest of child., including child unborn, residue of estate. Sd. wife to have use of entire estate during minority of child.

Overseers: Capt. Samll. Bowrne, John Lewellen.

Test: Capt. Francis Harbin, John Edwards, George Plater.

16. 29.

Donnell, Shute (nunc.), Calvert Co., 16th Aug., 1691;
24th Sept., 1691.

To Mrs. Jenkins and her husband, Richard, entire estate, excepting a legacy to Amey Granes.

Test: Lydia Cobb, Elizabeth Deliatt, Amy Granes, Robert Gates, James Clarke. 16. 29.

Bertrand, Paul, minister of the Gospel, Calvert Co.,

24th Mar., 1686-7;
—— —— 1691.

To wife **Mary,** 100 A., ''Cox-hay,'' on Patuxent R., and personal estate.

Test: Ant. Underwood, Martha Underwood, John Lowe.

16. 31.

Recorded by desire of Michael Morreen, none of test. being found.

Ladd, Capt. Richard, gent., Calvert Co.,   16th Mar., 1684; 10th Feb., 1691.

To nephew **John Rigden** (son to sister **Ellon**), land adj. to James Magroth's, and personalty; to be in charge of wife —— until 21 yrs. of age.

Goods in house, sent in by bro. **John** of Nowich, value £105, be sold and proceeds sent to him or his hrs.

To sister **Ellen Rigden** afsd., 100 A., ''Ladd's Desire,'' in the Western Branch.

'' bro. **John** afsd., £20 in full of any claim against estate.

'' the Church (newly built nr. the hornes upon The Clifts), dwelling plantation, ''Charles Gift,'' for maintenance of a minister to be settled by consent of Richard Smith, Jr., Thomas Tasker, Michaell Taney, John Hume. This excepts 100 A. sold to William Gambrell, planter.

'' wife ——, extx., residue of estate during life; at her decease 600 A., ''Groome's Lott,'' in western branch to nephew **John** afsd. Shd. sd. nephew die without issue, sd. lands to bro. **John** afsd. Shd. wife —— die intestate, her portion of ''Charles Gift'' afsd. to nephew **Thomas Forman,** chirurgeon.

Overseers: Bro.-in-law **Henry Rigden,** John Hume.

Test: John Griggs, John Mannyng, William Mitchell, William Harris.   16. 32.

Dawe (Daw), Nathan, of the Clifts, Calvert Co., 13th May, 1688; —— —— ——.

To wife **Mary,** extx., entire estate, real and personal, during life; at her decease as follows:

'' son **Edward,** real estate and ½ personal estate. Shd. sd. son die without issue, dau. **Mary** to inherit portion bequeathed him.

'' dau. **Mary,** ½ personal estate.

Test: Samuel Holdsworth, Jefferey Maneley, William Wilkinson, Thos. Howes.   16. 34.

Note—20th Jan., 1691. Letters of administration granted to within named **Edwd. Dowe** on estate of **Mary Dowe,** his mother, who died intestate, as well as on estate of father, **Nathan Dowe.**

Crawford, James, county chirurgeon, Calvert Co.,
26th Dec., 1691;
8th Jan., 1691-2.

> Ex. Joh. Mannying to see that each of child., ——, receive
> equal share of personal estate, and that real estate be
> divided bet. them when either of them come of age.

Test: John Holdsworth, William Marston, Richard Leake,
George Seley.   16. 35.

Note—Certain personalty allowed wife of **James Crawford.**

Gantt (Gant), Thomas, Calvert Co.,   18th Nov., 1691:
28th Jan., 1691.

> To wife **Ann,** extx., dwelling plantation —— and adj. lands
> during life; at her decease as follows:
> " eldest son **Thomas** and hrs., "Marsham's Rest" and
> "Pelerton," and to have at age of 17 the plantation now
> under care of John Martin, overseer, being pt. of afsd.
> lands.
> " dau. **Ann** and hrs., "Bullwick" at age of 18 or marriage.
> " dau. **Elizabeth** and hrs., "Edlowes Shoire" on Eastern
> Shore, Dorsettshere Co., at head of St. John's Ck., at age
> of 18 or marriage. Shd. any of afsd. child. die during
> minority or without issue, portion of deceased to pass
> to son **Edward** and hrs.
> " wife **Ann** and 4 child. afsd., personal estate.

Test: Tho. Brooke, John Smith, Sam. Peter.   16. 37.

Miles, Tobias, planter, Calvert Co.,   16th Aug., 1691:
18th Nov., 1691:
16th Mar., 1691.

> To son **John,** 400 A., "Miles End."
> " son **Tobias,** 100 A., "Brantry." Shd. he die before at-
> taining age of 18, sd. 100 A. to revert to son **John** and hrs.
> " daus. **Mary, Frances** and **Elizabeth,** each 50 A. of "Mill
> Runn." Shd. any of daus. die before marriage or age
> of 16, portion of deceased to surviving daus.
> " son-in-law **Edward Hood,** 1s.
> " wife **Elizabeth,** extx., personal estate absolutely, and use
> of 1/3 of "Miles End" during life.

Test: Capt. Henry Mitchell, Samll. Constable, Francis Maldin
(Mauldin), Richard Kent, Fran. Freeman.   16. 43.

Needham, William, Calvert Co.,   26th Oct., 1691;
3rd May, 1692.

> To wife **Mary,** extx., entire estate, excepting legacy to son
> **James.**

Test: Mathew Gautherin, Jno. Willymott.   16. 49.

Note—Letters granted on above estate to **Mathew Gautherin**
and **Mary**, his wife, extx. of above will.

Abington, John, of London, mcht.,   14th Jan., 1692;
                                             —— Nov., 1694.

Debt due to Richard Harrison of Md. to be paid.

To bro.-in-law **Dr. Mich. Carney,** debts due from him.

" sister Mirriell (wife of **Dr. Carney** afsd.), living at Stoake,
nr. Bristoll, Glocester Co., personalty now in possession
of Wm. Worrell.

" niece Mirriell (their dau.), £50.

" niece Mirriell Abington, £100.

Shd. either of afsd. nieces die before receiving legacy, sd.
money to return to estate.

To Mrs. Alice Nolinds, £100, and £150 yearly for maintenance
of her two sons, John and Charles. Shd. sd. Mrs. Nelenes
recover estate in Ireland left her by her father, now in
litigation with her bro., £100 yearly.

" godson John (son of **William Abington,** dec'd), £50 at
age of 21.

" John Pettitt, £50.

Estate in Maryland to be sold and proceeds divided among
child. of Mrs. Alice Nelmes, viz.: John, Charles and child
unborn.

Kinsman **John Abington** ex. and residuary legatee.

Test: Fenton Byune, H. Dennett, Thomas Freeman.   16. 64.

Richard Harrison and George Lingan afsd., exs. in Maryland.

Fary, Joseph,   2nd Feb., 1692;

To bros. **Francis** and **Robert,** 20s. each.

" mother Mary, extx., of London, widow, residue of estate
during life; at her decease to pass as follows:

" sister Mary, wife of **James Wagstaff,** ⅔.

" bro. **Charles,** ⅓.

Starting on voyage to Va., ship "Ruth."

Test: Wm. Broxton, Bej. Edmonds and his ser't., John Marreott.   16. 160.

From Baltimore City Land Office
Baltimore City Court House

Johnson, Capt. Henry,   16th May, 1689;
                                             13th June, 1689.

To sons **Henry** and **Joseph,** real and personal estate, equally.

Shd. either son die before age of 16, survivor to inherit portion of deceased. Shd. both die, estate to revert to wife
Elizabeth.

Ex.: Son **Henry**, assisted by his mother.

Test: James Mills, William Osborne, Abraham Blagg, Thomas Dalby.

R. M.—H. S. No. 1. 328.

Guest. Christopher, Balto. Land Office, Baltimore Co.,
17th Feb., 1690;
10th Mar., 1690.

Wife ——, extx. of estate, to divide same with child, ——.

To John Robinson and child of bro. **Richard Cromwell**, personalty; and to mother **Guest**, £5.

Test: John Brown, John Robinson, **Richard Cromwell**.

R. M.—H. S. No. 1. 331.

Yorke. William. of Birch R., planter. Balto. City Land Off., Baltimore Co., 23rd Nov., 1690;
5th Mar., 1690.

To 5 sons, **William,. Olliver, John, George** and **James**, real estate equally. Shd. any of sd. sons die before age of 16, survivors to inherit portion of dec'd.

Personal estate to be divided among all children ——, equally.

To wife **Mary**, extx., dwelling plantation on Bush R. during life and ⅓ pt. of personal estate.

Test: Wm. Duson, Phillip Collier, Edward Allely, John Hall.

R. M.—H. S. No. 1. 331.

Dowel, Edward, Baltimore Co., 30th Oct., 1690;
22nd Dec., 1690.

To son-in-law **Olliver Harriod**, 100 A., "The Rainge," Middle R., and personalty.

" dau.-in-law (stepdau.) **Unity Harriod**, 100 A., ——, on Middle R., and personalty.

" John Anderson, personalty and debts in tobacco due from him.

" Mary Harrison, 200 A., "Oglesby Chance," and residue of estate.

Exs.: Richd. Adams and Daniell Scott.

Test: James Maxwell, Mary Adams, Richard Adams, Jr.

R. M.—H. S. No. 1. 332.

Hemsted, Nicholas (nunc.), Balto. Co., 15th Nov., 1690;
2nd Dec., 1690.

Wife ——, extx., she to proceed in law with dau. of Thomas Thurstone for keeping testator from his right, both plantation and goods.

Test: Robert Love, William Gudgen, John Love, Roger Respenh.

R. M.—H. S. No. 1. 333.

Goldsmith, George, Baltimore Co.,   13th Mar., 1691-2;
                                             29th Apr., 1691-2.

To unborn child —— if a son, 650 A., ''Goldsmith's Rest,''
and personalty, and 70 A., ''Goldsmith's Inlargement.''
Shd. unborn child be a dau., afsd. tracts to dau. **Mary**
and hrs.

'' dau. **Mary,** 500 A., ——, at Gunpowder R., and 50 A. bou.
of Geo. Oglesby shd. unborn child be a boy. Shd. unborn
child be a girl, sd. child to inherit 500 A. bequeathed dau.
Mary, and personalty.

'' wife **Martha,** 200 A., ''Bonnington,'' Sassafras R., 100 A.,
''Robinhood's Forest,'' at hd. of Swan Ck., and ⅓ of
personal estate. Remaining ⅔ to dau. **Mary** and unborn
child ——.

Test: James Phillips, **Edward Bodell,** Edward Boothby.
                                         R. M.—H. S. No. 1. 339.

Note—Shd. wife marry again, bro.-in-law **Edward Bodell** to
have care of child.

Nicholls, John, Baltimore Co.,   4th May, 1691;
                                    —— —— ——.

To son **John,** personalty, and to the other 3 child., **Thomas,**
Mary and **Sarah,** personalty to be delivered to them by
their mother 7 yrs. after decease of testator.

Wife **Mary** extx. At her decease 50 A. to each child.

Test: Thomas Jones, Michael Judd, John Hathway, Robert
Oless.
                                         R. M.—H. S. No. 1. 345.

Hudson, Mathew,   27th Dec., 1688;
                                      —— —— ——.

To wife **Jane,** ''Birmans Forest,'' s. side Back R., and
H——_ lying on same side of sd. R. and personal estate
during her life; (not decipherable) reserving 100 A., ——,
''Joanasis Rainge'' to Joseph Perrgo.

Ex. Ebenezer Blackstone.

Test: —— Carrell, ——Gerrard. (Rest not decipherable.)
                                       R. M.—H. S. No. 1. 345.

Peverell, Daniell, of Spesutie Hundred, Baltimore Co.,
                                     22nd Mar., 1691-2;
                                     2nd May, 1692.

To dau. **Sarah,** entire estate, real and personal. Sd. dau. dying
without issue, wife **Hannah** to possess entire estate, absolutely.

'' wife **Hannah,** dower rights, and guardian of afsd. dau.
until of age or marriage.

Exs.: Wife **Hannah** and Samuel Browne.

Test: Thos. Hodges, Geo. Gannell, Bartholomew Hedge.

R. M.—H. S. No. 1. 350.

Jones, Robert, Baltimore Co.,   8th Nov., 1685:
6th Jan., 1690.

To landlord, Mr. George Gouldsmith, entire estate, with exception of personalty bequeathed to James Frinde.

Test: Richard Weakfield, Thomas Brown, John Mould.

R. M.—H. S. No. 1. 351.

Love, Robert, Sr., Baltimore Co.,   26th Mar., 1692:
7th June, 1692.

To son **John,** entire real estate. Shd. son **Robert** behave kindly toward his bros. and sisters, he to be given such a pt. of land as son **John** shall think fit.

Personal estate to be divided among all children at discretion of son **John,** ex.

Test: Saml. Sicklemore, Wm. Gredgeon, Jane Judd.

R. M.—H. S. No. 1. 354.

Hathway, John, of Bush R., Balto. Co.,   17th Mar., 1691-2;
30th Aug., 1692.

To George Smith, Sr., ex., tract on western br. Bush R., n. side of sd. branch. Patent for sd. land at William Elden's "Hogg Neck." Also 100 A., "Hathway's Addition," and personalty, including debt due from William Yorke and Thomas James, and personalty in poss. of Will. Pritchetts and Richard Ackew; also 130 lbs. tobacco for drawing conveyance bet. him and Thomas Preston, and 150 for drawing deed of gift for Charles Ramsey.

Codicil—18th March, 1691. Bond of Humphrey Jones assigned to use of testator. Bond of Michael Judd ordered to ex. afsd. George Smith to keep tract "Little Marloe" for own use.

Test: to codicil, Thomas Health, Robert Kess.

Test: Mathias Prosser, Wm. Osborn, Thomas Loe.

R. M.—H. S. No. 1. 355.

Beacher, Edith, of Patapsco R., Baltimore Co.,
23rd May, 1694;

———　———　———.

Son **Richard Gest (Gist), (Guest)** to care of bro. **Richard Cromwell** and Thomas Staly, they to have charge of his estate until he arrives at age of 21.

Test: Anna Oldton, Danl. Palmer, Ellinor Floyd.

R. M.—H. S. No. 1. 550.

INDEX

A

PAGE

Abbott, John 152, 234
Abbott, George 234
Abbott, Samuel 234
Abbott, Thomas 234
Abbott, William, ... 234
Abbot, Silvester 156
Abell, William 72, 127, 170
Abington, Ann 234
Abington, Andrew 234
Abington, John 234, 237
Abington, Mirriell 237
Abington, William 237
Abington Manor 50
Abitt, Lewiston 228
Abrahams, Isaac 148
Abrahams, Sophia 148
Ackew, Richard 240
Acquinkekas Hill 10
Acwith, Sarah 47
Acworth, Henry 49
Acworth, John............. 49
Acworth, Mary 49
Acworth, Richard 169
Acworth, Samuell 49
Acworth, Sarah 49
Acworth, William 58
"Acworth's Purchase" 49
Adames, Ann 14
Adames, Collins 14
Adams, Elianor (Elinor)..55, 75
Adams, Jacob 104
Addams (Adams), Jane...67, 231
Adams, Jean 63
Adams, John 223
Adams, Mary 238
Adams, Rachel 75
Adams, Richard 238
Adams, Thomas 166
Adams, William 231
Addersson, Thomas 206
Adderton, Jeremiah 201
Adderton, James 201
Adderton, Mary 201
Addison, Thomas 61, 211
"Addition of Gardiner's
    Grove" 128
"Addition" 108
Adkins, Elizabeth 114

PAGE

Adkins, Robert 114
Adkinson, Thomas 204
Adney, Moses 44
"Adventer" 65
Aford, William 142
Aires, Elizabeth 225
Aires, William 225
Aisquith, Elizabeth 197
Aisquith, George 197
Aisquith, Thomas 197
Asquith (Aisquith), William
                126, 197
Alavery, Faith 185
Alden, Andrew 217
Alderson, Simond 203
Aldridge (Aldeir), Rebekah. 179
Aldridge (Aldeir), Thomas.. 179
Alexander, Henry 192
Alexander, Mary 158
Alexander, Samuel 83
Alford, Ann 125
Alford, Edward 125
Alford, Elizabeth 125
Allchurch, Mary 73
Allely, Edward 238
Allen, Benja.............53, 220
Allen, Dorcas 57
Allen, Francis 192
Allen (Allean), Joseph...... 189
Allen (Allens), Mary....192, 197
Allen, Rebeckah 173
"Allen's Deceit" 111
Alley, John 23
All Faith Parish 29, 51
All Hallows Parish 47, 192
Allin, Thomas 61
Allison, John 141
All Saints 67
Alman, Thomas 131
Alvey, Joseph 13
Alvard, John 37, 203
"Aminedown" 193
"Amity" 83
"Anchor and Hope" 75
"Anchovis Hills" 39
Anderson, Edward 97
Anderson, Isaac 228
Anderson, Jane 91

PAGE

Anderson, James 228
Anderson, John 136, 238
Anderson, Lawrence 139
Anderson, Margaret 98, 228
Anderson, Mary 51, 139
Anderson, Thomas 22, 107
"Anderton" 217
Anderton, Francis 13
Anderton, James 13
Anderton, John 13
Anderton, Mary 13
Anderton, Sarah 13
Anderton's Addition 217
"Andower" 14
Andrews, Mary 33
Andrews, Nicholas 33
Andrews, Richard 33
Andrews, John 33
Andrews, Joseph 75
Angell, Wm..............24, 35
"Angellica" 143
"Anglese" 28
Angley, William 180
Ankrum, Mary 119
Ankrum, Richard 119
Annapolis, 26, 44, 108, 135,
  184, 196, 208, 212........ 217
Ann Arundle Manor........ 182
Annarundell River 31
Annimesax 49, 102, 153, 225
Annis, Thomas 97
"Annstroder" 68
Ansbee (Onsbee), Stephen... 233
Ansloe, John 214
"Arabia" 3
"Arcadia" 16, 66
"Archer's Hays" 91
"Archer's Pasture" 39
"Ardin's Adventure" 29
Ares, George 123
Ares, Mary 123
Arey, David 34
Arey, Deborah 34
Arey, Esther 34
Arey, John 34
Arey, Joseph 34
Arland, Ralph 197
Arland, William 197

PAGE

Armiger, Daniell 97
Armiger, John 97
Armiger, Robert 97
Armstrong, Francis 155
Arnelt, John 157
Arnold, John 228
Arnold, Ralph 170
Aron, Anne 187
Arthur, Alexander 141
Arthur, Mary 141
"Arthur's Choice" 79
Artley, Joseph 43
Ash, —— 194
Ash, William 139
Ashcom (Ashcombs), Charles
                        127, 211
Ashcom, Martha 127
Ashcom, Winifred 127
Ashe, Dorothy 18
Ashman, John....19, 97, 119, 216
Ashman, Richard 97, 119
Ashton, Thomas 132
Askew, Margaret 92
Askew, Michael 92
Askins, Edward 70, 139
"Assawamuh" 85
Atkinson, John 128
Atkinson, Neomy 57
"Atland" 133
Attkins, Mark 42
Attoway, Ann 70
Attoway, John 70
Attoway, Susanah 69
Attoway, Thomas 70
Attwood, Elizabeth 7
Attwood, Henry.......7, 27, 206
Attwood, John 7
Auld, James 9
Austen (Austin), Henry..44, 97
Austen, Joseph 192
Austin, William..........23, 163
Auston, John 10
Aveten, Anne 192
Aydelett, William 105
"Ayes Addition" 213
Ayling, James 164
"Ayres" 177

B

"Back Camp" 24
Back Creek..........11, 49, 131
Back Lingan 108
Back River 29, 51, 239
"Bacon Hall" 135
"Bacon Quarter" 154
Badger, William 40

Baggott, Mary 66
Baker, Charles 162
Baker, Francis 16
Baker, Isaac 234
Baker, James 188
Baker, John.........51, 71, 90
Baker, Nathan 56

PAGE

Baker, Sarah 56
"Bald Ridge" 153
Baldwin, Hester 26
Baldwin, James 26
Baldwin, John 26
Baldwin, Katharine 26
Baldwin, Thomas 26
"Baldwin's Chance" 26
Baldwin's Cr. 220
Ball, Ann 44
Ball, B.................... 63
Ball, Benjamin 122
Ball, Catherine 44
Ball, Edward 44
Ball, John 123
Ball, Michael 44
Ball, William 44
Ballock, Benjamin 225
Ballock, James 225
Ballock, Mary 225
Baltimore, Lady Margaret.. 20
Baltimore, Lord 107
Baltimore, Lord Charles.... 20
"Bangiah" 9
"Bangiah Manor" 9
Bangs, Joshua 133
Banister, John 114
Bankes, Geo............... 223
Banks, Bridget 186
Banks, Elizabeth 186
Banks, John 27
Banks, William 186
"Bank's Fork" 186
"Barbadoes" (Island of)
                 9, 48, 232
"Barbara's Choyce" 52
"Barbara's Inlet" 52
Barber, James 84
Barber, Luke 90, 134
Barber, Mary 84
Barber, Sarah 84
"Barber's Delight" 23
Bare Cr................... 51
Barens, William 153
Bare Poynt (or Leeds) Creek 150
Barker, Elizabeth 137
Barker, George 137
Barker, John 134, 136
Barker, Martha 137
Barker, Mary 137
Barker, William
        134, 136, 137, 224
Barkleton, Enoch.......... 106
Barley, James 25
Barman, Elizabeth 119
Barneby, John 136
Barnes, Anne 138
Barnes, Barbara 138

PAGE

Barnes, Benjamin 138
Barnes, Frances 62, 138
Barnes, Henrietta 138
Barnes, Henry 138
Barnes, John 171
Barnes, Richard 49
Barnes, Thomas 138
Barnet, William 179
Barnit (Barnett), Thomas
                 12, 203, 233
Barns, Mrs. 102
"Barnstaple" 216
Barnyeatt, John 225
Barrett, Alice 146
Barrett, Darby 218
Barratt, Edward 216
Barrett (Barratt), John
              8, 11, 146, 216
Barrett, Margaret 203
Barratt, Peter 216
Barratt, Thomas 203
"Barretts Addition" 146
"Barretts Delight" 146
Barrons, Alloner 72
Barrons (Barron), Ann...72, 213
Barron (Baron), Benjamin.. 109
Barron (Baron), Bridget.... 109
Barron, John 213
Barrons, Margaret 72
Barron (Baron), Martha.... 109
Barron (Baron), Mary...109, 189
Barrons (Barron), Rich...72, 150
Barron (Baron), Robert.109, 189
Barrons (Barron), Thomas.72, 213
"Barron Neck" 90, 144
"Barron Spot" 118
Barry, John 232
"Barrys Range" 205
"Bartaran" 149
Barter 180
Barton (Bartton), Elizabeth
                 80, 82
Barton (Bartton), Nathan 80, 82
Barton (Bartton), Rachel
   (Rachell) 80, 82
Barton, William 82, 174
Bartwith, Elizabeth 141
Bartwith, Frances 141
"Barwell's Hope" 181
Barwell (Barwill), John.... 181
Barwell (Barwill), Justinian. 181
Barwell (Barwill), Penelope. 181
Barwell (Barwill), Richard. 181
Bassett, John 202
"Batchelor's Delight" 227
"Batchelors Fortune" 143
"Batchellor's Adventure".. 159
Bateman, Abigall 81

PAGE

Bateman, Elizabeth 78
Bateman, Henry (Honeri).81, 111
Bateman, Ishll 167
Bateman, William 78, 81
Bath 13
Bathler Hall 30
Batie, John 110
Batie, Sarah 110
Batson, John 126
Battee, Fardinands 190
Battee (Batter), Samuel..36, 40
Battershell, Henry 16
Battershell, John 16
Battershell, Rachell 16
Battershell, William 16
Battle Creek 142, 211, 233
Batureius Point 156
Bavington (Banington), Eliza-
  beth 231
Bavington (Banington), Hugh 231
Bavington (Banington), John 231
Bavington (Banington), Jona 231
Bavington (Banington), Mary 231
Bavington (Banington), Rose-
  man 231
Bavington (Banington),
  Thomas 231
Bavington (Banington), Wil-
  liam 231
"Bawmarrigs" 25
Baxter, Edmund 29
Baxter, Hannah 148
Baxter, Mary 29
Bayard, Samuell 16
Bayley, Jacob 43
Bayley, Mary 43
Bayley, Thomas 43
Baylor, Bridget 126
Bayly, Thomas 185
Bay-neck 6
Bazell, Robert 56
Beach, John 11
Beach, Thomas 80
Beacher, Edith 240
Beachfield, Elizabeth 232
Beale, Alexander 17
Beal, James 196
Beale, John, 26, 29, 53, 82,
  89, 145, 185, 189........ 228
"Beale's Chance" 24
Beall, Charles 94, 135
Beall, Elizabeth 11
Beall, George 135
Beall, Mary 135
Beall, Ninian........11, 17, 135
Beall, Samuel 135
Beam, Christopher 108
"Beams Landing" 108

PAGE

Beam, Walter 108
Beans, Charles 53
Beans, Christopher 53
Beans, William 53
"Bear Neck" 26
Beard, James 122
Beard, John 122
Beard, Richard 172
"Beard's Dock" 221
"Beard's Landing" 53
Beauchamp, Dodgett 101
Beauchamp, Elizabeth 103
Beauchamp, Gray 101
Beauchamp, Hannah 101
Beauchamp, Isaac 103
Beauchamp, John 103
Beauchamp, Margaret 103
Beauchamp, Mary 103
Beauchamp (Beachamp),
  Sarah......101, 102, 103, 153
Beauchamp, Thomas 103
Beaumont, Richard 19
Beavan, Charles 41, 223
Beavans (Bevans), Thomas
  71, 216
Beaven, William 225
"Beaver Dam" (Beaver
  Dams)......38, 168, 197, 224
Beaver Dam Branch........ 31
"Beaver Dam Manor"..... 229
Bechamp, James 143
Beck, Edward 78
Beck, John 78
Beck, Jonathan 231
Beck, Lanslett 32
Beckwith, Ann 172
Beckwith, Henry 125
Beckwith, Nehemiah 125
Bedder, Richard 192
Bedder, William 192
"Bednall Green 50
Beesley, Abraham 118
"Belfast" 9, 151
Bell, Adam 51, 209
Bell, Ann 209
Bell, Antho............... 226
Bell, Charles 223
"Bells Gift" 228
Bell, Joseph 150
Bell, Richard 140, 185, 191
Bell, Thomas 226
Bellshair, Mary 66
"Belshew" 62
Belt, Jeremiah 31
Belt, John 31
Belt, Joseph....109, 122, 136, 211
Belt, Sarah 31
Bemberige, John 205

PAGE

Bencraft, Thomas 51
"Benjamin's Addition" 50
"Benjamin's Choyce" 50
"Benjamin's Discovery" ... 184
Bennett, Elizabeth 129
Bennett, Mary 164
Bennett (Bennet), Richard
144, 224
Bennett, Robert 185
"Bennet's Delight" 208
Benson, Edmond 26
Benson, Edward.........179, 190
Benson, Henry 59
Benson (Benton), John
12, 103, 166, 225 226
Benston, Thomas 226
Beraus, Mary 83
Beraus, William 83
Berry 173
Berry, Benjamin 41, 194, 223
Berry, George 146
Berry, James 37, 107, 160
Berry, Jeremiah 223
Berrey, Margaret 159
Berry, Mary 146, 223
Berry, Thomas 187, 205
Berry, Verlinda 223
Berry, William 8, 33
"Berry's Chance" 125
"Berry's Lott" 49
"Bersheba" 217
Bertrand, Mary 234
Bertrand, Paul 234
Besson, Nicholas 112
Best, Humphrey 60
Best, William 60
Beswick, Eunice 187
Beswick, George 186
Beswick, James 95
Beswick, Martha 187
Beswick, Richard 186
Beswick, Robert 187
Beswick, Silley 180
Beswick, Thomas.....33, 180, 186
Beswick, William 186
Betty, Arthur 8
"Betty's Lott" 76
Beven, Elizabeth 222
"Bever Marsh" 144
"Beverly" 45
"Bew Plains" 26
Bibber, Matthias Van...... 30
Bickerdike, Richard 212
Biddle, William 142
"Bigger" 23
Bigger, Ann 24
"Bigger's Chance" 23
Bigger, John 23

PAGE

Biggin, Abigall 83
Billingsley, Hannah 24
"Billingsley's Point" 40
"Billingsley's Swamp" 142
Billingsley, William 142
Billiter, Edward 138
Birch, Mary 221
"Birchley" 152
Birckhead, Abraham 50, 110
Birckhead, Nehemiah, 50, 109, 177
Birckhead, Mary 150
Birckhead, Solomon 50, 150
"Birckhead's Lott" 50
"Birckhead's Right" 50
"Birmans Forest" 239
Bishop, Rebecca 110
Black Wallnut Island....... 58
Black, William John....... 186
Blackborn, Edward 63
Blackborn, William 64
Blackburn, Edward 92
Blackester, Margaret 224
Blackiston, Ann 69
Blackiston, Elizabeth 69
Blackiston, John 69
Blackiston, Nehemiah 69
"Blackletakes Hermitage". 230
Blacklock, Thomas 194
Blackman, Thomas 170
"Blackshop" 86
Blackstone, Ebenezer 239
Blackwater R..........8, 75, 93
Blagg, Abraham 238
Blamer (Blamour), John
61, 157, 186
Blamer, Mary 61
Blangey, Elizabeth 208
Blangey, Jacob 21, 208
Blangey (Blangy), Lewis.20, 208
Blangery, Mary 208
Blay, William 219
"Blinkhorne" 37
Blockars, John 128
"Blomesberry" 67
Blunt, Benjamin 180
Blunt, Elizabeth 180
Blunt, Richard 180
Blunt, Robert 21, 180
Blunt, Samuel 180
Boarman, William 66
Boaston (Beason), Edward.. 231
"Bodell's Chance" 63
Bodell, Edward 239
"Bole Venture" 184
Bolt, Elizabeth 51
Bolt, Kenelm 212
Boltick, Mary 159
Bond, Benjamin 7, 161

PAGE

Bond, Benson 218
Bond, Elizabeth.......7, 50, 219
Bond, John........146, 161, 218
Bond, Peter 121, 161
Bond, Phinehas 219
Bond, Richard..50, 126, 161, 218
Bond, Sarah 219
Bond, Thomas, 146, 161, 210, 218
Bond, William 161
"Bond's Pleasant Hills"... 161
Bonnell, Izia.............. 109
Bonner, Elizabeth 76
Bonner, Rachel 76
Bonner, Theodorus 55, 76
Bonner, William 76
Bonney, Peter 162
"Bonnington" 239
Booker, Ann 133, 224
Booker, Martha 133
Boon, Jno................. 53
Booth, Jane 130
Booth, Margaret 107
Boothby, Charles 44
Boothby, Edward 239
Boots, William 231
Borden, Richard 112
Bordick's Creek 10
Bordley, Thomas 210, 220
Bork, Cislye 125
Bork, Rachel 125
Borman, William 139
Borrock, Jane 230
Bosley, Charles 79
Bosley, James 79
Bosley, John 79
Bosley, Joseph 79
Bosley, Mary 79
Bosley, Walter 79
Bosley, William 79
"Bosley's Expectation" ... 79
"Bosley's Pallace" 79
Bosman (Bozman), Ann.... 88
Bosman (Bozman), Blandina 88
Bosman (Bozman), Bridget. 88
Bosman (Bozman), George
                    45, 88, 153
Bosman (Bozman), John
                    86, 88, 220
Bosman (Bozman), Risden
    (Risdon) 88, 153
Bosman, Sarah 165
Bosman (Bozman), Thomas. 88
Bosman(Bozman), William. 88
Boson, Joseph 34
Bossom 112
Boston 209, 217
Boston, Esau 83, 166
Bourton, Joseph 185

Boswell, Mary 73
Bosworth, Daniell 14
Boteler, Alice 164
Boteler, Catherine 108
Boteler, Edward 108, 164
Boteler, Elizabeth 164
Boteler, Henry 108
Boteler, Martha 164
"Bottom of Forked Pt."... 38
Bouchelle, Petrus 15
Boucher, John 208
Boughton, Samuel 10
Bouland, Elizabeth 50
Bouland, William 50, 133
Boult (Bolt), Thomas, 128, 212
Bounds, Jonathan 12
Bounds, Sarah 12
"Bourn" 204
Bourne, Ambrose 62
Bourne, James 64
Bowditch, Ann (Anne)...58, 77
Bowditch, Robert 58, 77
Bowen, Charles 23
Bowen, Claxton 40
Bowen, David 211
Bowen, Elizabeth, 40, 211, 222
Bowen, George 40
Bowen, John 40
Bowen, Mary 178
Bowen, Milcah 40
Bowen, Solomon 100
Bowen (Bowin), William, 178, 165
Bowers, Elizabeth 163
Bowers, George 34
Bowers, John 163
Bowers, Mary 211
Bowes, George 205, 206
Bowles, David 126
Bowles, Isaac 146
Bowles, James 204
Bowles, Jane 204
Bowles, Katherine 126
Bowles, Mary 146, 169
Bowles, Tobias 172
Bowman, Samuell 123
Boxwell, Richard 8
Boyd, James 82
Boyde (Boyd), Adam....... 69
Boye, Abraham 213
Boye, Bowman 213
Boye, Elizabeth 213
Boye, Jane 213
Boye, John 213
Boye, Pigeon 213
Boye, Thomas 213
Bozman, Mary 217
Brabau, William 96
Bracy, Robert 85

PAGE

Bradford, John 110, 141
Bradie, William 48
Bradley, Thomas 164
Bradshaw, John 148
Bramble, John 116
Brambley, John 8
"Bramton" 214
Bran, Joseph 85
"Brandferd" 9
Brandt, Charles 12, 232
Brandt, Elizabeth 12
Brandt, Jacob 12, 232
Brandt, Marcus 232
Brandt, Randolph 232
Brandt, Sarah 12
Branford 89
Branklin, Henry 152
Brannock, John 32
Branock, Margaret 106
Brannock, Thomas....8, 95, 152
"Brantry" 236
Brantson, John 221
Brantson, Michael 221
Brassoure, Benjamin 176
Brassure, Thomas 176
Brattan (Bratten), Elizabeth 193
Brattan, James 154
Brattan (Bratten), John.... 193
Brattan, Quantan 193
Brattan (Bratten), Samuel.. 193
Brawner, Edward 138
Bray, Edward 15, 154
Bray, Martha 15, 154
Bray, Mary 15, 154
Bray, Pierce 15, 154
Breadey (Bredey), Charles.. 84
Breadey (Bredey), Owen.... 84
Breadey (Bredey), Pott..... 84
Breeding (Breed), Mathew.. 189
Breen, Richard 72
Brendner, Edward 80
Brent, Capt. George........ 33
Brent, Jane 33
Brent, John 39
Brent, Martha 33
Brent, Nicholas 33
Brent, Robert 33
Brent, William 33
Bresshier (Bresshear) (Bres-
  hire), Samuell....41, 42, 176
Brett (Britt), George
          133, 137, 139, 224
Brett (Britt), Henry
          133, 137, 191, 224
Brett, Richard 134, 224
Brett, Sarah 134
Brett, William 137, 139
"Brett's Addition" 224

PAGE

Brian, James 69
Briant, Dennis 29
"Brice's Hope" 76
"Brickyard" 145
Bridgeman, Elizabeth 51
Brightwell, Peter 11
Brinkworth, Edward 200
Brion, William 152
Briscoe, Alexander 34
Brisco, Anna 188
Brisco, James 188
Briscoe (Brisco), John, 19, 34, 188
Briscoe (Brisco), Mary, 34, 188
Briscoe, Philip (Philips)
          19, 51, 191
Briscoe, Susanna 191
Brisco, Thomas 188
Bristol 2, 54
Britain's Bay, 72, 123, 170, 173
Briver, Elias 78
Briver, Charles 78
Briver, Thomas 78
Briver, William 78
"Broad Creek," 20, 103, 110, 139
"Broadfield" 20
"Broad Knox Cr.".......... 20
"Broadneck" 201
Broad, Nich. 98
Broadway, Richard 44
"Brock" 17
Brock Branch 17
Brocke, Edward 17
"Brock Hall" 17
Brocklehorst, Anthony 129
Brome, Heneretta 233
Brome, John 38, 233
Brome, Martha 233
Brome, Winifred Margaret.. 233
"Brome's Bloome" 233
Bromley, Mile (Mich.)...... 1
Bronard, James 29
Brooke, Ann 131
Brook, Baker 211
Brooke, Charles 64, 131
Brooke, Clement 10
Brooke, Elinor 131
Brooks, Elizabeth 12
Brooke, Grace 64
Brooks (Brooke), Jane...12, 131
Brooks (Brooke), John
      12, 35, 93, 142, 211, 216
Brooke (Brook), Leonard, 131, 211
Brooks, Matthew 12
Brooke, Mr............... 163
Brooks (Brooke) (Brook),
  Richard 125, 132, 211
Brooke (Brooks), Robert,
          10, 64, 132

PAGE

Brooke, Roger 64, 142
Brook, Sarah 12, 211
Brooke, Thomas 10, 236
Brooke, William 234
"Brookfield" 28
"Brook's Discovery" 35
"Brooks Grove" 24
"Brook Hill" 108
"Brook Partition" 38
"Brooke Place Manor".... 64
"Brook Ridge" 37
Brooksbey's Point 190
Broom, Randall 70
Brothers United 45
Brotton, Elizabeth 36
Brotton, John 36
Brown, Alexander 212
Browne, Anthony 170, 173
Browne, Augustus 204
Brown, Calri 124
Brown, Charles 195
Brown, Deborah 214
Brown, Dorothy 37, 203
Browne, Edward 54, 62
Browne (Brown), Elizabeth
                    204, 212
Brown, Francis 67
Browne, Gabriel 204
Brown, George 212
Brown, Gustavus 1
Brown, Hannah 31
Brown, Hester 55
Brown, Jacob 67
Brown, James 35
Brown (Browne), John, 4, 31,
  40, 48, 62, 67, 85, 98, 204,
  212, 217................. 238
Brown, Jonathan 56
Browne, Joshua 31
Brown, Margaret 34
Brown, Maria 1
Brown, Mark 141
Brown, Martha 192
Brown, Mary 63, 74
Brown, Mathew 63
Browne, Peter 173
Brown Rachel 63
Browne, Robert 36
Bowrne (Browne), Samuell
                    234, 240
Brown, Sarah 63
Brown, Tarell 212
Browne (Brown), Thomas
      31, 158, 192, 204, 240
Browne, Valentine 31
Brown (Browne), William
            55, 122, 170, 183
"Brown's Entrance" 204

PAGE

Broxton, William 237
Bruff, Katherine 142
Bruff, Margaret 142
Bruff, Richard 142, 155
Bruff Thomas 142, 148
Brumbill, Nathll........... 195
Brune, Louis Deroch....... 36
"Brush Neck" 38
"Brushey Neck" 196
Bryan, Margaret 114
Brymer 34
Brymer, John 61
Brymer, William 34, 44
Bryning, John 88
Bryon, Patrick 159
Bryum, William 21
"Buchaneer Green" 83
Bucher, Elizabeth 82
Bucher, Francis 82
Buck, John 135
Buckingham, Katharine 216
Buchingham (Buckinham),
    Thomas 123, 216
"Buckinham" 87
"Buckland" 115
Buckley, Elizabeth 11, 60
Buckley, James 11, 60
Buckley, Margaret 60
Buckley, Nickolas 60
Buckley, Richard 60
Buckley, Robert 60
Buckley, William 60
Bucknam, John 226
Bucknam, Susanah 226
Bucknoll, John 44
Bull, Jacob 52
Bullen, John 94
"Bullens Right" 64
Bullett, Charles 195
Bullin, Thomas 181
Bulling Brook Creek....... 181
"Bullington" 40
Bullock, John 70, 206
Bullwick 236
Bulres Hills 44
Bumvally, Andrew 22
Burbage, John 25
Burch, Thomas 202
Burford, William 1, 185
Burgess, Edward 228
Burgess, Samuel 228
Burke, John 162
Burke (Burk), Mary, 23, 162, 219
Burke, Patrick 15
"Burlains Hill" 80
Burle, John 44
Burle, Mary 44
Burle, Rachell 44

PAGE

Burle, Sarah 44
Burle, Stephen 44
"Burmadus Hund" 105
Burn, Mary 122
Burnell, Jane 52
"Burrage" 177
"Burrage Blossom" 177
"Burrage's End" 177
Burross, Mary 111
Burroughs, Barbara 216
Burroughs, John 170
Burroughs, Mary 170
Burroughs, Richard.......18, 170
Burton, Ann 65, 92
Burton, Benjamin 178
Burton, Jane 65
Burton, Rebecka 120
Burton, William 65, 120
Busby, Charles 20
Busey, Charles 194
Busey, Edward 194
Busey, George 178
Busey, John 136, 194
Busey, Joshua 194
Busey, Paul 194
Busey, Samuell 194
Busey, Sarah 56, 194

PAGE

Bush, Ann 222
Bush R.............108, 238, 240
Bush, Thomas 222
Busick, Ann 117
Busick, James 117
Busick, Rebecca 117
"Busses Bridge" 45
Butcher, Mary 133
Butler, Ann 214
Butler, Cecil 233
Butler, Rupert .... 113'
Butler, Thomas 222
Butt, Dinah 27
Butt, Mary 27
Butt, Nicholas 27
Butt, Richard 27
Butt, Samuell 27
Butt, Thomas 27
Butterums, John 231
Butterworth, Isaac 146
Butterworth, Jane 131
Butterworth, Michaell 131
"Buttington" 108
Byfoot, William 94
Bynard, Thomas 120
Byune, Fenton 237

C

Cabbin Quarter 57
"Cabe" 55
Cabin Branch 39, 87
Cabin Cr. 180
Cabin Neck 52
Cabin Swamp 153
Cabinet, William 211
"Cacoway Point" 20
Cadell, John 226
Cadwallader, John 135
"Calead" 230
Caldwell, James 103
Caldwell (Caldwells), William
                        42, 153
"Calias" 93
Callaghanes, Ferd........... 187
Callinsworth, Dorothy 38
Calvert, Jane 77
"Calverton Manor" 38
Cambell, Dunkin 124
Cambell, James 212
Cambell, Thomas 188
Cambridge 142, 168
Camel, Margaret 73
Camell (Cammell), William
                        43, 113
Camill, Charles 124
Camill, Elizabeth 124

Campbell, Jane 71
Campbell, Richard 7, 169
Campbell, Walter 31
Camper, John 157
Camper, Thomas 9
Camwell, John 65
Canada, Charles 99
Canada, John 99
Canada, Mary 99
Candue, Elizabeth 78
Candue, Randall 78
Cannady, William 90
Cannell, Joseph 34
Canner, Thomas 168
Cannon, Elizabeth 161
Cannon, Rosanna 57
"Cannon Neck" 128
Cannon, Simon 161
Cantwell, Thomas 33, 97
Cape, John 13
Capell (Caple), Isabell, 123, 167
"Capthall" 64
Cardeau, Susanah 75
Carey, Thomas 30
Carleton, Thomas 20
Carleton, William 20
Carlile (Carlyle), Alexander
                        47, 177

PAGE

Carlsly, Elizabeth 104
Carlsly, Peter 104
Carlsly, Richard 104
Carlsly, Robert 104
Carlsly, Samuel 104
Carlsly, William 104
Carman, Thomas 160
Carney, Michael 237
Carney, Mirriell 237
Carpender, Joseph 147
"Carpenter's Point" 187
Carr, Elizabeth 167
Carr, Mary 167
Carr, Thomas 167
Carr, William 13
Carrell, ——— 239
Carrington, Timothy 97
Carroll, Charles, 40, 77, 107, 144
Carroll's Cove 128
Carselake, Benjamin 150
Carselake, Edward 150
Carselake, John 150
Carselake, Robert 150
Carter, Darby 192
Carter, James 138
Carter, John 49, 80, 103
Carter, Mary 47
Carter, Philip 47
Carter, Sarah 170
Carter, Valentine, 180, 181, 197
Cartwright, John.........21, 170
Cartwright, Margaret 170
Cartwright, Mary 21
Cartwright, Mathew 21
Cartwright, Peter 3, 21
Cartwright, Susannah 21
Carwick, Rebecca 205
Cary, Sary 34
Cary, William 107
Casey, Philip 151
Casley, John 34
Cassaway, Edward 150
Cassey, Elizabeth 4
Cassey, James 4
Cassey, John 4
Cassey (Carsey), Joseph.... 4
Castle, Mary 126
Castlea, David 199
Catherwood, Anne 42
Catherwood, Robert 42
Catholic (See Roman Catholic)
Catterwood, Margaret 38
"Catterton's Lott" 23
"Cattiron's Content" 45
Cattleing, Richard 184
Causine, Ignatius 2
Causine, William 2
Causine, John 2

PAGE

"Causin's Manor" 2
Cavinaugh, Margaret 205
Cavinaugh, William 205
"Cawdwell" 190
Cay, Jonathan 174, 189
"Cay's Folley" 165
Cecell (Cecil), Joshua....28, 40
"Cedar Neck" 9
Cedar Neck Cr............. 47
Chaires, Catherine 159
Chaires, James 159
Chaires, John 159
Chaires, Joseph 159
Chaires, Thomas 159
"Chairs Addition" 159
Chambers, Olife 83
Chambers, Richard 59, 83
Chambers, Thomas 199
"Chance" ("Chaunce")
    34, 38, 86, 93, 94, 118, 143, 207
"Chancellar's Manor"..... 197
Chancy, George 94
Chancy, Sarah 94
Chandler, Henry 205
Chandler, William, 3, 33, 72, 163
Channer, Charles 224
Chapell, John 17
Chapman, Anne 159
Chapman, Edward 42
Chapman, Elizabeth 3, 61
Chapman, John 3
Chapman, Richard 3, 159
Chapman, William 3
Chaptico Hundred 221
Charleton, Jane 63
"Charles and Benjamin"... 223
Charles Branch 53, 108
"Charles Gift" 235
"Charles Hill Land" 194
"Charles Lott" 147
Charlestown 53
"Charles Yates" 3
Charmes, Bridgett 90
"Cheinton" 204
"Chelsey" 126
"Cheney's Hazard" 38
Chesapeack Bay 209
Chesheir, John 27
Cheesman, John 77
Chester R., 18, 36, 38, 42, 52,
    78, 84, 101, 121, 149, 158,
    165, 181, 200............. 219
Chestertown 219
Cheston 128
Chestnut Meadow 160
Chew, Ann 177
Chew, Benjamin 50, 177
Chew, Elizabeth 40, 50

PAGE

Chew, Henry 40
Chew, John 50, 109, 177
Chew, Joseph 40, 50, 93
Chew, Mary 50, 56, 177, 219
Chew, Nathaniel 177
Chew, Samuell 50, 177
Chew, Sarah 177
Chew, William 177
"Chew's Right" 177
Chilan, Alexander 90
Child, Abraham 31, 44
Child, John 27
Child (Childe), Henry....50, 217
Childe, Margaret 217
Chiley, Samuel 222
China Moxson Creek 129
Chiseldyne, Cyrenius 212
Chiseldyne, Kenelm 212
Chiseldyne, Mary 212
"Chiva Chase" 77
Choptank R. (See Great
  Choptank R.)
"Chosen" 137
Christian, Mary 98
"Christian Temple Manor" 99
"Christopher's Lott" 186
Chubbard, Richard 220
Chunn, John 140
Church, The, 4, 5, 7, 17, 19, 29,
  40, 41, 51, 67, 69, 89, 140,
  144, 171, 179, 189, 197, 200,
  210, 231 235
Church, Philip 53
Church, Tabitha 53
Churn, Wilks 27
Cilley 208
Cinkkeeias Creek 152
Cissell (Chissell), James.... 98
Cissell, John 198
Cissell (Chissell), Mary 98
Cissell (Chissell), Ruth..... 98
Claggett, Thomas 223
Claleand (Clealeand), Alex-
  ander 199
"Clarcking's Wells" 38
"Clare" 66
Clark, Clement 22
Clark (Dennis), Denes...42, 101
Clarke, Edward............. 22
Clark, Elizabeth 69, 196
Clark, Elsey 196
Clarke (Clark), George
  99, 171, 208
Clarke, Grace 18
Clarke, Hannah 208
Clarke, Harman 221
Clarke, Henrietta 22
Clarke (Clark), James....69, 234

PAGE

Clarke, Joanna 77
Clarke (Clark), John
  22, 101, 125, 169, 221
Clarke (Clark), Mary
  16, 22, 101, 221
Clarke, Matthew 11
Clarke (Clark), Rebecka
  (Rebecca) 7, 77, 101
Clarke (Clark), Robert
  206, 216, 229
Clarke, Roger 8
Clark, Samuell 42
Clark, Sarah 101
Clarke, Susanna (Susannah)
  99, 171
Clarke (Clark), Thomas
  79, 141, 221
Clark, William 92, 101, 196
"Clarke's Purchase" 175
Clarkson, Elizabeth 66
Clarkson, William 139
Clarvo, Fran.............. 200
Clayland, Mr.............. 186
Clayland, W..............16, 185
"Clay's Neck" 121
Clayton, John 79
Clayton, Rachel 214
Clayton, Rosamond 79
Clayton, Solomon 160, 214
"Claxton" 121
"Clean Drinking" 140
Clegat, Deborah 25, 26
Clegatt, Edward 25
Clegatt, Elinor 25
Clegatt, Martha 25
Cleggatt, John 223
Cleland, Alex.............. 89
Clements, Abraham 100
Clements (Clemments), An-
  drew 99, 100
Clements, Charles 138
Clements, Elinor 73
Clements, Elizabeth 138
Clements, Francis 138
Clements, Jacob 100, 138
Clements (Clemment), Joseph
  138, 176
Clements, Rhafele 176
Clements, Rosomond 73
Clements Bay 51
"Clemfast" 155
Clem Town 198
"Clerk's Directions" 227
Clifton, Sarah 14
Clifts, The 8, 223, 234, 235
Clilan, Alex.............. 84
Climar, Charles 55
Climar, Johannah 55

PAGE

Climps, Mary 207
Clinkscales, Adam 213
Clinton, Elizabeth 184
Clinton, Elinor 184
Clocker, Alice 71
Clocker, Daniell 71
Clouds (Cloud), Benjamin
                        18, 147
Clouds, Mary 147
Clouds (Cloud), Nicholas
                18, 36, 147, 159
Clouds, Notlear 147
Clouds, Richard 147
Clouds, Sarah 147
Clouds, Hermitage 147
Clouthier, Jane 144
Clouthier, Robert 144
Clyd, Robert 205
Coale, Ann................. 32
Coale, Cassandra 177
Coale, Hannah 32
Coale, Margaret 32
Coale, Mary 32
Coale, Philip 177
Coale, Priscilla 32
Coale, Samuell 32
Coale, Sarah 32
Coale, Thomas 32
Coale, William 32
Coard, Anne 225
Cobb, Assibeth 154
Cobb, Lydia 234
Cobb, John 154
Cobb, Joseph 154
Cobb, Margaret 154
Cobb, Mary 154
Cobb, Nathaniel 154
Cobb, Samuel 154
Cobb, William 154
Cobble, William 12
Coch, William 101
"Cochells Hall" 72
Cockain, John 17
"Cockalds Point" 108
"Cock's Comb"............ 38
"Cock's Head" 38
Cockerel, Abraham 230
Cockerel, Elizabeth 230
Cockshutt, Thomas 67
Cody, Deborah 222
Coe, Jane 3
Coe, Richard 3, 19
Coffer, Mary 138
Coffer, Sarah 138
Coffer, Thomas 138
Cohow, Martha 184
Colakman, Derick 15
Colbrune, William 212

PAGE

"Cold Spring" 143
Cole, Edward 171
Cole, Eleanor 29
Cole (Coale), Elizabeth
                32, 143, 171, 177
Cole, John 70, 93
Cole, Mary 214
Cole, Richard 29, 214
Cole, Robt...............69, 171
Cole, Valentine 70
Coleburne, John 83
Colegate, Richard 4, 52
Coleman (Coalman), Charles
                        127, 234
Coleman, Richard 176
Coleman, Stephen 6
Coleman, Susanna 191
"Colerain" 107
Coley, Alice 179
Coligan, Hugh 48
Colke (Caulk), Jacob 136
Colke, Peter 157
Colke, Sarah 157
College of Virginia 112
Colley, William 33
Collier, Elizabeth 176
Collier, Phillip 238
"Collington" 11
Collington (Colington)
    Branch 9, 17, 135
Collins, Charles 88
Collins, Dennis 88
Collins, Frances 232
Collins, Francis 99
Collins, James 56
Collins, Jane 88
Collins, John 30
Collins, Margaret 148
Collins, Martha 214
Collins (Collings), Mary..14, 156
Collins, Matthew 43
Collins, Samuel 14
Collins, Thomas 65
Collings (Cullin), William
                        213, 228
Collson, Ann 30, 185
Collson, Eleanor 30
Collson, Elizabeth 185
Collson, George 185
Collson, Robert 30
Colly, William 121
Colt, Dorothy 147
Colt, Robert 86
"Combes Adventure" 14
Combs, Christopher 90
Combs, Edward 218
Combs, Elizabeth 218
Combs, William 218

PAGE

Comerford, Elizabeth 109
Comerford, George 109, 214
Comerford, Thomas 113
Comegies, Mary 207
Comegys, Cornelius 101
Comegys (Comegies), Edward
42, 101, 207
Comegys, Nathaniell 4
Comegys (Comeges), William
29, 231
"Common Garden" 22
Compton (Campton), John.. 191
Compton (Campton), Mathew 191
Comyers, William 219
Conant, Robert 17
"Confusion" 124
Conihane, Matthew 232
Connill, Elizabeth 30
Connolly (Connelly), Terrence
(Terence) 158, 225
Connoway, John 44, 190
Constable, George 220
Constable, Samuell 236
Connor, Arthur 94
Connor, Nathaniel 208
Conner (Connor), Philip, 21, 181
Connor, William 104
"Containing" 110
Contee, Alexander
1, 17, 138, 140, 191
Contee, John 220
Contee, Mary 19
"Content" 62
"Contention" 58, 103
"Conveniency" 193
Conyers (Conyer), Henry
30, 31, 228
Conyers (Conyer), Sarah, 31, 228
Coode, Ann 171
Coode, Jane 171
Coode, John 69, 171
Coode, Susannah 171
Coode, Thomas 171
Coode, William.......68, 171 212
Cooke, Bethe.............. 71
Cooke, Elinor 71
Cooke, Elizabeth 71
Cooke, Harklus 113
Cooke, Henry 71
Cooke (Cook), John......71, 185
Cooke, Margaret 71
Cooke, Mary 71
Cooke, Richard 113
Cooke, Robert 162
Cooke (Cook), Thomas...71, 95
Cooke (Cook), William, 65, 71, 116
"Cooks Cove" 204
"Cooke's Folly" 171

Cooksey, Samuel 171
Cooksey, Thomas 80
Coome, Elizabeth 139
Cooper, Christina Barbara.. 172
Cooper, Edward 99
Cooper, John (Jon.)......61, 194
Cooper, Mary 99
Cooper, Nicholas 61
Cooper, Penelope 61
Cooper, Philip 61
Cooper, Richard 73
Cooper, Thomas 73
Cooper, William 61
Cope, Ann 134
Copedge, Elizabeth 35
Copedge, John 35
Copedge, Philip 35
Corbett, Benonie 91
Corbett, Margaret 91
Corbin, Edward 146, 162
Corbin, Jane 162
Corbin, Nicholas 146
"Corke" 15
Corneliur, Peter 56
"Cornliv's Hills" 6
Cornwell, John 148, 166
"Correck Measure" 66
Corsica Cr................. 78
Cosden, Alphonso 211
Costin, Elizabeth 59
Costin, Isaac 59
Costin, Sarah 59
Costin, Stephen 59
Costin, Mary 59
Costin, Mathias 59
Costin, Rebecca 59
Costin, Roody 59
"Costin's Trouble" 59
Cottann, William 94
Cotman (Cottman), Benjamin
12, 46, 49
"Cottman's Swamp" 142
Cotton, Richard 220
Couland, William 85
"Could Harbor" 105
Coulson, Ann 123
Coulton, Marmaduke 147
Course, James 210
Coursey, Elizabeth, 128, 144, 187
Coursey, Henry 128
Coursey, James 16, 187
Coursey, Jane 21, 187, 210
Coursey, John 16, 187
Coursey, Otho 5
Coursey, William
5, 36, 52, 128, 144, 160
Coursey's Creek 144
Coursey's Neck 201

PAGE

"Coursey's Range" 62
"Coursey's Town" 36
"Coursey Upon Wye".... 128
Court House 6, 198
Courts, Charity 140
Courts, John 140
Covel, Sarah 153
"Covell's Cove" 228
"Covell's Troubles" 228
"Coventry" 155
Coventry Parish 83, 101, 154
Covington, Abraham 59
Covington, Jacob 129
Covington, Levin 207
Covington, Margery 39
Covington, Sarah 144
"Cowbrook" 93
"Cowes Six" 12
"Cow Garden" 168
"Cow Quarter" 85
"Cowsking" 61
Cox, Christopher 5
Cox, Cornelius 99
Cox, Elizabeth 14, 196
Cox, Jeffrey 118
Cox, John 99, 118
Cox, Joseph 5, 118, 169
Cox, Margaret 99
Cox, Mary 5, 196
Cox, Phillip 196
Cox, Rebecca 118
"Cox Town" 93
"Coxes Freehold" 64
"Cox-hay" 234
Coy, Joathan 89
Crabb, Thomas 136
"Crab Tree Neck"........ 55
Crad, Catharine 181
Crafford, Quinton 136
Craford, James 64
Craggs, John 162
Crampton, Henry 211
Crandle, Ester 206
Crandle (Candle), Francis... 206
Crane, Robert 189
Cranford, James 65
Cranley, Elinor 218
Crans, Hannah 122
Crawford, James 236
Craxson, John 4, 194
Craxson, Thomas 4
Craycroft, Mr............ 163
Creamer, John 144
"Credentia" 4
Creed, Elizabeth 92
Creed, Mary 93, 126
Creed, William 38, 92
Crew, Edward 34

PAGE

Cribb, Richard 215
Critchet, Frances (Alias
   Watkins) 15
Critchett, John 205
Critchett, William 133
Croft, Edward 31
Cromwell, Elizabeth 112
Cromwell, John 112
Cromwell (Crumwell), Joshua
                18, 19, 112
Cromwell, Rebeckah 180
Cromwell, Richard, 112, 238, 240
Cromwell, Thomas 112
Cromwell (Crumwell),
   William 18, 112
Cronch, Elizabeth 201
Cronean, Margaret 187
Croney, Daniel 180
Croney, John 180
Crooke, James 4
"Crooked Intention" 151
"Crooked Lane" 7
Crope, Joan 95
Crope, John 95
Crope (Croper), Thomas..95, 96
Cropper, Edward 165
Croree, William 198
Crosbie, James 48
Crosby, John 123
Cross, Elinor 220
Cross, James 198
Cross, Joshua 221
Cross, Mary 220
Cross, Thomas 221
"Crosshall" 171
Crouch, John 76
Crouch, Thomas 200
Crouley, Andrew 93
Crouley, Ann 93
Crouley (Crowley), Elinor
                93, 106
Crouley, Jacob 93
Crouley, John 93
Crouley, Joseph 93
Crouley, Lucy 93
Crouley, Rosannah 93
Crouley, Ruth 93
Crouley, Triphena 93
Crowelly, Timothy 90
Crowen, Daniel 228
Crowen, Katherine 228
Crowley, Daniell 106
Crowley, Elizabeth 107
Crowlie (Crowle), Cornelius. 87
Crowlie (Crowle), Ellinner.. 87
Crowlie (Crowle), Honor.... 87
Croxon, Jas............... 172
Cruchley, James 94

PAGE

Cruchley, Thomas 167, 181
Cruickshank, Alexander 120
Crump, Walter 174
Crumpton (Crumptin),
    Johanna 139
Crumpton (Crumptin),
    Francis 139
"Cuckold's Miss"........... 23
Cullen, Edmund 45
Cullen (Cullein), James..142, 228
Cullen (Cullin), John.....49, 228
Cullen, William 142
Culy, Samuel 126
Cumberbitch, Rebecca 135
"Cumberland" 162

PAGE

Cumming (Cummins), Mich.. 118
Cundon, Jas................ 158
Cunningham, John 145
Curey, Thomas 35
Curiven, George 233
Currier, Elizabeth 11
Currier, John 11
Curtis, James 102, 103
Curtis, Michael 51, 69
Cusack, George 130, 184
Cusack, Mary 130, 184
Cusack, Michall 130, 184
Cuttance, Josias 12
Cuttling, William 45
Cutts, John 61

D

Daffan, George 90
Dalby, Thomas 238
Daley, Pat................. 50
Daliner, Ka................ 172
"Dancing Branch" 176
Danes, Antho 78
Daniell, Frances 30
Daniell, Michel 65
Daniell, William 30
"Daniels Addition" 149
"Dansburry Hill" 173
Dansey, John 51
Dansey, Martha 51, 127
Dansey, Robert 51, 127
Dant, John 68
Dant, William 68
"Darby" 200
Dare, Nath................. 64
Dare, William 213
"Darland" 200
Darnall 9
Darnall (Darnell), Henry
                    9, 10, 110
Darnall, John 79
Darnall, Mr................ 125
Dashiel, Bridget 46
Dashiell, Elizabeth 177
Dashiell, George 177
Dashiell, Hast.............. 176
Dashiell (Dashiel), James,46, 176
Dashiell, Mathias 176
Dashiell, Rebeckah 177
Dashiell (Dashiel), Robert
                       46, 176
Dashiell, Sarah 177
Dashiell, Thomas 177
Dashiell, William 176
Dason, John 180
Dason, Mary 180
Davies' Creek 209

Davis, Ann 72
Davis, Briscoe 72
Davis, Easter 213
Davis, Edward 175, 216
Davis, Elizabeth 148
Davis, George 72
Davis, Henry 19
Davis, Isaiah 232
Davis, John
        49, 65, 72, 148, 155, 156
Davis, Margaret 98
Davis, Martha 65
Davis, Mary 72, 180, 185
Davis, Nicholas 40
Davis, Onor................ 98
Davis, Rachell 98
Davis, Richard 49, 106
Davis, Samuel 180
Davis, Sarah 49
Davis, Thomas
        49, 65, 98, 140, 163, 179, 180
Davis, Walter 198
Davis, William 20, 98, 123
Davis' Bridge 200
Davis' Inlet 49
"Davis Pharsalia" 158
Davison, Sara 148
Dawaoughte, Ann 152
Dawaoughte (Dawaoughate),
    Charles 152
Dawaoughate, George 152
Dawaoughate, John 152
Dawe (Daw), Edward...... 235
Dawe (Daw), Mary........ 235
Dawe (Daw), Nathan....... 235
Dawkins, Ann 37
Dawkins, Dorcas 30
Dawkins, James 30
Dawkins, Joseph 30
Dawkins, Maragarett 30

PAGE

Dawkins, Mary 30
Dawkins, Sarah 30
Dawkins, William 30, 37, 64
Dawson, Anne......148, 187, 226
Dawson, Cathrine 207
Dawson, Edward 122
Dawson, Elizabeth 149, 197
Dawson, Isabel (Eisbel).... 187
Dawson, James 148, 156
Dawson, John 187, 202, 226
Dawson, Jonas 187
Dawson, Jos. 151
Dawson, Mary 2, 139
Dawson, Nick...........61, 94
Dawson, Ralph 197
Dawson, Sarah 38
Dawson, Susanah 226
Dawson, Thomas 122
Dawson, William 197
Day, Ann 24
Day, Elizabeth 5
Day, George 24
Day, Jonn 24
Day, Lewcresia 189
Day, Margarett 24
Day, Mary 24
Day, Nich............... 5
Day, Robert 24
Day, Sarah 5, 143
Day, William 24
Deah, Richard 116
Deakins, John 53, 108
Deale 172
Deane, Charles 117
Deane, William 55
Deaver, Gilbard 65
Deavour, James 211
Decowdra, Martha 53
Deep Branch 120
Deford, Lewis 95
Delany (Dullany), William.. 62
Delaware Bay 85
Deliatt, Elizabeth 234
Delicourt, James 188
Dellebrook Mannor 211
Demillion, Anne 164
Deminit, Elizabeth 15
Deminit, James 15
Deminit, William 15
Denaly, Elizabeth 115
Denan, John 8
"Denby" 9
Denine, Elizabeth 233
Denine, Henry 233
Dennett, H................ 237
Dennis, Donnack 82, 155
Dennis, Elizabeth 82
Dennis, John 79, 82

PAGE

Dennis, Margaret 82
Dennis, Theopolus 82
Dennis, William 82
"Dennis' Purchase" 82
Denney, Peter 180
Denney (Denny), Sarah..180, 187
Denny, Anna 5
Denny, Charles 187
Denny, Christopher 5
Dent, Ann 59, 175
Dent, Elizabeth 226
Dent (Dentt), George, 2, 59, 175
Dent, Major 51
Dent, Rebeckah 59, 175
Dent, William 61
Denton, Vachell 26, 82
Denton, William 43
Deocan, James 78
Dermitt, Jos............... 162
Derrickson, Andreas 46
Derrickson, Benjamin 46
Derrickson, Joseph Andreas.. 46
Derrickson, Temperance 46
Derrickson, Samuel 46
Deucey, Margaret 40
Devall, Sarah 211
Deveres, Mich.............. 155
"Deviding Values" 199
Devinish, Ishmael 95
Dew, Ann 91, 92
Dew, John 91, 92
Dew, Patrick 91, 92
Dew, Rachel 91, 92
De Witt, John............. 10
Diall, Catherine 178
Diall, Denis 178
Diall, Hannah 178
Diall, Hester 178
Dickenson, Charles 156
Dickenson, Rebecca 156
Dickenson, William 7
Dickinson, Edward .... 126.
Dickinson, Isabella 113
Dickinson, James 120
Dickinson (Dickenson), John
                        126, 156
Dickinson, Judith 225
Dickinson, Samuel 120, 225
Dickinson, Sarah 126
Dickinson (Dickenson),
    Sidney 156
Dicks, Robt................ 75
Dickson (Dixon), Elizabeth. 62
Dickson (Dixon), John..... 62
Dickus, William 101
Digges, Charles 10, 125
Digges, Dudley 10
Digges, Edward 9

PAGE

Digges, Elizabeth 9
Digges, Mary 9
Digges, William 10
"Digges Point" 9
Diggs, Henry 204
Diggs, John 9
Diggs, Susanna Maria...125, 204
Dillgha, Jenny 152
Dillon, Thomas, 69, 73, 132, 173
Dinard's Point 171
Disharoone, Anne 76
Disharoone, John 76
Disharoone, Mary 76
Disharoone, Michael 76
Disharoone, Sarah 76
Disharoone, Rachell 76
Disharoone, William 76
Dison, Thomas 66
"Dispute" 96
"Ditteridge" 112
"Dividing Cr." 59, 115
"Dividing Hills" 198
"Dividing Run" 184
Dixon, William 103
Doagan, John 199
Doagan, Mary 199
Doagan, Thomas 199
Doagan, William 199
Dobson, James 121
Dobson, William 107
Dodd, Anne 2
Dodd, Mary 1
Doddson, John 26
"Dodson's Desire" 143
"Doggwood Springs" 72
Dohaty, Elizabeth 103
Dohaty, James 103
Dohaty, Janett 103
Dohaty, Katharine 103
Dohaty, Mary 103
Dohaty, Rose 103
Dohaty, Sarah 103
Dollar, Elizabeth 175
Donaldson, John 51, 109
Done, John 26
Donnell, Shute 234
Donnoghoe (Donoghue),
  Daniell 6, 14
Donnoghoe, Elinor 6
Donnoghoe, John 6
Donnoghoe, Matthew 6
Donnohon, Dan'll 155
Dorey, P.................. 214
Dorin, Charles 63
Dorin, Neomy 63
Dorrington, Joseph 27
Dorrington, Margaret 163
Dorrington, Mary 27, 75, 85

PAGE

Dorrington, Thomas 27
Dorrington, William 75, 168
Dormond, Cattran 86
Dorman, Henry 105
Dorman, Mathew 76, 105, 179
Dorman, Samuel 102
Dorrumple (Derrumple), John
  64, 164, 211
Dorrumple, William 142
Dorset, Ann 163
Dorset, John 163
Dorset, Mary 163
Dorsey, Acksah 25
Dorsey, Bazill 25
Dorsey, Benjamin 130
Dorsey, Caleb 25, 184
Dorsey, Deborah 25
Dorsey, Edward 25, 130
Dorsey, Frances 130
Dorsey, John 25, 130
Dorsey, Josh............... 130
Dorsey, Nicholas 130
Dorsey, Phillip 196
Dorsey, Pleasance 25
Dorsey, Richard 25
Dorsey, Samuell, 25, 26, 52, 185
Dorsey, Sophia 25
Dorsey, Thomas 130
"Dorsey's Adventure" 25
"Dorsey's Search" 25
Dossey, Edward 31
Dossey, John 31
Dossey, William 31
"Dottrage, Lettice" 213
"Double Creek" 144
"Doughtyes Hope" 150
"Doughtyes Lott" 150
Douglass, Anne 16
Douglass (Douglas), Benjamin
  59, 175
Douglass, George 16
Douglass, John 175
Douglas, Joseph 175
Douglass, Mary 71, 175
Douglas, Thomas 175
Douglas (Douglass), William
  15, 71, 131
Douse, Wm................. 117
Dover, William 131
Dowe (See Dawe)
Dowel, Edward 238
"Dowlsdall" 50
"Downdale" 222
Downes, Jeremiah 202
Downes, Jeremy 162
Downs, John 161
Downs, George 12
Downs, Kedimoth 161

	PAGE
Downs, Robert	47
Doyne, Elizabeth	130
Doyne, Ethelbert	184
Doyne, Jean	221
Doyne, Jessie	140
Draper, Lawrence	16
Draper, William	23
Dreadin, David	226
"Dressing Branch"	163
Drew, Antho	204
Drew, Margaret	204
Driskell, Dennis	178
Drummond, Rose	193
Drury, John	173
Dryden (Drayden), Isabella 185, 189	
"Drydocking"	123
Dryers, Samuel	31
Dublin	29, 114
"Duck Pye"	78
Ducks, Ann	104
Ducks, Elizabeth	86
Ducks, Grace	104
Ducks, John	104
Ducks, Rachel	104
Ducks, Robert	104
Duckett, Richard	62, 141, 186
Dudley, Richard	60, 205
Dudley, Thomas	205
Dudley, William	60
Duke, Andrew	30
Duke, James	30, 65
Dukes, Henry	145
Dukes, Susanna	145
Dulany, Catherine	54
Dulany, D.	19
Dullany, Darby	36
Dulsey (Dussey), Bryan	188
Dulton-Colt, Robt.	147
Dunavin (Donovan), James	88
"Dunbar"	28
"Dunbar and Bloomsberry"	172
Dunckly, Bassill	232
Dunckly, Rebekah	232
Dundee	200
Dunekin, George	230
Dunington, Ann	134
Dunington, Francis	133, 224
Dunington, Rebecca	133
"Dunn Back"	135
Dunn, Robert	78
Dunn, Stephen	64
"Dunsmore Heath"	158
Duplex, Ann	134
Duplex, Rebecca	134
Durbin, Christopher	161
Durbin, Thomas	161
Durden, Elizabeth	38
Durden, John	38
Durgee, Andrew	213
Durham Town	61
Duscol Derby	167
Duskey, Moses	114
Duson, William	238
Duvall, Mareen	17

E

	PAGE
Eadkin, Mary	140
Eager, John	161
Eagle, Saladine	190
Eareckson, Benjamin	214
Eareckson (Erreckson), Charles	57, 214
Eareckson, Elizabeth	214
Eareckson, John	214
Eareckson, Mathew	214
Earle, Anne	187
Earle, Carpenter	187
Earle, Elizabeth	187
Earle, James	187
Earle, Joseph	76, 160
Earle, Michael	187
Earle, Samuel	147
Early, Elizabeth	116
Early, John	116
"Early's Chance"	116
East Marsh Range	168
East Otwell	218
East Town	57
Easterling, John	38
Eastern Shore	165, 220, 236
Eats, Catharine	169
Eaty, Rachel	12
Eccleston, Margaret	169
Eccleston, Mary	141, 209
Edelen, Sarah	66
Eden, Henry	28
Edgar (Edger), Bridget	57
Edgar, Henry (Harre)	55
Edgar (Edger), James	55, 57, 75
Edgar, Tryphen	75
Edge, Margaret	54
Edge, Thomas	54
Edling, Richard	43
Edlos, Joseph	197
Edlowes Shoire	236
Edmonds, Alexander	109
Edmonds, Benjamin	237
Edmonds, Jas.	188
Edmondson, William	156
Edmonson, John	143

	PAGE
Edmonton	148
Edwards, Elizabeth	186
Edwards, John	234
Edwards, Joseph	29, 113
Edwards, Moses	146
Edwards, Richard	176
Edwards, Stourton	29
Edwin, Mary	55
Edwin, Michaell	55
Edwin, William	55
Eilson, Epr.	115
Elbert, William	95
Elden, William	240
Elder, John	217
Elderton, James	189
Eldridge, Jeremy	233
Elexsander, John	79
Elexsander, Robert	79
"Elizabeth's Delight"	9
Elk Ridge	25
"Elk Thickett"	228
Ellett, Thomas	11
Elletson, Rodger	163
Elliot (Eliott), Edward	8, 116
Elliot, Robert	211
Elliott, William	68, 192
Ellis, Ann	67
Ellis, Benjamin	230
Ellis, Hannah	159
Ellis, Jane	202
Ellis, John	230
Ellis Owen	41, 67
Ellis, Patrick	34
Ellis, Thomas	115
Ellis, William	125, 230
Ellit, Henry	106
Ellmes, William	6
Ellsing	117
"Ellson"	75
Ellt, Elinor	44
Ellt (Eltt), Henry	24, 65
Ellt, Mary	44
Ellt (Eltt), William	24, 44
Elt, John	24
Elzey, Arnold	114, 153
Elzey, Elizabeth	86
Elzey, Frances	86
Elzey, John	42
Elzey, Peter	86
Elzey, Sarah	114
"Emerby's Square"	157
Emerson, Alice	74
Emerson, Anna	74
Emerson, Elizabeth	197
Emerson, J.	74
Emerson, Katherine	74
Emerson, Redman John	74
Emerson, Richard	74

	PAGE
Emerson, Thomas	74, 197
"Emissex"	47
Emnit, Elizabeth	12
Emory, Ann	145
Emory, Arthur	145, 197, 198
Emory, John	122
Emos, Thomas	108
"Enden Spring"	35
England(See Gr. Britain)	
English (Engelich), Alex.	90
English, Anne	227
"Enlargement"	181
Ennalls Bartholomew	168
Ennalls, Elizabeth	167
Ennalls, Henry	168
Ennalls, John	168
Ennalls, Joseph	167
Ennalls, Sarah	169
Ennalls, Thomas	167
Ennalls, William	216
Ennall's Creek	168
"Ennalls' Inheritance"	168
"Ennalls' Outlet"	168
"Ennalls Purchase"	168
"Ennalls Reserve"	167
Ennises, William	216
Ensey, John	163
Esgate, Stephen	158
Estey, Richard	136
Eunall, William	54
Evan, Job.	4
Evans, Abigall	56
Evans, Anne	213
Evans, Anthony	120
Evans (Evins), Curtis	158
Evans, David	24, 165
Evans (Evens), Edward, 80, 110
Evans (Evins), Elizabeth, 148, 158
Evans (Evins), Griffith, 158, 182
Evans, Jane	129
Evans (Evens), John, 54, 109, 148
Evans (Evens), Joseph, 149, 156
Evans, Mary	192
Evans, Suener	24
Evans, Thomas	191, 213
Evans, William	57, 93, 125
Everett, Jane	160
Everitt, Rachel	159
Evins, Jeffrey	119
Ewbanks, Ann	7
Eubanks (Ewebanks), Richard	7, 174
Ewbanks (Ewebanks), Thomas	118, 174
"Exchange"	117, 153
Exell, Samuel	169
Exell, Sarah	169
Eyton, Richard	2

F

PAGE

Fairbanck, Ann 9
Fairbanck (Fairbank) (Farebank), David 9, 151
Fairbanck, Hannah 9
Fairbanck (Fairbank) (Farebank), John 9, 151
Fairbank, Elizabeth 151
Fairbank (Farebank), Mary Ann 151
Fairbrother, Thomas 135
Fairfax, John 3
"Fairfields" 12
"Fairhaven" 85
Fall, Abraham 213
Fall, John 213
Fall, Mary 213
Fanning, Benja............. 43
Fanning, Edward 21
Fanning, Mary 230
Farfax, John 191
Farlie (Farloe), Creek.....6, 29
Farmeorth (Farmleorch), Elizabeth 199
Farmer, Elizabeth 7
"Farnham" 126
"Farney Hill" 199
Farnile, John 211
Farr, Edward 51
Farr, John 199
Farrels, Agnes 169
Farrels, Daniels 169
Farroll, Richard 232
Fary, Charles 237
Fary, Francis 237
Fary, Joseph 237
Fary, Mary 237
Fary, Robert 237
Faulkinn, Ann 122
Faulkinn, John 122
Faulkinn, Mary 122
Faulkinn, Peter 122
Faulkinn, Valentine 122
Faulkinn, William 122
Feabus, George 86
"Fearborrough" 224
Fearnly (Fernly), Henry... 233
Feddeman, Mary 150
Feddeman, Philip 150, 168
Feddeman, Richard 168
Fellengame (Fillengame), John 198
Fellengame (Fillengame), Richard 198
Fellengame (Fillengame), Sarah 198
Fellows, John 149

PAGE

"Fellowship" 142
Fendall, John 3, 178
Fenwick, Cuthbert 13, 229
Fenwick, Elizabeth 64
Fenwick, Enoch 13, 229
Fenwick, Ignatius 13, 229
Fenwick, John 13, 229
Fenwick, Richard 13, 229
Ferrill, Frances 136
Ferrill, Mathew 136
"Ferry Point" 220
Field, Ann 97
Field, Edward 51
Fielder (Filder), Barbary... 192
Fielder (Filder), William... 192
"Findone" 137
"Fisher's Choyce" 8
Fisher, Abraham 127
Fisher, Alexander 75
Fisher, Dorrington 8
Fisher, Elizabeth 75, 188
Fisher, Isabella 195
Fisher, Mark 75, 106
Fisher, Mary 8, 76
Fisher, Rachell 8
Fisher, Sarah 8, 181
Fisher, Thomas 75, 181
Fisher (Fish), William
16, 195, 206
"Fishbourn's Landing" 118
Fishing Bay 58
Fitchew (Ficzchew), Walter 95
Fitzharbert, Harry 233
Fitzpabuck, Charles 6
Fitz Redmond, William 217
"Five Pines" 56
Fitzgarritt, Rachell 34
Fitzgerald, Margaret 42
Fizgerrald, Rachel 100
Fizhew, Ann 100
Flanesey, Margaret 222
Fleharty, Francis 30
Fleming, Ellis 24
Fleming, John 85
"Flent" 153
Fletchell, Anne 110
Fletchell, Elizabeth 110
Fletchell (Fletchall), Thomas
110, 141, 162
Fletcher, Dorothy 5
Fletcher, Michael 5
Flolerty, John 230
Flowers, John 57, 141
Flowry (Flowers), John..... 8
Floyd, Ellinor 240
Floyd, Jasper 126

	PAGE
Foard, William	123
Folson, Amy	180
Foning, Benony	3
Foning, Hannah	3
Fooke, Gerard	61
Fookes, William	168
"Foole Play"	147
"Forbearance"	145
"Forcett's Plains"	160
Ford, John	173
Forde, Leah	167
Ford, Rachell	34
Ford, Robert	22, 34, 173
Fordham, Benjamin	217
Fordham, Lydia	217
Fordman, Benjamin	135
Fordman, John	135
Fordman, Joseph	135
Fordman, Lydia	135
Fordman, Margaret	135
Fordman, Richard	135
Fordman, Sarah	135
Foreman, Arthur	230
Foreman, Charles	230
Foreman, Elizabeth	230
Foreman, John	230
Foreman, Margaret	230
Foreman, Robert	230
Foreman, William	225, 230
"Forest of Dane"	126
Forman, Thomas	235
Forrest, Richard	208
"Forrest Landing"	46
Forrester, Mary	217
Forrester, Peter	217
Forster (Foester) (Foster), Ann	97, 119, 169
Forster (Foester), Wm.	97, 119
Forward, Jonathan	220
Foskell, Elizabeth	32
Foster, Alice	158
Foster, Elinor	228
Foster, James	98
Foster, John	168
Foster, Phoebe	169
Foster, Mary	168
Foster, Rebecca	169
Foster, Sarah	169
Fountaine (Fantain), John	13, 153, 212
Fountaine, Marcy	13, 104
Fountain, Mary	212
Fountaine (Fountain), Nicholas	13, 212
Fowler, Ann	203
Fowler, Daniel	203
Fowler, John	44
Fowler, Priscilla	221
Fowler, William	141
Fowset, Ann	85
"Fox Hill"	96
Foy, Hannah	24
"Frampton" ("Framtum")	158
Francis, Mary	202
Francis, Thomas	202
"Frankford"	16
"Frankford's Addition"	16
Franklin, Bridgett	165
Franklin, Robert	45
Fraser, Ann	1
Fraser, John	138
Fray, Charles	94
Fray, Jane	94
Fray, William	94
Frawner, Mary	3
"Freebornes Progress"	145
Freeborne, Richard	26, 145
Free Schools	5, 210
Freeman, Fran	236
Freeman, Henry	233
Freeman, John	32
Freeman, Thomas	237
Freeman, William	136
French, James	73
French, Mary	36
French, Samuell	36
French, Thomas	4, 36
French, Zerubabell	36
"Friend's Choice"	48
"Friend's Discovery"	49
Friends (See Quakers)	
"Friendship"	123, 129
"Friendship Rectifyed"	142
Frinde, James	240
Frisby, Ann	6
Frisby, James	6
Frisby, Richard	6
Frisby, Stephen	6
Frisby, William	6
"Frisby's Conveniency"	6
"Frisby's Purchase"	6
Frith, Henry	185
Frith, Rebecca	185
"Frogg Hall"	171
Full, George	192
"Fuller"	143
Fulston, Richard	29
Furgusson (Ferguson), Elizabeth	8, 184
Furgusson, George	8
"Furn's Choice"	153
Fyffe, Gil	134

G

	PAGE
Gage, John	90
Gahart, Peter	18
"Gahead"	209
Galahaw, Katherine	73
Gale, Benjamin	39
Gale, Elizabeth	18
Gale, John	39
Gallaway, William	15
Galloway (Gallaway), Richard	32, 33, 183
Galloway, Samuell	45
Galloway, Sophia	183
Gambrell, Anne	190
Gambrell, William	235
Gannell, George	240
Gantt(Gant), Anne	123, 236
Gantt (Gant), Edward	236
Gantt (Gant), Elizabeth	123, 196, 236
Gant, James	123
Gant, John	123
Gant, Mary	123
Gant, Mathew	123
Gardiner, Ann	128
Gardiner, Clements	128, 171
Gardiner, Edward	59
Gardiner (Gardner), Elizabeth	128, 163
Gardiner, Henrietta Maria	128
Gardiner, James	214
Gardiner, John	123, 128
Gardiner, Mary	128, 214
Gardiner, Richard	128
Gardiner, Susannah	128
Gardiner, Wilfraid	128
Gardiner, William	221
"Gardiner's Grove"	128
"Gardiner's Purchase"	126
Gardner, Alexander	38
Gardner, Biningman	163
Gardner, Frances	38
Gardner, Joseph	163
Gardner (Gardiner), Luke	163, 204
Gardner, Ralph	163
Gardner, Samuel	163
Gardner, Tebbra	38
Garfoot, Charles	231
Garland, Randall	10
Garman, Stephen	61
Garner, Ann	179
Garner, Matthew	164
Garretson, Garrett	204
Garrett, Amos	18, 196
Garris, George	178
"Garrison Plain"	121

	PAGE
Garrison Ridge	4, 161
Gartrell (Garterell), John	94
Gassaway, Susanna	40
Gassaway, Thomas	36, 40
Gates, John	66
Gates, Joseph	66
Gate, Katharine	12
Gates, Robert	234
Gattes, Richard	206
Gaudy, John	36, 75
Gauskins Point	121
Gauslin, Hannah	201
Gautherin, Mary	237
Gautherin, Mathew	237
Gemmett, Grace	1
Gendaron, Mark	83
"George's Desire"	108
"Georges Park"	182
Gerrard, ——	239
Gerrard, John	17
Gesep, Joseph	90
Getward, Rebecca	136
Gibb (Gibbs), John	37, 170
Gibbon (Gibbins), John	153, 166
Gibson, Alice	98
Gibson, Anne	149
Gibson, Jacob	149, 227
Gibson, James	24, 207
Gibson, Katherine	69
Gibson, Richard	149
Gibson, Sophia	149
Gibson, William	69
Gibson, Wookman (Woolman)	112, 227
Giddins, Benjamin	60
Giddins, Catherine	60
Giddins, Elizabeth	48
Giddins, M.	61
Giddins, Mary	47
Giddins, Maurice	60
Giddins, Thomas	47
Giffard, Douglas	175
"Gilbert's Adventure"	16
Gilbert's Bridges	3
Gilbert, Hannah	16
Gilbert, Michaell	16
Gilbert, Thomas	16
Giles, Elizabeth	143
Giles, Rachel	211
Gill, Jane	121
Gill, Steven (Stephen),	121, 161
Gillespie, George	48, 172, 189
Gillimore, Torle	21
Gillis, John	77
"Gilmort's Fields"	198
"Gilmort Hills"	198

PAGE

Ginkens, Jane 170
Ginkins, Jean 170
Giraus, James 103
Giraus, Mary 103
Giraus, Robert 103
"Girl's Portion" 184
Gist, Edith 112
Gist, Richard 112
Gist, Zippora 112
Gittings, Mary 217
Givan, Robert 49
"Glaids Addition" 179
Glanvill, John 219
Glanvill, Martha 219
Glanvill, Mary 219
Glanvill, Nathaniel 219
Glanvill, Rachel 219
Glanvill, Stephen 219
Glanvill, William 6, 219
Glass, Christopher 77
Glaze, John 163
Glebe Land 67
"Gledling Pt." 39
Glen, Ann 52
Glen, Jacob 16
Glen, John 218
Glen, William 5
Glives, George 230
Gload, Ambrose 35
Gloid, Rachell 36
Glover, Thomas 126
Glover, William 61
Godfry, Mary 134
Godfrey, William 30, 120
Goding, Mary 148
Godman, Jno............... 68
Godsgrace, John 24
"Godumne" 117
Godwin, Jos................ 47
Gody, Margaret 12
Goforth, Sarah 8
Goforth, William 158
Goforth, Willoby 7
"Golden Grove".......125, 204
"Golden Race" 39
Goldhawk, George 21
Goldsberry, Edward 170
Goldsberry, John 170
Goldsberry (Gouldberry),
    Margaret 170
Goldsberry, Robert 170
Goldsberry, William 170
Goldsborgh, Margaret....... 122
Goldsborgh, William 122
Goldsborough (Goulds-
    borough), Robert.......6, 200
Goldsmith (Gouldsmith),
    George 239, 240

PAGE

"Goldsmith Inlargement".. 239
Goldsmith, Martha 239
Goldsmith, Mary 18, 239
"Goldsmith's Rest"........ 239
Goldsmith, Thomas Notley
    (Nottley) 18, 43, 51
Goletie, Thomas 3
Goley, John 203
Gooch, John 1
"Good Intent" 66
"Good Luck"...37, 65, 136, 162
Goodman, Ann 118
Goodman, Francis 10
Goodman, Rebecca 21
Goodman (Godman), Thomas
    21, 94, 113, 181
Goody (Gody), William...3, 12
Goose Cr................42, 88
"Goosey's Addition" 23
"Goosey's Choice" 2, 23
"Goosey's Comeagain" 23
"Goosey's Lott" 23
"Gorden's Delight" 176
Gordon, Mary 49
"Gotherd's Folley" 11, 12
Gott, Anthony 27
Gott, Capell 27
Gott, John 27
Gott, Matthew 27
Gott, Richard 26, 161, 183
Gott, Robert 26, 27, 123
Gott, Samuell 27
Gott, Sarah 27, 183
Gottrell, Amos 138
Gough, James 18
Gouldsberry, John 32
"Gover's Hills" 40
Grady (Gredy), Owen 88
Graifan, Thomas 196
"Gramer's Chance" 50
Granes, Amey (Amy),....... 234
Granges, William 210
"Grasin Creek" 209
Grasty, Ann 198
Grasty, Samuel, 125, 133, 198, 209
Gray, Andrew 138
Gray, Elizabeth 138
Gray, George 24
Gray, Isabel 75
Gray, Jacob.........55, 57, 75
Gray (Grey), John
    48, 82, 117, 138, 153, 179, 215
Gray, Joseph 225
Gray, Judith 140
Gray, Miles 153
Gray, Mr.................. 166
Gray, Thomas 138
Gray, William 38, 82

	PAGE
Gray, Zachariah	179
Grayham, Thomas	27
Greace (Grace), John	196
Greace, John Clark	196
Grear, Annanias	41
Grear, Benjamin	41
Grear, Henry	41
Grear, James	41
Grear, John	41
Grear, Joseph	41
Great Branch	88
Great Britain, 5, 40, 48, 89, 94, 99, 112, 114, 120, 123, 132, 134, 137, 162, 167, 181, 210, 217, 220	223
Great Choptank Parish	56
Great Choptank R., 81, 135, 143, 168, 181, 186, 218, 220, 233	
"Great Hopes"	45
"Great Neck"	180, 196
Green Anne	73
"Green Branch"	213
Green, Charity	66
Green, Elizabeth	14, 58
Green, Henry	43
Green, James	34, 71
Green, John	189
Green, Mary	71
"Green Oak"	125
Green, Richard	87
Green, Sarah	30
Green, Thomas	71
Green, William	97
"Greenfield"	76
Greenfield, ——	14
Greenfield, Elizabeth	127
Greenfield, James	39
Greenfield, Jone	39
Greenfield, Martha	39
Greenfield, Mary	51, 127
Greenfield, Micajah	39
Greenfield, Thomas	39, 51
Greenfield, Thomas Truman 29, 39, 127, 212	
Greenfield, Truman	172
Greenhill Town	193
Greenwell, Catherine	73, 99
Greenwell, Charles	18
Greenwell, Grace	17
Greenwell, Henry	18
Greenwell, Ignatius	18
Greenwell, James	17, 18
Greenwell, Jane	18
Greenwell (Greenwill), John 18, 99, 172	
Greenwell, Justinian	18
Greenwell, Stephen	18
Greenwell, Thomas	18
Greenwell, William	18
"Greenwidge"	176
Gregory, John	23
"Grey's Chance"	143
Grey, Edward	82
Grey, Francis	82
Grey (Gray), James	82, 225
Grey, Richard	82
Grey, Thomas	82
Griggs, John	235
Griffin, Anne	178
Griffins, Charles	208
Griffin, James	62
Griffin, Judith	125
Griffin (Griffen), Lewes (Lewis) 55, 57	75
Griffin, Oliver	178
Griffen, Richard	201
Griffen, Thomas	201
Griffen, Williams	143
Griffiith, Elizabeth	210
Griffith, John	209
Griffith, Mary	209
Griffith, Mathew	21
Griffith, Samuel	56, 91, 92, 210
Griffith, William	94
Groase, Sarah	115
"Groome's Lott"	235
Groome, William	212
Groon, Richard	39
Grose, Elizabeth	11
Grove, Robert	132
Groves, George	2
Groves, John	2, 59
Groves, Mary	2
Groves, Matthew	2
Groves, William	2
Grundy, Margaret	181
Grunwin, Thomas	197
Gudgen (Gudgeon), William 238, 240	
Guest, ——	238
Guest, Christopher	238
Guest, Edith	112
Guest (Gest) (Gist), Richard	112, 240
Guibert, Elizabeth	69
Guine, Thomas	162
"Guins Falls"	121
Guithine, Mary	120
Guithins, Benjamin	120
Guithins (Guitthins), Morris	120
Gulick, Nicholas	165
Gumley, Deborah	84
Gumley, James	84
Gunby, John	225
"Gunner's Harbor"	78
Gunpowder Falls	146

. PAGE

Gunpowder R.
15, 51, 79, 108, 197, 239
Gunthrope, Jonathan 36
Gunthrope Sam'll 36
Gurr, Jonathan 216
"Gutriges Choice" 180
Guyther, Dorothy 90
Guyther, Mary 90
Guyther, Nicholas 172
Guyther, Owen 90
"Guyther's Purchase" 71
Guyther, Sarah 90

PAGE

Guyun, John 2
Gwinn (Guin), Ann 40, 53
Gwyn, Hannah 78
Gwyn, James 78
Gwyn, John 78
Gwyn, Robert 78
Gyles, Richard 192
Gyllot, Abraham 83
Gyllot, George 83
Gyllot, John 83
Gyllot, Mary 83
Gyllot, William 83

H

Haa, George 117
"Haccots Chance" 87
Hackett, Elizabeth 117
Hackett, Litia 117
Hackett, Michael 146
Hackett, Nicholas 218
Hackett, Oliver 117
Hackett, Theophilius 117
Hacket (Hackett), Thomas
36, 117
Hackney, Margaret 209
"Hadden" 186
Hadder, Anthony 202
Hadder, Mary 202
Hadder, Sarah 202
Hadder, Worring 202
Haddock, James 9, 139, 220
Hagan, James 98
Hagan, Thomas 98
Hages, John 124
Hagoe, Ignatius 66
Hagoe, James 66
Hagoe, Mary 66
Hagoe, Thomas 66
Hagoe, William 66
Haking (Hackins), Robert.. 205
Halayrd (See Hillyard).
Haley, Rosehana 126
Halfpenny, Francis 36
Halkmer, John 205
Hall, Abraham 188
Hall, Ann 150
Hall, Aquila 162
Hall, Benjamin 9, 218
Hall, Dorothy 202
Hall, Edward
128, 148, 149, 162, 188
Hall, Elihu 93
Hall, Elisha 93, 218
Hall, Elizabeth 220
Hall, Francis 9
Hall, George 202
Hall, Henry 127, 215

Hall, James 188
Hall, Jane 202
Hall, John
1, 13, 19, 39, 162, 188, 238
Hall, Joseph 67
Hall, Mary
47, 93, 148, 179, 188, 218
Hall, Richard 93, 133
Hall, Robert...109, 149, 207, 220
Hall, Sarah........ 93, 148, 218
Hall, Thomas 149, 188
Hall, William 149
"Hall's Choice" 50
"Hall's Harbour" 149
"Hall's Hills" 93
"Hall's Lott" 50
"Hall's Mount" 93
"Hall's Ridge" 93
Halsall, John 142
Halsall, Ruth 142
Hamphrey's Creek 162
"Hambleton" 23
Hambleton, Andrew 136
Hambleton's Branch 96
Hambleton, David 82
Hambleton, Edward..60, 73, 122
Hambleton, Elizabeth 73
Hambleton, Margaret 73
Hambleton, Sarah 73
Hambleton, William
6, 9, 73, 148, 151, 186
Hambrooke, John 75
Hambrooke, Mary 75
Hamilton, A 36
Hamilton, Alexander 9
Hamilton, Andrew 94, 211
Hamilton, Anne 16
Hamilton, Jane 130
Hamilton, Mary 211
Hamilton (Hableton) (Ham-
illton),William 19,71,145, 162
Hammitt, John 216
Hammon (Hamon), Anne... 160

PAGE

Hammon, Edward 178
Hammon (Hamon), Elizabeth 160
Hammon (Hamon), James... 160
Hammon (Hamon), Jean.... 160
Hammon (Hamon), John 160, 178
Hammon (Hamon), Richard
148, 160
Hammon (Hamon), Thomas 160
Hammon (Hamon), Walter.. 160
Hammon (Hamon), William. 160
Hammond, John 123, 164, 179
Hammond, Thomas 4
Hampton, John 25, 115
Hampton, Mary 59
"Hampstead" 209
"Hamsted" 233
Hanah, Mrs. 68
Hancock, Charity 126
Handy, Elizabeth 192
Handy, William 192
"Hangman's Folly" 78
Hanson, Ann 17
Hanson, Benjamin 17, 22
Hanson, Frederick 53
Hanson, George 52, 54, 210
Hanson, Hans 53
Hanson, Jacob 22
Hanson, John 17, 140
Hanson, Mary 17
Hanson, Robert 17, 118, 140
Hanson, Samuell
17, 134, 140, 175, 178
Hanson, Sarah 17, 22
Hanson, Thomas 22
Haper, John 229
"Haphazard" 30, 131, 151
"Happata Venture" 164
"Harbert's Chance" 175
Harbert, Sarah 175
Harbert, Vitus 205
Harbert, William 12, 175
Harbin, Francis 234
Harde, Elizabeth 184
Harde, George 184
Harde, Ignatius 184
Harde, John 184
Harde, William 184
"Hardfortune" 23
Hardick, Sarah 110
Hardin (Harden) (Harding),
Edward 60, 120, 217
Hardin, John 182
Harding, Thomas 175
"Hardshift" 98, 131
"Hardship" 211
Hardy, Ann 19
Hardy, George 19
Hardy, Henry 19, 119

"Hardy's Purchase" 19
Hardy, William 70
Hargess, Abraham 97
Hargess, Francis 97
Hargess, Thomas 97
Hargess, William 97
"Hargess Hope" 97
Hargrave, Isaac 231
Harlock, Edward 233
Harmon, Henry 32
"Harmless" 75
Harnack 153
Harney, Philip 73
Harp, Joseph 19, 145
Harper, Edward 59
Harper, Francis 59, 212
Harper, Henry 59, 137
Harper, James 233
Harper, John 59
Harper, Mary 137
Harper, Richard 59
Harper, Samuel 57, 75
Harper, Sarah 59
Harper, William 59
Harrell, William 107
Harrington. Elias 43
Harriod, Olliver 238
Harriod, Unity 238
Harris, Ann 121, 143
Harris, Benjamin 44
Harris, Caleb 48
Harris, Catharine 204
Harris, Edward 112
Harris, Elizabeth...175, 182, 113
Harris, Esther 48
Harris, George 143, 144, 178, 223
Harris, Isaac 121
Harris, James....21, 48, 132, 210
Harris, Jeremiah 48
Harris, John 48
Harris, Joseph 44, 223
Harris, Judith 48
Harris, Loyd 41
Harris, Mary 121
Harris, Patience 48
Harris, Peter 72, 73
Harris, Priscilla 48
Harris, Rhoda 121
Harris (Harriss), Robert 48, 115
Harris, Sarah 48
Harris (Harriss), Thomas
112, 175
Harris (Harriss), William
44, 182, 192, 235
Harris, Workman 121
"Harris' Lott" 187
"Harris' Venture" ("Ad-
venture") 48

	PAGE
Harris' Hundred	196
Harrison, Abigail	151
Harrison, Alice	151
Harrison (Harryson), Anne	139, 224
Harrison, Benjamin	151
Harrison, Cathrine	191
Harrison, Charles	32
Harrison, Dorothy	218
Harrison, Elizabeth	50, 224
Harrison, Frances	224
Harrison, George	175
Harrison, James	151
Harrison, John	94, 151
Harrison, Joseph	61, 82, 130, 151, 185, 191
Harrison, Marmaduke	14, 118, 156
Harrison, Mary	238
Harrison, Rachael	224
Harrison, Richard	9, 33, 50, 61, 237
Harrison, Robert	9, 151
Harrison, Samuell	50, 93
Harrison, Sarah	93, 151
Harrison, Thomas	35
Harrison, William	151, 224
Harrison, Violetta	138
"Harrison's Lott"	50
"Harrison's Pasture"	50
Harrow, John	119
Harrow, Peter	119
Harry, Edward	3
Hart, Arthur	229
"Hart's Content"	229
Hart, Elinor	229
Hart, Mary	229
Hart, Mercy	229
Hart, Richard	229
Hart, Robert	229
Hartlew, Joseph	84
Harvey, Charity	114
Harvey, James	74
Harvey, Thomas	92, 97
Harwood, John	57, 70, 156, 192, 207
Harwood, Mary	207
Harwood, Peter	14
Haskell, Michael	230
Hassell, Katharine	216
Hastins, George	146
Hastins, John	109
Hastins, Mary	146
"Hatfield Hills"	72
Hathway's Addition	240
Hathway, John	239, 240
"Hatton"	7
Hatton, Mr.	3
Hatton, Thomas	197
"Hatton's Point"	1
Hause, John	97
"Hausloop"	19
Hawes, Thos.	119
Hawkins, Elizabeth	137, 144
Hawkins, Ernault	144
Hawkins, Henry Holland	137
Hawkins, John	52, 109, 122, 137, 144
Hawkins, Joseph	84
"Hawkins' Pharsalia"	36, 128
Hawkins, William	38
Hawton, Benjamin	134
Hawton, John	134
Hawton, Joseph	134
Hay, James	29
Hay, Mary	212
Hayes, John	128
Hayman, Charles	105
Hayman, Henry	105
Hayman, Isaac	105
Hayman, James	105
Hayman, John	105
Hayman, Sarah	105
Haynes, Hez.	204
Hayward, Francis	169
Hayward, John	169
Hayward (Haywood), Richard	195
Hayward, Thomas	75, 168
Hazlehurst, Benjamin	136
Head, Ann	23, 207, 220
Head, Bigger	24, 207, 220
Head, Charity	207
Head, Katharine	24, 207
Head, Kendall	23
Head, Mary	24, 207, 220
Head, William	23, 108, 141, 207
Headen, Ann	29
Headon, John	29
Healder, William	126
Health, Thomas	249
"Healy's Plantation"	118
Heard, Elizabeth	171
Heard, John	198, 199
Heard, Mary	18
Heard, William	199
Heath, Abraham	105
Heath, Jas.	177
Heath, John	102
Heath, William	50
Heathcot, Ann	224
Heather, Ephraim	193
Heathman (Hathman), Allexander	133, 174
Heathman, Anne	133
Heathman, Frances	133
Heathman, John	133

PAGE

Heathman, Margaret 133
Heathman, Mary 133, 174
Heathman, Thomas 133
Hebb, Jeane 90
Hebb, John 126
Hebb, Mathew I............ 191
Hebb, Priscilla 126, 191
Hebb, Thomas 90, 191
Hebb, William 70, 126, 191
Hedge, Bartholomew 240
Heharty, Steven 180
Heighe, Samuell 214
Heirs, Eugen 90
Hellen (Hellin), David...63, 178
Hellin, James 178
Hellin, John 178
Hellin, Penelope 178
Hellin, Peter 178
Hellin, Richard 178
Hellin, Susanna 178
Hemsley, Anne 220
Hemsley, Mary 19, 220
Hemsley, Philemon 220
Hemsley, Vincent 52, 78
Hemslev, William 220
"Hemsley's Brickland" ... 36
Hemsted, Nicholas 238
Henderson, Jacob 5
Henderson, William.....104, 105
Hendrickson, Milderatt 230
Henebry, Edward 53
Henly, Daniel 171
Henly, Elizabeth 41
Hennard, Richard 210
Henrick, John 195
Henrix, Henry 149
Henry, Helen 114
Henry, Hugh 114
Henry, Jannet 114
Henry, John 11, 15, 114
Henry, Catherine (Kather-
  ine), ...65, 92
Henry, Mary 115
Henry, Robert Jenkins 115
Henry, William 161
"Henry's Addition" 115
Henson, Benjamin 138
Henson, Col. 88
Henson, James 206
"Hens Roost" 100
Herald, William 124
Herbert, Phillip 98
"Herds Mountains" 3
Hergesson, Susannah 82
"Heriford" ("Herriford")
  95, 190
Herman, Casparus Aug...... 89

PAGE

Herman, Ephraim Augustine
  89, 100
Herring Bay 177
Herring's (Herring) Cr.
  40, 50, 155, 177, 195
Hesme, Thomas 155
Hew, Henry 119
Hews, Hororah 158
Heyerd, Thomas 15, 30
"Hiccory Plaines" 109
"Hickory Hills" 197
"Hickory Hollow" 198
"Hickory Ridge" 55
"Hicors Hallows" 127
Hicks, Roger 100
Hide, Jonathan 52
Higan, Elizabeth 125
Higgins (Higgens), Thomas
  13, 26
Higgs, Christopher 150
"Highfields Addition" 205
Higheway, Hanah 114
Highway, Jacob 114
Highway, Jasper 114
Higman, Thomas 103
Higton, Jon. 139
Hill, Abell 32
Hill, Charles 225
Hill, Clement 42, 110
Hill, Edward 228
Hill, Elce 46
Hill, Frances 67
Hill, Henry 28, 44
Hill, Hutten 166
Hill, John 67
Hill, Joseph 221
Hill, Richard 46
Hill, Susannah 27
Hill, William 50
"Hill's Chance" 32
"Hill's Neck" 228
"Hillaley" 128
Hillarey, Ellinor 164
Hillary, Thomas 223
Hillyard (Halyard), Edward 90
Hillyard, Frances 90
Hillyard, Jane 90
"Hinchingham" 6, 209
Hinton, Samuel 29, 59, 146, 162
Hindman, Jacob 5
Hindman, James 4
Hindman, Mary 4
Hindman, William 5
Hissett, Ann 222
Hissett, Elinor 222
Hissett, Elizabeth 222
Hissett, Jane 222
Hissett, Johanna 222

PAGE

Hissett, Philip 222
Hissett, Rose 222
Hitchcock, George 79
Hitchcock, John 129
Hitchcock, Sarah 129
Hixham 20
Hoard, William 110
Hobbs, Ann 32
Hobbs, Robert 32
Hobson, John 75
Hockley Cr. 81
Hodge, Robert 202
Hodges, John 78
Hodges, Tamer 55
Hodges, Thomas 240
Hodgin, John 76
"Hogg Pen" 37
"Hog Quarter" 229
"Hogg Neck" 240
"Hogg's Norton" 25
Hogin, Ester 141
Hogin, John 141
Hogin, Margaret 141
Hogin, Richard 141
Holladay (Holliday), George
                    7, 197
Holladay, Leonard 40, 182
Holbrook, Dorrity 38
Holbrook, Jos. 38
Holbrook (Holbrock), Thomas 192
"Holden" 5
"Holden's Addition" 5
"Holden's Range" 5
"Holdsworth" 218
Holdsworth, Isabella 234
Holdsworth, John 234, 236
Holdsworth, Samuel 234, 235
Holdsworth, Thomas 18, 218
Holeadger (Holaiger) (Hol-
  endger), Philip 79, 100
Holland, Anthony 27
Holland (Holand), Jacob 123, 167
Holland, John
            68, 78, 106, 155, 187
Holland, Richard...106, 155, 165
Holland, Thomas 227
Holland, William 17
"Holland's Hills" 50
Hollingshead, Mary 44
Hollingsworth, Edward 224
Hollingsworth, William 147
Hollum, Joana 83
Hollum, John 83
Holmes, Edward 41
Holmstead, Richard 222
Holshott, John 36
Holsill, George 194
Holsill, John 195

PAGE

Holsill, Ruth 195
"Holt's Divising" 80
Houlton, John 4
Hollyday, Jonahan 126
Hollyday, James 39
Holyday, Mary 136
Homes, Joseph 74
Homes, Richard 152
Honggos Cr. 225
Hood, Edward 236
Hood, Thomas 190
Hood, William 190
Hooke, Elizabeth 68
Hooke, William 212
Hooper, Anne 75
Hooper, Henry 169
Hooper's Neck 178
Hope, Elizabeth 2
"Hopewell" 29, 105
Hopewell, Agnes 233
Hopewell, Ann 233
Hopewell, Frances 188, 191
Hopewell, Francis 70
Hopewell, Hugh....188, 206, 233
Hopewell, Richard 209, 233
Hopewell, Susannah 233
Hopewell, Thomas 76
Hopkins, Anne 13, 148
Hopkins, Benjamin 78
Hopkins, Denis (Dennis)
        74, 118, 157, 185, 204
Hopkins, Edward 13
Hopkins, Elizabeth 13, 157
Hopkins, Gerrard ...,.....17, 32
Hopkins, James 157
Hopkins, Joseph 70, 77, 157
Hopkins, Margaret 143
Hopkins, Nathaniel 78
Hopkins, Robert 70, 115, 157
Hopkins, Sarah 53, 78
Hopkins, Susannah 13
Hopkins, Thomas 148
Hopkins, Thomasin 17
Hopkins, William 12
"Hopp" 204
Hopper, Daniel 124
Hopper, David 113
Horn, Henry 133
Horn, James 133
Horn, Jenny 188
Horne, Constelvus 45
Horne, Margaret 45
Horne, Sarah 45
Horne, William 45
Horner, George 88
Horney, Juliana 149
"Hornisham" 50
Horsey, John 31

PAGE

Horsey, Nathaniel 45
Horsey, Stephen...... 31, 45, 153
Hosier (Hossier), Henry
                    84, 107, 181
Hoskins, Ann 119, 129, 163, 227
Hoskins, Ballard 129
Hoskins, Bennett 129, 163
Hoskins, George 128
Hoskins, John 171, 227
Hoskins, Martha 129
Hoskins, Mary 129
Hoskins, Oswald 129, 163
Hoskins, Phillip 119, 129
Hoskins, William 21, 129, 130
"Hoskins' Lott" 129
Hospital Run 178
Houldin, Richard 112, 226
Houlson, Abraham 36
Houlson, Andrew 36
Houlson, Eals 37
Houlson, Henry 36
Houlson (Houlton), John.... 36
Houlson, Thomas 36, 37
Hoult, Obadiah 131
"Houndslow's Addition"... 22
Howard, Benjamin 135
Howard, Bernard 165
Howard, Charles 81, 145
Howard, Cornelius 81, 145
Howard, Edmund 2
Howard, Elizabeth.....2, 59, 175
Howard, George 2
Howard, James 145
Howard, John 2, 81
Howard, Joseph 26, 82
Howard, Margaret 2
Howard, Martha 146
Howard, Mary 145, 165
Howard, Michael 167
Howard, Rebecka 59
Howard, Samuel 82, 145
Howard, Sarah 173
Howard, Thomas
              2, 59, 81, 145, 193
Howard, William Stevens 2, 59
Howard, William
          84, 97, 137, 146, 174
"Howard's Addition" 81
"Howards Chance" 152
"Howard Forest" 146
"Howard's Gift" 173
"Howard's Heirship" 81
"Howard's Hills" 81
"Howard's Mount" 173
Howe, John 30
Howe, Sarah 179
Howe, Thomas 96, 174, 175, 179
Howes, Charles 63

PAGE

Howes, Edward 63
Howes, Henry 63
Howes, Jane 63
Howes, Susannah 63
Howes (How), Thomas..234, 235
Howell, Christiam 186
Howell, Thomas....117, 152, 186
Howell, William 186
Howitt (Hewitt), Caleb 162
Howkins, Aron 84
Howkins, Elizabeth 84
Howkins, Joseph 84
Howkins, Ruth 84
Howkins, Thomas 84
Hubart, Humphrey 32
Hudson, Anthony 10
Hudson, Henry 82
Hudson, Jane 239
Hudson, Mathew 239
Hudson, Thomas 114
Hueit, Hannah 54
Hues, Sarah 89
Hugh, Even 119
Hughes, Thomas 17
Hulse, William 170
Hume, John 235
Hunger R. 180
Hungerford, Mary 174
Hunt, Jobe 91, 143
Hunt, John 91, 186
Hunt, Mr. 223
Hunt (Huntt), Thomas 72, 91, 143
Hunt, William 228
Hunter, Margaret 209
Hunter, Richard 131
Hunter, Samuel 160
Hunter, Thomas 209, 222
Hunter, William
     10, 33, 97, 163, 194, 200
Hunting Cr. 108, 217
"Hunting Neck" 197
"Hunting Quarter" 90
"Huntington" 155
"Huntington's Addition"... 155
"Huntington Grange" 155
"Hurd's Camp" 4
Hurdle, Robert 28
Hurlock, Sarah 217
Hurrell, Alexander 183
Hurtt, Edward 16
Husband, Hannah 207
Husband, James 207
Husband, John 207
Husband, Thomas 207
Husband, William 207
"Husborne Forest" 46
Huskins, Edward 21
Hussey, Mich'll 23, 37, 62

PAGE

Hutchins, Catherine 22
Hutchins, Frances 22, 216
Hutchins, John 22, 214
Hutchins, Quill 22
Hutchins (Hutchings), Robert, ...22, 216
Hutchins (Hutchings), William 22, 216
Hutchinson, Gavin 25
Hutchinson, John 7
Hutchinson, Mary 8
Hutchinson, Margaret 137
Hutson, Jonathan 212
Huttson, Thomas 107

Hutton, Charles 132
Hyat, Barbara 52
Hyatt, Charles 176
Hyde, John 171
"Hyerdier Lloyd" 106
Hyett, Barbara 221
Hyland, John 231
Hyland, Millice 231
Hyland, Nicholas 213, 231
Hynde, Jane 10
Hynde, Thomas 10
Hyne, Charles 32
Hynson, Thomas 78

I

Iglul Island 195
Imbert, Andrew 5
Imbert, Elizabeth 5
"Indian Gyant's Sepulcher" 108
Ingram, John 38, 54
Ingram, Mary 38, 62
"Inlargement" 3
Insley (Insly), James 229
Iredale, Francis 114
Ireland 237
Ireland, Ann 151

Ireland Cr. 56
Ireland, John 103, 227
Ireland, Samuel 151
Irvine, George 189
Irvin (Irving), John 30, 177
Island of Barbadoes 232
Island Cr. 37, 58, 64, 74, 106, 218
Island Marsh Cr. 96, 218
"Island Neck" 233
"Island Plains" 108
Israell, John 14

J

Jacks, Barbary 70
Jacks, Elizabeth 70
Jacks, Richard 70
Jacks, Thomas 70
Jackson, Barbara 52, 221
Jackson, Faith 74
Jackson, Francis 52, 221
Jackson, George 52, 221
Jackson, Jacob 186
Jackson, James 112, 185
Jackson, Jane 186
Jackson, John 74
Jackson, Joseph 52, 221
Jackson, Sarah 185
Jackson, Thomas 52, 221
"Jackson's Venture" 185
"Jacobs Cr." 100
Jadwyn (Jadwin), Jeremiah
                        23, 224
"Jamaica" 137
James, Ellinor 7
James, Hannah 175
James, John 7, 41, 175
James, Mary 175
James, Thomas 240
"James Inspection" 7
Jameson, Thomas 224

"Jane's Armour" 150
Janes, John 114
Janney, Randall 63
Jarbo, John 199
Jarboo (Jarboe), Peter 206
Jarrard, Graves 117
"Jasper's Lott" 52, 144
Jeames, Alexander 118
Jeane, Joanna 206
Jeane, John 206
Jeane, Thomas 206
Jeanes, Ann 224
Jeanes, Edward 224
Jeanes, Elizabeth .....,..... 224
Jeanes, Joseph 224
Jeanes, Mary 224
Jeanes, William 224
Jefferson, Weedon (Weldon)
                  41, 207, 220
Jenefer, Michall 125
Jenifer, Daniel 194
Jenifer's Gift 208
Jenkins, Mattheu 203
Jenkins, Mary 171
Jenkins, Mrs. 234
Jenkins, Rachell 36

PAGE

Jenkin (Jenkins), Richard 135, 234
Jenkins, Susanna 171
Jenkins, Thomas 203
Jenkins, Walter 203
Jenkins' (Jenckins) Cr...... 168
Jennings, Ann 43
Jennings, Bartholomew 43
Jennings, Elizabeth 89
Jennings (Jenings), Henry 89, 201
Jennings, Joseph 43
Jennings, Mary 43
Jennings, Thomas 89
Jenzakin Cr. 86
Jerman, Job 25
Jerson, John 82
Jessup (Jesup), Joseph 199
Jessup (Jesup), Mary 199
Jesuit 9
Joanes, Sarah 8
"Joanasis Range" 239
Jobson, Easter 136
Jobson, John 136
Jobson, Michael 136
Jobson, Philip 136
Joce, Thomas 198
Johnins, Miles 228
Johns, Abraham 142, 222
Johns' Addition 143
Johns, Aquilla 143
Johns, Isaac 143, 223
Johns, Kensey 143
Johns, Mary 7, 123
Johns, Priscilla 222
Johns, Richard 50, 142, 222
Johns, Rebecca 143
Johns, Thomas 143
Johns, William 123
Johnson, Albert 147
Johnson, Andrew 196, 207
Johnson, Arthur 148
Johnson, Barbary 32
Johnson, Charity 225
Johnson, Daniel 65
Johnson, Elinor 196
Johnson, Elizabeth 237
Johnson, Frances 65
Johnson, George 107
Johnson, Henry 56, 92, 237
Johnson, Jacob 196
Johnson, Jean 102
Johnson (Jnoson), John 27, 52, 175, 196
Johnson, Joseph 94, 237
Johnson, Katharine 177
Johnson, Leonard 148
"Johnson's Lot" 176

PAGE

Johnson, Luke 105
Johnson, Mary 37, 127, 142, 173
Johnson, Michael 196
Johnson, Peter 148
Johnson, Richard 201
Johnson, Robert.....47, 115, 148
Johnson, Samuell 46, 71, 164, 170
Johnson, Steven 196
Johnson, Susannah 31
Johnson, Thomas 37, 201
Johnson, William 127, 201
Johnston, Anne 113
Johnstone (Johnson), Archibold (Archibald) 89, 130, 176 208
Johnston, Benjamin 113
Johnston (Johnson), Elizabeth 113, 196............ 237
Johnston, Francis 94
Johnston, James 113
Johnston, Joseph 113
Johnston, Robert 113
Jolle, Thomas 121
Jolle, Timothy 126
"Joneses Addition" 162
Jones, Alice 225
Jones, Ann 11, 60, 230
Jones, Barbara 3
Jones, Benjamin 65, 230
Jones, Blanch 195
Jones, Catherine 227
Jones, Charity 187
Jones, Charles 3, 53, 97, 135, 233
Jones, David 65
Jones, Edward 135, 197
Jones, Elenor 180
Jones, Elizabeth 53, 65, 148, 195, 230
Jones, Evan 39
Jones, Francis 151
Jones, Giles 195
Jones, Grace 195
Jones, Henry 89
Jones, Humphrey 240
Jones, Jacob 65
Jones, Jane (Jerere) 53, 56, 111, 150, 195
Jones (Joanes), John 20, 22, 27, 124, 174, 178, 195, 215, 227, 229 230
Jones, Jonathan 215
Jones, Lewis (Lewey) 149, 150, 215, 227
Jones, Mary 53, 65, 124, 215, 227, 230
Jones, Morgan 195
Jones, Peter 230
Jones, Phil 123, 207

PAGE

Jones, Rachel 230
Jones, Richard 11, 32, 74, 203, 227
Jones (Joanes), Robert..230, 240
Jones, Rowland (Roland) 99, 227
Jones, Samuel 227
Jones, Temperance 65
Jones, Thomas
  1, 6, 52, 124, 198, 215, 221, 239
Jones, William 15, 20, 23, 65,
  67, 100, 107, 168, 179, 195, 230
Jones Falls 4, 79
"Jones Fancy" 219
"Jones Neck" 52
Jonings, Barbara 221
Jonings, Elizabeth 221
Jonings, John 221
Jonsson, Arch 79
Johnsson, Margaret 79
Jordan (Jordain), Elizabeth
  51, 89
Jordan, Francis 51
Jordan (Jordain), Gerard
  (Gerrard) (Geratt) (Jer-
  ad)..........18, 51, 89, 90
Jordan, Jesse 89
Jordan, John 89, 232

PAGE

Jordan (Jordon) (Jordian),
  Justinian (Justinen)
    18, 51, 90
Jordan, Mrs. 232
Jordan, Rebecca 131
Jordan, Theodore 89
Jordan (Jordain), Thomas
    51, 89, 131
Jordan, Samuel 89
Jordan's Branch 61
Jorden Folly 121
Joseph, William 51
"Joseph's Place" 30
"Joseph's Reserve" 30
"Joshemon" 115
Jowles, Henry Peregrine..51, 212
Joy, Charles 229
Joy, Peter 229
Joys, Thomas 222
Jubb, Robert 44
Judd, Jane 240
Judd, Michael 239, 240
Judrell, John 117
Juers, James 94
"Jugothorp" 140
"Juxta Stadium Aureolum" 39

K

Keadle, Zachariah 213
Kearn, Barnaby 40
Keave, Elinor 90
Keeas, John 224
Keech, Elizabeth 137
Keech, Martha 137
Keen (Keene), John 180, 233
Keene, Richard......41, 223, 234
Keene, Mary 233
Keith, Alexander 146
Keith, John 146
Keld, Elinor 60
Keld (Kelld), John 60
Keld, Mary Hebb 60
Keld, Simon 60
Keld, Thomas 60
Kellam, John 225
Kellam, Joshua 225
Kellam, Mary 225
Kellam, William 222
"Kellam's Choice" 225
Kellton, Thomas 6, 220
Kellam, Tabitha 156
Kelly, Daniel 171
Kelly, James 148, 150
Kelly, Patrick 81
Kemole, Mary 162
Kemble, William 162
"Kemp's Beginning" 101

Kemp, James 54
Kemp, John 54
Kemp, Mary 54
Kemp, Thomas 54
Kempston, Ann 56
Kempton, Richard 231
Kenecey, Francis 34
Kendeloe, Thomas 206
Keneday, Anne 230
Kenedy, John 217
Kendrickson, John 87
Kennerly, Jos. 152
Kennerly, Joshua......8, 31, 58
Kennett (Kennitt), John ... 182
Kennett, Samuel 182
Kennett (Kennitt), William 182
Kenny (Kenney), Elizabeth 32
Kenny (Kenney), Joseph.... 32
Kenny (Kenney), Samuell... 32
Kenny (Kenney), William.. 32
Kent, Absalom 167
Kent, Grace 167
Kent, Henry 167
Kent, Mary 167
Kent, Richard 236
Kent, William 167
Kent Island 20, 36, 54, 62,
  68, 78, 111, 121, 147, 180,
  208 214

PAGE

Kenton, James 67
Kenton, John 67
Kenton, Lidia 67
Kenton, Rebecka 67
Kenton, Solomon 67
Kenton, Thomas 67
Kenton, William 67
Kersey, John 121
Kersey, Mary 156
Kersey, Tabithey 140
Kesey, Timothy 219
Kess, Robert 240
Kibble, William 141
Kicke, John 13
Kid, William 108
Kid's Levell 108
Kidder, James...30, 31, 125, 138
Kilburne, Charles 52
"Killeray" 23
Killingsworth, Elizabeth 42
"Killkenny" 147
Kimball, David 219
Kindelan, Thomas 51
King, Adam 209
King, Ann 61, 188
King, Charles...65, 188, 206, 209
King, Christopher 75
King, Edward 206
King, Elizabeth 188
King, Henry 161, 215, 216
King, Hugh 206
King, Isaac 15
King, Jacob 15
King, Jane 206
King, John
    74, 91, 97, 158, 188, 200, 206
King, Joseph 158
King, Juliana 198
King, Mary 75, 161, 188
King's Misfortune 216
King, Peter 15
King, Robert 115
King, Sarah 15, 198
King, Sophia 198
King, Susannah (Susan) 15, 188
King, Thomas 188, 189, 194
King, William......161, 188, 189
King and Queen Parish..... 171
King's Cr. 84
Kingsale 108, 181

PAGE

Kingsale's Addition 181
Kingstowne 181
"Kingsberry" 161
Kininmount, Alexander 150
Kininmount, Benjamin ..149, 155
Kinnimont, Elizabeth 13
Kiniston, Deborah 28
Kinler, John 47
Kinnerstone, Marg. 228
Kirby, Anne 112
Kirby's Addition 111
Kirby, George 138
Kirby, James 111
Kirby, Mary 112
Kirby, Sarah 112
Kirby, Thomas 231
Kirby, Walter 111
Kirby, William 79, 111, 231
Kirk, Bridget 226
Kirk (Kirke), John
    58, 95, 117, 138, 225
Kirk, Sarah 226
Kirke, William 23
Kirwan (Carrawen), Jane.. 116
Kirwan (Carrawen), John... 116
Kirwan (Carrawen), Mary.. 116
Kirwan (Carrawen), Mat-
    thew 116
Kitely, Sarah 196
Kiteley (Kitely), Thomas... 196
"Kitt's Choice" 3
Knatchbull, Horton 113
"Knaves Choyce" 29
Knight, Christopher 84
Knight, Mary 206
Knight, Richard 48
Knight, Stephen 99
Knowles, Catherine 14, 71
Knowles, Henry 14
Knowles, Jas. 76
"Knowle's Purchase" 14
Knowlman (Knolman), An-
    thony 29
Knowlman, John 29
Knowlman, Rachell 29
Knowlman, Richard 29
Knox, Alexander 153
Kranivit (Kranivet), Oliver
    33, 68
Kyard, Hannah 184

L

Lacon, Francis 81
Lacon, William 157
Ladd, John 235
Ladd, Richard 235
Ladd's Desire 235

Lake, Jane 116
Lake, Mary 116
Lake, Robert 116
Lamar, Ann 11
Lamar, John 11

PAGE

Lamar, Thomas 11
Lamb, Elizabeth 31
Lamb, John 31, 190
Lamb, Margaret 31
"Lambert" 23
Lambert, Joseph 4
Lanahan, John 43
"Lancaster" 110
Lancaster, Benjamin 100
Lancaster, Catherine 100
Lancaster, Elloner 100
Lancaster, George 100
Lancaster, Henry 100
Lancaster, John 194
Lancaster, Philip 100
Lancaster, William 100
Lancastershire 4
Lancelot, Jane 51
Landon, Capt. 210
"Landover" 24
Lane, Benjamin 50
Lane, Darby 121
Lane, Elizabeth 33
Lane, Harrison 50
Lane, John 41
Lane, Joseph 50
Lane, Richard 50, 57
Lane, Samuell 33, 50
Lane, Sarah 33, 50
Lane, Walter 83
Lane, William 23, 82, 83
Lang, Robert 36
Langcake, Francis 165
Langford's Bay
    6, 20, 21, 128, 200, 210, 219
"Langford's Neck" 52
Langham, Annastatia....127, 170
Langham, William 72, 170
Langley, John 35, 201
Langley, Joseph 28, 35
Langley, Rachell 35
Langley, Sarah 35
Langrill, James 58
"Langworth Point" 69
Lanham, Josiah 210
Lanman, William 133
Lann (Lane), Easter 22
Lann (Lane), John 22, 23, 41, 48
Lann (Lane), Judith 22
Lann (Lane), Mary 23
Lann (Lane), Walter 22
"Lann's Delight" 22
Larey (Lary), Dan'll 192
Larey (Lary), Joshua 192
Larey (Lary), Mary 192
Larey (Lary), Willmoth
    (Welmoth) 192

PAGE

Larogue, Isaac 112
Larramore, Margaret 213
Larrance (Laurance), George 167
Lashly, Eals 122
Lashly, John 122
Latcham, Elizabeth 182
Lattemore, Mary 232
Latton, Thomas 89
Law, Amos 179
Laws, Catherine 20
Law's, George 47
Law's, John 47
Law's (Laws), Robert....20, 47
Laws, William 20
Lawrence, Benjamin 183
Lawrence, Henry 159
Lawrence, Mary 159
Lawrence, Rachel 183
Lawrence, Richard 159
Lawson, Elizabeth 80
Lawson, John....5, 132, 147, 209
Lawson, Thomas 80
Lawson, William 80
Lawton (Laton, Latton),
    Anne 199
Lawton (Laton, Latton),
    Jemine 199
Lawton (Laton, Latton),
    John 199
Lawton (Laton, Latton),
    Joseph 199
Lawton, Mary 199
Lawton (Laton, Latton),
    Thomas 199
"Lawyer's Discovery" 216
Layfield, Thomas 83, 85
Layton, Alice 76
Lazenby, Robert 126
Leach, Alice 1
Leach, Elizabeth 1
Leach, Jeremiah 91
Leach, John 1
Leach, Margaret 1
Leach, Mary 1
Leach, Samuel 1
Leafe (Leaf), Richard ...91, 92
Leake, Richard 236
Leck, John 165
Lecompte (Lecompt), John
    106, 152, 156
Lecompte, Joseph 106
Lecompte, Mary 106
Lecompte, Moses 106
Ledyatt, John 233
Lee, Elinor 48
Lee, John 16
Lee, Luke 201

PAGE

Lee, Mary 192
Lee, Phillip 214
Lee, Samuell 201
Lee, Thomas 169
Lee, William 61
Lee, Winifred 224
Leeds, John 118
"Leeth" 227
Leigh, Dorothy 90, 172
Leigh, John 173
Leigh, Mary 172
Lemarr (Lemar), Charles 73, 122
Lemmen, Ardis 195
"Lentley" 159
"Letchworths Chance" 143, 222
Lets, John 90
Leu, Dolle 90
Levena, Rice 23
Levenigh, Hendreick Van... 15
Levin, Robert 79
Lewellen, John 234
Lewis, Town of........... 32
Lewis, —— 137
Lewis (Levis), Abraham.... 187
Lewis (Levis), Ann 187
Lewis (Levis), Elizabeth 137, 187
Lewis (Levis), Glode....... 187
Lewis, Grace 11
Lewis (Levis), Jane 187
Lewis, James 171
Lewis (Levis), John........ 187
Lewis (Levis), Thomas
        1, 6, 161, 187
Lewis (Levis), William...42, 187
Lidster, William 103
Lilley, Thomas 29
Lillinston (Lilleston) (Lil-
   lingstone), Carpenter 4, 88, 187
Lillingston, Frances 4
Lillingstone, Mary 187
"Limbrick" 149
Linch, Anne 59
Linch (Lynch), Mary 59, 145, 179
Linch, Patrick 59
Linch, Robuck 59
Linch, William 59
Lindall, Katharine 146
Lines, George 142
Lindsay, David 220
Lindy (Linday), Thomas.... 200
"Lingan's Adventure" 108
Lingan, George 237
Lingan (Lingham), Thomas
        164, 169
Lingan, Thomas 108
Linkhorn, John 100
"Linnath" 25
Linton, Susannah 89

PAGE

Lipkin Cr. 176
Liston, Edward 41
"Litchfield" 94
"Little Belew" 45
Little Choptank R. 76, 117, 125
Little Duck Cr. 230
"Little Marloe" 240
"Little Run" 146
Little, Thomas 64
"Littleton" 26
Littleton's Creek ....,.... 82
"Little Wells" 177
"Littleworth" 20
Liverpool 114, 123
Lloyd, Edward.....1, 5, 158, 200
Lloyd, James 200
Lloyd, Philemon 200, 220
Lloyd, Rebecca 200
Lloyd, Richard 200
Lloyd, Sarah 200
Lloyd, Thomas 138
"Lloyd Town" 200
Loadin (Loador) (Loaden),
   Richard 81
Lockerman, Govert 209
Lockerman, Govin 58
Lockerman, Nicholas 141
Lockerman, Sarah 209
"Lockwood's Adventure".... 227
"Locust Thicket" 37
Lodge, Rev. Thomas....... 54
Loe, Thomas 240
"Loer Landing" 93
Loker, Francis 197
Loker, Thomas 197
London 132, 167, 181, 205,
   210, 220, 223 228
Londontown 26, 228
Lone, John 55
Long (Longue), Ann 41, 166
Long, Anthony 200
Long, Benjamin 41, 223
Long (Longue), Dan....102, 166
Long, David 83, 102
Long, Elizabeth 41, 111
Long, Jane 41
Long, Jeffey (Jeoffry) (Jeff-
   rey) 102, 103, 166
Long (Longue), John
        102, 166, 181
Long, Mary 41, 45, 103
Long, Randolph 83, 102
Long, Sarah 181
Long, Susanna (Susannah)
        41, 122
Long, Thomas
   41, 79, 181, 218, 223

PAGE

Long (Longue), William
166, 181, 218
"Long Hill" 176
"Long Lane" 223
"Long Point" 218
"Long Reach" 130
"Long Ridge" 103
"Long Town" 49
"Long Week" 128
Longue, Samuel 166
Loramur, William 54
Lord, Edward 199
Lord, Francis 104
Lord, James 157
Lord, John 157
Lord, Judith 157
Lord, Mary 157
Lord, Rosanna 157
"Lord's Chance" 157
"Lordship's Favor" 91
Louring (Loering), William.. 99
Louther, Richard 7
Lovdy, Sarah 217
Love, John 199, 238, 240
Love, Robert 238, 240
Love, Thomas 129
Loveday, John 4
Lovelidge, John 120
"Lovepoint" 54
Low (Lowe), John.......66, 235
Lowder, Charles 96
Lowder, John 106
Lowe, Ann 125, 204
Lowe, Bennett 125, 204
Lowe, Dorothy 125, 204
Lowe, Elizabeth....125, 204, 217
Lowe, Henrietta Maria 125
Lowe, Henry.......125, 131, 204
Lowe, John 225
Lowe, Nicolas (Nicholas)
125, 141, 180, 182, 204, 217
Lowe (Loe), Thomas...125, 240

PAGE

Lowe, Mary 125, 204
Lowe, Vincent 217, 220
Lower Plantation 218
"Lowerey's Rut" 64
Loyd, Roderick 51
Loyd, Sarah 51
Loyd's Point 183
Luckett, Massey 97
Luckett, Samuell 29
"Lucky" 121
Luddingham (Luddenham),
Ann 149
Luddingham (Luddenham),
Edward 149
Luddingham, Isaac 149
Luddingham (Luddenham),
John 149
Luddingham (Luddenham),
Mary 149
Luddingham (Luddenham),
Rebecca 149
Ludwigg, William 217
Luke, Amy 225
Luke, Isaac 225
Luke, Mary 225
Lun (Lunn), John 57, 75
Lundy, John 165
Lurkey, John 144
Lurtey, Nich. 112
Lurty, Nicholas 33
Lusby, Jacob 221
Lusby, John 221
Lusby, Mary 26
Lusby, Robert 26
Lyle, William 44
"Lyn" 7
Lynch, Robert 29
Lynn (Line), Elizabeth 1
Lynn (Line), Francis 1
Lynn (Line), Margery 1
Lynn (Line), Richard 1

M

Macartley, Timothy 208
Macbride, David 219
Mace, Henry 203
Macham (Mahy), Edward... 161
Machartie, Capt. 89
Machee, Daniel 217
Machentee, Margaret 79
Machetee, Edmond 72, 73
Machetee, Frances 73
Machetee, James 72, 73
Machetee, Patrick 72, 73
Machetee, Rosemond 72, 73
Machey, Alexander 99

Machgill, D. 96
Machintosh, John 201
Machon, Deborah 114
Machon, James 114
Machoo, Paul 132
Mack, John 30
Mackall, Ann 96, 174
Mackall, B. 18
Mackall, Benjamin 96, 174
Mackall, Dorkass 96
Mackall, James
18, 38, 64, 65, 96, 174
Mackall, John........14, 96, 174

PAGE

Mackall, Mary 96, 174
Mackall, Susannah 174
Mackartey, Denis 202
Mackdaniel, Thomas 101
Mackdowell, Mary 65
Mackdowell, William 65
Mackeel, Edmund 13
Mackell, Clare 125
Mackery, William 78
Mackey, James 129
Mackgill, Grace 64
Mackginney, Michael 11
Mackhone, Timothy 101
Mackinel, John 81
Macklaine, Hector 19
Mackleane, Lochle 30
Macklin, Elizabeth 124
Macklin, Mary 124
Macklin, Robert 124
Mackmahan, Derby 149
Mackmore, James 46
Mackneal, Alice 102
Mackneal, Hugh 102
Mackneal, Katherine 102
Mackmillington, Mary 229
Macnemara (Machemara),
    John 219
Macomas, John 3
Maconchie (Machonchie),
    William......17, 138, 139, 140
Macwell, Samuel 161
Maddox (Maddux) (Madux),
    Ann 43, 105
Maddox, Jane 43
Maddox, John.......1, 3, 43, 134
Maddox, Margaret 43
Maddox, Notley 18, 42
Maddox, Samuell 42, 227
Maddux (Madux), Alexander
    104, 105, 153
Maddux, Daniel 104
Maddux, Elinor 104
Maddux (Madux), Elizabeth
    104, 105
Maddux (Madux), Lazarus
    104, 105, 153
Maddux (Madux), Mary 104, 105
Maddox (Madux), Nathaniel 105
Maddox (Maddux), Sarah
    43, 104, 134
Maddux (Madux), Thomas
    104, 105
Maddux, William 42, 104
Maden, John 88
Maeding, Catherine 88
Magdaniel, Allen 92
Magee, John 141
Magill, Daniell 113

PAGE

Magnell, John 87
Magothy R. 122, 196
MaGowen, Henry 216
Magraugh (Megrath), Jean
    (Jane) 133
Magreger, Margaret 82
Magroth, James 235
"Magyes Joynter" 210
Magruder, Elinor 41
Magruder, Nathaniell 39
Magruder, Robert 41
Magruder, Samuell 41, 223
Magruder, Sarah 41
Mahaine, Robert 202
Mahaney, Thomas 54
Mahaney, Timothy 54
Mahany, Dennis 73
Mahun, Edward 179
"Maiden Bower" 171
Maiton, Leonard 147
Maiton, Mary 147
Maiton, Susanna 147
"Make Peace" 153
Makey (Macky), Elizabeth.. 97
Makey (Macky), James..... 97
Makings, Peter 8
Maldin (Mauldin), Francis.. 236
Malihan, Daniell 84
Malohan, Liza 84
Malohan, William 84
Malow, Margaret 37
Maloyd, Charles 147
Malven, Robert 86
Man, George 182
Man, William 54
"Manchester" 3
Manders, Cecisley 180
Maneley, Jefferey 235
Manghoin, Jeane 196
Mankester's Craft 194
Mankin, Josiah 119
Mankin, Margaret 203
Mankin, Stephen 203
Manly, John 213
Manning (Mannyng), John
    64, 124, 213, 234, 235, 236
Manning, Joseph 2, 124
"Mannings Discovery" 124
Manokin, River 104
"Manor Plantation" 59
Mansell, Grace 113
Mansell, Robert 113
Mansell, Thomas 9, 29
Mansfield, Thomas 6
Manzey, Margaret 232
Marcarty, John 19
Marcer, Thomas 207
March, Timothy 231

PAGE

Margaret, Winifred 233
"Margarett's Delight" 14
"Margaret's Fancy" 152
Mariate, Eliner 31
Marin, Charles 106
Mark, John 202
Markero, Thomas 100
Marlborough.... 93, 108, 164, 223
"Marley Lott" 50
Marloe, John 30
Marr, James 7
Marray, Jabes 112
Marrett, Isaac 106
Marrett, Mark 106
Marrett, Philies 202
Marrett, William 202
Marritt (Marett), Frances.. 98
Marritt (Marrett), John..98, 202
Marriott, Augustine 190
Marriott, Emanuel 190
Marriott Marreott), John
                      190, 237
Marriott, Joseph 190
Marriott, Mark 76
Marriott, Sarah 76, 190
Marriott, Silvanus 190
Marron, Elizabeth 225
Marsey, Nicholas 4
Marsgate 200
Marsh, Alice 84
Marsh (Mash), Elizabeth
                      52, 80, 144
Marsh, John 53
Marsh (Mash), Mary 52
Marsh (Mash), Sarah....52, 144
Marsh (Mash), Thomas 52, 80, 144
Marshall, Adria 83
Marshall, Adrian 83
Marshall, Ann 214
Marshall, Elizabeth 78, 83
Marshall, George 83
Marshall, John 93
Marshall, Margaret 222
Marshall, Mary 222
Marshall, Samuel 83
Marshall, Sarah 15
Marshall (Marchell), Thomas
                      83, 105, 222
Marshall, William 78
"Marshars Point" 12
"Marshey Point" 12
Marshy Ck................ 58
Marston, William 236
Martin, Anne 1, 191
Martin, Domick 109
Martin, Eleanor 135
Martin, Elizabeth...157, 191, 234

PAGE

Martin, George 47, 114
Martin, Isabell 234
Martin, James 191, 234
Martin, John...97, 135, 137, 236
Martin, Margaret 191
Martin, Michael 137
Martin, Sarah 49
Martin, Thomas 157
Martin, William 191
"Martin's Addition" 32
"Martinton" 32
"Marumscolt" 103
"Mary's Duckdome" 30
"Mary's Green" 1
"Mary's Lot" 115
Mason, Elinor 68
Mason, Elizabeth 121
Mason, John......18, 71, 99, 171
Mason, Joseph 68
Mason, Mary 68, 69, 99, 171, 200
Mason, Mathers (Matha)
  (Mathew)....68, 99, 171, 172
Mason, Richard 68
Mason, Robert 99, 172
Mason, Solomon 68
Mason, Stratford 172
Mason, Susanna 99
"Mason's Purchase" 171
Mather, George 21
Mathews, Anne 218
Mathews, Esther 124
Mathews, Grace 129
Mathews, Thomas 124
Mathews, William 218
Mathole, James 49
Mattapany R. 171, 195
Mattason, John 56
Mattawoman 138
Mattershaw, Elizabeth 34
Mattershaw, George 34, 37
Mattews, Henry 22
Mattews, Roger 22
Matthews, Sarah 22
Matthews, William 33
Mattingly, Ann 69
Mattingly, Charles 69
Mattingly, Elizabeth 69
Mattingly, Ignatius 69
Mattingly, James 68
Mattingly, Luke 69
Mattingly, Thomas 68
Mattingly, William 69, 94
"Mattingly's Purchase" ... 68
Mattinly, Ruth 171
"Matypynie Landing" 105
Maudsley (Mondsley), James 180
Maudsley (Mondsley), Mary 180
Mauldin, Francis 213, 231

PAGE

Mawdesley, John 41
Maxwell, James 238
Maxwell, William 48
May, John 133
May, Mary 133
Maynard, Sarah 201
Maynadier, Daniel 94
Mayo, Samuel 83
"Mazereen Hall" 56
McClester, Charles 193
McClester, Daniell 114
McClester, John 114, 193
McClester, Joseph 114
McClester, Margret 114
McClester, Martha 114
McClester, Neale 114, 193
McRagh, Jane 85
McRagh, John 85
McRagh, Mary 85
McRagh, Owen 85
McRagh, Robert 85
McRagh, William 85
Mead, William 91, 196
Meakin, James 132
Meare, Abraham 183
Meare, Isaac 183
Meare, James 183
Meare, Martha 183
Meare, William 183
"Meares" 143
Meares, Elizabeth 205
Mears, John 215
Mecay, Alexander 79
Mecay, Anne 79
Mecay, George 79
Mecay, John 79
Mecay, Martha 79
Mecay, Robert 79
Medford, Bullwin 210
Medford, George 210
Medford, Maccall 210
Medford, Rachell 210
Medford, Thomas 210
Medley, John 123
Meed, Ann 123
Meed, Benjamin 122
Meed, Francis 122
Meed, John 122
Meed, William 122
Meekins, Abraham 184
Meekins (Meekin), John
            174, 184, 187
Meekins, Richard 184
Meekins, Sarah 184
Meekins, William 184
"Meekin's Chance" 184
"Meekins' Hope" 184
Meeks, Francis 97, 101

PAGE

Meeks, James 101
Mehony, Denis 204
Mehony, Mildred 204
"Melinda" 4
Melmill, David 156
Mercer, Elizabeth 81, 111
Mercer, Jacob 81, 111
Mercer (Mercy), John 81, 103, 111
Mercer, Mary 81, 111
Merchant, Joseph 95
Merchant, William 95
"Merchant's Outlet" 95
Mercier, Francis 52
Merefield, Elizabeth 60
Merer, William 86
Meriday, John 43
Merraday, Sarah 179
Merredith, Anne 198
Merredith (Merideth), William 198
Merrick, James 55
Merricks, John 149
Merriken, Charles 208
Merriken, Comfort 27
Merriken, Grace 27
Merriken, Hugh 27
Merriken, John 27
Merriken, Joshua 27
Merriken, Mary 27
Merriken, Sarah 27
Merrydeth, Elizabeth 75
"Mershan's Rest" 236
"Metten" 155
Mezick, Benjamin 165
Mezick, Isaac 165
Mezick, Jacob 165
Mezick, John 165
Mezick, Joseph 165
Mezick, Joshua 165
Mezick, Julin 165
Mezick, Mary 165
Mezick, Nehemiah 165
Mezick, Priscilla 165
Mezick, Sarah 165
"Michael and William" 13
"Michells Chance" 228
Michen, William 117
"Middle Green" 61
"Middle Ridge" 4
Middle River 94, 238
"Middle Town" 48
"Middlesex" 58
Middleton, Elizabeth 137
Middleton, George 146
Middleton, William 137
Midford, John 181
Milbourn, Sarah 231
Milbourn, Stephen 231

PAGE

Milby, Joseph 200
Miles, Edward 2
Miles, Elizabeth 211, 236
Miles, Frances 236
Miles, Francis 73
Miles, James 238
Miles, John 236
Miles, Mary 53, 73, 236
Miles, Nicholas 170
Miles, Tobias 236
"Miles End" 236
Mill——, Ralph 14
Miller, Adam 194
Miller, Ann 126
Miller, Anne 201
Miller, Arthur 230
Miller, Elizabeth 7, 8, 182
Miller, George 182, 194
Miller, Grace 63, 164
Miller, Jacob 29
Miller, John 126, 152
Miller, Jon. 201
Miller, Joseph 182
Miller, M. 7
Miller, Margaret 174
Miller, Martha 7
Miller, Mary 7, 194
Miller, Rebecca 126, 201
Miller, Richard 69
Miller, Robert 7, 158
Miller, Sarah 182
Miller, Thomas 182
Miller, William.....63, 158, 182
Millington, Ruth 57, 75
Millington, Samuel 57
Millmon, Mary 126
Millmon, Nicholas 126
Millmon, Thomas 126
"Mill Road" 5
"Mill Road Addition"..... 5
Mill Runn 236
Mills, David 218
Mills, Elizabeth 232
Mills, Ellinor 176
Mills, James 238
Mills, John 41, 68, 176
Mills, Nicholas 123
Mills, Peter 68
Mills, Richard 176, 183
Mills, Robert 86, 115, 176
Mills, Selliner 176
Mills, William 39, 68, 176,
                        183, 192
"Millstones" 121
"Mills Town" 39
Milton, Mary 87
Mings, Edward............. 91
Mings, Mary 91

PAGE

"Mingses Chance" 91
Minner, Peter 168
Mitchell, Benjamin 46
Mitchell, Henry 236
Mitchell, John 46, 151
Mitchell, Mary 46, 64, 154
Mitchell, Oliver 28
Mitchell, Randolph 154
Mitchell, Richard 168
Mitchell, Thomas 176
Mitchell, William 235
Mitford, Mary 112
Mitford (Mittford), William 112
Moacrinick, Francis 205
Mobberley, Edward 194
Mobley, Rebecca 211
Mochon, Thomas 88
Moettig, Godfrey 8
Mogbee, Brock 17
Mogbee, Mathew 17
Mogg, Richard 127
Mogua, Richard 83
Monat, James 228
Monatt, John 126
Moncester (Mankester),
    James 194
Moncester (Mankester),
    Mary 194
Moncester (Mankester),
    Prudence 194
Moncester (Mankester), Wil-
    liam 194
Mondy, John 95
Monk, Mary 14
Monkester, Elizabeth 194
Monokin 86
Monro, Rebecca 18
Monro, Robert 18
Monroe, Catherine 159
Monroe, Duncan 159
Monroe, Elizabeth 159
Monroe, John 159
Monroe, Sarah 160
Montgomery, Catherine..... 24
Moor, Ann 154
Moore, Charles 124
Moore, Clair 98
Moore, Edith 124
Moore, Hannah 124
Moor (More), John 61, 154
Moore, Juliana 124
Moore, Norest 124
Moore, Rebecca 124
Moore (More), Richard 68,
                        106, 124
Moor (More), Sarah..26, 68, 154
Moore, Semour 54, 97
Moore (Moor), Thomas...20, 154

PAGE

"Moorfields" 57
Mooth, Thomas 54
More, Mary 147
More, Priscilla 61
More, Tabitha 47
"More's Hope" 37
Morecraft, John 123
Morees, Morris 103
Morgan, Anne 232
Morgan, Edward 90, 99
Morgan, James 121
Morgan, John 54, 121
Morgan, Margarett (Mar-
  grett) 24, 133
Morgan, Mary 90, 232
Morgan, William 36
Morgans, Richard 99, 133
Morgin, Thomas 91
Moreen, Michael 235
Morris, Edward 25
Morris, Elenor 82
Morris, Jeremiah 82
Morris, Joseph 25
Morris, Parthenia 25
Morris, Thomas 25
Morris, William 25
Morriss, John 46
Morriss, Manasses 47
Mortemore, Elizabeth 18
Mortemore, John 18, 207
Morton, John 119
Morton, Thomas 113
Morwood, William 134
Moseley, Robert 71
Mosley, Robert 172
Mosly, Barbara 164
Moss, Edmund 179
Moss, Ralph 179

PAGE

Moss, Robert 179
Moss, Thomas 179
"Mothers Delight" 147
Motton, John 209
Mould, John 240
"Mt. Calvert" 53, 108, 135
"Mount Misery" 68
"Mount Pleasure" 180
"Mount Silley" 95
Mountsier, William 159
Moy, Richard 127
Mudd, Sarah 33, 130
Mudy Creek 101
Muffetts Island 233
Muguane (Mugunane), Wil-
  liam 102
"Mulberry Grove" 193
Mulberry Island 58
Mulken, Timothy 42
Mullican, Daniell 35
Mullakin, Joanna 152
Mullikin (Mullakin), Alice.. 151
Mullikin (Mullakin), John
  151, 152
Mullikin (Mullakin), Sarah 151
Mumford, Sarah 156
Munday, Henry 146
Munfield, John 54
Munn (Mann), William 58
"Murphes Choyce" 179
Murphy, James 101
Murphy, Roger 160
Murumrenough, Sarah 31
Musgrave, Susanna 178
Musgrove, Charles 80
"Musketo Hammock" 47
Musselbrook, James 11
Myrsby, Sarah 187

N

Nailer, George 11
Nailer, Martha 11
Nairne (Nearne) (Nane)
  (Naire), Robert 15, 193, 226
Nalk, Charles 97
Nanjemy Cr. 42
Nanticoke R. 58, 59, 86, 153
Nanticoyne, Manor of...... 167
"Narborough" 96
"Nathaniell's Point 200
Neale, Ann 55
Neale, Anthony....10, 72, 73, 97
Neale, Roswell 194
Neale, Charles 98, 199
Neale, Edward 9, 55
Neale, Elizabeth 174
Neale, Francis 8, 55

Neale, Hannah 54
Neale, Henry 9
Neale, James 194
Neale, Jerimy 55
Neale, Jonathan 55
Neale (Neall), John......29, 174
Neale, Martha 54
Neale (Neal), Mary...10, 33, 55
Neale, Oswell 33
Neale, Pa. 196
Neale, Raphael 132, 194
Neale, Samuel 55
Neale, Thomas 149
Nearne, James 226
Neatkin, Mr. 209
"Necessity" 115
Neck Pastime 118

PAGE

Needells (Needle), John 187
Needham, James 236
Needham, Mary 236
Needham, William 236
Neighbor, Francis 183
Neighbor, Mary 183
"Neighborly Kindness" 117
Nesley, Aaron 199
Nevet, Elinor 68
Nevitt, Francis 127
"New Designe" 53, 125
New England 70, 209, 217
"New France" 20
"New Scotland" 60
Newman, Dennis 121
Newman, George 194
Newport 139
"Newport Paywell" 19
Newton, Edward 152
Newton, Thomas 75
New Yarmouth 209
Newtown Hundred 188
Nicholan, Isaac 127
Nicholls, John 239
Nicholls, Mary 17, 239
Nicholls, Sarah 239
Nicholls, Thomas 239
Nichols (Nicholes), Henry.5, 200
Nichols, Joshua 4
Nicholson, Anne 228
Nicholson, Benjamin 227
Nicholson, Edward 227
Nicholson, Elizabeth 228
Nicholson, James 238
Nicholson, Joseph 227
Nicholson, Roger 165
Nicholson, Samuel 227
Nicholson, Sarah 225
Nicholson, William 227
"Nicholson's Manor" 227
Nickols, Robert 70
Nickolson (Nichelston), Fran-
  ces (Francis), 159, 170, 185
Nickolson, John......70, 159, 179
Nickolson, Patrick 159
Nickolson, Susannah 159
Nickolson, Thomas 159
Nicolls (Nicols), Isaac
                    125, 126, 202
Nileson, William 230
Nilson (Nelson), Hugh 193
Niner, Patrick 88
Noads, Ann 18
Nobell (Noble), Elizabeth
                        137, 224
Noble, Elizabeth 134

PAGE

Noble, George 109
Noble, John 46
Noble, Jonathan 115
Noble, Jos. 163
Noble, Robert 220
Noble, William 86, 102
Noddall's Brand 80
Noe, Samuell 43
Noells, Anne 152
Noell, Bazell 152
Noells (Nowell), Eleanor.... 152
Noells (Nowell), Elizabeth.. 152
Noells (Nowell), John 152
Nolinds (Nelenes) (Nelmes),
  Alice 237
Nolinds, Charles 237
Nolinds, John 237
Nolson, James 92
Norrice (Norris), John..110, 179
Norrice, Susannah 110
Nonrie, Elizabeth 159
"Normington" 186
Norris, Clare 179
Norris, Henry 3
"North Bendon and Todd". 148
North Carolina 115, 202, 203
"North Paterton" 47
"North Yarmouth" 167
"Northampton" 116
"Norton" 211
Norton, Andrew 134
Norton, Cornelius 134
Norton, John 59
"Norwell's Pocaty" 152
Norwood, John 14
Nottingham Town 39
Nouland, William 201
Novell, Jane 162
Nowell, Bazwell 56, 156
Nowell, Elianor 156
Nowell, Hannah 56
Nowell, James 56, 156
Nowell, Margaret 156
Nowell, Septimus 56
Nuby, Barnett 26
Numan, Mary 19
Numan, William 19
Numbers, James 99, 129
Numbers, Peter 99
Nuthall, Breaht 18
Nuthall, Elinor 18
Nuthall, John 18
Nuton, Joseph 16
Nutt, Thomas 16
"Nutwell's Adventure" ... 40
Nuttwell, James 41

O

	PAGE		PAGE
O'Cahan, John	16	Orme (Oram), Robert	
O'Caine, Judith	134		28, 41, 162, 176
Odeton, Richard	119	Orme, Sarah	28
Offett, Edward	17	Orphin, Thomas	21
Offett, James	17	Orrell, John	126
Offett, John	17	Orrick, Ezekiel	28
Offett, Mary	17	Orrick, James	28
Offett, Thomas	17	Orrick, Mary	28
Offett, William	17	Orrick, Priscilla	28
Ogg, George	4	Orsborne, Hannah	180
Ogilby, Patrick	108	Orton, Thomas	122
Ogilvie, Margaret	217	Osberne, Richard	216
Ogilvie, Patrick	217	Osborne, Elizabeth	176
Oglesby Chance	238	Osborne, Thomas	176
Oglesby, George	239	Osborne (Osborn), William	
Olandman (O'Landman), De-			238, 240
num	133	Osborne (Osborn), William	
Olandman (O'Landman),			13, 94
Mary	133	Osbourne, Edward	121
Oldham, Hannah	179	Ottis, John	209
Oldham, John	179, 218	Oulford, Mary	187
Oldton, Anna	240	Outen, Sabro	195
"Oldton's Garrison"	4	"Outlet"	96
Oless, Robert	239	Outten, John	104
"Olive Branch"	31	Owen, Joseph	183, 212
Olliver, William	39	Owens, John	134
Ollover, Ann	119	Owens, Mary	220
Olman, William	128	Owens (Owings), Richard...	71
O'Neale (O'Neall), Peter ...	72	Owens, Ruth	71
Onsbee, Elizabeth	233	Owens, Steven	71
Organ, Matthew	121	Owens, William	50, 149
Orme, Aaron (Aron)	28, 182	Owings (Owens), Sarah...	14, 71
Orme, John	28, 176, 182	Oydolett, Margarett	195
Orme, Morris	148	"Oyle of Beasom"	56
Orme, Moses	28, 176, 182	"Ozburn's Lott"	108

P

	PAGE		PAGE
Paca, Aquila	146	Parish, Edward	167
Padimson, John	180	Parke, Robert	6
Padgett, Thomas	41	Parker, Elizabeth	24, 39
Pain, Elizabeth	126	Parker, Fielder	24
Paine, William	102	Parker, Gabriel	14, 39
Pairpoint, Mahittable	227	Parker, Henry	155
Palmeer, Daniel	240	Parker, Jan.	89
Palmer, Jacob	149	Parker, Judith	69
Pamatuck, Isaac	209	Parker, Mary	24
Pamer, Oliver	100	Parker, Richard	79
Panter, Dorothy	20	Parker, Robert	14, 71
Panter, John	19	Parker, Thomas	21
"Panter's Den"	20	Parker, William Henry	24
"Paradise"	209	"Parker's Point"	181
Parck, Mary	8	"Parker's Thicket"	149
Pardice, Christopher	195	Parkinson, Jos.	162
"Pardonaram"	106	Parrandie, Jas.	80
Parette, Math.	91	Parrandie, John	80

PAGE

Parrare, Thomas 197
Parrish, John 33
Parsons, Abigail 16
Parsons, Agnes 16
Parsons, Alexander 113
Parsons, Benjamin 16
Parsons, Catharine 89
Parsons, Charles 16, 70
Parsons, Cosmas 29
Parsons, David 113
Parsons, Edward 70
Parsons, Elizabeth 68, 70
Parsons, Jan. 89
Parsons, John 16, 70
Parsons, Joseph 16
Parsons, Margaret 89
Parsons, Mary 70, 89
Parsons, Nicholas 16
Parsons, Phillis 70
Parsons, Robert 70
Parsons, Samuel 16, 147
Parsons, Solomon 16
Parsons, Thomas 68
Parsons, William 89
"Parson's Chance" 16
"Partnership".......37, 111, 181
"Paschall's Purchase" 215
"Pascuum" 40
Patapsco Neck 145
Patapsco R.
  14, 27, 79, 81, 145, 183, 240
Patrick, John 24
Pattesons (Pateson), Jacob.. 229
Pattison, John 4, 182
Pattison, Mary 44
Pattison, Sarah 182, 218
Patton, David 94
Patton, Elinor 77
Patton, James 77
Patton, John 77
Patton, Mary 77
Patton, Robert 77
Patton, Sarah 77
Patton, Thomas 77
Patton, William 77
Patuxent 25, 31, 40, 51, 130, 175
Patuxent R. 26, 31, 37, 50,
  108, 130, 136, 156, 178,
  183, 197, 228, 233........ 234
Paul, Ann 115
Paul, Charles 115
Paul, Elizabeth 115
Paul, George 115
Paul, Jacob 115, 209
Paul, Joseph 209
Paul, Martha 209
Paul, Mary 115
Paul, Peter 209

PAGE

Paul, Robert 115
Paul, William 115
Pawquapsie 209
Paxton, Martha 122
Payne, Charles 173
Payne, Ezekiel 174
Payne, Hannah 201
Payne, Henry 174
Payne, Isaak 201
Payne, James 174
Payne, John 175
Payne, Leonard 174
Payne (Paine), Mary 22, 174
Payne, Peter 173
Payne, Sarah 201
Payne, Thomas 174, 201
"Peach" 153
Peacocke, Edward 226
Peale, Sarah 77
Peale, Thomas 155
Pearce, Anne 230
Pearce, Benjamin 207
Pearce, D. 7
Peirce (Pearce) (Pierce),
  Elizabeth 81
Pearce, Gidian 230
Pearce, John 215
Peirce (Pierce), Thomas 81
Pearce, Williams 215
Pearson, Elizabeth 11
Pearson, Francis 11
Peck, Daniel 158
Pecock, William 37
Peety, John 225
Peirpoint, Amos 179
"Pelerton" 236
Pemberton, Benjamin 181
Pemberton, James 181, 187
Pemberton, John....60, 181, 187
Penington, Henry 136
Peninton, Tytus 190
Penn, John 1
Pennington, Joseph 43
Pennsylvania 15, 32, 36, 63,
  90, 99, 135, 141.......... 148
Penny, James 119
Pennywell, Richard 156
Penrice (Pinrice), John 15
Peopell, John 116
Perrahawkin 48
Perrgo, Joseph 239
Perry Neck 96
Perry (Pery), Hugh 6, 88, 139
Perry, Joseph 40
Perry (Perrie), Robert ...46, 77
Perry (Pery), Samuell....88, 139
Perry (Pery), Thomas....10, 139
Perry (Pery), William...138, 139

	PAGE
"Pershoar"	115
Person, Martha	8
Pery, Anne	139
Pery, John	139
Pery, Mary	139
Pery-Neck	156
Peteete, John	40
Peter, Samuel	236
Peterson, Andrew	99
Peterson, Harmon	95
Peterson, Rebecka	95, 117
"Pettibones Rest"	44
Pettitt, John	237
"Petton"	7
Petuxet, John	209
Peverell, Daniell	239
Peverell, Hannah	239
Peverell, Sarah	239
"Pheasant Tree"	39
Phelpes, John	53
Philadelphia	36, 63, 135, 141
Philips, Ann	8
Philips, Benony	8
Philips, James	22, 52, 112, 239
Philips, William	8
Phillips, Edward	142
Phillips, John	83
Phillips, Mary	76
Phillips, Phillip	76
Phillips, Robert	4, 124
Phillips, Thomas	124
Phillip's Range	216
Phillpott, Edward	177
Phillpott, Eleanor	178
Phillpott, John	178
Phillpott, Mary	178
Phillpotts, Parle	52
Philpott, Charles	174, 178
Philpott, Elizabeth	174
Phinice, Richard	170
Phippard, John	67
Phippard, Mary	67
Phippard, Ursilla	67
Phippard, William	67
Phoenix, Dinah	10
Phoenix, Edward	10
Pickett, Elizabeth	120
Pickett, John	28
Pickett, Mary	120
Pickett, Mathew	120
Piereville, John	35
Pierce, Gideon	53
Pierce, John	81
Pierson, Simon	146
Pigeon House Creek	19
Pigatt, Nathaniell	20
Piggott, John	56
Pigman, Ann	200

	PAGE
Pigman, Catherine	200
Pigman, Elizabeth	200
Pigman, Grace	200
Pigman, John	200
Pigman, Mason	200
Pigman, Sarah	200
Pike, Archabel	180
Pike, Mildred	180
Pile, Richard	42, 109
"Pileswood Lane"	17
Pillington, Gabriel	100
"Pimberton's Good Will"	46
Pindar, William	36
Pinder, Joseph	30
Piper, Isaac	193
Piner, Thomas	169, 219
Piscattaway (Piskathaway)	110, 113
Pisto, Philip	145
Pitt (Pitts), John	86, 107, 169
Pitt, Rebecca	107
Pitts, Ann	86
"Pitts Bridge"	185
Pitts, Charles	75
Pitts, Elizabeth	86
Pitts, George	86
Pitts, Jane	86
"Plain Dealing"	84, 147
Planner, William	103
"Planter's Delight"	94
Plantmer, Capt.	166
Plater, George	234
Plesto, Dorothy	169
Plesto, Edward	169
Plesto, John	169
Plomfeilde, Jas.	188
Plowden, Edmund	18
Plowden, George	13
Plummer, Samuel	109
Plummer, Thomas	109
Plunket (Plinket), Thomas	138
Poape, William	42
Pockhiccory Ridge	186
Pocomoke	15, 114, 154, 193
Pocomoke R.	76, 105, 115
Polke, William	227
Pollard, Tobias	116
Pollet, Margarett	50
Pollet, Thomas	50
Pollett, William	227
Pomokey	10
Poluck Creek	10
Ponder, Richard	159
Pool (Poole), Edward	152
Pool, Richard	65
Pool, Thomas	59
Poore, Richard	216
Poor, the	39, 50, 51, 194

PAGE

Poor, William 152
"Poor Man's Industry" 113
Pope, Elizabeth 57
Pope (Widow) 70
"Popingay" 50
Poplar Hill Church 51
Poplar Hill Hundred....126, 164
Poplar Island 58
"Poplar Neck" 68, 98, 228
"Popler Levell" 224
"Pork Hall" 50
Porter, Elizabeth 155
Porter, Francis 155, 157
Porter, Giles 7
Porter, Hugh 82, 155
Porter, James 157
Porter, John 34, 155, 157
Porter, Joseph 157
Porter, Joshua 155
Porter, Katharine 155
Porter, Lawrence 157
Porter, Mary 155
Porter, Peter 190
Porter, Rachel 155
Porter, William 155
Portobacco............2, 9, 119
Portobacco Church 130
Posey, Benjamin 80
Posey, Bolaine 80
Posey, Francis 80
Posey, John 80
Posey, Mary 2, 80
Potomac R. 69, 82
Pott, John 53
Pott, Joseph 53
Pott, Maj. 210
Pott, William 52
Pottenger, John 11
Pottenger, Samuel 11
Potter, Elizabeth 173
Pottobone, Thomas 44
Poulson, Cornelius 129
Poulton, John 127
Powell, Anne 111
Powell, Daniell 107
Powell, Elizabeth 77
Powell, Gary 152
Powell, George 111
Powell, Howell ...107, 181, 203
Powell, James 111
Powell, John......70, 76, 107, 111
Powell, Joseph 70
Powell, Judith 111
Powell, Levin 76
Powell, Margaret 76
Powell, Rachell 111
Powell, Richard 124
Powell, Susannah 107

PAGE

Powell, Thomas 111
Powell, William 14, 76
"Powell's Addition" 76
' Powell's Inheritance 70
"Powell's Lott" 76
"Powell's Recovery" 76
Power, Joseph 171
Powers, George 157, 158
Pratt, Jane 181
Presbury, Joseph 79
Preston, Anne 7, 8
Preston, John 7, 217
Preston, Jone 8
Preston, Thomas 240
Preston, William 56, 217
Prestwood, Thomas 185
Price, Benjamin 167
Price, Elizabeth 5, 33, 97
Price, Hannah 167
Price, Isabelle 123
Price, Johanna 140
Price, John........167, 169, 197
Price. Juliannah (Juliana)
    33, 97
Price, Mary....33, 123, 167, 183
Price, Mordecai 167
Price, Prudence 218
Price, Rachel 167
Price, Robert 33
Price, Sarah 167
Price, Stephen 167
Price, Thomas 5, 97, 167, 197, 224
"Prickard" 226
Prickell Pear Creek........ 28
Pride, Abell 32
Prise, Edward 94
Pritchard, Jane 131
Pritchard, Mary 131
Pritchard (Prickard), Wil-
    liam 72, 131
Pritchett, Richard 125
Pritchetts, William 240
Prittchett, Thomas 48
Proctor, Walter 224
Proprietary Rent 210
Prossér, Mathias 240
Protestant 69, 158
Protestant Church.....19, 69, 158
"Prouses Point" 151
"Providence" 34, 115
Pruitt, John 158
Pryer, Jacob 100
Pryer, John 100
Pryer, Philip 100
Pryer, Sarah 100
"Puddington" 228
"Puddington Harbor" 228

PAGE

Pull (Pell), James 126
Pullin, Jonn 156
Punning, John 129
Purnall, John 148, 212
Purnell, Thomas 105, 192

PAGE

Purrock, James 135
Pursell, Patrick 76
Puttneck, William 119
Puzey, William 102
Pye, Charles 10

Q

Quakers 12, 33, 34, 40, 50, 56,
    77, 84, 86, 87, 93, 100, 107,
    120, 143, 177, 181, 205.... 222
Queen (Ann)'s Town....160, 186

Queen, John 113, 205
"Quick Sale" 215
Quinton, Walter 60, 73, 76

R

Rablin, David 27
"Raccoon Point" 166
"Racliff (Ratcliff) Cross"
    36, 209
Rackliff (Rackliffe), Nath.
    213, 225
Racten, Thomas 78
"Radner" 51
Raggs, Frances 124
Raggs, Sarah 124
Raggs, John 124
Ragon, John 42
Rakes, William
    21, 54, 63, 79, 112, 147, 208
Ramsey, Charles 240
Ramsey, John 97
Ramsey, Thomas 3
Randall, John 74
Randall, Robert 169
Randall, Thomas 121
"Range" 96, 132
Rankin, Elizabeth 126
Rankin, John 126
Ransom (Ransome) George
    28, 175, 182
Ransom, Ignatius 176, 182
Ransom, Joseph 176, 182
Ransom, Richard ... 176, 182
Ransom, William....28, 176, 182
Ranter's Ridge 31
Rasin, Elizabeth 100
Rasin, John 100
Rasin, Philip 100
Rasin, Thomas 100
Rassom (Russam), Elizabeth. 206
Ratliff, Jacob 221
Ratcliff, Richard 14
Ratcliffe, Francis 113
Ratcliffe, Rachel 165
Ratfif, Mary 194
Rathenbury, Hannah 112
Rathenbury, Margaret 112
Rattenbury, John 184

"Rattlesnake" 1
"Rattle Snake Hill" 35
Rawley (Rawly), William 54, 97
Rawley, Samuel 97
Rawlings, Anthony 57, 125
Rawlings, Deborah 196
Rawlings, Dorothy 202
Rawlings, Elizabeth 75
Rawlings, Henry 111
Rawlings (Rawlins), John
    162, 179, 202
Rawlings, Richard 196
Ray, Daniell 189
Ray, James 142
Ray, John 22, 141
Ray, William 141
Raye, Alexander 148
Raymond, John 44, 83
Raymond, Susannah 44
Read, Ann 132
Read, David 210
Read, George 7
Read (Reid) (Reed), John
    128, 132, 162, 169
Read (Reed), Owen..61, 163, 184
Read, William 22, 132
Reading, Timothy 80
Readman, John 91
Reagen, Philip 188
Reavell (Revell), Alice...... 166
Reavell (Revell), Charles.... 165
Reavell (Revell), Mary 166
Reavell (Revell), Randall... 165
Reavell (Revell), William... 165
Reaves, Daniel 141
Reaves, Ellinor 141
Reaves, John.............. 141
Reaves, Mary 51
Reaves, Thomas 51, 141
"Red House" 207
"Red Lyon's Branch"...52, 144
Reddish, John 101
Redgrave, Abraham 34, 210

PAGE

Reed, Benjamin 37
Reed, Easter 212
Reed, Elizabeth 212
Reed, Hugh 37
Reed, Mary 212
Reed, Pierce (Pearce) 212
Reed, Thomas 228
Reed, Walter 212
Reeder (Reedar), Benjamin
  70, 128
Reeder (Reedar), Elizabeth. 128
Reeder (Reedar), Richard... 128
Reeder, Simon 128
Reeves (Revves) (Reves)
  (Rives), Thomas....2, 21, 227
Reeves (Reves) (Rives), Ub-
  gate 2, 227
Reeves (Reves), William 161, 227
Reformed Protestant Re-
  ligion 162
"Refuge" 108
Regan, Timothy 130
Register, Robert 55
Register, Sarah 55
Rehoboth Inlet 47
Renells, Andrew 107
Rensha, Ann 20
Rensha, Samuell 20
Renshaw (Rensher), Ann 47, 211
Renshaw, Joseph 68
Renshaw, William 110
Rensher, Bridgett 30
Rensher, Thomas 30
Respenh, Roger 238
Restell, Elizabeth 219
Reston, Edward 42
"Retalliation" 39
"Revell" 123
Reves (Rives), Mary 227
"Reviving Spring" 5, 121
Reynolds, Henry 70
Reynolds, John 30, 121
Rhodes, Abraham 197
Rice, Catherine 148
Rice, Ralph 148
"Rich Thicketts" 1
Rich, William 182
Richards, John 85
Richards, William 24
Richardson, Ann 90
Richardson, Bridgett 90
Richardson, Daniell 54, 183
Richardson, Ebener 90
Richardson, Elizabeth 63
Richardson, Hannah 148
Richardson, Henry 221
Richardson, John 63, 202
Richardson, Margaret 183

PAGE

Richardson, Nich.....73, 90, 197
Richardson, Thomas 221
Richardson, William
  32, 33, 46, 50, 63, 92, 148, 183
Riche, John 75
Richetts, John 32
Richmond 5
Ritchie (Richie), David..154, 226
Richson, Joseph 57
Rickan, Jeremiah 101
Rickards, Elizabeth 47
Rickards, John 47
Rickards, Jones 47
Rickards, Philip 47
Ricketts, William 32
Ricks, Abigail 13
Ricks, John 13
Riddell, George 141
Riddell, John 141
Riddley, Walter 120
Rider, John 97
"Riders" 201
Ridgby, John 192
Ridgley, Deborah 25, 26
Ridgeley, Charles 25, 26
Ridgeley (Ridgely), Henry
  94, 130
Ridgely, Robert 184
Ridgeley, William 25
"Ridle" 156
"Ridley" 151
Rigby, Arthur 148
Rigbye, Nathaniel 177
Rigden, Ellen 235
Rigden, Henry 235
Rigden, John 235
Riggen, Ambrose 48
Riggin, John 102
Riggin, Stephen 102
Riggs, James 110
Riggs, John 190
Right, Jeremiah 154
Ringgold, Thomas 147
Ringold, Charles 101
Risteau, John 185
Roach, Abigal 153
Roach, Arabella 153
Roach, Elizabeth 153
Roach, Mary 153
Roach, John 153
Roach, Hannah 153
Roach, Michael 153
Roach, Nathaniel 153
Roach, Rebecca 153
Roach, Samuel 153
Roach, Sarah 153
Road (Rhode) River........ 202
"Roadway" 200

PAGE

Roales, John 35
Roales, William 35
Roberson (Robson), Eliza-
    beth 49
Roberson, John 49
Roberson, Rachel 201
Roberson, Robert 226
Roberts, Anne 17
Roberts, Edward 1, 135
Roberts, Elizabeth 64, 118
Roberts, Henry 17
Roberts, Jacob 64
Roberts, James 64
Roberts, John 17
Roberts, Priscilla 143
Roberts, Richard 8
Roberts, Robert 143
Roberts, Ruth 64
Roberts, William 215
Robertson, Daniell 50
Robertson, James 212
Robertson, Mary 229
Robeson, Hannah 77
Robinhood's Forest 239
Robins, Elinor 205
Robins, Elizabeth 205
Robins, Henry 113
Robins, James 113, 205
Robins, Margaret 113
Robins, Thomas 113, 205
Robinson, David 218
Robinson, Francis 124
Robinson, James 231
Robinson (Roberson) (Rob-
    ertson), John 11, 49, 60,
    85, 180 238
Robinson, Jon. 187
Robinson, Joseph 85
Robinson, Joshua 85
Robinson, Judith 218
Robinson, Mary...35, 85, 93, 187
Robinson, Michael 85
Robinson, Peter 4, 85
Robinson (Robson), Richard
    15, 62
Robinson, Solomon 218
Robinson, Stephen 123
Robinson, Thomas 85
Robinson, Thomas Godsgrace
    35, 91
Robinson (Robeson) (Rober-
    son), William 32, 35, 49,
    60, 77, 85................ 114
Robinson's Purchase 85
Robson, Andrew 185
Robson, Charles 8
Robson, Elizabeth 62
Robson, Jas. 158

PAGE

Robson, John 57, 62
Robson, Mary 8, 62
Robson, Mathew 62
Robson, Richard 62
Rock, John 76
Rock Creek 135, 227
"Rock Hall" 17
"Rock of Dumbarton" 135
"Rockey Point" 228
Rockhould, Thomas 207
Roe, Morty 54
Rogers, David 57
Rogers, Elizabeth 14, 99, 140, 171
Rogers (Rodgers), John
    53, 140, 162
Rogers, Joseph 14
Rogers, Mary 14
Rogers, Nich. 145, 161
Rogers, Richard 140
Rogers, Roadham (Rodham)
    140, 172
Rogers, Samuel 14
Rogers, Thomas 26, 33
"Roger's Increase" 81, 145
Rolph, John 16
Roman Catholic Church 9, 11,
    33, 130, 184, 194, 198, 204,
    205, 221, 224............ 229
Ronge, Paul 120
Rookwood, Edward 139
Rookwood, Mary 139
Rookwood, Thomas 139
Roorock, William 88
Rooxbey, John 217
Ror, Joseph 45
Rose, Basell (Basoll)....30, 138
Rose, Charles 5
Rose, Jane 17
Rose, Mary 221
Rose, Richard 109
"Rose's Purchase" 109
Rosenquist, Alexander 215
Rosenquist, Andrew 231
Ross, William 46
Rossin, Robert 90
"Rotterdam" 42, 168
Round, Edward 193
Round, James 193
Round, Mary 193
Round, Samuell 48
Round, William......48, 177, 193
Rouse, John 142
"Rowclift" 224
"Rowder" 19
Rowe (Roe), Abigale 67
Rowe, Edward 218
Rowe (Roe), William 67
Rowles, William 201

PAGE

Royston, John 146
Rozer, Eliza 10
Rozer, Notley 9
Rozier, John 197
Ruff, Richard 52
Ruley, Rebecca 28
Rumley, Ann 57
Rumsey, Charles 130
Rumsey, Edward 131
Rumsey, Katherine 131
Rumsey, William 130
Russell, Elizabeth 148, 155
Russell, James 119

PAGE

Russell, Mary 155
Russell, Michael 148, 155
Russell, Rebecca 148, 155
Russell, Sarah 155
Russell, Thomas 66, 155
Russell, William 155
Russh, Susannah 16
Russh, Thomas 16
Rust, Richard 22
Ruth, Margery 75
Ruth, Thomas 43
Ryan, William 46
"Rycraffs Choyce" 66

S

Saintclaire, Priscilla 51
Saintclaire, Robert 51
Saintclar (Saint Clare), Rob-
    ert 3, 202
Salleman, Robert 199
"Salleys" 51
Salsbury, Elizabeth 43
Salsbury, James 43
Salsbury (Solsbury), John
            34, 36,   43
Salsbury, Joseph 43
Salsbury, Mary 43
Salsbury (Soldesbury), Pate-
    grew (Pettygrew) 8, 106
Salsbury, Samuel 43
Salsbury, Thomas 43
Salsbury, William 43
Salten, Jude 72
Salter, John 36
Salt Store House 39
Samnell, Peter 58
Samonds, William 46
Sample, Mary 22
Sampson, Henry 133
Sampson, Jeremiah 133
Sampson, Sarah 133
"Sam's Beginning" 135
Samson, Constant 29
Samson, John 29
Samson, Richard 29
"Samson's Addition" 29
Samuell, Peter 114
Samuells, Ann 49
Samuells, (Samuell), Richard
            49, 114
Sanders, Eleanor (Elinor)
            139, 226
Sanders, Elizabeth 28
Sanders, George 100
Sanders, James 11, 36
Sanders, Jane 36
Sanders, John 21, 123, 226

Sanders, Joseph 28
Sanders, Mary 49, 52, 139
Sanders, Mathew 123, 226
Sanders, Peter 151
Sanders, Prudence 61
Sanders, Richard 49
Sanders, Robert 123
Sanders, William
        90, 123, 182, 226
"Sander's Folly" 226
Sandford, Stephen 80
Sands, Elizabeth 118
Sands, Judith 118
Sands, Mary 118
Sands, Robert 118
Sands, Sarah 118
Sands, Susannah 118
Sands, Thomas 118
"Sands His Lot" 118
Sandys, William 131
Sanford, Jas. 179
Sappington, Margarett 99
"Sarah's Delight" 228
Sardy, Jane 221
Sare, John 75
Sassafras R. 6, 38, 132, 239
Sassafrax 99
"Saturday Work" 2
Sauser (Saser), Benjamin.19, 47
Sauser (Saser), John........ 47
Sauser, Panter 19, 47
Sauser, Thomas 19
Sauser (Saser), William..19, 47
"Sauser's Addition" 47
"Sauser's Folly" 47
Savage, Thomas 105
Savidge, Thomas 7
Sawell, Cuthbert 13
"Scagspring" 43
Scamper (Scamport) (Scam-
    pord), Jane 41, 42

PAGE

Scamper (Scamport) (Scampord), Peter 41
Scanterbury 207
Scholfield, Benjamin 46, 193
Scholfield, Henry 154
Schoolfield, Joseph 46
Schools 21, 109
Scieatie 198
"Scilla" 62
Scisell Meeeting House..... 100
Scorry (Scurre), Thomas.... 207
"Scotch-mans Wonder".... 209
"Scotland" 27, 126
Scott, Alexander 72
Scott, Ann 48
Scott, Daniell 238
Scott, Edward 78, 169, 210
Scott, John 85
Scott, Martha 169
Scott (Scutt), Mary..14, 37, 78
Scott (Scot), Robert
          18, 29, 51, 132
Scott, Sophia 148, 156
Scott, Walter 99
Scott, William........6, 21, 196
Scriven, John 177
Scrogin, John 59
Scully, Margaret 34
Scurlock, Richard 53
Seady, Anthony 105
Seager, John 73, 201, 209
Searson, Widow 51
Second Ck.........9, 151. 186
Sedwicks, Elisha 211
Sedwicks, Grace 211
Sedwicks, Joshua 65
Seikes, John 90
Seley, George 236
Semmes, Mary 97
Semms (Sims), Eleanor..... 139
Semms (Sims), Elizabeth.... 139
Semms (Sims), Francis 139
Semms (Sims), Marmaduke. 139
Semms (Sims), Ruth........ 139
Serman, Thomas 49
Seth, Charles 43
Severerne (Severenes), John. 97
Severn River 179
Sewell, Henry 190
Sewence, John 43
Sexton, Patrick 160
"Shadewell" 55
"Shadewell's Addition" ... 55
Shahan, Bridgett 9
Shakley, Benjamin 140
Shakley, Edward 140
Shakley, Elizabeth 140
Shakley, Francis 140

PAGE

Shakley (Shekertie), John.. 140
Shakley, Mary 140
Shakley, Michael 140
Sharin, Mary 159
Sharp, Elizabeth 30
Sharp, John 30, 31
Sharp, Mary 30
Sharp (Sharpe), Peter
          8, 156, 158, 225
Sharp, Robert 30
Shary, Job 166
Shavers, Abraham 145
Shavers, Susanna 161
Shaw, Christopher 162
Shaw, Elinor 60
Shaw, Geofrey Mathew 187
Shaw, James 162
Shaw, Margaret 162
Shaw, Mary 33, 114
Shaw, Mathew 60
Shaw, Thomas 114
Shaw, Wiliams 162
Shaw, —— 35
Sheeld, Catherine 147
Sheeld, Edmond 147
Sheele, Mary 21
Sheele, William 21
Shehe, David 47
Sheircliffe, John 72
Shepard, William 214
"Shepard's Forrest" 190
Sheppard, Catherine 22
Sheppard, Pearsivall 162
Sheredine, J. 93
Sheredine, Thomas 161
Sherrine, Abraham 144
Sherwood, Daniel 148
Sherwood, Elizabeth 107
Sherwood, Frances 148
Sherwood, Francis 148
Sherwood, John 107
Sherwood, Philip 148
"Sherwood Neck" 148
Shiler, Jane 119
Shiles, John 30
Shiles, Thos. 30
Shillingsworth, William 10
Shilton, Thomas 57
Shirclef, John 198
Shirley, Katherine 73
Shirley, Richard 73
"Shirley's Point" 209
"Shoal Creel" 168
Shoebrooke, Thomas 67
Shoklee (Shokley, Ann..... 85
Shoklee (Shokley), David.. 84
Shoklee (Shokley), Elinor.. 85

PAGE

Shoklee (Shokley), Eliza-
    beth 85
Shoklee (Shokley), John... 85
Shoklee (Shokley), Mary.... 85
Shoklee (Shokley), Richard. 84
Shoklee (Shokley), William. 84
"Shore Ditch" 157
Short, Anne 226
Short, Christopher 57
Short, Daniel 226
Short, George 226
Short, Thomas 202
Shorter, Elizabeth 93
Shorter, William 93
"Showan Hunting Ground" 51
"Shrimp's Neck" 80
Shropshill, Jane 150
Sicklemore, Samuel 240
"Siles Chance" 129
Sillavan (Swillavant), Dan-
    uell 35, 63
Sillavan (Swillavant), Pris-
    cilla 35, 63
Sikes, Thos. 84
Simckclair, Mary 19
Simme, William 228
Simpson, Ann 234
Simpson (Sympson), Ignatius 43
Simpson (Sympson), James. 43
Simpson, Jeremiah 234
Simpson, John 234
Simpson (Sympson), Mary.. 43
Simpson (Sympson), Thomas
                16, 43, 234
Simpson (Sympson), William
                    43, 140
"Simpson's Supply" 226
Simson, James 226
Sinckclair, Mary 19
Sinckleare, Robert 179
Sinclair, Magins 19
Sinclaire, Alexander 114
Sinefield 34
Sinett, Garrett 129
Sinklar, William 100
Sinnett, John 9
Skannahone, George 185
Skantlebury, Thomas 156
Skeen, Rachel 12
Skein, Robert 20
Skellden, Edward 191
Skidmore, Edward 88
Skidmore, Joseph 88
Skidmore, Rebecca 88
Skinner, Addtonton (Adder-
    ton) 14, 24, 35, 63
Skinner, Andrew 74, 150

PAGE

Skinner, Ann (Anne)
            14, 59, 150, 174
Skinner, Clarke 14
Skinner, Dorothy 150
Skinner, Elizabeth 150, 174
Skinner, John 79, 158
Skinner, Mary 150, 174
Skinner, Richard 150
Skinner, Robert 14, 174
Skinner, Thomas 59
Skinner, William
            14, 24, 35, 96, 174
Skippers, John 234
Skirvan, William 46
"Slow" 95
Sluter, Henry 15
Slve, Gerard 199
Slve, Jon. 3
"Small Hogs" 191
Smallshaw, John 112
Smallwood, James 26
Smallwood, Leadstone 26
Smallwood, Mary 26
Smallwood, Prier 26
Smallwood, Thomas 26
Smeathers, James 78
Smith, Alice 146
Smith, Andrew 125
Smith, Ann..61, 66, 142, 201, 206
Smith, Anthony 123
Smith, Archibald 154
Smith, Av. 95
Smith, Barbary 38
Smith, Basill 142
Smith, Benjamin 142
Smith, Cassandra 183
Smith (Smyth), Charles
                7, 29, 128
Smith, Chas. Somerset....38, 67
Smith, Daniel 188
Smith, Dorothy 128, 142, 173, 218
Smith, Edward 48, 109
Smith, Eleanor 142
Smith, Elias 136
Smith, Elizabeth 21, 37, 61,
    142, 172, 173, 206........ 214
Smith, Esq. 62
Smith, George 154, 240
Smith (Smyth), Henry 13
Smith, James
        62, 77, 142, 154, 201, 219
Smith, John (Jon) 8, 48, 61,
    62, 93, 109, 134, 136, 142,
    184, 194, 195, 196, 201, 212,
    214, 218 236
Smith, Jos. 91, 173, 210
Smith, Mareen 48

PAGE

Smith, Margarett (Margaret) 197, 214
Smith (Smyth), Martha 61, 142, 169, 209
Smith, Mary..109, 142, 201, 214
Smith, Mathew 62
Smith, Peter 173
Smith, Philomon 201
Smith, Priscilla 136
Smith, Rebecca 154
Smith, Renatus 214, 220
Smith, Richard 23, 37, 235
Smith, Robert 48, 213, 214
Smith, Roger 142
Smith, Rousby 38
Smith, Samuell 61, 100, 119, 142, 163, 219
Smith, Sarah....61, 154, 164, 219
Smith, Susannah 173
Smith (Smyth), Thomas 21, 48, 54, 56, 62, 91, 130, 146, 169, 209, 210............ 236
Smith, Walter 37, 96
Smith, William 48, 74, 136, 183, 195, 206
"Smith's Conveniency" 38
"Smith's Fort" 37
"Smith's Forrest" 37
"Smith's (Smyth's) Meadows" 21, 209
"Smith's Purchase" 226
Smithson, Owen 90
Smithson, Thomas 5
Smock, Henry 25
Smoot, Ann 174
Smoot, Barton 174
Smoot, Rachell 2
Smoot, Richard 134
Smoot, Sarah 178
Smoot, Thomas 174
Smoot, William 174
"Smoot's Purchase" 1
Smuelling, Randall 48
"Smyth's Desert" 209
"Smyths Venture" 209
Snowden, Elizabeth 32
Snow Hill 14, 115, 193
Sollers, John 38
Sollers, Robert 177
Sollers, Sabrett 218
"Solomon's Friendship" ... 96
Somerland, John 31
Somerset Parish 42
Somersett, Charles 91
Sommers, Benjamin 47
Sommers, John 47
Sommers, Mary 48
Sommers, Thomas 47

PAGE

Sommers, William 47
"Something" 186
"Somthingworth" 19
Sothoron, Ann 221
Sothoron, Benjamin 221
Sothoron, John Johnson..... 221
Sothoron, Mary 221
Sothoron, Richard 221
Sothoron, Samuel 221
South, John 131
"South Louthian" 23
"Southrich" 224
South R. 70, 179
"South River Quarter" 25
Soward, John 44
Soward, Mary 44
Soward, William 44
Spalding, Honour 171
Sparks, Capt. 88
Sparrow, Anne 203
Sparrow, Elizabeth 203
Sparrow, John 202, 203
Sparrow, Kensey 202
Sparrow, Matilda 203
Sparrow, Sarah 182
Sparrow, Solomon 182, 202
Sparrow, Thomas 202
"Sparrow's Nest" 183
"Sparrow's Rest" 202
Speak (Speake), Bowling 119, 163, 184
Speak, Mary 119
Spence, James 151
Spence, Magnus (Magnis) 120, 151
Spencer, Charles 157
Spencer, Edward 129
Spencer, Jervis 231
Spesutie Hundred 204, 239
Spink, Cathrine 199
Spink, Eliner 199
Spink, Teclo 199
Spinke, Clement 198
Spinke, Edward 72, 127, 170
Spinke, Elizabeth 127, 170
Spinke (Spink), Francis 127, 198, 199
Spinke, Henrieta 198
Spinke, Henry 72, 110, 123, 127, 165, 170, 174........ 198
Spinke, Leocresia 198
Spinke, Margaret 127, 198
Spinke, Mary 127, 198
Spinke, Monica 198
Spinke, William 127
"Spinkies Rest" 198
Sporne (Snorne), Nicholas 93, 164, 233

PAGE

Sprigg, Thomas 18
Springnall, John 158
"Spring Close" 118
"Springg Garden" 57
Sproul, Nicholas 40
Spry, Elizabeth 13
Spry, Thomas 14
Spurier, Thomas 206
Squires, John 71
Squires, Sarah 71
Squires, Thomas 71
St. Clement's Hundred ...69, 171
"St. Edmonds" 97, 119
St. George's Hundred....126, 201
St. George's Parish 204
St. Ignatius Chappell 198
St. Innigoes Church 205
"St. James" 66
St. James Parish 7
"St. John's" 80, 97, 120
St. John's Creek 236
St. Lawrence R. 123
St. Leonard's Creek 37, 175
St. Martin's River..59, 115, 166
St. Mary's City 172
St. Mary's Hundred 126
St. Michaell's Hundred 188
St. Michaell Town 232
St. Michael's Creek 157
St. Michael's Parish
    5, 149, 200, 226
St. Michael's R. 148, 150, 157, 200
St. Omers College 10
St. Paul's Parish..4, 67, 144, 210
St. Peter's Neck 86
St. Peter's Parish 33
St. Richard's Mannor 209
"St. Thomas" 29
Stacey, John 71
Stacey, Mathew 81
Stallings, Richard...164, 167, 219
Staly, Thomas 240
"Stanaway's Lucky Chance" 115
Standforth, Elizabeth 127
Standforth, Joseph Whips... 127
Standforth, Philothea 127
Stanford, Margaret 95
Stanford, Mary 125
Stanford, Susannah 56
Stanford (Stanforth), John
    95, 127, 195
Stanley, Jacob 67
"Stanley's Choice" 67
Stannard (Stunnard), Abell. 24
Stapleford, Robert 7, 8
Stapleton, John 119, 184
Starkey, Edward 186
Starling, Hannah 102

PAGE

Starling, John 102
Starrat, John 76
Start, Elizabeth 158
Start, Ephraim 158
Start, John 158
"Stedmore" 37
Steele (Steal), Francis (Fran-
    ces) 81, 231
Steele, John 109
Steele, Mary 109
Steele, Rebecca 81
Steele, Thomas 81
Steele, William 109
Stennet, John 38
Stephens, Abigail 12
Stephens, Ann 12
Stephens, Hanna 12
Stephens, Isaack 12
Stephens (Stevens), John 12,
    20, 21, 31, 56, 75, 86, 151,
    205 215
Stevens (Stephens), Richard
    11, 12
"Stephen's Conquest" 12
"Stepney" 134
Stepney Parish 47, 49
Stevens, Charles
    20, 74, 80, 158, 186
Stevens, Edward 86
Stevens, Elizabeth 86, 215
Stevens, Francis 54
Stevens, Isaac 141
Stevens, James 80
Stevens, Kezia 80
Stevens, Magdalen Maud.... 215
Stevens, Sarah 28, 56, 215
Stevens, Tabbither 86
Stevens, Thomas 215
Stevens, Walter 152
Stevens (Stephens), William
    61, 125, 190, 215
"Stevens Plains" 186
Stevenson, Edward 4, 79
Stevenson, Mary 79
Stevenson, William 166
Steward, Alex. 44
Steward, Charles 63
Steward, David 63
Steward, Margarett 44
Stewart, John 46, 75
Stewart, Thomas 75
"Stillington" 207
Stinchecomb, Nathaniell 44
Stitts, Isaac 48
Stitts, Robert 48
Stockdall, Edward 45, 103
Stockdall, Jean (Boyce) 45
Stockdall, Jane 45

PAGE

Stockett, Thomas 204
Stockley, John 47
Stockley, Mary 47
Stockley, Thomas 47
Stockley, William 47
"Stock Range" 200
Stockwell, Thomas....45, 49, 102
Stoddart, Elizabeth 110
Stoddert (Stodert), James 94, 211
"Stokebardolph" 39
Stokes, John 204
Stone, Martha 137
Stone, Mathew 174
Stone, Mr. 37
Stone, Thomas 130, 136
Stone, Rachell 174
Stone Island 37
"Stonesby" 233
Stonestreet, Thomasin 51
"Stony Hill" 16
Storey, Joana 58
Story, James 58
Story, Joseph 41
Story, Marmaduke.......149, 174
Story, Walter........19, 119, 175
Stoughton, William 114
Stourten, William 88
Stourton, Margery 29
Stourton, Robert 29
Stratfoord, Joseph 216
"Strickland's Rest" 222
"Strife" 126, 174, 186
Strutton, George 167
Strutton, Mary 167
Stuart, William 63
Stubbs, John 120
Studd, Thomas 31
Studham, Thomas 157
Stump, Thomas 162
Sturgess, John 166
Sturges, Jonathan 47
Sturmey (Sturney), Catherine
                        35, 63
Sturmey (Sturney), William
                        35, 63
"Suckia Swamp" 61
Sudfif, John 194
Sudler, Joseph 180
Sulevane, Susannah 43
Sullivane, Agnes 219
Sulivann, Jenerate 195

PAGE

Sulivant, Ann 91
Sulivant, Darby 91
Sullivant (Sulivane), Dennis
                    28, 197, 219
Sulivant, Elizabeth 91
Sulivant, Jeremiah 91
Sulivant, Joseph 91
Sumerland, John 201
Summerlin, Margaret 201
"Summerly" 84
Summers, Sarah 152
Sumner, Margaret 102
Sunderlin, John 38
"Sunken Ground" 104
Sunkey, Thomas 27
"Surveyors Forrest" 5
Sury, Elizabeth 183
"Susetren" 230
Susquehannah Hundred 55
Susquehanna R. 66, 156, 231
Sutcliff, Joshua 24
Sutten (Sutton), John
                    17, 148, 158
Sutton, Mr. 155
Sutton, Robert 54, 121
Sutterfield, Edward 62
Sutterfield, William 62
Suttle, Ann 3
Suttle, Elizabeth 3
Suttle, John 3, 139
Swale, William 51
Swan, Elizabeth 164
Swan, George 164
Swan, James 164, 199
Swan (Swann) Cr.
                6, 27, 55, 204, 239
"Swan Island" 6
Swan Point 6
Sweale, William 172
Swearingen, Samuell 27
Sweatman, William 78
Sweeney Her 70
Sweeney, Terren (Taren)
                    89, 109, 231
Sweeney (Sweeny), Wm..... 89
Sweet, Sarah 52
Swinger, Alexander 148
"Swineyard" 43
Swynley, Thomas 28
Symonds, Charles 15

T

"Tack's Point" 218
Tait, John 176
Talbott (Tabott), Edward... 189
Talbott (Tabott), Elizabeth. 189

Talbott (Talbot) (Tabott),
    John 54, 86, 189, 190
Talbott, Katharine 4
Talbott, Margarett 4

PAGE

Talbott (Tabott), Mary..... 189
Talbott (Tabott), Richard... 189
Talbott (Tabott), Sarah.... 189
Talbot, Thomas 4
Talbott, William 4
"Talbott's Angles" 32
Tallott, Mathew 179
Taney, Catherine 22
Taney, Jane 172
Taney, Mary 22
Taney, Michll. 142, 235
Taney, Thomas 142
Taneyhill, James 175
Tanyhill, John 28
Tanyhill (Taneyhill), Sarah
                          28, 175
"Tarcell's Neck" 75
Tarent, Leonard 132
Tarent, Mary 132
"Tarkill" 20
Tarvert, John 89
Tasker, Ann 18
Tasker, Thomas 235
Tat—, Matthew 14
Tatam, John 195
Tate, John 204
"Taunton" 212
Tavern Creek 6
Tayler, Rebecca 216
Taylor, Abrm. 120, 151, 157, 213
Taylor, Ann 21, 127
Taylor, Catherine 225
Taylor, Dorothy 141
Taylor, Elinor 141
Taylor, Elizabeth....21, 141, 204
Taylor, Francis 215
Taylor, George 182
Taylor, Grace......21, 127, 188
Taylor, Henry 18, 188
Taylor, Ignacius 127
Taylor, Isabel 204
Taylor, James....127, 188, 203
Taylor, Jane 67
Taylor, John...166, 188, 203, 213
Taylor, Jonathan 120
Taylor, Joseph 203
Taylor, Margaret 83
Taylor, Martin 202
Taylor (Tayler), Mary 21, 26, 46
Taylor, Nebuchadnezer....66, 95
Taylor, Rachel 188
Taylor, Robert 37
Taylor, Ruben 66
Taylor, Sam'l........66, 95, 145
Taylor, Sarah 140
Taylor, Thomas
        8, 56, 127, 138, 141, 203
Taylor, Upgate 21

PAGE

Taylor (Tayler), William
                     21, 46, 141
"Taylor's Chance" 203
"Taylor's Coast" 40
"Taylor's Island" 106
"Taylor's Ridge" 157
Tazewell, Wm. 192
Teach, John 153
Teall, Ed. 145
Tedman, Phil. 95
Tench, Edw. 117
Tengell, Sarah 154
Tenison, Abraham 98
Tenison, Absolem 98
Tennerly, Phillip 182
Tennisson, Mary 12
Tervervild (Terbifield), Gil-
  bert 197
"Thabush Manning" 234
Thacker, Margaret 186
Thacker, Mary 186
Thacker, Samuel 186
Thacker, Wm. 64
Tharley, Sam 80
Tharpe, Wm. 60
"The Addition"...209, 224, 231
"The Addition to Cool
  Spring" 167
"The Adjoyner" 198
"The Adventure" 55, 131
"The Angle" 182
"The Angles" 108
"The Beach" 47
"The Branch" 198
"The Chance" 223
"The Clifts" 235
The Clifts Burying Ground.. 223
"The Defence" 222
"The End of Controversy" 31
"The Exchange" 76
"The First Part of Free
  Gift" 38
"The Folly" 90
"The Forrest" 96
"The Fox" 173
"The Grove" 132
"The Hills" 1, 175
"The Hope" 148
"The Island" 6
"The Levell".............. 223
"The Middle" 76
"The Parting Path" 29
"The Plaines" 4, 210
"The Purchase" 143
"The Rainge" 238
"The Recovery" 136
"The Release" 101
"The Reserve" 14

	PAGE
"The Ridge"	108
"The Ripe"	133
"The Schoolhouse"	96
"The Tanyard"	1
"The Vineyard"	189
"The Wedge"	175
"The Widow's Purchase"	31
"The Woodyard"	168
"The World's End"	224
"The Young Man's Adventure"	32
Theobalds, Mary	140
Therenton (Thorneton), Wm.	58
Thomas, Anne	156
Thomas, Benony	10
Thomas, Edmond	74, 197
Thomas, Edward	40
Thomas, John	57
Thomas, Katharine (Catherine)	10, 58
Thomas, Mary	58
Thomas, P.	190
Thomas, Trustam	74
Thomas, William	57, 70, 156, 169, 189, 203
Thomas and Anthony's Choice	172
Thompkins, John	12
Thompson, Alse	34
Thompson, Andrew	49
Thompson (Tompson), Ann.	106
Thompson, Augustine	36, 111
Thompson, Barbara	72
Thompson, Charity	119
Thompson (Tompson), Chas.	106
Thompson (Tompson), Christopher	122, 162
Thompson, Dan'll	34
Thompson (Tompson), Elizabeth	35, 106
Thompson (Tompson), Frances	106
Thompson, George	35, 126
Thompson (Tompson), James	22, 98, 133, 170, 171, 180, 199
Thompson, Jane	2
Thompson (Thomson), Jennet	120
Thompson, Johanna	35
Thompson (Tompson), John	106, 213
Thompson (Tompson), Joseph	106
Thompson, Margaret	35, 180, 189
Thompson, Mary	120, 213
Thompson, Michael	72
Thompson, Mildred	165
Thompson, Richard	120
Thompson, Sarah	26, 36, 106, 120
Thompson, Sebastion	180
Thompson, Thos.	37, 120
Thompson (Tompson), Walter	10, 109
Thompson (Tompson), Wm.	72, 120, 163, 205
"Thompson's Addition"	106
"Thompson's Choice"	223
Thornley, Thos.	170
Thornton, Elizabeth	138
Thornton, Mary	74
Thornton, Wm.	138
Thornwell, Leath	56
Thornwell, Mary	56
Thornwell, Robert	56
Thornwell, William	56
Threhearne, John	102
Threisby, Rhodah	187
Thrill, Elizabeth	34
Thrill, Joseph	34
"Thrimby Grange"	200
Thurley, Richard	90
Thurrel, Mr.	11
Thurstone, Thomas	238
Tibbs, William	161
"Tidenton"	32
Tilden, John	169
Tiler, Jonathan	215
Tiler, Martha	215
Tiler, Thomas	215
Tilghman, Anna Maria	147
Tilghman, Henrietta Maria	147
Tilghman, Madan	5
Tilghman, Mary	147
Tilghman, Richard	132, 147, 169, 187
Tilghman, Wm.	147
Tillman, Hans	81
Tilman, Ann	86
Tilman, John	86
"Timber Neck"	178
Tingle, Samuel	155
Tinkers Branch	113
Tinsone, James	82
Tippin, Ann	23
Tippin, Mary	23
Tippin, William	23
Tippit, Thos.	43
Tipton, Thomas	215
Tipton, William	167, 215
Tobey, Cornelius	136
Tobin, Cornelius	167
Tobin, Elinor	167
"Todcaster"	218
Todd, Christopher	51
Todd, Dorothy	75
Todd (Tood), Elizabeth	52, 190
Todd, Martha	52
Todd (Tood), Michell (Michel)	115, 116, 229

PAGE

Todd, Philip 51
Todd, Robert 51
Todd, Thomas 51
Todd, William 51
"Todd's Plaines" 161
Toddadill, Mathew 109
Tolles, Roger 197
Tollson, Andrew 21
Tollson, Richard 21
Tolson, Francis 186, 224
Tom, Eliza 37
Tom, William 37
Tompson, Cuthbert 194
Tompson, Josiah 213
Tood, Anne 190
Tood, Lance 190
Tood (Todd), Margaret..116, 190
Tood, Mary 190
Tood, Richard 190
Toole, Jane 15
Toole, Patrick 15
"Touloon" 194
Tovey, Elizabeth 54
Tovey, Mary 54
Tovey, Mr. 209
Tovey, Samuell 54
"Tovey's Lott" 54
Towgood, Josiah 110
Town Neck 51
Town Point 89
Townley, John 196, 214
Townley, Mary 214
Townsend, James 107
Townsend, Jane 83
Townsend, John 83
Townsend, Rebekah 155
Townsend, Sarah 83
Townson, Rich 179
Townson, Tho. 221
"Towtenfields" 220
Traenes, James 84
Train, James 49
Transquaking River 167
Travis, Elizabeth 176
Travis, John 176
Travis, Mary 176
Travis, Seliner 176
Travis, William Mills...... 176
Tredhaven Crk......13, 179, 217
Tredhaven R. 74
Trego, Jno. 152
"Trent Neck" 40
Trevilion, John 158
Trew, Elace 7
Trew, Elizabeth 7
Trew, John 7
Trew, Mary 7
Trew, William 7, 42

PAGE

Trewman, Vincent 24
Trice, Abraham 49
"Triller" 222
Trimble (Trimbell), Eliza-
   beth 185, 189
Tripe, Abraham 83
Trippe, Jno. 32
Troth, Elizabeth 143
Trott, Elizabeth 217
Trott, Thomas 217
Trotten, Luke 161
Trotten, Rose 161
Truman, Edward 172
Truett, James 156
Truett, Sarah 156
Truitt, Geo. 25
Truitt, John 25, 178
Truman (Trueman), Henry
                       172, 233
Truman, James 172
Truman, Jane 172
Truman, Sarah 172
Truman, Thomas 172
"Truman's Acquaintance".. 39
"Trumping" 209
Tubman, Geo. 137
Tubman, Richard 137
Tubrid, Edward 43
Tuckahoe 9, 22, 55, 67, 81,
   144, 158, 181, 203........ 224
Tuckahoe Crk. 62, 107, 128
Tuckahoe Meeting House
                   120, 181, 205
Tucker, Ann 65
Tucker, John 65, 109
Tucker, Nath. 145
Tucker, Sarah 145
Tucker, Thos......38, 65, 123, 181
Tull, Benja. 12
Tull, Elizabeth 182
Tull, John 102, 182
Tulley, Hannah 159
"Tulley's Neck" 214
"Tullye's Delight" 144
Turbervile, Gilbert 205
Turbot, Elizabeth 198
Turbutt, Foster.....112, 144, 218
Turbutt, Marion 144
Turbutt, Michael 144
Turbutt, Samuel 144
Turbutt (Turbot), Wm.
                  129, 144, 198
"Turkey Hill" 206
"Turkey Island" 228
"Turkey Neck" 94
"Turkey Park" 157
Turlo (Turlie), William..... 197
Turner, Anne 206

PAGE

Turner, Edward......54, 206, 215
Turner, Elizabeth 175
Turner, Gidion 63
Turner, Johana 64
Turner (Turners), Jno.
   11, 51, 62, 63, 98, 109, 178, 206
Turner, Joseph 206
Turner, Mary 206
Turner, Richard 224
Turner, Sarah 51
Turner, Sol. 109
Turner, Thomas 63, 206
Turner, Widow 178
Turner, Wm.....54, 178, 206, 214
Turpin, John 153
Turpin, Mary 153
Turpin, William 153
"Turvey" 22

PAGE

Turville (Turvile), John
                182, 213, 225
"Tuscatacat" 209
Twiford (Twyford), Richard. 44
Twigger, Jno. 46
Twilly, Robert 103
Tyler, Robert 38, 141
Tyndale, Athelstand 2
Tyndale, Mrs. Hester 2
Typpett, Nicho. 7
Tyre, James 53
Tyrwhitt, Anne 232
Tyrwhitt, Charles 232
Tyrwhitt, Frances 232
Tyrwhitt, George 232
Tyrwhitt, Margarett 232
Tyry, Anna 217

U

"Ueubert" 96
Umgreville, Chas. 20
"Umtiguint" 110
Underwood, Ant. 235
Underwood, Martha 235
Underwood's Choice 188
"Unduce" 49
"Upholden" 9
"Upland" 67
"Upland Addition" 67
"Upper Cock Town"....... 38

"Upper Deal" 208
Upshaw, William 132
Upshur, Mary 86
Usher, Elizabeth 28, 35
Usher, George 28
Usher, Jean 28
Usher, Jno. 28
Usher, Mary 28
Usher, Sarah 28
Usher, Thos. 28

V

Vale, Jno. 152
"Vale of Misery" 229
Valentine, George....44, 121, 184
"Valley of Jehosophat".... 37
Vanbibber, James 99
Vanderford, Chas.....68, 73, 144
Vanderford's Branch 158
Vandervourt, George 96
Vanderwerf, Rich ..:....... 81
Vanheck, Jno 6
Vaughan, Prudence 117
Vaughan, Wm. 49, 117
"Vaux's Land" 5
Vernon, Chr. 7, 27
Vernon, Thomas 20
Vestry 210
Veze (Veazey), Chas....... 105
Veze (Veazey), Elizabeth... 105
Veze (Veazey), George 105

Veze (Veazey), John 105
Veze (Veazey), Nathaniell.. 105
Veze (Veazey), William..... 105
"Viana" 87, 101
Vicars, Elizabeth 152
Vicars, John 152
Vickars, Rachell 8, 152
Vickors (Viegers), Thos..... 31
Vienna 167
Vinall, Hanah 68
Vinall, Stephen 68
Vinecome, William 31
"Vines Neck" 38
Vinnicom, Jane 142
Vinson, John 31
Virginia
   40, 51, 52, 112, 132, 225, 237
Voss, Thos. 158
Vowles, James 206

W

PAGE		PAGE
Wade, Robt. 200		Waple, Elizabeth 119
Wade, Samuell 5		Waple, John 118
Waford, Wm. 142		Waple, Osmond 118
Wagstaff, James 237		Waple, Sarah 118
Wagstaff, Mary 237		Ward, Ann 48
Wakefield, Abel 12		Ward, Cornelius 48
Waldron, Chas. 129		Ward, Henry 123
Wale, Edward 165		Ward, James 102, 226
Wale, Elias 165		Ward, Jno. 40
Wale, Elizabeth 165		Ward, Margaret 123, 226
Wale, John 165		Ward, Matthew Tilghman
Wale, Nathaniel 165		118, 148, 200
Wale, Rackliff 165		Ward, Samuel 48
Wale, Turvile 165		Ward, Thos. 48, 102, 162
Walker, Ann 173		Ward, Wm. 99
Walker, Dan 62		Warfield, Alexander.....179, 183
Walker, George....72, 73, 79, 216		Warfield, Benjamin 183
Walker, James 173, 177		Warfield, Elizabeth 183
Walker, Mary 173		Warfield, Jno. 145, 179
Walker, Richard 170, 173		Warfield, Joshua 183
Walker, Robt.............43, 107		Warfield, Lydia 183
Walker, Thos. 123, 173, 195, 198		Warfield, Rachel 183
"Walker's Chance" 13		Warfield, Richard 145, 183
Wall, Alexander 95		Warfield, Ruth 183
Wall, Jno. 17, 207		Warfield, Sarah 183
Wall, Joseph 106		"Warfield Forrest" 183
Wall, Mary 95		"Warfield's Range" 183
Wall, Rachel 106		Waring (Warring), Basil..39, 94
Wall, Thomas 95		Waring, Martha 39
Wall, William 95		Warman, Stephen 228
Waller, John 20		Warner, Edw. 207
Waller, Major 20		Warner, Geo 78, 132
Walley, Isaac 126		Warner, Saml............... 221
Walley, Mary 126		Warner, William 215
Wallis, Samuel 87, 178		"Warplesdon" 96
Wallis, Wm. 86		Warram, Wm. 213
"Wallop's Neck" 46		Warren, Anne... 1
Wallstorne, London 103		Warren, Barton 174
Walston, Thomas 102		Warren, Jno. 1
Walter, John 40		Warren, Judith 1, 19
Walters, Christopher 70		Warren, Mary 1
Walters, Rebecka 69		"Warren's Discovery" 1
Walton, Alisha 155		Warrick, James 174
Walton, Elizabeth 106		"Warsester" 195
Walton, Hannah 106		Warum, William 231
Walton, John 105		Wason, Francis 205
Walton, London 46		Waters, Rich'd 12
Walton, Mary 106, 195		"Waterford" 49
Walton, Rachel 154		Watkins, Basiel 179
Walton, Rebecca 106		Watkins, Elizabeth 11
Walton, Sarah 106, 195		Watkens, Frances 133
Walton, Wm. 106		Watkins, Gassaway 11
Wamsley, Sarah 196		Watkins, John..11, 129, 179, 190
Wane, Chas. 113		Watkins, Mary 179
Wanill, Susanna 215		Watkins, Nicholas 11
"Wanister" 98		Watkins, Thomas 179

PAGE

Watson, Robt. 105
Watters, John 213
Wattes Creek 135
Watts, Alexander 33
Watts, Ann (Anne), 20, 152, 196
Watts, Edward 146
Watts, George 152
Watts, John 20, 45, 146, 152, 193
Watts, Peter........71, 152, 208
Watts, Stephen 208
Watts, Thomas 208
Watts, Wm.......71, 90, 196, 208
Wattson (Whatson), Benony 58
Wattsoṅ (Waston), Francis
58, 167
Wattson (Whatson) (Watson),
Robert 58, 105
Wattson (Whatson), William 58
Wattson's Purchase 61
Waughop, Ann 172
Waughop, Elizabeth 208
Waughap, Mary 208
Waughop, Thos. 172, 208
Wayger, Wm. 70
Weakfild, John 217
Weakfeild, Richard 240
Weathertee, Jas. 77
Weaver, Rich. 207
Webb, Comfort 166
Webb, Elizabeth 166
Webb, Esther 166
Webb, Henry 166
Webb, James 205
Webb, Jno. 156, 205
Webb, Joseph 216
Webb, Mary 166
Webb, Park 205
Webb, Peter 216
Webb, Rebecca 205
Webb, Richard.....120, 182, 205
Webb, Sarah 215, 216
Webb, Sophia 166
Webb, Tabitha 166
Webb, William 166
Webster, John 146
Webster, Rich.......58, 117, 142
Webster, Thos.......72, 163, 188
"Wedge Mill" 197
Wedge River 197
Weeb, Elizabeth 54
Weems, Elizabeth 63
Weer, Robt. 82
Welding (Welden), Thomas.. 175
Welch, Ann 73
Welch, Elinor 73
Welch, John 17, 73
Welch, Katherine 73
Welch, Thos. 73, 188

PAGE

Welch, Thomasin 17
Welch, William 214
"Well Close" 197
Wellch, Silvester 94
Wellett, Edward 11
Wellman, Elizabeth 183
Wellman, Joseph 129, 183
Wellman, Martha 129
Wellman, Michael 129, 183
Wellman, Thos. 129, 183
Wells, Elizabeth 186
Wells, Frances 186
Wells, George 177, 186
"Wells Hill" 177
Wells, James 146
Wells, Jane 4, 20
Wells, Jno......4, 20, 36, 63, 208
Wells, Joseph 186
Wells, Mary 17, 186
Wells, Nathan 186
Wells, Robert 186
Wells, Rich. 179
Wells, Sarah 186
Wells, Thos. 17, 186
Wenables, John 46
Wenables, Joseph 46
Wenables, William 46
"Wenfield" 62
West, Anthony 45
West, Cattiron (Catoron).... 45
West, Elizabeth 45, 221
West, J. 31, 153
West, John 45, 48, 153
"West Marsh Range"....... 167
West, Mary 45
West, Randall 45, 48
West, Richard 21
West, Stephen 221
West, Thomas 45, 153
"West Wells" 177
West, William 45
Westall, Ann 185
Westall, George 185
Westall, John 185
Westall, Richard 185
Western Branch 235
Western Shore 177, 220, 222
"Westminster" 145
Westminster Parish 190
Weston Branch 136
"Westward" 13
Wetharell, Edward 138
Wetharell, Elizabeth 138
Wetharell, Grace 138
Wetharell, Henry 213
Wetharall, John 138
Wetharell, Wm. 138

PAGE

Wetherington (Withington)
John 219
Whaley, Jno. 150
Wharton, Chas. 102
Wharton, Elizabeth 137
Wharton, Henry.........130, 184
Wharton (Whorton), Mary
10, 86, 102
Wharton, William 102
Whartown, Elizabeth 133
"Whealler's Chance" 190
Wheatley, Anne 110
Wheatley, Elizabeth 110
Wheatley, Francis 110
Wheatley, James 109
Wheatley, John 109
Wheatley, Joseph 110
Wheatley, Mary 110, 184
Wheatley, Sampson 31
Wheatley, Susannah 110
Wheatley, Thomas 110
Wheatley, Winifride 110
Wheatley, Wm. 31, 166
"Wheatley's Meadows".... 109
Wheeler, Grace .... 62 '
Wheeler, Jno. 41, 42
Wheeler, Thos. 73
Wheeler, Benj. 204
"Wheeler's Branch" 94
Wheeler, Charles 58, 233
Wheeler, Elizabeth 204
Wheeler, Isaac 86
Wheeler, Luke 199
Wheller, Sarah 86
Whetherly, Elizabeth 49
Whetherly, James 49
Wheatherly, Sibell 22
Whetherly, Wm. 49
"Whetstone" 47
Whiler, Luke 90
Whipps, Elizabeth 56
Whipps, John 56
White, Ambrose 85
White, Anne 196
White, Archibald 15, 154
White, Cathrine (Kathrine). 193
White, Cornelius 134
White, Dennis 9
White, Elizabeth 225
White, James 225
White, Jno. 15, 111, 154, 193, 214
White, Mary 9
White, Precella 193
White, Rose 193
White, Richard 225
White, Sarah 193
White, Sassiah 193
White, Stevens 193

PAGE

White, Tabitha 193
White, Wm. 85, 112, 154, 193, 225
White, Wm. Halthom....... 80
"White Field" 104, 128
"White House Neck"...... 200
"White Marsh" 186
"White Tree Branch"...... 186
"White Wine and Claret".. 25
"White's Rest" 143
"Whiteaker's Purchase".... 25
Whitehead, Fran. 15
Whitehead, Rich. 44
Whitehead, Wm. 44
Whittaker, Wm. 121
"Whittacar's Ridge" 3
Whitticar, Abraham 3
Whitticar, Charles 3
Whitticar, Elizabeth 3
Whitticar, Hannah 3
Whitticar, Isaac 3
Whitticar, Jno. 3
Whitticar, Peter 3
Whitticar, Sarah 3
Whittington, Charity 65
Whittington, Francis 64
Whittington, Jno. 36
Whittington, Mary 65
Whittington, Wm.......9, 64, 193
Whore Kill Town 32
Whorekill Crk. 115
Wickes, B. 63
Wickham, Nathaniel 176
Wickocomaco Crk. 11
Wickocomyco (Wickacomo-
co) R................3, 192
Wicks, Anna 54
Wicks, Benjamin 54, 63
Wicks, Joseph .....'......54, 63
Wicks; Mary 54
Wicks, Sam'll 54
"Widows Mite" 110
"Widow's Purchase" 57
Wigg, Richd. 190
Wight, Ann 39
Wight, John 39
Wikley, Michael 21
Wild, Peter 161
Wilde, John 101
Wilde, Mary 101
Wiles, Thos. 55
Wilkinson, Ann 162
Wilkinson, Elizabeth 143
Wilkinson, James 179
Wilkinson, Phillisanah 162
Wilkinson, Robert 162, 179
Wilkinson, Sophia 162
Wilkinson, Tamar.......162, 179

PAGE

Wilkinsson (Wilkinson) (Wilkeson), William 22, 80, 162, 179, 216 235
Wilkisson (Wilkinson) (Wilkenson), John 22, 119, 143, 163
Willard, Jno. 174
Willet (Willett), Edward 136, 223
Willey, Frances 57
William and Ann 207
William's and Mary's Parish 89
Williams, Abraham 160
Williams, Benja. 26
Williams, Charles 227
Williams, Eleanor 160
Williams, Elizabeth 92, 118, 173, 193
Williams, George 160
Williams, Hannah 103
Williams, Henry 160
Williams, Henry Price..... 160
Williams, Isaac 160
Williams, Jacob 233
Williams, James 23
Williams, Jane 19
Williams, Jno. 7, 202
Williams, Jos. 92
Williams, Mark 149, 174
Williams, Mary 42, 160
Williams, Matthew 161
Williams, Nathaniel 192
Williams, Phillodelphy 141
Williams (William), Thos. Nath'll...............46, 202
Williams, Thomas 74, 103, 128, 202, 212, 214
Williams, Wm. 97, 102, 143
Williams' Addition 228
William's Branch 150
William's Folly 202
William's Hope 102
Williamson, Alex. 6, 53
Williamson, Grace 187
Williamson, Jacob 90
Williamson, James 92
Williamson, Sam'll....43, 51, 221
Willicoxon (Willicoxen), John 61
Willicoxon (Willicoxen), Lewis 61
Willicoxon (Willicoxen), Magdalen 61
Willicoxon (Willicoxen), Thomas 61
Willimott, James 63
Willinger, Jno. 81
Willis, Andrew 168
Willis, Elizabeth 23, 83
Willis, Grace 23

PAGE

Willis, James 104
Willis, John 23, 101
Willis, Richard 56, 101
Willis, Sarah 57
Willis, Thomas 83
Willis, Wm. 21, 23, 43
Willisey, Philip 172
Willkinson (Wilkinson), Chris. 36, 43, 145
Wilkisson, Catherine 22
Willmott (Wilmote), John 161, 216
Willmot's Choice 125
Willoughby, Jno. 27
Wills, Ozias 80
Willson, Abigall 58
Willson, Alexander 43, 192
Willson, Andrew 58
Willson, Catherine 22
Willson, David 49
Willson (Wilson), Eph.....45, 49
Willson, Francis 192
Willson, James 120, 159, 192, 230
Willson (Wilson), Jno. 23, 42, 67, 80, 157, 169
Willson, Jone 192
Willson, Margaret 85, 159
Willson (Wilson), William 21, 49, 83, 139, 159
Willy, Dianna 57
Willy, John 57
Willy, Katherine 57
Willymott, Ann 63
Willymott, Elizabeth 63
Willymott, John.....63, 233, 237
Willymott, Thos. 63
Willymott, Wm. 63
Wilmore, Simon 146
Wilmote, Jane (Jean)....... 216
Wilmote, Richard 216
Wilson (Willson), Anne...80, 192
Wilson, Elizabeth 80
Wilson, Janus 108
Wilson, Joseph 108
Wilson, Joshua 108
Wilson (Willson), Josiah 10, 53, 108, 220
Wilson, Lingen 108
Wilson, Martha 108
Wilson, Mary 186
Wilson, Priscilla 167
Wilson (Willson), Thomas 58, 176
Winchester 20
Winchester Moyety 52
Winder, Elizabeth 46
Winder, Jean 45
Winder, John 45
Winder, Rachell 46

	PAGE
Winder, Thomas	46
Winder, William	46
Windsor, Thos.	163
Wine, Elizabeth	45, 137
Wine, Henry	137
Wine, Francis	137
Wine, Jno.	59
Wine, Mary	137
Wingate, Judy	57
Wingate, Mary	57
Winkapin Neck	183
Winlock, Wm.	68, 79
Winn, Ephraim	159
Winn, Tho.	230
Winnett, George	51
Winnfield	214
"Winser Cassell"	45
Winsett, Jno.	206
Wintersell, Amelkey	74
Wintersell, Catherine	74
Wintersell, Elinor	74
Wintersell, Elisha	74
Wintersell, Jane	74
Wintersell, Joshua	74
Wintersell, Margaret	74
Wintersell, Susanah	74
Wintersell, Thomas	74
Wintersell, William	74
"Wintersell"	74
"Wisbick"	9
Wise, Abigail	158
Wise, Anthony	158
Wise, Christopher	158
Wise, Diannah	51
Wise, John	158
Wise, Rich'd	51
Wise, Samuel	158
Wiseman, John	73
Wiseman, Robert	73
Witcherly, Thos.	99
Witershell, Mary	84
"Wolfs Harbour"	19
Wolfe's Quarter	37
Wolles	227
"Wollring Field"	3
Wombell, Peter	99
Womsley (Wamsley), Richd.	196
Wood, Ambrous	6
Wood, Ann	42, 102
Wood, Elijah	42
Wood, Elizabeth	160, 218
Wood, Hannah	42
Wood, Jane	42
Wood, Joana	16
Wood, Jno.	37, 42, 185
Wood, Jonathon (Jonathan),	98, 119
Wood, Margaret	42

	PAGE
Wood (Woods), Robert	99, 102, 222
Wood, Sarah	42
Wood (Woods), William	6, 218
Woodall, John	87
Woodard, Benja.	8, 152
Woodel, John	169
Woodel, Martha	169
Wooden, Elizabeth	183
Wooden, John	183, 190
Wooderd (Woodard), James.	8
Woodfield, Thos.	27
Woodland, Elizabeth	116
Woodland, John	116
Woodland, Mary	116
Woodland, Rich.	116
Woodland, Wm.	116
Woodman's Neck	200
Woodro, Joseph	224
Woods (Wood), James	148, 166, 185
Woods (Wood), Jasper	201
Woods Quarter	125
Woods, Thos.	104
Woodward, Amos	196
Woodward, Ann	133
Woodward, Johanna	164
Woodward, John	133
Woodward (Wooderd), Jos...	8
Woodward, Mary	164
Woodward, Rachel	164
Woodward, Thomas	164
Woolcoat (Woolcott), John..	8
Woolcoat (Woolcott), Sarah.	8
Wooldhave, Joseph	24
Woolefood, James	168
Woolford, Roger	152, 169
Woolford, Sarah	169
Wooly Trap Crk.	104
Wooten, Turner	228
Wootton, W.	31
Worinall, Basil	94
Worinall, Mark	94
Wormesly, Elizabeth	196
Wornel, Edward	169
Wornel, Sarah	169
"Worrell"	70
Worrell, Edw.	147
Worrell, Wm.	179, 237
Worrick, Jas.	165
Worthington, Alice	42, 114
Worthington, Sam'll..	30, 42, 114
Worthington, Will	179
Wrench, Wm.	96, 161
Wright, Anne	67, 96
Wright, Charles	96
Wright, Edward.	96, 124, 159, 161
Wright, Hairclough	96

	PAGE
Wright, Henry	43
Wright, John	96
Wright, Joseph	28
Wright, Mary	122
Wright, Nath.	95
Wright, Rachell	96
Wright (Write), Sarah....34, 192	
Wright, Solomon......66, 96, 124	
Wright, Thos.	192
Wright, Thomas Hynson 23, 62, 96	
Wrightson (Writson), John 5, 121	
Wrightson (Writson), Mary 5, 121	
Writson, Catherine	121
Writson, Deborah	121
Writson, Francis	121
Writson, Margaret	121
Writson, Thomas	121
Wroughton, Josiah	115
Wyatt, Anne	87
Wyatt, Elizabeth	87
Wyatt, Johanna	87
Wyatt, John	87
Wyatt, Jos.	155
Wyatt, Rachel	87
Wyatt, Rebecca	87
Wyatt, Sarah	87
Wye, R........112, 150, 160, 200	
Wyetts, Nicholas	2

Y

	PAGE
Yardly, John	42
Yates, Charles 3,	53
Yates, Lydia 3, 134	
Yates, Robert 3,	53
Yates (Yeates), Wm.	199
Yearley, Wm.	27
Yeate, Benjamin	145
Yeate, Eleanor	145
Yeate, Elizabeth	145
Yeate, George	145
Yeate, John	145
Yeate, Joshua	145
Yeate (Yate) (Yates), Mary 145, 184, 188	
Yeate, Rachael	145
Yeate, Samuel	145
"Yeates Contrivance"	145
Yokley, Mycall	94
Yopp, Charles 37, 203	
Yopp, Jane 37, 203	
Yopp, Roger........37, 189, 203	
Yopp, Sarah 37, 203	
Yopp, Susanna	189
"York"	13
Yorke, George	238
Yorke, James	238
Yorke, John	238
Yorke, Mary	238
Yorke, Olliver	238
Yorke, William 238, 240	
Yorkson, York	99
Yorkshire	5
Young, Ann	37
Young, Benjamin	164
Young, Constance	20
Young, David	34
Young, Elizabeth	164
Young, Francis 93, 164	
Young, George 35, 164	
Young, Henry 93, 164	
Young, John	164
Young, Jos.	196
Young, Mary 110, 164	
Young, Sam'l	221
Young, Sarah	34
Young, William 110, 113, 162, 164	
"Young Richard"	190
Younger, Humphrey	78
"Young's Attempt"	164
Youons, Jane	74